THE SOCIAL SCIENCE OF CINEMA

THE SOCIAL SCIENCE
OF CINEMA

Edited by

James C. Kaufman

and

Dean Keith Simonton

OXFORD
UNIVERSITY PRESS

OXFORD
UNIVERSITY PRESS

Oxford University Press is a department of the University of Oxford.
It furthers the University's objective of excellence in research, scholarship,
and education by publishing worldwide.

Oxford   New York
Auckland   Cape Town   Dar es Salaam   Hong Kong   Karachi
Kuala Lumpur   Madrid   Melbourne   Mexico City   Nairobi
New Delhi   Shanghai   Taipei   Toronto

With offices in
Argentina   Austria   Brazil   Chile   Czech Republic   France   Greece
Guatemala   Hungary   Italy   Japan   Poland   Portugal   Singapore
South Korea   Switzerland   Thailand   Turkey   Ukraine   Vietnam

Oxford is a registered trademark of Oxford University Press in the UK
and certain other countries.

Published in the United States of America by
Oxford University Press
198 Madison Avenue, New York, NY 10016

© Oxford University Press 2014

Library of Congress Cataloging-in-Publication Data
The social science of cinema / edited by James C. Kaufman, Dean Keith Simonton.
    pages cm
Includes bibliographical references and index.
ISBN 978–0–19–979781–3
1. Motion pictures.   2. Motion pictures—Social aspects.   3. Motion pictures—Psychological
aspects.   I. Kaufman, James C. editor of compilation.   II. Simonton, Dean Keith editor of
compilation.
PN1995.S558 2013
791.4301—dc23
2013017333

9 8 7 6 5 4 3 2 1
Printed in the United States of America
on acid-free paper

James would like to dedicate his work on this book to a fellow
movie (and graphic novel) buff, who is also a colleague,
mentor, advocate, scholar, and loved and trusted friend:

Dr. Jonathan A. Plucker

Dean would like to dedicate his work to the memory of two persons
who sparked his cinematic curiosity when he was still a teenager:

his high school drama coach, Stan Johnson,

who uttered a few words as Lt. Cunningham
in John Ford's *What Price Glory?*

and his stepfather, Keith R. Williams,

who conducted the music for Charlie Chaplin's *Limelight*

—both films appearing in 1952.

CONTENTS

SECTION THREE: *The Production*

SECTION FOUR: *The Reception*

ACKNOWLEDGMENTS

The editors would like to thank Lori Handelman (formerly of Oxford) and Joanna Ng and Abby Gross from Oxford University Press.

CONTRIBUTORS

Pawan V. Bhansing
University of Amsterdam
  Business School
Amsterdam, The Netherlands

Kaitlin L. Brunick
Department of Psychology
Cornell University
Ithaca, New York

Joshua Butler
Iceblink Films
Los Angeles, CA

Gino Cattani
Department of Management and
  Organizations
Stern School of Business—New York
  University
New York, New York

Tomas Chamorro-Premuzic
Department of Psychology,
  Goldsmiths, University of London
Department of Psychology, University
  College London
New York University in London
London, United Kingdom

Marc Choueiti
School for Communication and
  Journalism
University of Southern California
  Annenberg
Los Angeles, California

Annabel Cohen
Department of Psychology
University of Prince Edward Island
Prince Edward Island, Canada

Gerald C. Cupchik
Department of Psychology
University of Toronto Scarborough
Toronto, Ontario

James E. Cutting
Department of Psychology
Cornell University
Ithaca, New York

Jordan E. DeLong
Department of Psychology
Cornell University
Ithaca, New York

Joris J. Ebbers
University of Amsterdam
 Business School
Amsterdam, The Netherlands

Victor Fernandez-Blanco
Departmento de Economica
University of Oviedo
Oviedo, Spain

Simone Ferriani
Dipartimento di Scienze Aziendali
Universita' di Bologna
Bologna, Italy

Victor Ginsburgh
ECARES, Brussels and CORE
 Louvain-la-Neuve
University of Brussels
Brussels, Belgium

Thalia R. Goldstein
Department of Psychology
Pace University
New York, New York

Amy Granados
School for Communication and
 Journalism
University of Southern California
 Annenberg
Los Angeles, California

Allègre L. Hadida
University of Cambridge Judge
 Business School and Magdalene
 College
Cambridge, United Kingdom

Michelle C. Hilscher
Department of Psychology
University of Toronto Scarborough
Toronto, Ontario

Anne Hsu
Department of Psychology, University
 College London
London, United Kingdom

Andrea Kallias
Department of Psychology
Goldsmiths, University of London
London, United Kingdom

James C. Kaufman
University of Connecticut
Neag School of Education
2131 Hillside Road
Storrs, CT 06269-3007

Iain Pardoe
Department of Mathematics and
 Statistics
Thompson Rivers University
Kamloops, British Columbia,
Canada

Katherine M. Pieper
School for Communication and
 Journalism
University of Southern California
 Annenberg
Los Angeles, California

Juan Prieto-Rodriguez
Departamento de Economía
University of Oviedo
Oviedo, Spain

Dean Keith Simonton
Department of Psychology
University of California, Davis
Davis, California

Stacy L. Smith
School for Communication and
    Journalism
University of Southern California
    Annenberg
Los Angeles, California

Sheila Weyers
Center for Operations Research and
    Econometrics
Université catholique de
    Louvain-La-Neuve, Belgium

Nachoem M. Wijnberg
University of Amsterdam
    Business School
Amsterdam, The Netherlands

THE SOCIAL SCIENCE OF THE CINEMA: FADE IN

Ever since motion pictures first landed on screen, there have been many key questions that the studios and laypeople have tried to answer. What makes a movie an Oscar winner? How does one movie become a hit and another movie flop? Why do some films earn critical acclaim while other films become critical turkeys or bombs? How do audiences perceive film? What makes a movie resonate with a viewer? Are we unduly influenced by negative behaviors on screen? These questions have spurred debates, discussions, and many theories. Until the past two decades, however, it was quite rare to have the issues approached from a scientific viewpoint.

Today, the empirical study of movies is reaching a golden age. Top researchers from psychology, economics, sociology, business, and communications have all tackled the question of how movies work. Our goal in compiling this book was to reach out across disciplines to find the best empirical research being done on the movies, from the spark of creation to the results of the final product.

Like nearly everyone, we love the movies and often follow-up our film watching with a rigorous discussion of the strengths and weakness of whatever movie we watch. This book, to us, is the ultimate act of figuring out the mystery behind the movies—what makes them so memorable to us, what has made them the leading works of art for the past century, and how this art intersects with the business of making money.

Roger Ebert once said that most people do not consciously look at movies. Fewer people still have tried to scientifically study them. We believe that you will find the essays that follow insightful and thought-provoking, and we hope that you enjoy them as much as we have.

James C. Kaufman
Dean Keith Simonton

THE SOCIAL SCIENCE OF CINEMA

THE CREATION

WRITING FOR SUCCESS

SCREENPLAYS AND CINEMATIC IMPACT

Dean Keith Simonton

The screenplay or script has a very paradoxical place in the cinematic art. On the one hand, the writers who create screenplays tend to be among the more obscure members of the core film crew (cf. Pritzker & McGarva, 2009). Only those writers who produce and direct their own films, such as Woody Allen or Ingmar Bergman, are likely to be featured on the movie theater's marquee. As further proof: How many of us can name the writers behind our favorite movies? How many of us can identify the writers nominated for best writing Oscars just last year?

On the other hand, when moviegoers are surveyed about what sends them to the movie theater, they will often point to the story as a critical determinant of preference (De Silva, 1998). Moreover, both film critics and industry professionals appear to agree because all movie awards that have any value will include honors for best screenplay. Indeed, it is common to have two separate award categories, one for best original screenplay and the other for best adaptation. The former is "written directly for the screen," whereas the latter is based on "material previously published or produced"—to use the words of the Academy of Motion Picture Arts and Sciences, which bestows the Oscars.

Filmmakers are well aware of the critical contribution of the script. Even though the screenplay operates "behind the scenes," it is what defines those scenes. It describes both the action and the dialogue in a very direct manner (e.g., one page of script equals one minute of screen time). It provides not just the basis for the actors' performances, but also the foundation for almost everyone and everything else involved in preproduction, production, and post-production (e.g., the addition of special effects). It should come as no surprise, then, that script constitutes the single most important component of cinematic success (Simonton, 2011). By "success," I mean much more than box office or financial performance: Success also includes critical acclaim and movie awards beyond honors for best screenplay (Simonton, 2007, 2009b). Furthermore, several distinct attributes of the script have crucial repercussions for these multiple success criteria. It is to these attributes and their cinematic consequence that I devote the bulk of this chapter. At the chapter's close, however, I impose a few caveats. Although the screenplay's contributions are often underappreciated, we have to be careful not to overstate or oversimplify. The script's impact is subtle and complex.

Attributes

Not surprisingly, scientific research on screenplays has concentrated on their more obvious distinguishing features. These are (a) the film's running time, (b) the film's genre or broad story type, (c) the rating the film received from the Motion Picture Association of America (MPAA), (d) the type and intensity of "mature content" depicted in the film, (e) whether the film is a sequel to or remake of a previous film, (f) whether the film is based on a true story about a person or event, and (g) whether the film is based on an original script or an adaptation and, in the latter case, the source of the adaptation. Where appropriate, these attributes are defined with respect to the final theatrical release rather than with either the preproduction script or the later video/DVD version. For example, the MPAA rating a film received during its theatrical distribution can often differ from the later "director's cut" (Simonton, 2011). With that in mind, each of these script attributes will be examined with regard to three criteria of cinematic success: box office impact, movie awards, and critical acclaim. When appropriate, I will include production costs or budget to put the three main criteria in perspective (cf. Simonton, 2005a).

Runtime

The research reported in this chapter concentrates on English-language, live-action, feature-length narrative films (Simonton, 2011). That is, most investigations omit foreign-language films, animations, shorts, and documentaries to reduce sample heterogeneity and thereby render the remaining films more comparable. Nonetheless, such standard cinematic products can still vary greatly in length. For example, one study of 1,006 films released between 2000 and 2006 obtained a range of from 71 minutes to 3 hours and 51 minutes (Simonton, 2009a). Of course, most running times fall somewhere between these two extremes. In fact, the average duration is a little less than 2 hours (Simonton, 2004b, 2005b). Nevertheless, the variation is substantial enough to have considerable consequences for all three criteria of cinematic success.

Box Office Impact. Consumers report a strong preference for longer films (Holbrook, 1999). Given the cost of a theater ticket, it appears that moviegoers want to get their money's worth. In line with this desire, the film's duration is positively associated with earnings on the first weekend of release and with the final gross earnings at the end of the theatrical run (Simonton, 2005b). So, one might wonder why most films are not 3-hour extravaganzas. One possible answer is simple: Longer films cost more to make (Simonton, 2005b, 2009a). Hence, a shorter film can actually turn a better profit than a longer film. To illustrate, *My Big Fat Greek Wedding* (2002) lasts only 95 minutes, but it cost only $5 million to produce; it grossed $241 million, rendering it one of the more profitable films in 2002.

Film Honors. The critics and professionals who vote on award winners concur with consumers: More is better. In particular, longer films are more likely to receive best picture honors (Simonton, 2005b; see also Simonton, 2009a). The most recent Oscar winners in this category offer examples: *The King's Speech* (118 minutes), *The Hurt Locker* (131 minutes), *Slumdog Millionaire* (120 minutes), *No Country for Old Men* (122 minutes), *The Departed* (151 minutes), *Crash* (113 minutes), *Million Dollar Baby* (132 minutes), *The Lord of the Rings: The Return of the King* (201 minutes), *Chicago* (113 minutes), and *Gladiator* (155 minutes). Given that the typical feature film during this period lasts 108 minutes, not one is shorter than the norm (Simonton, 2009a).

Better yet, the film's runtime is positively associated with the number of nominations and awards received in other award categories (Simonton, 2005b; see also Simonton, 2009a). These categories are dramatic (directing, acting, writing, and editing), visual (cinematography, art production, costume, and makeup), technical (special visual effects, sound effects editing, and sound mixing), and music (score and song). Long films provide everyone in the cast and crew sufficient opportunity to show what they can do. In contrast, short films give talents and technicians insufficient breathing space. Hence, the longest of the films just listed, the third and last installment of *The Lord of the Rings*, got more than a best picture statuette. The film also took home ten Oscars in the categories of writing, directing, editing, art production, costume design, makeup, visual effects, sound mixing, score, and song. Only in acting did the film fail to pick up a major honor.

Critical Acclaim. Film critics appear to agree with both moviegoers and award voters: Film length is positively correlated with the critics' evaluations (Simonton, 2005b, 2009a). This relation holds for both critics' judgments published during the film's theatrical run and the assessments that appear after the film becomes available as a video or DVD. For instance, the 201-minute *The Lord of the Rings: The Return of the King* averaged 4.9 stars out of 5 in standard video/DVD guides, a half star or more higher than the films that were nominated for best picture Oscars in the same year: the 137-minute *Mystic River* received 4.4 stars; the 138-minute *Master and Commander: The Far Side of the World*, 4.4 stars; the 102-minute *Lost in Translation*, 4.2 stars; and the 141-minute *Seabiscuit*, 3.9 stars. Presumably, the rationale for this positive association is the same as holds for box office and film honors. The cast and crew are granted more latitude to show their stuff. The screenwriter, especially, is granted ample time to develop the characters and storyline, thus avoiding flat cardboard figures and gaping plot holes.

Before going on to the next script attribute, I should indicate an oddity. The film's duration is the only variable that is positively associated with all three criteria of cinematic success. Other attributes are far less consistent in impact, as will become apparent in the following sections.

Genres

Story type is a central attribute of any screenplay. Genre also determines many other script traits. Genre is perhaps second only to runtime as a determinant of the cinematic experience. To be sure, "genre" is not a single variable but rather a very large number of separate "dummy" variables coding which genre a a given film belongs to. Indeed, there are literally dozens of such genre categories, such as drama, comedy, romance, musical, action, adventure, fantasy, science fiction, thriller, mystery, film noir, horror, western, and more. That said, most empirical investigations concentrate on the small number of genres that dominate the film inventory, such as drama and comedy (Simonton, 2011). The reason for this focus is statistical. Dummy variables encoding relatively rare genres, such as film noir, will have too little variance to have stable predictive value. This problem is aggravated by the fact that smaller categories will often overlap with other categories, thus reducing the unique variance that can be explained. Keeping this in mind, how does genre affect box office impact, film honors, and critical acclaim?

Box Office Impact. Many investigators have indicated that a film's genre affects its performance in the box office. For instance, some research has confirmed the popularity of comedy, romance, fantasy, sci-fi, and horror films (Litman, 1983; Litman & Kohl, 1989; Simonton, 2005b; Sochay, 1994; Wyatt, 1994). Other genres seem less consistently relevant to consumer tastes, such as war, western, mystery, crime, and film noir (Walls, 2005b). Sometimes moviegoer will buy a theater ticket for a film in a particular genre and other times not, so that the various preferences cancel out. Cinematic tastes are also not stable across time or constant across cultures. For example, comedies do not do very well when they cross cultural boundaries (e.g., Lee, 2006).

All of these peculiarities notwithstanding, one genre stands out most consistently and strongly as antithetical to good box office performance: drama (Chang & Ki, 2005; Collins, Hand, & Snell, 2002; Litman & Kohl, 1989; Simonton, 2005b; Sochay, 1994; cf. Walls, 2005b). Light entertainment, not weighty enlightenment, is what most movie consumers seek (Holbrook, 1999; see also Anast, 1967). Dramas open on fewer screens, have much lower earnings on the first weekend, and have an appreciably lower gross at the end of their domestic run (Simonton, 2004a, 2004b; see also Chang & Ki, 2005; Litman & Kohl, 1989; Prag & Casavant, 1994; Simonoff & Sparrow, 2000; cf. Sochay, 1994). What renders this antidrama bias so curious is that a substantial proportion of releases represent this very category: Frequently, dramas represent close to half of the total annual releases (Simonton, 2004b). So why do filmmakers create dramas in the first place? One plausible answer is that dramas are relatively inexpensive to produce: There is a negative association between dramatic scripts and the film's final production costs (Simonton, 2005b).

Film Honors. The drama genre's low production cost is not its only asset: Films in this genre are most likely to get best picture awards from most major organizations (Simonton, 2005b; see also Simonton, 2009a). Dramas are also most highly correlated with awards and nominations for directing, writing, and acting—the core honors bestowed by most societies and associations. In contrast, dramas are less prone to receive honors for such technical achievements as visual effects, sound effects editing, and sound mixing (Simonton, 2005b; see also Simonton, 2009a). The absence of these latter honors helps us understand why dramas can cost less to produce: A great drama can be shot with no special effects whatsoever.

Other genres also bear some connection with film honors (Simonton, 2005b; see also Simonton, 2009a). Romances are also common candidates for best picture awards and nominations. Moreover, like dramas, romances also are inclined to receive recognition for directing, acting, and writing. Yet, unlike dramas, romances have a higher probability of earning nominations and awards for visual and music achievements. Great love stories invite lush cinematography, sets, costumes, makeup, and music, whether score or song. A classic example was *Doctor Zhivalgo* (1965), which won Oscars for best art direction-set decoration, best cinematography, best costume design, best music score, and best writing.

Two final observations are due (Simonton, 2005b; see also Simonton, 2009a). First, comedies have *lower* odds of earning recognition in the visual, technical, and music categories. This genre appears to rely on wit alone to achieve cinematic ends. Second, musicals are the most likely to win honors for score and song—not a big surprise—but also have some advantage with regard to visual honors. The best musicals often feature first-rate production values. To illustrate, *An American in Paris* (1951) won Oscars in art direction-set decoration, cinematography, and costume design, in addition to best music.

Critical Acclaim. Film critics appear to prefer dramas just as much as those who vote for movie awards. This positive correlation holds for both film reviews published during the film's theatrical run and those that do not appear until after the film becomes available in video or DVD format (Simonton, 2005b; see also Holbrook, 1999; Simonton, 2009a). The preference for the dramatic genre seems to reflect a long-standing aesthetic bias toward serious drama. For example, Shakespeare's tragedies are more highly acclaimed than are his comedies and romances (Simonton, 1986). *Hamlet, King Lear, Othello*, and *Macbeth* are more famous than *Midsummer Night's Dream, Taming of the Shrew*, and *Twelfth Night*. This hierarchy goes back to the beginning of drama in ancient Athens. Of the four great playwrights of ancient Greece—Aeschylus, Sophocles, Euripides, and Aristophanes—the last, the creator of comedies rather than tragedies, is viewed as the lesser figure (Simonton, 1983).

Uniquely, the Hollywood Foreign Press Association bestows two sets of awards (the Golden Globes) in the best picture and best lead acting categories, one set for drama and the other for musical or comedy. Yet only the first set of awards has a high likelihood of corresponding to the Oscars given in the same categories (Pardoe & Simonton, 2008). It is therefore interesting that film critics, in addition to liking drama better than comedy, also seem to dislike musicals. At least, the musical genre is negatively associated with the ratings received in movie guides (Simonton, 2005b), perhaps because musicals do not look or sound as good on most home entertainment systems.

MPAA Ratings

Since 1968, the MPAA has rated films on a qualitative scale ranging from accessible to all moviegoers to permitted only for moviegoers who are 18 and older. Although the rating system has evolved since then, the current version goes as follows: *G* (general admission), *PG* (parental guidance advised), *PG-13* (parents strongly cautioned because some material may be inappropriate for children under 13), *R* (restricted, children under 17 are not admitted without an accompanying parent or adult guardian), *NC-17* (no one 17 and under admitted), and *Not Rated* (mostly used for foreign-language films that slowly navigate the art-house circuit). The MPAA rating considers a wide array of content attributes, including violence, intense battle sequences, gore, frightening or disturbing images, nudity, sensuality, sexual content, sexual references, crude sexual humor, simulated or graphic sex, language, profanity, tense situations, mature themes, alcohol abuse, drug abuse, teenage drinking, and even bad sportsmanship—all very crucial aspects of a typical film script. These attributes also have rather differing repercussions for the diverse indicators of cinematic success.

Box Office Impact. Movie consumers have a distinct dislike for films that contain objectionable or offensive content (Holbrook, 1999). This distaste shows up in box office performance: Those films that make the most money are most often those with the most accessible MPAA ratings, especially PG-13 (Chang & Ki, 2005; Collins, Hand, & Snell, 2002; De Vany & Walls, 2002; Medved, 1992; Ravid, 1999; Sawhney & Eliasberg, 1996; Simonoff & Sparrow, 2000; Simonton, 2005b, 2009a; cf. Delmestri, Montanari, & Usai, 2005; Litman & Ahn, 1998; Terry, Butler, & De'Armond, 2005; Walls, 2005a). In stark contrast, R-rated films are far more likely to become financial flops with respect to both short- and long-term box office returns. Such films open on fewer screens, earn less on the first weekend, and obtain a smaller domestic gross by the end of the theatrical run. One investigation estimated that R-rated films released in the early 2000s saw a $12 million decrement in gross earnings relative to films with MPAA ratings of PG-13 or lower (Terry, Butler, & De'Armond, 2005).

These contrasts prove most curious: Films that are accessible to the widest audiences, according to the MPAA rating, and especially the highly accessible G rating, are relatively rare, whereas the R rating is often the most common, followed closely by PG-13. Indeed, roughly 50 percent of mainstream films coming out in a given year often fall into the R category (Chang & Ki, 2005; De Vany & Walls, 1999; Wyatt, 1994). Thus, this R-rated movie paradox parallels the drama genre paradox mentioned earlier. Filmmakers are most prone to make serious films with "mature content" that make them ill-suited for a big showing in the box office. This is not to say that R-rated films cannot make money; rather, it is difficult to have an R-rated blockbuster.

Film Honors. One possible motivation for the high output of R-rated films is that filmmakers are waiting for award season. What a serious film loses in money might be compensated in prestige. And, in fact, R-rated films are more likely to receive nominations and awards in the dramatic categories, namely, writing, directing, acting, and editing (Simonton, 2005b; cf. Simonton, 2009a). As observed earlier, honors in these categories are most conspicuously correlated with critical acclaim. Nonetheless, this strategy has significant drawbacks as well: R-rated films do not have a higher likelihood of earning best picture awards or even nominations, and such films actually have a lower likelihood of receiving honors in the visual, technical, and music award categories (Simonton, 2005b; cf. Simonton, 2009a). In other words, R-rated films are less likely to be honored for art direction, costume design, makeup, visual effects, sound effects editing, sound mixing, score, and song.

The other MPAA ratings are connected to different award categories (Simonton, 2005b; cf. Simonton, 2009a). Films rated PG-13 are less likely to receive kudos in the dramatic categories but are more likely to earn honors in the technical categories (e.g., teen-oriented action flicks with an abundance of striking special effects). PG-rated films score highest in the visual and music categories (e.g., many family-oriented films, such as *Mary Poppins*). And, last, G-rated films are more likely to earn honors for music, whether for score or song, but are less likely to earn honors in the dramatic categories (e.g., kids' musicals).

Critical Acclaim. The critics are somewhat ambivalent about films with distinct MPAA ratings. On the one hand, some researchers have found that film critics prefer R-rated cinema (Simonton, 2005b; see also Holbrook, 1999). This preference appears both in the reviews written during the film's theatrical run and in the reviews published after the film's video/DVD release. In contrast, although a PG-13 rating has no correlation, positive or negative, with critical acclaim, the G and PG ratings are negatively associated with those evaluations, especially with movie guide assessments.

On the other hand, other studies have found no correlations, positive or negative, between an R rating and critical acclaim (Simonton, 2009a). Why the difference? Scrutiny of the two sets of inquiries reveals that those supporting a positive association used samples confined to films that earned major award nominations, whereas those that failed to find any relation used samples that were more representative of the general population of theatrically released films. Hence, an R rating only seems useful in discriminating the critical judgments of elite films. If so, then we must again raise the question: Why make an R-rated film? The box office costs are not compensated by critical acclaim except for a subset of releases each year.

Sex and Violence

Although MPAA ratings provide handy indicators of a script's mature content, the ratings suffer from a major liability: Any given rating may be bestowed for several quite contrasting reasons. To illustrate, consider the five films nominated for the 2008 best picture Oscar. Although all five earned an R rating, *The Reader* received it for "some scenes of sexuality and nudity"; *Milk* for "language, some sexual content, and brief violence"; *The Curious Case of Benjamin Button* for "brief war violence, sexual content, language, and smoking"; *Frost/Nixon* received it for "some language"; and *Slumdog Millionaire*, the film that actually won, for "some violence, disturbing images, and language." Obviously, sex, violence, language, smoking, and disturbing images all played different roles in the judgment that children could not watch the film unless accompanied by an adult. Thus, it becomes necessary to examine the effects of particular types of "adult," "mature," "objectionable," or even "exploitative" content—with special focus on "sex and violence."

Box Office Impact. It is a truism to say that "sex sells." Indeed, this supposed truth became a key plot element in Blake Edwards's *S.O.B.* (1981): The producer opts to turn a family film that financially flopped into a box office hit by inserting scenes in which a female actor known for her wholesome image appears nude on the screen. Edwards had his own wife—Julie Andrews of *Mary Poppins* fame— bare her breasts for the first time on the silver screen. Yet her exposure did not save the movie. In fact, empirical research has shown that the more sex, the less sales (Cerridwen & Simonton, 2009; see also Thompson & Yokota, 2004). For the most part, sexual content, including nudity and sensuality, is inconsistent with good cinema economics. This negative effect holds not only for domestic gross—where it might be dismissed as residual US Puritanism—but also for the presumably more liberal audience in the United Kingdom, as well as for earnings worldwide. Although the data show that "sex is cheap" in the sense that films with graphic sex and nudity cost less to make, films with such content are still less likely to turn a profit. These negative effects appear even after adjusting for the MPAA rating (Cerridwen & Simonton, 2009). Hence, the unprofitability cannot be attributed to the fact that fewer persons are allowed to see the movie.

Nor are sex and nudity the only mature content that drive moviegoers away from the theaters. Consumers are also adverse to alcohol and drug use, as well as to profanity and smoking (Cerridwen & Simonton, 2009). If the filmmaker really wants to make money at the box office, violence provides the best means, particularly if accompanied by guns and other weapons, by frightening scenes with corresponding scary or tense music, and with plenty of "jump scenes" for shock value (Cerridwen & Simonton, 2009; see also Thompson & Yokota, 2004). There's nothing like the violent villain unexpectedly appearing out of a dark corner to get the adrenaline rush that sends some masochistic moviegoers back for more. Curiously, although graphic sex and nudity do not help a film turn a profit, more modest PG-13 level sexuality, combined with eye-catching but not gory violence, offers a more profitable formula for success (Ravid & Basuroy, 2004). The James Bond flicks, with their parades of action heroes and sexy heroines, seem to provide models for financial success.

Film Honors. If strong sex doesn't sell, then it seems reasonable to ask why it's there. One potential explanation could be that sex and nudity provide some boost during the award season. Perhaps such serious content makes the film seem like a more serious contender—or at least inspire more award voters to see the film. The single empirical study addressing this issue focused on Oscar and Golden Globes (Cerridwen & Simonton, 2009). In each case, nominations and awards were counted in the categories of best picture, director, screenplay, and male and female leads and supporting. The outcome was somewhat complex. Although graphic sex and nudity were negatively correlated with receiving such recognition, sexual content, when accompanied by profanity, smoking, drinking, and drug abuse, could enhance the probability that a film would receive Oscar and Golden Globe honors. The researchers speculated that this cinematic package might appear "artsy" or "edgy" in a way that echoes the often more daring film fare that enters the United States from Europe. Nevertheless, if the aim is to win kudos from the Academy or the Hollywood Foreign Press Association, a better choice is to make films that grapple with difficult topics and issues, particularly those that might display tense family scenes.

The relation between violence and movie awards is less subtle: With respect to the Oscars, such content is irrelevant one way or another (Cerridwen & Simonton, 2009). That same null impact holds for other content variables closely associated with violence, such as blood and gore, disrespectful or bad attitude, and guns and weapons. Furthermore, films that feature lots of violence and fear are less inclined to receive Golden Globe recognition. Hence, the only incentive for violent content is box office cash, not trophy gold.

Critical Acclaim. Perhaps mature content is put in a film to satisfy the tastes of film critics. After all, the latter make their living reviewing hundreds of movies per year. Becoming sated with mainstream imagery, critics might get desperate for something truly novel or shocking. Unfortunately, this explanation does not fit the data. The critics do not seem fond of sex and violence either (Cerridwen & Simonton, 2009; see also Ravid & Basuroy, 2004). Moreover, this twofold antipathy holds for both those critics who review films during their theatrical release and those who pass judgment after the film has entered the market on video or DVD.

So if critics do not like sex and violence, what mature content do they like? Apparently, film critics prefer films that feature frightening scenes, smoking, tense family situations, and serious topics to talk about (Cerridwen & Simonton, 2009). Seriousness seems more significant than sensationalism.

Sequels and Remakes

Although a proverb says "familiarity breeds contempt," it has long been known that the opposite is more often the case: Repeated exposure produces liking

(Bornstein, 1989). Screenwriters can take advantage of this fact by writing scripts that are strongly connected with the scripts used in previous films, especially films that were widely successful in the box office. The most obvious way of connecting one film to another is through the remake. For example, the 1998 *Psycho* was a virtual shot-by-shot recreation of Hitchcock's classic 1960 *Psycho*, the only major change being the use of color photography. Another route to the same end is the sequel, in which the protagonist and some other characters are carried over from one film to the next. This not only saves the screenwriter some effort, but it can also guarantee a celebrity a life-long source of income. Perhaps the most conspicuous example is Sylvester Stallone in *Rocky* (1976), *Rocky II* (1979), *Rocky III* (1982), *Rocky IV* (1985), *Rocky V* (1990), and *Rocky Balboa* (2006).

But do sequels and remakes really enjoy more cinematic impact?

Box Office Impact. Filmmakers like sequels for good reason: Such movies have a somewhat higher probability of making money than do original films (Basuroy, Chatterjee, & Ravid, 2003; Chang & Ki, 2005; Collins, Hand, & Snell, 2002; De Vany & Walls, 1999; Litman & Kohl, 1989; McKenzie, 2009; Prag & Casavant, 1994; Ravid, 1999; Sawhney & Eliasberg, 1996; Simonton, 2005b, 2009a; Terry, Butler, & De'Armond, 2005; Wyatt, 1994; but see Litman, 1982; Sochay, 1994). Sequels open on a larger number of screens, bring in more box office on opening weekend, enjoy more extended theatrical runs, and end up earning a more impressive domestic gross. Sequels do suffer a financial drawback, however: Their production costs are higher than normal (Simonton, 2005b, 2009a). It seems that there is a strong expectation that the sequel will outdo the special effects of its predecessor. In addition, the lead actors can command progressively more money for their services. According to the Internet Movie Database, Arnold Schwarzenegger received $75,000 for *The Terminator* (1984), $15,000,000 for *Terminator 2: Judgment Day* (1991), and $30,000,000 for *Terminator 3: Rise of the Machines* (2003). Meanwhile, the budgets for the three films enlarged from $6,400,000 to $200,000,000, indicating that Schwarzenegger's percentage of the cost grew from 1 percent to 15 percent. This budget increase meant that the series became progressively less profitable, with the box office not entirely recovering the enhanced expenses.

Remakes might make more business sense than sequels. If consumers liked the original, why would they not enjoy an updated version with contemporary stars, state-of-the-art techniques, and script enhancements? Yet the economics of remakes are less outstanding than sequels (Simonton, 2005b; cf. Simonton, 2009a). Unlike sequels, remakes do not have substantially bigger budgets than other films. Although remakes are like sequels in that they open on more screens, earn a bigger first weekend, and attain a higher gross than average, they do not usually achieve the same magnitude of box office success as sequels do. It remains to be determined whether the lower costs compensate for the lower returns.

Film Honors. I mentioned earlier that sequels are inclined to cost more to make, and I conjectured that some of those increased costs may be ascribed to enhanced special effects. This conjecture is supported by the facts: Sequels have a high likelihood of receiving nominations and awards in the technical categories, namely, visual effects, sound effects editing, and sound mixing (Simonton, 2005b; cf. Simonton, 2009a). Yet those kudos are the only advantages because sequels also have lower prospects of earning recognition for best picture or dramatic achievements, such as best screenplay, best direction, and best acting (Simonton, 2005b; cf. Simonton, 2009a). Of these deficits, it is likely writing that is most adversely affected. Having to create a sequel must stifle the creative imagination of most screenwriters. Unlike the writer for the first film, who is free to create characters and plots with relatively few constraints, the writer of sequels must restrict his or her creativity to what is consistent with the first version. This restriction even applies when the same creator writes both the original and the sequel. Writers become imprisoned in a cell of their own design.

Remakes also have a definite liability with respect to movie awards and nominations (Simonton, 2005b; cf. Simonton, 2009a). Indeed, they are even worse off than sequels because remakes do not even receive recognition in the technical categories. In addition, like sequels, remakes have a lower probability of receiving recognition the dramatic categories. Obviously, the writer cannot earn much praise for updating a screenplay for a remake. The directing and acting may be handicapped as well. Often a film good enough to inspire a remake will also feature performances that are hard acts to follow. The remake of *Psycho* offers ample illustrations of how the actors could not live up to their predecessors in Alfred Hitchcock's original version.

Critical Acclaim. Given what we already know, it is easy to guess how the critics feel about sequels and remakes: Critics like neither (Simonton, 2005b, 2009a). This antipathy holds for the reviews published at the beginning of the theatrical run, as well as for after the release of the video/DVD. Critical disdain is also more potent for sequels than for remakes. Hence, film critics seem to side with those who bestow the nominations and awards for best picture and in the major dramatic honors. With respect to the criteria that really matter, sequels are less prone to be worth seeing than the original films that inspired them. To illustrate, consider the following films and their sequels (averaged movie guide ratings on 5-star scale in parentheses; from Simonton, 2011): *The French Connection* (4.8) and *The French Connection II* (2.8); *The Sting* (4.5) and *The Sting II* (1.8); *Conan the Barbarian* (3.1) and *Conan the Destroyer* (2.3); *The Blair Witch Project* (2.9) and *Book of Shadows: Blair Witch 2* (1.9); *2001: A Space Odyssey*

(5.0) and *2010: The Year We Make Contact* (3.0); *Men in Black* (3.9) and *Men in Black II* (2.6); and *The Matrix* (3.9), *The Matrix Reloaded* (3.5), and *The Matrix Revolutions* (2.5). The fall from grace for each successive film can amount to a star or more. Sequels almost inevitably run out of ideas. I know of only two major exceptions (Simonton, 2011). First *The Godfather* (4.9) was surpassed by *The Godfather, Part II* (5.0), albeit the decline appeared in *The Godfather, Part III* (3.8). Second, in *The Lord of the Rings* trilogy, we obtain the following rating (Simonton, 2011): *The Fellowship of the Ring* (4.5), *The Two Towers* (4.7), and *The Return of the King* (4.9). However, this second example is probably the exception that proves the rule. *The Lord of the Rings* films were all adapted from J. R. R. Tolkien's classic, and all three were filmed together rather than separately. In the main, it requires some special circumstances for a sequel surpass its predecessor.

True Stories and Biopics

Sometimes a script can be considered a "remake" of a different sort; namely, a remake of a true story—thus, *Chariots of Fire* (1981) which tells the actual story of two British track athletes who competed in the 1924 Summer Olympics. One special case of a "fact-based" film is the biopic, which narrates the life of some notable person. Famous examples include *Ray* (Charles) (2004), *Ed Wood* (1994), *Gandhi* (1982), *Patton* (1970), *Lawrence of Arabia* (1962), *Viva Zapata!* (1952), *Ivan Groznyy I* (*Ivan the Terrible, Part One*; 1942), *Queen Christina* (1933), and *Napoléon* (1927). In these examples, the "title characters" of the biopic are obvious, but, at other times, the subject is not so evident. *Beautiful Mind* (2001) deals with the life of the Nobel laureate John Nash. Given how often true stories and biopics are produced, we inquire whether they have any special advantages as business or as art.

Box Office Impact. The production of true stories and biopics cannot be justified by their box office performance (Simonton, 2005b; see also Simonton, 2009a). On the contrary, such films have poorer odds of doing well on opening weekend, and biopics are less prone to open in wide release. Their overall domestic gross does not arise above mediocrity. The only positive in the financial picture is that true stories and biopics have somewhat lower production costs, albeit the savings are small. Interestingly, moviegoers seem a bit more attracted to true stories in general than they are to biopics in particular. Do biopics come across as just another high school history lesson?

Film Honors. Whenever a particular script attribute does not predict box office success, it often gains points from an aesthetic perspective. In the Golden Age of Hollywood, films based on true stories and biographies were frequently the basis for prestige products that aspired more to status than profits. That motive persists. First, such films have a higher probability of earning nominations and awards in the dramatic and visual categories (Simonton, 2005b). That is, true stories and biopics are more prone to get recognition for writing, directing, acting, editing, cinematography, art production, costume design, and makeup. The last award category becomes especially critical when a protagonist must undergo noticeable aging in the process of telling his or her life story. In addition, true stories seem to have an edge with respect to best picture honors (Simonton, 2005b). *Gandhi* illustrates some of these virtues. In addition to winning the best picture Oscar, it won Oscars for best writing, directing, lead actor, editing, cinematography, art direction and set decoration, and costume design, plus it got an Oscar nod for makeup. Even so, scripts based on real events or persons do not have an advantage in the technical and music categories (Simonton, 2005b). Perhaps this null effect means that the film's weight is supposed to be carried solely by the "truth" or the "facts." Special visual and sound effects, as well as outstanding scores and songs, may be seen as superfluous if not distracting.

Critical Acclaim. Even though film critics seem a bit more ambivalent than the award voters, true stories appear more likely to receive positive evaluations (Simonton, 2005b; Simonton, 2009a, 2011). This critical preference shows up in the evaluations published early in the film's theatrical run, but becomes even more prominent in the movie guide ratings that appear after the videos/DVDs become available. Although this critical tendency holds for true stories in general, the positive correlation is not nearly so conspicuous for biopics. However, because biopics represent only about half of all true stories, it is conceivable that this particular type is not common enough to have the same repercussions for critical evaluations (or movie awards as well). In addition, biopics most often narrate the lives of illustrious people, whereas true stories often treat less historic events, such as notorious homicides—such as *In Cold Blood* (1967), *The Black Dahlia* (2006), or *Zodiac* (2007). Neither the killers nor their victims have any claim to fame beyond the vicious crime that linked their fates. Indeed, only in the first film are the murderers actually known by name.

Adaptations

Many professional and critical organizations distinguish between two very different types of writing. On the one hand are original scripts that present a story created specifically for the big screen. On the other hand are adaptations, in which the script is based on some previous work conceived for some medium other than cinema. Adaptations can be quite heterogeneous in their origins (Simonton, 2011). In particular, the prior work can entail (a) plays, such as the many films based on William Shakespeare (e.g., *Hamlet* [1948]); (b) novels or short stories, such as the numerous films adapted from Jane Austen or Charles Dickens (e.g., *Pride & Prejudice* [2005]); (c) nonfiction, such as *The Last Emperor* (1987; from Henry Pu yi's autobiography); (d) opera, operettas, and musical theater, such as *The Sound of Music* (1965); (e) religious scriptures and epic poems, such as *Beowulf* (2007); and (e) comic books, television shows, and video games, such as *Superman* (1978), *Star Trek: The Motion Picture* (1979), and *Lara Croft: Tomb Raider* (2001), respectively. Whatever the specifics, adaptations are very common. In one investigation fully 46 percent of the sampled films were adaptations (8 percent plays, 28 percent novels, 2 percent other fiction, 5 percent nonfiction, and 3 percent other material; Simonton, 2005b).

Here, I address the question of whether adaptations are more or less likely to exhibit cinematic impact. Yet that's not the only question worth addressing. What type of adaptation is best: plays, novels, TV shows, or some other source? Does the quality of the source matter? For example, does it make a difference whether the script is based on a literary classic, a Broadway hit, a best seller, or a prestigious prizewinner? And, last, does it matter whether the author of the original material contributed to the cinematic adaptation? Should the playwright or novelist participate? Alternatively, is the adaptation best left to expert screenwriters?

Box Office Impact. At a general level, adaptations do not seem to enjoy the same box office performance as original screenplays. In particular, no differences are observed with respect to production costs, the number of screens on opening weekend, the first-weekend gross, or the final domestic gross (Simonton, 2005b; cf. Chang & Ki, 2005; see also Simonton, 2009a). At a more specific level, however, adapted scripts do suffer relative to their original counterparts. The economic disadvantages are twofold: First, play adaptations open on fewer screens, earn less on their first weekend of release, and pull in a smaller domestic gross in comparison to original scripts (Simonton, 2005b). Adapted plays are likely too strongly linked with art rather than entertainment. In addition, when a play makes its way to the movie theater it often looks too stagy and claustrophobic to take full advantage of an artistic medium that encourages the liberal use of space and time. A play's emphasis on the word—dialogue and monologue—may also prove a negative in a cinematic rendition.

Second, the original author's active involvement in writing the adaptation only makes the product worse (Simonton, 2005b). No matter what the specific source—whether play, novel, or TV show—its original creator seems to interfere with producing a marketable screenplay. The more involvement, the higher the amount of interference. A screenplay with the author as sole adaptor is less likely to make money than is a screenplay with the author as co-adaptor. To be specific, films based on author adaptations are inclined to open on fewer screens and to bring in a smaller first weekend gross. Perhaps the original author remains too preoccupied with preserving "artistic integrity" to respond pragmatically to economic necessity.

All told, a producer should spurn play adaptations, and especially those adaptations in which the dramatist wrote or co-wrote the screenplay. Tom Stoppard's experience with his *Rosencrantz & Guildenstern Are Dead* may prove typical of an author-adapted play that flopped in the box office when adapted as a film script.

Film Honors. So far, it appears that it should be difficult to secure financial backing for an adaptation because the producers may not recoup their investment at the box office. Yet we have witnessed multiple times when movie awards do not always correspond to financial performance. The same lack of correspondence holds here, too (Simonton, 2005b; cf. Simonton, 2009a). First, screenplay adaptations have a higher probability of receiving nominations and awards for best picture, the likelihood increasing even more if the original source was either a novel or a nonfiction book. Second, adaptations have a higher probability of obtaining nominations and awards in the dramatic categories—like screenplay, direction, and acting—a correlation particularly strong for nonfiction adaptations. Third, adaptations feature a higher probability of receiving nominations and awards in the visual categories, an effect strongest for novels and nonfiction. In addition, adaptations of literary classics are positively associated with recognition in the visual categories. A script adapted from a novel by Austen or Dickens offers many opportunities for great cinematography, art production, costume design, and makeup. For instance, *Pride & Prejudice* (2005) received nominations in all four visual categories.

Nonetheless, if the goal is to garner as many awards as possible, adaptations do have some liabilities as well (Simonton, 2005b; cf. Simonton, 2009a). First, adaptations from novels are less inclined to receive recognition in the technical categories, and adaptations from plays are less inclined to receive recognition in the technical and music categories. Evidently, such literary adaptations put more emphasis on film as art and less on movies as entertainment. Second, adaptations in which the original author participated in the writing are also less likely to yield films that receive nominations and awards in the technical categories. It may be that when original authors enjoy some control over the final screenplays, they are more likely to veto the insertion of distracting special effects and other technological wizardry. That said, adaptations are more apt to gain honors in the cinematic categories that count the most.

Critical Acclaim. I have indicated many times that film critics are most inclined to concur with the award voters rather than with the movie ticket buyers. That inclination also shows up with respect to this script attribute, albeit the agreement is not perfect (Simonton, 2005b; cf. Simonton, 2009a). The principal concurrence is that critically acclaimed films are more likely to be adaptations from material from some other medium. Furthermore, critics appear particularly fond of literary classics. Last, of the different sources of adaptations, nonfiction works also show the strongest positive effect. The latter pair of findings seems contradictory because filmable nonfiction works are seldom literary classics. Edward Gibbon's *The History of the Decline and Fall of the Roman Empire* can be counted as a classic work of nonfiction literature, but nobody is going to make a movie adapted from its massive volumes. Hence, it is better to conclude that non-fiction works and literary classics offer two independent sources of adaptations that earn high praise from film critics.

One last curiosity is worth noting: Critical sleepers have a higher probability of being adaptations of bestsellers, whether fiction or nonfiction (Simonton, 2009c). That is, such films receive higher critical evaluations after release as DVDs or videos than the same films received during their theatrical run. This may suggest that later critical appraisals are better informed by critics actually reading the bestseller on which the script was based.

Caveats

We have just seen that numerous script attributes are positively or negatively associated with one or more criteria of cinematic success, whether box office impact, film honors, or critical acclaim. Although the size of the inventory may be impressive, I must be careful not to claim too much. The scientific research has certainly not reached the point at which I can quit my day job and earn a better income as a Hollywood script consultant. This caution is dictated by the following three considerations.

First, the predictive power of these attributes is not sufficiently high to make secure forecasts (Simonton, 2011). To illustrate, one investigation explained 35 percent of the variance in domestic gross, 9 percent of the variance in best picture honors, and 19 percent of the variance in critical evaluations using script attributes as predictors (Simonton, 2005b). Although these figures certainly tell us that the screenplay is important, the amount of variance explained is still smaller than would be required to make predictions that producers could use to avoid taking huge risks. Even in the case of domestic gross earnings, where over a third of the variance is accounted for, the predictive precision is not great enough to ensure that a film would be a blockbuster rather than a flop.

Second, the script success relationships reviewed so far are moderated by a host of other factors, so that a positive correlation under one set of conditions might become a negative correlation under another set of predictions. For instance, the impact of certain script attributes is contingent on the film's genre. In particular, although "sex doesn't sell" with respect to mainstream adult cinema (Cerridwen & Simonton, 2009), sex does sell with respect to family films (Simonton, Skidmore, & Kaufman, 2012). But, of course, this statement refers to different levels of sexuality and nudity. The sex in a film rated R or NC-17 is of a rather different kind than that in a film rated G, PG, or even PG-13. Thus, the title character in *WALL-E* putting on a bra over his eyes because he thinks it is goggles is not comparable to what goes on in *Lust, Caution*, or *The Dreamers* (examples of which I refrain from mentioning here). When filmmakers "push the envelope" in family films, they are pushing a different envelope than are those who produce films for mature audiences. Nor is genre the only moderator. For example, the predictive utility of different script characteristics varies according to how select is the sample of films: The predictors for films in general are not identical to films that have received nominations for major awards (Simonton, 2005b, 2009a). What differentiates the mediocre from the elite need not be the same as that differentiating the core-elite from the peripheral-elite.

Third and last, any film aficionado can easily protest that a vast number of script attributes have been omitted from consideration. For the most part, researchers have concentrated on those characteristics that are most easily assessed, such as genre and MPAA rating (Simonton, 2011). More subtle aspects of the protagonist, as well as of the storyline, have been largely ignored (but, for exceptions, see Beckwith, 2009; Eliashberg, Hui, & Zhang, 2006). Thus, it should make a difference whether the main character is sympathetic or repugnant, just as it should make a difference whether the screenplay has enormous plot holes or numerous clichés. These admissions only mean that investigators still have a lot of work to do. Yet what we can still say for sure is that the film's narrative does matter. The best films tell a great story.

References

Anast, P. (1967). Differential movie appeals as correlates of attendance. *Journalism Quarterly, 44*, 86–90.

Beckwith, D. C. (2009). Values of protagonists in best pictures and blockbusters: Implications for marketing. *Psychology and Marketing, 26*, 445–469.

Bornstein, R. F. (1989). Exposure and affect: Overview and meta-analysis of research, 1968-1987. *Psychological Bulletin, 106*, 265–289.

Cerridwen, A., & Simonton, D. K. (2009). Sex doesn't sell—nor impress: Content, box office, critics, and awards in mainstream cinema. *Psychology of Aesthetics, Creativity, and the Arts, 3*, 200–210.

Chang, B. -H., & Ki, E. -J. (2005). Devising a practical model for predicting theatrical movie success: Focusing on the experience good property. *Journal of Media Economics*, *18*, 247–269.

Collins, A., Hand, C., & Snell, M. C. (2002). What makes a blockbuster? Economic analysis of film success in the United Kingdom. *Managerial and Decision Economics*, *23*, 343–354.

De Silva, I. (1998). Consumer selection of motion pictures. In B. R. Litman (Ed.), *The motion picture mega-industry* (pp. 144–171). Boston: Allyn and Bacon.

De Vany, A., & Walls, W. D. (1999). Uncertainty in the movie industry: Does star power reduce the terror of the box office? *Journal of Cultural Economics*, *23*, 285–318.

De Vany, A., & Walls, W. D. (2002). Does Hollywood make too many R-rated movies? Risk, stochastic dominance, and the illusion of expectation. *Journal of Business*, *75*, 425–451.

Delmestri, G., Montanari, F., & Usai, A. (2005). Reputation and strength of ties in predicting commercial success and artistic merit of independents in the Italian feature film industry. *Journal of Management Studies*, *42*, 975–1002.

Eliashberg, J., Hui, S. K., & Zhang, Z. J. (2006). From storyline to box office: A new approach for green-lighting movie scripts. Working paper, The Wharton School, University of Pennsylvania.

Holbrook, M. B. (1999). Popular appeal versus expert judgments of motion pictures. *Journal of Consumer Research*, *26*, 144–155.

Lee, F. L. F. (2006). Cultural discount and cross-culture predictability: Examining the box office performance of American movies in Hong Kong. *Journal of Media Economics*, *19*, 259–278.

Litman, B. R. (1983). Predicting success of theatrical movies: An empirical study. *Journal of Popular Culture*, *16*, 159–175.

Litman, B. R., & Ahn, H. (1998). Predicting financial success of motion pictures: The early '90s experience. In B. R. Litman (Ed.), *The motion picture mega-industry* (pp. 172–197). Boston: Allyn and Bacon.

Litman, B. R., & Kohl, L. S. (1989). Predicting financial success of motion pictures: The '80s experience. *Journal of Media Economics*, *2*, 35–50.

McKenzie, J. (2009). Revealed word-of-mouth demand and adaptive supply: Survival of motion pictures at the Australian box office. *Journal of Cultural Economics*, *33*, 279–299.

Medved, M. (1992). *Hollywood vs. America: Popular culture and the war on traditional values* (1st ed.). New York: HarperCollins.

Pardoe, I., & Simonton, D. K. (2008). Applying discrete choice models to predict Academy Award winners. *Journal of the Royal Statistical Society: Series A (Statistics in Society)*, *171*, 375–394.

Prag, J., & Casavant, J. (1994). An empirical study of the determinants of revenues and marketing expenditures in the motion picture industry. *Journal of Cultural Economics*, *18*, 217–235.

Pritzker, S. R., & McGarva, D. J. (2009). Characteristics of eminent screenwriters: Who *are* those guys? In S. B. Kaufman & J. C. Kaufman (Eds.), *The psychology of creative writing* (pp. 57–59). New York: Cambridge University Press.

Ravid, S. A. (1999). Information, blockbusters, and stars: A study of the film industry. *Journal of Business, 72*, 463–492.

Ravid, S. A., & Basuroy, S. (2004). Managerial objectives, the R-rating puzzle, and the production of violent films. *Journal of Business, 77*, S155–S192

Sawhney, M. S., & Eliasberg, J. (1996). A parsimonious model for forecasting gross box-office revenues of motion pictures. *Marketing Science, 15*, 113–131.

Simonoff, J., & Sparrow, I. (2000). Predicting movie grosses: Winners and losers, blockbusters and sleepers. *Chance, 13* (3), 15–24.

Simonton, D. K. (1983). Dramatic greatness and content: A quantitative study of eighty-one Athenian and Shakespearean plays. *Empirical Studies of the Arts, 1*, 109–123.

Simonton, D. K. (1986). Popularity, content, and context in 37 Shakespeare plays. *Poetics, 15*, 493–510.

Simonton, D. K. (2004a). Film awards as indicators of cinematic creativity and achievement: A quantitative comparison of the Oscars and six alternatives. *Creativity Research Journal, 16*, 163–172.

Simonton, D. K. (2004b). Group artistic creativity: Creative clusters and cinematic success in 1,327 feature films. *Journal of Applied Social Psychology, 34*, 1494–1520.

Simonton, D. K. (2005a). Cinematic creativity and production budgets: Does money make the movie? *Journal of Creative Behavior, 39*, 1–15.

Simonton, D. K. (2005b). Film as art versus film as business: Differential correlates of screenplay characteristics. *Empirical Studies of the Arts, 23*, 93–117.

Simonton, D. K. (2007). Is bad art the opposite of good art? Positive versus negative cinematic assessments of 877 feature films. *Empirical Studies of the Arts, 25*, 143–161.

Simonton, D. K. (2009a). Cinematic success, aesthetics, and economics: An exploratory recursive model. *Psychology of Creativity, Aesthetics, and the Arts, 3*, 128–138.

Simonton, D. K. (2009b). Cinematic success criteria and their predictors: The art and business of the film industry. *Psychology and Marketing, 26*, 400–420.

Simonton, D. K. (2009c). Controversial and volatile flicks: Contemporary consensus and temporal stability in film critic assessments. *Creativity Research Journal, 21*, 311–318.

Simonton, D. K. (2011). *Great flicks: Scientific studies of cinematic creativity and aesthetics.* New York: Oxford University Press.

Simonton, D. K., Skidmore, L. E. & Kaufman, J. C. (2012). Mature cinematic content for immature minds: "Pushing the envelope" versus "toning it down" in family films. *Empirical Studies of the Arts, 30*, 143–166.

Sochay, S. (1994). Predicting the performance of motion pictures. *Journal of Media Economics, 7,* 1–20.

Terry, N., Butler, M., & De'Armond, D. (2005). Determinants of domestic box office performance in the motion picture industry. *Southwestern Economic Review, 32,* 137–148.

Thompson, K. M., & Yokota, F. (2004). Violence, sex, and profanity in films: Correlation of movie ratings with content. *Medscape General Medicine, 6*(3), 3–54.

Walls, W. D. (2005a). Modelling heavy tails and skewness in film returns. *Applied Financial Economics, 15,* 1181–1188.

Walls, W. D. (2005b). Modeling movie success when "Nobody knows anything": Conditional stable-distribution analysis of film returns. *Journal of Cultural Economics, 29,* 177–190.

Wyatt, J. (1994). *High concept: Movies and marketing in Hollywood.* Austin, TX: University of Texas Press.

2

SELL-BY DATE?

EXAMINING THE SHELF LIFE AND EFFECTS OF FEMALE ACTORS IN POPULAR FILMS

Stacy L. Smith, Amy Granados, Marc Choueiti, and Katherine M. Pieper

We live in a post-feminist world. Right? After all, two women did contend for positions in the executive branch during the 2008 presidential race, and Nancy Pelosi was the Speaker of the US House of Representatives for 4 consecutive years. In addition to politics, females are making gains in both educational and employment arenas. *USA Today* (Marklein, 2010) reported that females earn more bachelor's degrees than do their male counterparts. Furthermore, women now comprise roughly half of the American workforce (Boushey, 2009, p. 33). Given this, Maria Shriver (2009, p. 6) and the Center for American Progress recently declared that the United States is now "a woman's nation." Women not only work as much as men but some have asserted that they control roughly 80 percent of the purchasing decisions in the home (Barletta, 2006).

Despite these steps forward, it seems that some segments of society are still sitting idle (or taking steps back) in terms of gender equality. In 2007, *Vanity Fair* writer Christopher Hitchens declared that females aren't as funny as men (notwithstanding the recent box office success of *Bridesmaids* and Tina Fey's best-selling book *Bossypants*). That same year, on the heels of lackluster box office performances by Jodie Foster's *The Brave One* and Nicole Kidman's *The Invasion*, Nikki Finke asserted that Warner Brothers' president of production said the company was done making female-driven films (Finke, 2007). Humor and bankability aside, female actors and industry insiders indicate that being "fuckable" is still a factor affecting male content creators' casting decisions (Cuban, Wagner, & Arquette, 2002).

Against the backdrop of these inconsistent societal trends, the aim of this chapter is to review research on the status of females in one cultural industry: popular films. Toward this goal, the chapter is divided into three main sections. First, the content analytic work on gender roles in motion picture content is reviewed. The aim of this section is to document the portrayal of gender on the silver screen. Given the infrequency and stereotyping of females, the second section focuses on reasons for these skewed depictions. Rather than relying on the press, anecdotal evidence, or speculation, the results of a recent qualitative study interviewing more than one hundred industry leaders about gender hegemony in popular studio films are delineated. The third section focuses on effects. In light of content patterns, the last segment of the chapter covers research on the consequences for youth of consuming stereotypical and/or sexualized cinematic content.

It is important to note three caveats at the outset of this chapter. The first pertains to the time frame of the content analytic research reviewed. Only studies conducted between 1990 and present day are discussed. Consequently, this is *not* a historical overview of empirical research on females in film because anything published pre tent-pole/high concept is not relevant in today's market forces. The second is that this review takes an audience-based approach, with the child consumer in mind. Young viewers may be more susceptible to some types of media effects: as a result, the chapter privileges content studies on family films and primarily focuses on research involving participants younger than 21 years of age. The third is that we have already written a recently published overview on theorizing and effects of sex-role stereotyping (Smith & Granados, 2009). Rather than rehash the same literature, here, we focus our review narrowly on three potential outcomes and point the reader to our aforementioned chapter for a more detailed analysis of theoretical mechanisms.

Content Patterns

Over the past 5 years, our research team has conducted multiple studies on the prevalence and portrayal of males and females in popular films (e.g., Smith & Choueiti, 2011a,b; Smith & Choueiti, 2010a,b; Smith, Choueiti, Granados, & Erickson, 2008; Smith & Cook, 2008; Smith, Pieper, Granados, & Choueiti, 2010a). Some of these studies have been funded by Academy Award® winner Geena Davis' See Jane Program and others have been subsidized by the Annenberg School for Communication and Journalism. Several consistent trends have emerged across this body of work, to which we now turn.

The first trend is that gender equity still does not exist in popular films. Looking at 122 fictional English-language G-, PG-, and PG-13-rated films theatrically released between September 5, 2006 and September 7, 2009, Smith and Choueiti (2010b) coded every discernible on-screen speaking character. A total of 5,554 distinct characters were evaluated, with 29.2 percent female and 70.8 percent male. Similar results were obtained across a sample of 400 popular G-, PG-, PG-13-, and R-rated films released between 1990 and 2006 (Smith & Cook, 2008). The results showed that only 27 percent of speaking characters in that study were female. Other research has documented that female characters can occupy anywhere from 25 to 33 percent of roles (Bazzini, McIntosh, Smith, Cook, & Harris, 1997; Lauzen & Dozier, 2005; Powers, Rothman, & Rothman, 1996; Smith & Choueiti, 2011a and b).

Some variation exists in the portrayal of gender by Motion Picture Association of America (MPAA) rating. In Smith and Choueiti's (2010b) study of 122 films, a significant but trivial difference (less than 5 percent) was observed by rating. As rating increased, the percentage of females slightly decreased (G = 32.4 percent, PG = 30 percent, PG-13 = 27.7 percent). We also found the same significant but trivial tendency across the 400-film study (Smith & Cook, 2008), with the ratio of males to females by rating as follows: G = 2.5:1; PG = 2.6:1; PG-13 = 2.8:1, and R = 2.9:1.

The second trend reveals that there has been no change in the percentage of females in popular films over time. Combining two of our datasets and coding additional general audience movies, we assessed gender prevalence in popular films released between January 1, 1990 and September 7, 2009 (Smith & Choueiti, 2010b). Every first-run G-rated film ($n = 150$) in this period was examined, as well as 148 PG films and 150 PG-13 films. All re-releases were removed prior to analysis. Separating the films into roughly 3–5 year blocks of time (see Table 2.1), we found no significant change within rating ($p < .05$).

Looking at the bottom row of Table 2.1, less than a 1 percent change has occurred from 1990–95 to 2006–09. Significant but trivial deviation (less than

Table 2.1 Percentage of Female Characters in G, PG, and PG-13 Films by Time

Rating	1990–1995	1996–2000	2001–2006	2006–2009
G	29.9%	27.4%	28.7%	32.6%
PG	28.3%	29.8%	28.1%	30.0%
PG-13	26.6%	28.4%	25%	27.7%
Total	28.7%	28.3%	26.9%	29.3%

Films were theatrically released between January 1, 1990 and September 7, 2009. For the third epoch, the cutoff date was September 4, 2006 and the start date for the fourth epoch was September 5, 2006.

5 percent) also was observed in our assessment of gender prevalence across 150 Academy Award® Best Picture nominated films (Smith et al., 2008) between 1977 and 2006: 1977–86 (27.2 percent female), 1987–96 (28.9 percent female), and 1997–2006 (25.4 percent female). Interestingly, though, our recent follow-up to this study (Smith, Choueiti, & Gall, 2012) found a significant increase in the percentage of females (32.6 percent) in Academy Award® Best Picture nominated films from 2007 to 2010.

Turning from prevalence to the way in which characters are portrayed, the third trend is that females are more likely to be hypersexualized than are their male counterparts. Across 122 G, PG, and PG-13 films, females are more likely than males to be shown in sexy (tight and/or revealing) attire (24 percent vs. 4 percent), partially naked or showing exposed skin between mid chest and upper thigh region (18.5 percent vs. 5.6 percent), and/or beautiful (14 percent vs. 3.6 percent).[1] Females are also more likely than males to be depicted with a small waist (22.9 percent vs. 4.5 percent), leaving little room for a womb or any other internal organ. In animation (e.g., Jasmine in *Aladdin*), female waist sizes are so small that sometimes they approximate the circumference of the character's upper arms! The presence of a large chest or unrealistic body ideal (hourglass for females, inverted triangle for males) did not differ meaningfully by gender.

The fourth trend pertains to fulfilling traditional roles, which is more characteristic of females than males. Smith and Cook (2008), examining parental status of characters across 400 films, found a higher percentage of females (52.2 percent) than males (40.4 percent) were caregivers. This gender gap has closed a bit more recently, with Smith and Choueiti's (2010b) results revealing that 54.7 percent of females and 47.6 percent of males were typecast as parents. No difference emerged in the percentage of males and females portrayed as relational partners. This may be due to the fact that Hollywood is beginning to depict females more equitably in a diverse range of roles. Alternatively, it may be the case that the economic success of "bromance" and male-driven romantic comedies facilitates casting more males in domesticated contexts.

Research also reveals that occupations are often sex linked. Examining frequency of employment across 101 popular G-rated films released between 1990 and 2005, Smith et al. (2010a) found that a higher percentage (but not significantly different) of males (55.2 percent) than females (48.2 percent) were depicted with an occupation. Almost a fifth of the working females (16.2 percent) were shown in traditionally male occupations whereas only 2.3 percent of the working males were shown in traditionally female ones. Hence, there are very few counter-stereotypical role models, especially for younger male viewers.

A larger gender gap was observed more recently, when Smith, Choueiti, and Stern (2011a) coded occupation across every first-run theatrical G-rated film ($n = 21$) released between 2006 and 2009. In this study, 58 percent of males held a job but only 32 percent of females did. A higher percentage of females than males were shown in professional jobs or white-collar careers. Although this may seem like progress, females were noticeably absent in other prestigious occupational domains. In contrast to males, not one female was depicted working in the medical sciences (e.g., medical doctor, dentist, veterinarian), executive business suites (e.g., CEO), law, or politics. More optimistically, females (just like their male counterparts) were shown employed in the hard sciences and as astronauts/pilots. Evaluating eighty-eight films from 2002, Lauzen and Dozier's (2005) results revealed that among major characters, a higher percentage of males than females held occupational power in their 30s ($M = 73$ percent vs. $F = 63$ percent, $p < .10$), 40s ($M = 82$ percent vs. $F = 66$ percent, $p < .05$), and 50s ($M = 86$ percent vs. $F = 68$ percent, $p < .10$).

The last trend involves ageism, with females being presented as younger than their male counterparts. In the 2006–09 study, we found that a higher percentage of females than males were younger than 21 (20.5 vs. 12.5 percent) and 21–39 years of age (54.3 vs. 49.3 percent). Among characters 40–64 years of age, the pattern is opposite, with 33.7 percent of speaking roles filled by males and 20.2 percent filled by females. Minimal differences in age by gender emerge for characters 65 years or older (males = 4.4 percent, females = 5 percent). Other studies document somewhat similar age by gender effects (Bazzini et al., 1997; Lauzen & Dozier, 2005; Smith & Choueiti, 2010a; Smith & Choueiti, 2011b).

Overall, gender plays a role in the prevalence and portrayal of males and females in popular films. Not only are females infrequently portrayed when one considers that they comprise roughly half of the US population, but they also tend to be either young and sexy (e.g., "sex pot") or old and domesticated (e.g., "sex not"). The latter suggests that there is clearly a "sell-by date" for females in film and that their typical shelf life is roughly 40 years.

Reasons for Stereotyping Females in Film

What accounts for the prevalence and portrayal of females in family films? In a recent interview study (Smith, Granados, & Choueiti, 2011b; Smith, Granados, Choueiti, Erickson, & Noyes, 2011c) funded by the Geena Davis Institute for Gender and Media, we asked 108 male (60.2 percent) and female (39.8 percent) industry leaders about some of the just-mentioned trends. Content creators had, on average, a little more than 23 years of experience (*range* = 4–46 years) in the film industry and their mean age was 47.13 years (*range* = 30–65 years). The qualitative interviews were audio recorded, transcribed, and then subjected to analysis. In total, we captured nearly 90 interview hours (i.e., more than 2 full work weeks) and transcribed over 1,000 pages.

Prevalence

After presenting industry leaders with the percentage of females across 300 top-grossing G, PG, and PG-13 films from 1990 to 2006, we asked, "Why do you think that females represent less than 30 percent of all speaking characters?" Spontaneous answers were content analyzed by two independent judges. Six major reasons emerged (see Table 2.2), with "positive male market forces" being the most frequently cited answer to this question (43.7 percent). This referred to the bankability of male leads, male-oriented genres, and/or male stars. More male than female industry leaders gave this response (48.3 vs. 37.2 percent). As a point of comparison, not quite a fifth of participants referred to "negative female market forces" in their answers (18.3 percent males, 11.6 percent females; see Table 2.2). This response is surprising, given the recent box office success of female-driven films (e.g., the *Twilight* franchise, *Alice in Wonderland,* or *Hunger Games*) and the movie industry's tendency to focus on replicating the immediate past when green-lighting films for the near future.

What does research reveal about the relationship between box office and gender of lead characters and/or casts? To date, a few studies have been conducted (e.g., Garrison, 1971; Wallace, Seigerman, & Holbrook, 1993), with only two directly and recently answering this question. Using the one-hundred top-grossing films worldwide in 2007, Lauzen (2008, p. 2) examined the box office prowess of female-oriented films (i.e., a protagonist or notable female in an ensemble) versus male-oriented films. Female movies, in comparison to male movies, had—on average—lower production costs, sold fewer tickets, and initially played in fewer theatres. However, Lauzen (2008) notes "When the size of the budget is held constant, films with female protagonists or prominent females in an ensemble cast earn similar box office grosses...as films with male protagonists...the differences in box office grosses are not caused by the sex of the protagonist but by the size of the budget" (p. 2).

Smith, Weber, and Choueiti (2010b) conducted a similar analysis using the one-hundred top-grossing domestic movies from 2007. These scholars put female films to a much more stringent test, however. Only those narratives that featured a girl/woman as the protagonist ($n = 18$) or co-lead ($n = 2$) were categorized as female-driven. In addition to leads, more than ten production, distribution, and exhibition variables were examined. Using structural equations, Smith et al.'s (2010b) models accounted for 45–70 percent of the variability in ticket

Table 2.2 Examples of Industry Leaders' Spontaneous Responses Within Reason

Reason	Industry Leader Responses
Positive Male Market Forces	**43.7%**
Director	Comic books are generally very male-oriented and those have become some of the biggest grossing films out there.
Producer	[T]hey try to make material that is...the least risk possible and that tends to be genre films, a lot of male-driven things that they know can make money overseas no matter what the domestic box office is so they feel safer betting their money.
Producer	I would say that it's easier to finance films with men. The research, you know, that's been done, people who then tell you how much money you can get for your film, it's always the male lead, you know, that has the bigger box office.... There's more action films and the action films have more men and there's more animated films with male leads.... Well, we're told that male characters sell. I don't necessarily believe that, so.
Director	Stories with men sell better.
Male-Dominated Industry	**32.0%**
Executive	The majority of the screenwriters are male...
Casting	In part, because we work in a male-driven industry.... We're in an industry where writers are predominantly male, directors are predominantly male so they are more likely to tell male-oriented stories.
Director	The directors and writers are predominantly male.... I've read about what percentage of the WGA is female and it's very small...
Director	It's sort of a reflection of how many women are...in...the creative roles.... And that's kind of a top to bottom thing; I mean I notice that in animation, too.... All the way down the line through production, it's predominantly male.

(*continued*)

Table 2.2 (Continued)

Reason	Industry Leader Responses
Male Target Audience	20.4%
Executive	Because studios are targeting boys.
Executive	[T]his assumption that the ticket-going audience is fourteen-year-old boys.
Director	They cater to the guy audience.
Producer	[S]adly and largely…it is teenage boys who most often go to the theater and most often go over and over again and…as a result of that fact studios make movies for that demographic.
Males Resist Females' Stories	17.5%
Producer	The research that everybody cites is that girls will go to the movies boys go to but boys are too embarrassed to go to the movies girls go to.
Executive	[I]t's easier to get women to see men movies, than it is to get men to see women movies.
Writer	A male audience will go to watch a male character, a female audience will go to watch a male character; a male audience is not going to watch a female character so, it's just a commercial, purely business decision.
Producer	Women will go see…movies about men or women. But men like to see more male-driven material. I think a lot of times when on a date night, you know, a woman will concede to see a horror film before a man'll concede to see a romantic comedy, which would be a more female-driven film.
Negative Female Market Forces	15.5%
Producer	It's possible that there are plenty of scripts written that are more women-centric that studios just don't make for economic reasons.
Producer	Money. It's [a] perception that a woman cannot open a film.
Executive	Historically, films with female protagonists…have sometimes flopped and there's an aversion, I think, to those films.

(continued)

Table 2.2 (Continued)

Reason	Industry Leader Responses
Writer	If it were very easy to make stupid money with female leads there would be a[n] absolute flood of female lead movies.... I think those people are interested absolutely in making money and if doing it easily with a female lead would happen, there would be female lead movies all the time.
Cultural Influences	8.7%
Casting	[I]t's a male-based society...
Director	Male-dominated world

Excerpts are from Smith et al. (2011). Changing the status quo: Industry leaders' perceptions of gender in family films. Report prepared for the Geena Davis Institute for Gender in Media, Los Angeles, CA.

sales. In short, the three strongest predictors (direct, indirect paths) of box office performance (domestically, internationally) were production costs, distribution density, and critics' reviews. Gender of lead character or gender composition of casts played a small to nonsignificant role in the financial performance of films. Together, the results from these two studies cautiously suggest that female-driven films may not be the box-office poison that some purport. Given that both of these studies focused on 2007 films and theatrical ticket sales, more research is needed before definitive claims can be made about the financial impact of characters' gender in movies both in the short-term (box office performance) or long-term via other distribution windows (DVD, TV/cable broadcasting, ancillary products).

Differing little by gender of study participant, the second reason for the infrequency of females in film (32 percent) is "male-dominated industry." This seems to be right on point, as the ratio of males to females in above-the-line positions of director, producer, or writer was 4.88:1 across 122 films released between 2006 and 2009. Only 7 percent of directors ($n = 144$), 13 percent of writers ($n = 432$), and 20 percent of producers ($n = 989$) were female.

Can having a female in one of these gatekeeping positions make a difference in the frequency of girls/women on-screen? To answer this question, we bifurcated the sample of films featuring a female director versus those with only male direction. The same thing was done with writers and producers. We then looked at the percentage of females on-screen in each category. The percentage of girls/women on-screen increases significantly when a female is involved in directing (Fdir = 35.1 percent of speaking characters are female vs. Mdir = 28.8

percent) or writing (Fwriter = 36.4 percent vs. Mwriter = 26 percent). Producer gender also has a significant but less pronounced association (less than 5 percent) with the percentage of female characters on-screen. These trends are some-what consistent with those observed across 150 Academy Award® Best Picture (Smith et al., 2008) nominated films or the one-hundred top-grossing films from 2007 (Smith & Choueiti, 2010a), 2008 (Smith & Choueiti, 2011a), and 2009 (Smith & Choueiti, 2011b).

There are at least two possible explanations for these findings. It may be that behind-the-scenes females are more mindful of including female actors across the population of speaking characters (i.e., writing background characters who are female, flexible casting with small parts). Or, it may be the case that studio executives feel more comfortable giving female-driven properties to female writers and/or directors. As a result, the types of films females get the opportunity to direct and/or write may be narrow in scope (e.g., romantic comedies, dramas) and limited in terms of earning potential (see Writers Guild of America, West, 2011; also Smith, Pieper, & Choueiti, 2013).

The third reason that content creators gave for the lack of females in film per-tained to the target audience: males. More than 20 percent of content creators said that males are more frequent moviegoers than females, males are more likely to determine which movies are selected, or the industry targets the male con-sumer (see Table 2.2). This reason was cited by a higher percentage of female (25.6 percent) than male (16.7 percent) participants. Data from the MPAA (Motion Picture Association of America, 2011, 2010, 2009) sheds light on atten-dance patterns by gender. In 2009, US females purchased 55 percent of movie tickets whereas US males purchased 45 percent. Females bought 50 percent of the tickets sold in 2010, however. Similar gender findings emerged in 2011. These domestic statistics reveal that females go to the box office just as much as their male counterparts.

The fourth reason (17.5 percent) suggests that males are more discriminat-ing than females when selecting movies. Girls will watch stories about boys, but boys will not watch stories about girls. Female content creators (30.2 percent) were more likely than their male counterparts (8.3 percent) to spontaneously give this response. However, when we asked participants a follow-up question and inquired if this specific reason accounted for the infrequency of females in film, more than 95 percent of those interviewed said "yes" or "maybe." This is surpris-ing, given that content studies show that females comprise *more than half* of all teen speaking characters in popular teen-oriented movies (Behm-Morawitz & Mastro, 2008; Stern, 2005). In our own study of 122 top-grossing films, females occupied 44.2 percent of all teen roles. Despite what content creators say, stories with a large percentage of female characters are not repelling the young male demographic from the box office.

What is also interesting is that this claim has not been rigorously tested by social scientists. Surveys have had children or emerging adults report their "favorite" TV characters (Hoffner, 1996; Hoffner & Buchanan, 2005) and/ or rate their level of identification with popular TV figures (Miller & Reeves, 1976; Reeves & Miller, 1978). Hoffner and Buchanan (2005) found that undergraduates are more likely to wishfully identify with and perceive themselves as similar to same sex characters. With younger viewers, other studies (Hoffner, 1996; Miller & Reeves, 1976; Reeves & Miller, 1978) show that same-sex character identification (including choice of favorite character) is stronger for boys than girls. Furthermore, females are more likely to cite male characters as favorites and/or identify with them than males are to cite female characters (Miller & Reeves, 1976; Reeves & Miller, 1978). Somewhat similar gender-based patterns have been observed among youngsters selecting heroes/ heroines (Holub, Tisak, & Mullins, 2008; Gash & Conway, 1997). Hoffner (1996, p. 390; Hoffner & Buchanan, 2005, p. 329) summarizes two potential explanations for these asymmetrical gender findings: (1) there are more active and interesting roles for male than female characters on TV/film, and (2) culture is more intolerant of boys/men embracing stereotypically feminine qualities than of girls/women embracing stereotypically masculine ones.

Experimentally, a slightly different picture emerges. Holding base stories constant but varying protagonist gender (among other factors), Jose and Brewer (1984) found that character liking and perceived similarity was gender-linked but story enjoyment was not. Put differently, the average story liking was independent of the lead character's gender across male and female elementary school-aged participants. Showing short movie clips (*Beauty & the Beast*; *Teenage Mutant Ninja Turtles*) of G-rated films to 3- to 9-year-olds, Oliver and Green's (2001) results reveal that enjoyment was interactively influenced by participants' gender and whether they labeled the clips stereotypically for males or females. If the participants did not stereotype the content, no differences by gender in enjoyment were reported—which is similar to Jose and Brewer's (1984) findings. Labeling the clips stereotypically (e.g., "a male film," "a female film"), however, *decreased* enjoyment significantly for those participants watching clips featuring an opposite-sex protagonist. It must be noted that these findings emerged across participants' self-reports but not facial responses of enjoyment. Given the paucity of research in this area, future studies are needed to understand when children begin stereotyping motion picture content and how content (i.e., genre, music, themes, setting) and environmental factors (i.e., parents, siblings, peers, marketing of films) independently and interactively contribute to this process.

The final reason cited by our study participants was culture. A small percentage of individuals pointed to larger patterns of societal patriarchy (see Table 2.2).

Consistent with this reason, diverse feminist scholars have hailed the social and political advances of the women's movement (Baumgardner & Richards, 2000) while acknowledging that girls and women continue to experience the consequences of patriarchy at home, in the workforce, and in society at large (MacKinnon, 2003; McRobbie, 2009). To illuminate this point, consider the following statistics: only ninety (16.8 percent of 535) women were seated in the US Congress as of February 2012 (see Center for American Women and Politics, 2012); at American Fortune 500 companies, women hold only eighteen (3.6 percent) CEO positions (CNNMoney, 2012). As these data points reveal, women are still noticeably absent from two powerful cultural arenas (i.e., politics, business).

It is interesting to note that these six reasons were roughly the same ones given by the content creators for the lack of female lead characters (as opposed to all speaking characters) in popular family films. It is possible that industry leaders were not thinking about the entire population of speaking characters with regard to gender balance. In fact, almost a third of the study participants indicated spontaneously that they would not notice if a film or screenplay featured female characters in roughly 50 percent of all speaking roles. As such, another reason for the infrequency of females in film may be that content creators (males *and* females) simply do not pay attention to gender imbalance on-screen.

Sexualization

In the same study, industry leaders also were asked about the sexualization of girls/women in family films (Smith, Granados, & Choueiti, 2011b). After showing content creators two figures depicting gender differences (i.e., sample-wide across 300 G, PG, PG-13 films, comparison of live-action and animated females in 100 G-rated films) across multiple hypersexualization measures we asked, "Why do you think females are more likely to be sexualized than males in animated formats?" Again, open-ended responses were transcribed and coded by two independent judges.

Seven reasons emerged from the content creators' responses, with the first pointing to culture (45.1 percent) or "references to what individuals and/or society likes, desires, or expects with regard to physical appearance" (Smith, Granados, & Choueiti, 2011b, p. 2). Stated differently, movies simply mirror life. Females (63.9 percent) were more likely to give this reason than were males (30.4 percent). Some examples from the content creators' interviews include:

It goes back to that darn Barbie drat her....of course little girls are attracted to beautiful women figures and they wanna be beautiful and sexy...because men find sexy beautiful. So even at a young age women wanna be sexy because it's what men like. (Producer)

Why has the Barbie Doll endured all these years? Clearly, it's not just young men or men that are drawn to that. Girls are drawn to it, too. And again I think that harkens back to what is perceived as a societal ideal. (Casting director)

I think in society women are sex objects and men are pursuers. (Producer)

Do child consumers prefer sexy cinema characters? Although recent research reveals that sexualized content in theatrically released motion pictures "Doesn't Sell—Nor Impress!" (Cerridwen & Simonton, 2009, p. 200), less empirical work has been done on the pull of hypersexualized characters on young consumers. Social cognitive theory suggests that attractive characters are potent role models that can foster attention (Bandura, 1986).

The alluring quality of attractive faces seems to begin very early in life, as laboratory research reveals that 6- to 8- month-old infants show more visual attentiveness to attractive female faces than to unattractive ones (Langlois et al., 1987). Subsequent studies document that 12-month-olds interacting with a stranger wearing an attractive mask demonstrate *more* liking and play behavior and marginally *less* resistance than those interacting with a stranger wearing an unattractive mask (Langlois, Roggman, & Rieser-Danner, 1990). Follow-up research shows that 12-month-old boys and girls play (measured by length of contact) with an attractive female doll significantly more than a highly similar unattractive one. Other studies illustrate that 6-month-olds are drawn to slides depicting desirous faces of (1) males and females, (2) Caucasian and African-American women, and (3) adults and infants (Langlois, Ritter, Roggman, & Vaughn, 1991). The magnetism of attraction has been explained using prototype processing. According to Rubenstein, Kalakanis, and Langlois (1999), "Prototype models predict that mathematical averageness in a face is considered attractive because of its similarity to the abstracted central tendency that people store as a category representation" (p. 854). Data collected via laboratory experiments with 6-month-olds supports this theorizing (Rubenstein et al., 1999).

Television studies with children also establish the lure of attractive characters. Physical attractiveness or good looks is a significant predictor of boys' and girls' TV character identification and/or parasocial relationships (Hoffner, 1996; Reeves & Miller 1978). Other research with college-aged females only shows a same-sex effect (Hoffner & Buchanan, 2005).

To date, we are not aware of any study that reveals that the *sexiness* of cinema characters, rather than—or in addition to—their attractive appearance, affects child viewer–character liking/identification. One study (Morawitz, 2007), which actually manipulated the presence or absence of sexually revealing attire on an attractive female protagonist in a popular video game (i.e., *Tomb Raider: Legend*, 2006), found no difference in undergraduate participants' ratings of game enjoyment or character attractiveness between the two conditions (sexy attire/attractive Lara vs. nonsexy attire/attractive Lara). Operationalizing sexiness as a small waist, Götz (2008) showed a representative sample of 1,055 children 3–12 years old three manipulated images of two female TV characters with varying waist-to-hip (WHR) ratios and asked them to select which one they liked best. The majority of children preferred female characters (i.e., Bibi Blocksberg, Cloe from *Bratz*) with an average waist size (WHR = 0.8 or 0.7, respectively). This research suggests that although kids may be drawn to attractive media characters, adding "sexiness" may not increase appeal. Clearly, more experimental research in this area is needed.

The second reason was "roles females play," which was spontaneously cited by 35.7 percent of the content creators and deviated little by gender (Males = 36.2 percent, Females = 35.1 percent). This category was inclusive of the role, function, and appearance associated with the construction of female characters in animated films (Smith et al., 2011b). Not surprisingly, in our own qualitative analysis (Smith & Cook, 2008) of thirteen female-driven G-rated animated and live action films theatrically released between 1937 and 2006, more than 90 percent focused on love and romance, greater than 33 percent included an extreme makeover, and more than 66 percent showed females being put on display for a social presentation. The latter types of depictions may not only foster viewers' gaze of G-rated gals but reinforce among young girls and boys the heteronormative tendency to objectify females (see Fredrickson & Roberts, 1997). Here are some examples of the content creators' responses:

It's the fantasy for young. It's the sort of princess fantasy. (Producer)

I think it's the roles they're playing. It's the characters they're playing. (Producer)

If I'm thinking about a typical Disney film, which is all about fairytale, fairytale love presenting this ideal. This ideal love, this ideal relationship, this ideal everything is painted in this idealistic including, the female body. (Executive)

The third reason for the sexualization of females points to gender imbalance in the production of animated films. A full 23.3 percent of the content creators indicated that it is a boy's club, with more females (27 percent) offering this reason than males (20.4 percent). Consistent with this explanation, less than a fifth (17.3 percent) of all animation guild members in 2006 were female across more than ten different job titles such as directors, writers, art directors, layout, and 3D animators and modelers (Smith & Cook, 2008, p. 21). The percentage of *working* female content creators in animation is much lower than these union-based statistics, however. For this chapter, we examined the biological sex of every credited director and screenwriter across each fully or partially animated first-run G-rated film theatrically released between January 1990 and September 2009.[2] Across eighty-seven movies, only 1.44 percent of directors (2 of 139) and 13 percent of writers (71 of 541) were female. Animation is largely a male bastion, with a ratio of 8.315 males to every 1 female working in this arena.

The fourth reason pertains to the art form of animation, which capitalizes on exaggeration. The only limitations in this craft reside in the minds and imaginations of inspirational sketch artists. As Wells (1998, p. 188) states, "Cartooning has always been informed by the tradition of caricature, that both operates as a *satirical mechanism* which makes comment through its exaggeration of certain physical traits, and *as a design strategy*, which concentrates on redefining and exaggerating aspects of the body or environment, for purely *aesthetic* purposes" (emphasis original). Just under a fifth of the content creators (19.8 percent) mentioned that the art form may contribute to hypersexualization. Very little difference was observed between genders (Males = 20.4 percent, Females = 18.9 percent). Examples from the transcripts include:

> You can draw Snow White with a 13 inch waist and no one has to really fit into a corset. So, you can even take it further, cause you can. (Director)

> You say sexualized and I think that some people would also say 'idealized.' Like that's the ideal, this hourglass form being pretty, and being very toothsome....You can make something as idealized as you want to...you're not beholden to what people actually really look like. (Director)

> Oh my God because you can draw what you want. You can idealize what you draw. (Director)

The history of animation was the fifth most frequently cited response (18.8 percent), with some variation among male (20.8 percent) and female content creators (16.2 percent). For this category to be coded, industry leaders may have focused on precedent-setting characters/films or the traditions set in motion from early animation. In the earliest Disney films (i.e., *Snow White, Pinocchio*), animation tasks were performed almost entirely by men. Females were relegated primarily to the inking and painting departments. Dozens of young women were involved in the production of these early feature-length films, but rarely received screen credit although they served a crucial function in bringing the animators' vision to life (Thomas, 1935; Zohn, 2010). Excerpts from the content creators' interviews include:

> Again, I think you're following a tradition going back to *Snow White and the Seven Dwarfs*.... There is an idolized version of how princesses or animated female leads should look and therefore it—there's a continuation—it could go from Snow White on to Ariel and Jasmine and the latest is Disney in the '90s and now the shape of these characters has not really changed at all. (Producer)

> Just the tradition of Barbie and Cinderella, I mean, they've always looked that way. That's what we grow up with thinking is pretty. And that's what a fairy looks like or a princess looks like. (Writer)

> I guess you go back to the Disney movies like *A Little Mermaid*, is that kind of what's going on? I think that a lot of times those are traditional fairytales and I think that the way those characters have been drawn throughout the ages... I mean it's changed a little bit but it's kind of remained the same, the mermaid has always had a bikini on.... I think it would kind of be more shocking and take someone out of the story more if all of a sudden their physique was changed... from what it had been for years and years in fairytales. (Director)

The last two reasons were cited by less than 15 percent of the industry leaders. Content creators' fantasy (e.g., 11.6 percent; story artists' drawings reflect their own perceptions of the ideal female or idealized females are what they enjoy drawing) was marshaled as a reason, which was mentioned by more females (18.9 percent) than males (6.1 percent). Short cut (5.8 percent) or story artists relying on easily recalled past images of animated females to inform their current drawings was the seventh and final reason. This explanation was only cited by male content creators (10.2 percent).

In sum, industry leaders gave seven different reasons for the sexualization of animated characters that supposedly carry two X chromosomes. What is interesting, however, is that many of the content creators we interviewed believed that such depictions could impact younger audiences. Of those asked "Do you think that seeing sexualized characters in animation affects child viewers?," 84 percent said "yes." Among those giving an affirmative response, 41.7 percent indicated that viewing can function as a form of "social learning" (e.g., "I think it forms imagery of ideals for both boys and girls. We do respond to what we see in our stories, and it does affect how we view our own sex and the opposite sex"), and 46.4 percent said exposure can influence expectations and/or desires about idealized appearance and body image (e.g., "They either take note of it or they go 'ah, this is how a woman's meant to look…'"; "I think it makes girls feel insecure, that they don't look like that. I think it makes them overly conscious of their bodies"). As such, these topics are the focus of the next section of this chapter.

Effects

Given what we know about the portrayal of females in film, the next question to ask is what effect does viewing have on developing youth? The purpose of this section is to answer this very query focusing on two areas: stereotyping and body image. Much of this work, particularly with the first criterion, is approached theoretically from a social cognitive (Bandura, 1986), cultivation (Morgan, Shanahan, & Signorielli, 2009), or gender schema (Calvert, 1999) perspective. These mechanisms are reviewed elsewhere. So, we tailored this section to focus narrowly on effects. Also, most of the research reviewed here draws on studies examining the effects of exposure to other media (TV, magazines, books) because so little empirical work has been conducted on film.

Stereotyping Effects

Sex Roles. Noting exceptions (Perloff, 1977; Repetti, 1984) and mixed findings (Signorielli, 1989), research indicates that TV may play a part in cultivating stereotypical gender role outcomes for viewers across the lifespan. Some studies show that heavy TV viewers have more conventional sex role beliefs than do light viewers (e.g., Frueh & McGhee, 1975; Volgy & Schwarz, 1980). Signorielli and Lears (1992) found an association between viewing and believing that some household chores should be gender linked—particularly among boys. A few studies have observed a relationship between viewers' media diets and negative attitudes about females (Zuckerman, Singer, & Singer, 1980 [girls only]). With multiple controls, Behm-Morawitz and Mastro (2008) found that, among emerging adults, viewing teen movies was a significant and *negative* predictor of "attitudes toward women's rights" (p. 140). Affinity for teen characters/films was a significant *positive* predictor, however. Thus, identification with teen characters/films—some branded as "mean girls"—may actually moderate viewers' real-world attitudes and beliefs about women in society.

Given the nature of surveys, it must be noted that causal order of exposure and stereotyping effects cannot be determined. Longitudinal and naturalistic research can help shed some possible light on the time order issue, however. Kimball (1986) found that adolescent males (measures = behaviors, jobs) and females (measures = peer, authority relations) became more traditional 2 years after the introduction of TV to a Canadian town. Using multiple controls, Morgan (1982) found that Time 1 TV exposure was a significant and positive predictor of Time 2 sexism among sixth- to tenth-grade girls from higher socio-economic status (SES) groups. Over a 6-month period, Morgan and Rothschild (1983) found that TV viewing had a significant and positive association with stereotypical attitudes toward household chores on eighth-graders from lower SES groups, with fewer friends, and with access to cable. Morgan (1987) found that early TV viewing predicted more stereotypical attitudes 6 months later for males whose chore behavior was *less* stereotypically masculine and for females whose chore behavior was *more* stereotypically feminine.

Experimental research has set out to determine whether exposure to counter-stereotypic images of gender portrayals can reduce sex-role stereotyping. Some studies reveal that children exposed to nontraditional content evidence less conventional play behavior (McArthur & Eisen, 1976 [boys only]), attitudes about women (Pingree, 1978 [except eighth-grade boys]), attitudes toward and beliefs about activities (Flerx, Fidler, & Rogers, 1976; Vaughan & Fisher, 1981), and characteristics (Davidson, Yasuna, & Tower, 1979).

Summing up, the research reveals that TV exposure can contribute—under some conditions—to sex-role or counter-stereotyping. Consistent with this conclusion, Herrett-Skjellum and Allen's (1996) meta-analysis reveals that the relationship between TV viewing and acceptance of sex-role stereotyping across survey ($r = .075$) and experimental ($r = .207$) research is small and significant.

Occupation Research. Studies have assessed TV's contribution to children's and adolescents' occupational knowledge (e.g., DeFleur & DeFleur, 1967; Jeffries-Fox & Signorielli, 1979), aspirations (e.g., Signorielli, 1993; Wright et al., 1995), and perceptions of careers (e.g., Potts & Martinez, 1994). This body of work reveals that TV can play a role in occupational socialization. Here, we are interested in whether media exposure is related to children's sex typing of jobs. Some, but not all (Meyer, 1980), evidence suggests that it may be (Beuf, 1974).

Wroblewski and Huston (1987) found that heavy viewing of TV shows that depict females traditionally and light viewing of those that depict females in non-traditional careers significantly predicted fifth- and sixth-grade girls' willingness to consider feminine TV jobs. Kimball's (1986) naturalistic study found that boys cultivated more traditional perceptions of careers for males and females after 2 years of TV viewing. Indeed, a meta-analysis of surveys (Herrett-Skjellum &

Allen, 1996) found a small to medium ($r = .22$) correlation between TV viewing and gender stereotyping of occupations.

Just as some research suggests that exposure to nontraditional depictions may mitigate sex-role stereotyping, a few studies report similar findings for occupational attitudes or beliefs. Surveying third- through sixth-graders, Miller and Reeves (1976) found that participants accurately recognizing TV women working in counter-stereotypical careers (i.e., police officer, park ranger) rated those nontraditional jobs as more "appropriate" for females than did participants who could not accurately recognize such characters.

Experimental evidence also reveals the effects of exposure to traditional and/or nontraditional information on children's and adolescents' thoughts and attitudes (Ashby & Wittmaire, 1978; Greene, Sullivan, & Beyard-Tyler, 1982). Flerx et al. (1976) found that those five-year-olds exposed to a short nontraditional film or book were more likely to accept females in counter-stereotypical jobs than were those exposed to a traditional book both immediately after viewing and 1 week later. Counter-stereotyped responses, under certain conditions, have been documented after exposing children and/or adolescents to commercials (O'Bryant & Corder-Bolz, 1978; Pingree, 1978 [except eighth-grade boys]) or popular UK police dramas (Gunter & McAleer, 1991) featuring women in nontraditional jobs. A field experiment has also examined the impact of *Freestyle*, a TV show created to reduce gender stereotyping among preadolescents. Although the program had little consistent impact on "pre-occupational activities" (Johnston & Ettema, 1982, p. 147), viewing plus discussion of the show "increased their estimates of the proportion of women in traditionally male jobs and correspondingly reduced their estimates of the proportion of women in traditionally female jobs" (p. 172).

Research with adult participants has found that exposure to stereotyped images can impact females' evaluation of activities, objectives, and even task performance. Schwarz, Wagner, Bannert and Mathes (1987) found that females exposed to advertisements featuring domestic portrayals were *less* likely to hold a positive orientation toward civic engagement than females who had not yet seen the ads. Females viewing ads depicting objectified women did not differ from females in the control condition on the same outcome, however. Geis, Brown, Jennings (Walstedt), and Porter (1984) found that female undergraduates who watched traditional ads subsequently placed less of an emphasis on achievement compared to homemaking in essays about their future. Women who saw nontraditional ads mentioned achievement themes significantly more often than women who saw traditional ads. Similarly, Jennings (Walstedt), Geis, and Brown (1980) compared females viewing traditional and nontraditional ads. The results showed that those in the nontraditional condition exhibited more independence and were judged more self-confident than those in the traditional condition. Scholars have argued that stereotyped commercials act as triggers that can reinforce, inhibit, or broaden women's social roles.

More recent work has explained similar effects using *stereotype threat*, which is the process by which females' performance on male-dominated tasks may be unconsciously self-sabotaged when traditional views about women are made salient. Davies, Spencer, Quinn, and Gerhardstein's (2002) experiments show that when compared to women viewing nontraditional or neutral ads, those women seeing stereotypical portrayals scored lower on a math test (studies 1 and 2), answered a smaller number of math problems (study 2), and demonstrated less interest in quantitative fields (study 3). As the authors state, "cultural stereotypes question women's ability to succeed in any traditionally masculine domain" (p. 1617). In these studies, priming a self-relevant stereotype immediately impacted women's performance and aspirations in a typically male-dominated field. With repeated exposure, females may not only underestimate their mathematical aptitude but narrow their career prospects based on similar misperceptions.

The research just reviewed shows that viewing traditional and nontraditional portrayals in the media affects thoughts, attitudes, and behaviors. This relationship may be moderated by intervening variables. Because societal proscriptions of acceptable masculine behavior may be more narrow and rigid than those for feminine behavior, it is not surprising that some studies (Frueh & McGhee, 1975; Vaughan & Fisher, 1981) and reviews of research (Huston, 1983, p. 407) reveal that boys are more sex typed than girls. Not all research supports this perspective (Signorella, Bigler, & Liben, 1993). The type of measures used, initial beliefs before exposure, and age of the participant may affect stereotypical responding. Particularly for the last category, it may be the case that the effects of different types of traditional and nontraditional portrayals change over the course of development (see Smith & Granados, 2009). Children who are post-gender constancy (i.e., understand that biological sex does not change) may pay greater attention to and be more affected by stereotypical depictions involving same-sex characters than those who have not achieved this cognitive milestone. With time and maturity, children also will begin to comprehend a broader array of verbal (i.e., sexist comments, innuendo) and/or visual examples (i.e., domesticity, sexual harassment) of stereotypical and counter-stereotypical attitudes and actions.

In addition to these viewer characteristics, the type of genre consumed may play an independent or interactive role in teaching and/or reinforcing gender-linked or counter-stereotypical attitudes, beliefs, and/or behaviors (Repetti, 1984; Zuckerman et al., 1980). Length of exposure to the media may also be an important factor. For instance, a single or short exposure to a counter-stereotypical portrayal (e.g., male nurse) of a highly ingrained social role (e.g., male doctor) may not impact some children's immediate perceptions (see Cordua, McGraw, & Drabman, 1979; Drabman et al., 1981). Extended viewing of nontraditional casting or even mediation by caregivers while younger children view stereotypical content (see Nathanson, Wilson, McGhee, & Sebastian, 2002) may be needed to increase acceptance of nonconventional roles for males and females in society.

Due to the popularity of youth-oriented genres such as princess films and comic book movies, future scholars would do well to examine how young viewers relate to these traditional images. If stereotyping effects can be found in response to commercials, TV shows, and highly edited films, it becomes important to examine the role of family films that are embraced by the masses at the box office and brought into the home via DVDs, action figures, books, clothing, and untold other models of masculine and feminine ideals.

Body Image Effects

Because of the hypersexualization of females in film noted earlier, two areas of research seemed particularly relevant to review: (1) studies focusing on females' self-objectification (SO), and (2) research focusing on thin/attractive media models on females' body image concerns more broadly. In terms of the former, Fredrickson and Roberts (1997) have proposed objectification theory. According to this view, a large portion of society legitimates or sanctions the sexualization of women. Sexualization occurs directly or vicariously (i.e., media portrayals) through visual scrutiny of females' bodies. Objectification that is sexual in nature occurs when "women are treated *as bodies*—and in particular, as bodies that exist for the use and pleasure of others" (p. 175). When females internalize this third-person perspective, SO may take place, which can contribute to increased cognitive awareness and/or surveillance of the body. Consequences of SO include (p. 181–185), but are not limited to, body shame, anxiety, and decreased task performance (e.g., Calogero, 2004; Fredrickson, Roberts, Noll, Quinn, & Twenge, 1998; Quinn, Kallen, Twenge, & Fredrickson, 2006; Roberts & Gettman, 2004).

A variety of contexts (e.g., wearing a swimsuit vs. a sweater) and messages (e.g., sentence task) have evoked SO in the lab, including exposure to mediated images of females (Harrison & Fredrickson, 2003; for no effect, see Morawitz, 2007). To illustrate, Harper and Tiggemann (2008) found that female participants viewing ads with attractive and thin women experienced more state SO immediately after than did female participants viewing control ads.

Survey research has looked at the direct and indirect relationships between media exposure and SO or SO and partner objectification. Morry and Staska (2001, p. 269) found that females' consumption of fashion magazines was positively related to adopting the media's skewed standard of thinness, which, in turn, was positively related to heightened SO. Unexpectedly, Zurbriggen, Ramsey, and Jaworski (2011) found no signigicant relationship between SO and sexy media exposure. Path analyses showed that sexy media viewing had a marginal positive association with partner objectification. Additionally, partner objectification was negatively related to relational satisfaction.

Longitudinally and with multiple controls, Aubrey-Stevens (2006a) found that Time 1 viewing of "sexy" TV content was a significant and positive predictor of Time 2 trait SO for females and males. The results also showed that trait SO was a significant and *negative* predictor of viewing sexy TV a year later. Exploring moderators of the sexy media–SO link, Aubrey-Stevens (2006b, p. 167) found that among females with low self-esteem, viewing of alluring media at Time 1 was a *positive* and significant predictor of trait SO at Time 2. Females high in self-esteem, however, evidenced an overtime *negative* relationship between trait SO and viewing sexy content. Even a media literacy intervention (*Slim Hopes*) designed to raise awareness and reduce the negative effects of sexualized portrayals can unintentionally evoke SO in females (Choma, Foster, & Radford, 2007). Using the same film, however, another intervention revealed no difference between control and treatment conditions on other body image outcomes (Irving & Berel, 2001).

In addition to the research on SO, dozens of studies have looked at the impact of thin media models on adult and adolescent females. A few meta-analyses (Groesz, Levine, & Murnen, 2002; Holmstrom, 2004) have been conducted and yielded somewhat mixed findings. Recently, Grabe, Ward, and Hyde (2008, p. 460) assessed more than seventy studies and found a small to moderate negative effect of media consumption on outcomes including body dissatisfaction and thin ideal internalization. Scholars (see Harrison & Hefner, 2008) have evoked a few theoretical mechanisms (e.g., social comparison, modeling, cultivation) to explain how media may be one variable, among others (e.g., parents, peers), that directly and/or indirectly contributes to negative effects (Stice, Schupak-Nueberg, Shaw, & Stein, 1994). Intervening variables (e.g., preexisting body dissatisfaction, age, race, genre, social support) also may independently or interactively affect media–body image linkages (see Harrison & Hefner, 2008).

The just-cited research has focused primarily on adolescents and adults. Other studies have begun to examine media's impact on elementary school-aged children. This is particularly important because many girls begin to desire a thinner physique around age 6 (e.g., Ambrosi-Randić, 2000; Dohnt & Tiggemann, 2004,

2006a,b). Not surprisingly, studies show that media can play a role in girls' body dissatisfaction. Although there are inconsistencies in results across media (e.g., Clark & Tiggemann, 2007), a growing corpus of research shows that viewing or valuing media images/popular thin ideals is associated with girls' weight concerns (e.g., Field et al., 1999; Taylor et al., 1998), eating disorder symptomatology (e.g., Moriarty & Harrison, 2008), and body esteem (e.g., Dittmar, Halliwell, & Ive, 2006).

To date, only one study could be found that examines the impact of thin characters in animated films on young girls' body dissatisfaction. Hayes and Tantleff-Dunn (2010) randomly assigned 3- to 6-year-old girls to view roughly 14 minutes of animated film clips featuring appearance incidents (i.e., verbalizations and/or actions) or animated clips of TV shows and films without appearance incidents. Immediately after viewing, no short-term differences emerged by condition on girls' body dissatisfaction ratings.

What accounts for these counterintuitive findings? There are at least a few possible explanations. First, a manipulation check was not conducted to see if children detected differences in appearance-related incidents across the viewing conditions. Given that younger children have more difficulty than older children in comprehending auditory information and drawing inferences from story content (Rolandelli, Wright, Huston, & Eakins, 1991; Thompson & Myers, 1985), they may not have attended to or encoded many of the beauty-centric comments in the treatment condition. Second, and because TV and film animation features sexualized characters with unrealistically small waist lines (see Smith & Granados, 2009), it may be the case that the females across the treatment and control conditions were just variations of different slim body types (e.g., hourglass vs. lollipop). Third, and as articulated by the researchers, the experimental and control groups were exposed to beauty-centric toys prior to post-test ratings of body satisfaction. Viewing appearance-related stimuli may have wiped out the treatment effect. Clearly, more research is needed to explore the impact that animated digitized dames are having on the socialization of girls' body image concerns.

Conclusion

Overall, the aim of this chapter was to review what we know about females in film. In terms of prevalence, females seem to be grossly underrepresented behind the camera and on-screen. When girls and women are shown, it is sometimes in a traditional or sexualized light. Viewers are exposed to these types of portrayals at a very young age, with animated content providing a "sexy socialization" to societal expectations for girls and women. Among some consumers, short-term or extended exposure to stereotyped or sexualized depictions can contribute to ill effects.

The chapter illuminates a few major gaps in our knowledge, three of which we highlight here. We still know very little empirically about the role of film in children's development, despite the fact that cinematic content produced in the United States and exported globally may affect many children's upbringing. Most stimuli in experiments have relied on TV content, magazines, or commercials. Yet, cinematic content creators can airbrush or computer enhance animated and live-action female and male bodies to perfection. Exposure to such extreme physical ideals of beauty, along with the fact that children often watch the same movies again and again during childhood (Dobrow, 1990; Mares, 1998), may contribute to young viewers forming skewed schemas or prototypes of attractiveness, as well as expectations of how girls and women should look and act. Scholarship investigating film—along with marketing of cross-platform content (e.g., books, video games, interactive websites)—would aid our understanding of the role of media in the lives of youth.

Another area needing empirical attention pertains to the relationship among studio executives and on-screen portrayals. The lack of females on-screen may have something to do with the biological sex of individuals running the multinational companies that fund studio projects. Recently, the White House Project Report (2009) showed that only 16 percent ($n = 7$) of the forty-four individuals in leadership or executive positions across the major, independent, and mini-major studios were female. Clearly, the dearth of female speaking characters on-screen may also have something to do with the fact that few women have broken through the celluloid ceiling in Hollywood. Of those who have, some may be high in social dominance (see Umphress, Smith-Crowe, Brief, Dietz, & Watkins, 2007) and thus make conscious and unconscious decisions that reinforce and perpetuate gender hegemony. Qualitative studies are needed that document the experiences of women and men working in the executive suites of multinationals, as well as of how individual differences in employees may support and/or thwart the vertical integration of females in key gatekeeping studio positions.

Although our focus here has been on screen portrayals and behind-the-scenes employment, we still know very little about the psychological consequences for female actors routinely playing sexualized and stereotyped roles in Hollywood films. Yet the literature reviewed herein reveals that females are susceptible to SO and negative effects. One study of undergraduate females found that even the mere *anticipation* of male gaze can heighten body shame and appearance concerns (Calogero, 2004). Given that most film directors and cinematographers are male (Smith et al., 2013), as are many photojournalists at red carpet events, working female actors may often find themselves in job-related situations (i.e., auditioning, filming, press on major movie release) in which they expect to be objectified. How women navigate these situations psychologically and interpersonally, the impact SO may have on their work-related performance, and individual difference characteristics that may increase or decrease negative effects are all fertile soil for quantitative and qualitative inquiry.

In conclusion, females are still marginalized and sexualized in motion picture content. More research is needed to understand the barriers that face women within entertainment, as well as the effects of exposure to skewed and stereotypical media representations on male and female child consumers.

Acknowledgments

The authors would like to thank Julia Ormond for contributing to the title of this paper as well as for insightful guidance on industry research.

Notes

1. Attractiveness captured verbal statements (i.e., "he is hot!") and nonverbal actions (e.g., cat calls) made by characters that communicate the physical desirousness of other characters.
2. For another study, we had investigated gender in the total population of G-rated films. Using this sample, we gathered the writing and directing credits for each film from IMDbPro on May 22, 2012. The biological sex of every individual receiving credit in these categories was confirmed using online sources. Names listed more than once within a category were not double coded.

References

Ambrosi-Randić, N. (2000). Perception of current and ideal body size in preschool age children. *Perceptual and Motor Skills, 90*(3), 885–889.

Ashby, M. S., & Wittmaier, B. C. (1978). Attitude changes in children after exposure to stories about women in traditional or nontraditional occupations. *Journal of Educational Psychology, 70*(6), 945–949.

Aubrey, J. S. (2006a). Effects of sexually objectifying media on self-objectification and body surveillance in undergraduates: Results of a 2-year panel study. *Journal of Communication, 56*(2), 366–386.

Aubrey, J. S. (2006b). Exposure to sexually objectifying media and body self-perceptions among college women: An examination of the selective exposure hypothesis and the role of moderating variables. *Sex Roles, 55*(3/4), 159–172.

Bandura, A. (1986). *Social foundations of thought and action: A social cognitive theory.* Englewood Cliffs, NJ: Prentice Hall.

Barletta, M. (2006). Women control about 80 percent of household spending: A look at the numbers. *TrendSight: Marketing to Women.* Retrieved from http://www.trendsight.com/view/40/204/

Bazzini, D. G., McIntosh, W. D., Smith, S. M., Cook, S., & Harris, C. (1997). The aging woman in popular film: Underrepresented, unattractive, unfriendly, and unintelligent. *Sex Roles*, *36*(7/8), 531–543.

Baumgardner, J., & Richards, A. (2000). *Manifesta: Young women, feminism, and the future*. New York: Farrar, Straus and Giroux.

Behm-Morawitz, E., & Mastro, D. E. (2008). Mean girls? The influence of gender portrayals in teen movies on emerging adults' gender-based attitudes and beliefs. *Journalism and Mass Communication Quarterly*, *85*, 131–146.

Beuf, A. (1974). Doctor, lawyer, household drudge. *Journal of Communication*, *24*(2), 142–145.

Boushey, H. (2009). The new breadwinners. In H. Boushey & A. O'Leary (Eds.), *The Shriver report: A woman's nation changes everything* (pp. 31–67). Washington DC: Center for American Progress.

Calogero, R. M. (2004). A test of objectification theory: The effect of the male gaze on appearance concerns in college women. *Psychology of Women Quarterly*, *28*(1), 16–21.

Calvert, S. (1999). *Children's journeys through the information age*. Boston: McGraw Hill.

Center for American Women and Politics. (2012). *Women in U.S. Congress 2012*. Retrieved from http://www.cawp.rutgers.edu/fast_facts/levels_of_office/documents/ cong. pdf

Cerridwen, A., & Simonton, D. K. (2009). Sex doesn't sell—nor impress! Content, box office, critics, and awards in mainstream cinema. *Psychology of Aesthetics, Creativity, and the Arts*,*3*, 200–210.

Choma, B. L., Foster, M. D., & Radford, E. (2007). Use of objectification theory to examine the effects of a media literacy intervention on women. *Sex Roles*, *56*(9/10), 581–591.

Clark, L., & Tiggemann, M. (2007). Sociocultural influences and body image in 9- to 12-year-old girls: The role of appearance schemas. *Journal of Clinical Child & Adolescent Psychology*, *36*(1), 76–86.

Cordua, G. D., McGraw, K. O., & Drabman, R. S. (1979). Doctor or nurse: Children's perception of sex typed occupations. *Child Development*, *50*, 590–593.

CNNMoney. (2012). *Career advice from Fortune 500's women CEOs*. Retrieved from http://money.cnn.com/galleries/2012/fortune/1204/gallery.500-women-ceos-on-the-glass-ceiling.fortune/

Cuban, M. (Executive Producer), Wagner, T. (Executive Producer), & Arquette, R. (Director). (2002). *Searching for Debra Winger* [Motion picture]. United States of America: Immortal Entertainment.

Davidson, E. S., Yasuna, A., & Tower, A. (1979). The effects of television cartoons on sex-role stereotyping in young girls. *Child Development*, *50*(2), 597–600.

Davies, P. G., Spencer, S. J., Quinn, D. M., & Gerhardstein, R. (2002). Consuming images: How television commercials that elicit stereotype threat can restrain women academically and professionally. *Personality & Social Psychology Bulletin*, *28*(12), 1615–1628.

DeFleur, M. L., & DeFleur, L. B. (1967). The relative contribution of television as a learning source for children's occupational knowledge. *American Sociological Review*, *32*(5), 777–789.

Dittmar, H., Halliwell, E., & Ive, S. (2006). Does Barbie make girls want to be thin? The effect of experimental exposure to images of dolls on the body image of 5- to 8- year old girls. *Developmental Psychology*, *42*, 283–292.

Dobrow, J. R. (1990). The rerun ritual: Using VCR's to re-view. In J. R. Dobrow (Ed.), *Social and cultural aspects of VCR use* (pp. 181–193). Hillsdale, NJ: Erlbaum.

Dohnt, H. K., & Tiggemann, M. (2004). Development of perceived body size and dieting awareness in young girls. *Perceptual and Motor Skills*, *99*(3), 790–792.

Dohnt, H. K., & Tiggemann, M. (2006a). Body image concerns in young girls: The role of peers and media prior to adolescence. *Journal of Youth and Adolescence*, *35*(2), 141–151.

Dohnt, H. K., & Tiggemann, M. (2006b). The contribution of peer and media influences to the development of body satisfaction and self-esteem in young girls: A prospective study. *Developmental Psychology*, *42*(5), 929–936.

Drabman, R. S., Robertson, S. J., Patterson, J. N., Jarvie, G. J., Hammer, D., & Cordua, G. A. (1981). Children's perception of media-portrayed sex roles. *Sex Roles*, *7*(4), 379–389.

Field, A. E., Cheung, L., Wolf, A. M., Herzog, D. B., Gortmaker, S. L., & Colditz, A. (1999). Exposure to the mass media and weight concerns among girls. *Pediatrics*, *103*(3), e36.

Finke, N. (2007, October 5). Warner's Robinov bitchslaps film women: Gloria Allred calls for Warner's boycott. *Deadline Hollywood*. Retrieved from http://www. deadline.com/2007/10/warners-robinoff-gets-in-catfight-with-girls/

Flerx, V. C., Fidler, D. S., & Rogers, R. W. (1976). Sex role stereotypes: Developmental aspects and early intervention. *Child Development*, *47*(4), 998–1007.

Fredrickson, B. L., & Roberts, T. (1997). Objectification theory: Toward understanding women's lived experiences and mental health risks. *Psychology of Women Quarterly*, *21*(2), 173–206.

Fredrickson, B. L., Roberts, T., Noll, S. M., Quinn, D. M., & Twenge, J. M. (1998). That swimsuit becomes you: Sex differences in self-objectification, restrained eating, and math performance. *Journal of Personality and Social Psychology*, *75*(1), 269–284.

Frueh, T., & McGhee, P. E. (1975). Traditional sex role development and amount of time spent watching television. *Developmental Psychology*, *11*(1), 109.

Garrison, L. C. (1971). *Decision processes in motion picture production: A study of uncertainty*. Unpublished doctoral dissertation, Stanford University.

Gash, H., & Conway, P. (1997). Images of heroes and heroines: How stable? *Journal of Applied Developmental Psychology*, *18*, 349–372.

Geis, F. L., Brown, V., Jennings (Walstedt), J., & Porter, N. (1984). TV commercials as achievement scripts for women. *Sex Roles*, *10*(7/8), 513–525.

Götz, M. (2008). Do children want skinny cartoon characters? Test of kids' preferences for different body shapes. *Televizion, 21*, 20–21.

Grabe, S., Ward, L. M., & Hyde, J. S. (2008). The role of the media in body image concerns among women: A meta-analysis of experimental and correlational studies. *Psychological Bulletin, 134*(3), 460–476.

Greene, A. L., Sullivan, H. J., & Beyard-Tyler, K. (1982). Attitudinal effects of the use of role models in information about sex-typed careers. *Journal of Educational Psychology, 74*(3), 393–398.

Groesz, L. M., Levine, M. P., & Murnen, S. K. (2002). The effect of experimental presentation of thin media images on body satisfaction: A meta-analytic review. *International Journal of Eating Disorders, 31*(1), 1–16.

Gunter, B., & McAleer, J. (1991). Television police dramas and children's beliefs about the police. *Journal of Educational Television, 17*, 81–101.

Harper, B., & Tiggemann, M. (2008). The effect of thin ideal media images on women's self-objectification, mood, and body image. *Sex Roles, 58*(9/10), 649–657.

Harrison, K., & Fredrickson, B. L. (2003). Women's sports media, self-objectification, and mental health in black and white adolescent females. *Journal of Communication, 53*(2), 216–232.

Harrison, K., & Hefner, V. (2008). Media, body image, and eating disorders. In S. L. Calvert & B. J. Wilson (Eds.), *The handbook of children, media, and development* (pp. 381–406). Malden, MA: Blackwell.

Hayes, S., & Tantleff-Dunn, S. (2010). Am I too fat to be a princess? Examining the effects of popular children's media on young girls' body image. *British Journal of Developmental Psychology, 28*(2), 413–426.

Herrett-Skjellum, J., & Allen, M. (1996). Television programming and sex stereotyping: A meta-analysis. *Communication Yearbook, 19*, 157–185.

Hitchens, C. (2007, January). Why women aren't funny. *Vanity Fair*. Retrieved from http://www.vanityfair.com/culture/features/2007/01/hitchens200701

Hoffner, C. (1996). Children's wishful identification and parasocial interaction with favorite television characters. *Journal of Broadcasting & Electronic Media, 40*, 389–402.

Hoffner, C., & Buchanan, M. (2005). Young adults' wishful identification with television characters: The role of perceived similarity and character attributes. *Media Psychology, 7*, 325–351.

Holmstrom, A. J. (2004). The effects of the media on body image: A meta-analysis. *Journal of Broadcasting & Electronic Media, 48*(2), 196–217.

Holub, S. C., Tisak, M. S., & Mullins, D. (2008). Gender differences in children's hero attributions: Personal hero choices and evaluations of typical male and female heroes. *Sex Roles, 58*, 567–578.

Huston, A. C. (1983). Sex-typing. In E. M. Hetherington & P. H. Mussen (Eds.), *Handbook of child psychology: Socialization, personality, and social development* (vol. 4, pp. 387–467). New York: Wiley.

Irving, L. M., & Berel, S. R. (2001). Comparison of media literacy programs to strengthen college women's resistance to media images. *Psychology of Women's Quarterly*, *25*, 103–111.

Jennings (Walstedt), J., Geis, F. L., & Brown, V. (1980). Influence of television commercials on women's self-confidence and independent judgment. *Journal of Personality & Social Psychology*, *38*(2), 203–210.

Jeffries-Fox, S., & Signorielli N. (1979). Television and children's conceptions of occupations. In H. S. Dordick (Ed.), *Proceedings of the sixth annual telecommunications policy research conference* (pp. 21–38). Lexington, MA: Lexington Books.

Johnston, J., & Ettema, J. S. (1982). *Positive images*. Beverly Hills, CA: Sage.

Jose, P. E., & Brewer, W. F. (1984). Development of story liking: Character identification, suspense, and outcome resolution. *Developmental Psychology*, *20*, 911–924.

Kimball, M. M. (1986). Television and sex-role attitudes. In T. M. Williams (Ed.), *The impact of television: A natural experiment in three communities* (pp. 265–301). Orlando, FL: Academic Press.

Langlois, J. H., Ritter, J. M., Roggman, L. A., & Vaughn, L. S. (1991). Facial diversity and infant preferences for attractive faces. *Developmental Psychology*, *27*, 79–84.

Langlois, J. H., Roggman, L. A., Casey, R. J., Ritter, J. M., Rieser-Danner, L. A., & Jenkins, V. Y. (1987). Infant preferences for attractive faces: Rudiments of a stereotype? *Developmental Psychology*, *23*, 363–369.

Langlois, J. H., Roggman, L. A., & Rieser-Danner, L. A. (1990). Infants' differential social responses to attractive and unattractive faces. *Developmental Psychology*, *26*, 153–159.

Lauzen, M. M. (2008). *Women @ the box office: A study of the top 100 worldwide grossing films*. San Diego, CA: Center for the Study of Women in Television and Film.

Lauzen, M. M. (2012). *The celluloid ceiling: Behind-the-scenes employment of women on the top 250 films of 2011*. San Diego, CA: Center for the Study of Women in Television and Film.

Lauzen, M. M., & Dozier, D. M. (2005). Maintaining the double standard: Portrayals of age and gender in popular films. *Sex Roles*, *52* (7/8), 437–446.

MacKinnon, C. (2003). Afterword. In C. MacKinnon & R. Siegel (Eds.), *Directions in sexual harassment law* (pp. 672–704). New Haven, CT: Yale University Press.

Mares, M. L. (1998). Children's use of VCRs. *The ANNALS of the American Academy of Political and Social Science*, *557*, 120–131.

Marklein, M. B. (2010, January 26). College gender gap remains stable: 57 percent women. *USA Today*. Retrieved from http://www.usatoday.com

McArthur, L. Z., & Eisen, S. V. (1976). Television and sex-role stereotyping. *Journal of Applied Social Psychology*, *6*(4), 329–351.

McRobbie, A. (2009). *The aftermath of feminism: Gender, culture and social change*. London: Sage.

Meyer, B. (1980). The development of girls' sex-role attitudes. *Child Development*, *51*(2), 508–514.

Miller, M. M., & Reeves, B. (1976). Dramatic TV content and children's sex-role stereotypes. *Journal of Broadcasting, 20*(1), 35–50.

Morawitz, E. (2007). Effects of the sexualization of female characters in video games on gender stereotyping, body esteem, self-objectification, self-esteem, and self-efficacy. Doctoral dissertation, University of Arizona. Retrieved from http://proquest.umi.com/pqdlink?did=1372038221&Fmt=6&clientId=5239&RQT=309&VName=PQD

Morgan, M. (1982). Television and adolescents' sex role stereotypes: A longitudinal study. *Journal of Personality & Social Psychology, 43*(5), 947–955.

Morgan, M. (1987). Television, sex-role attitudes, and sex-role behavior. *Journal of Early Adolescence, 7*(3), 269–282.

Morgan, M., & Rothschild, N. (1983). Impact of the new television technology: Cable TV, peers, and sex-role cultivation in the electronic environment. *Youth & Society, 15*(1), 33–50.

Morgan, M., Shanahan, J., & Signorielli, N. (2009). *Growing up with television: Cultivation processes.* In J. Bryant & M. B. Oliver (Eds.), *Media effects: Advances in theory and research* (3rd ed., pp. 34–49). New York: Routledge.

Moriarty, C. M., & Harrison, K. (2008). Television exposure and disordered eating among children: A longitudinal panel study. *Journal of Communication, 58*(2), 361–381.

Morry, M. M., & Staska, S. L. (2001). Magazine exposure: Internalization, self-objectification, eating attitudes, and body satisfaction in male and female university students. *Canadian Journal of Behavioural Science, 33*(4), 269–279.

Motion Picture Association of America. (2009). *Theatrical market statistics.* Los Angeles: Author.

Motion Picture Association of America. (2010). *Theatrical market statistics.* Los Angeles: Author.

Motion Picture Association of America. (2011). *Theatrical market statistics.* Los Angeles: Author.

Nathanson, A. I., Wilson, B. J., McGee, J., & Sebastian, M. (2002). Counteracting the effects of female stereotypes on television via active mediation. *Journal of Communication, 52*(4), 922–937.

O'Bryant, S. L., & Corder-Bolz, C. R. (1978). The effects of television on children's stereotyping of women's work roles. *Journal of Vocational Behavior, 12*(2), 233–244.

Oliver, M. B., & Green, S. (2001). Development of gender differences in children's responses to animated entertainment. *Sex Roles, 45* (1/2), 67–89.

Perloff, R. M. (1977). Some antecedents of children's sex-role stereotypes. *Psychological Reports, 40*(2), 463–466.

Pingree, S. (1978). The effects of nonsexist television commercials and perceptions of reality on children's attitudes about women. *Psychology of Women Quarterly, 2*(3), 262–277.

Potts, R., & Martinez, I. (1994). Television viewing and children's beliefs about scientists. *Journal of Applied Developmental Psychology, 15*(2), 287–300.

Powers, S., Rothman, D. J., & Rothman, S. (1996). *Hollywood's America: Social and political themes in motion pictures.* Boulder, CO: Westview Press.

Quinn, D. M., Kallen, R. W., Twenge, J. M., & Fredrickson, B. L. (2006). The disruptive effect of self-objectification on performance. *Psychology of Women Quarterly, 30*(1), 59–64.

Repetti, R. L. (1984). Determinants of children's sex stereotyping: Parental sex-role traits and television viewing. *Personality & Social Psychology Bulletin, 10*(3), 457–468.

Reeves, B., & Miller, M. M. (1978). A multidimensional measure of children's identification with television characters. *Journal of Broadcasting, 22*(1), 71–86.

Roberts, T., & Gettman, J. Y. (2004). Mere exposure: Gender differences in the negative effects of priming a state of self-objectification. *Sex Roles, 51*(1/2), 17–27.

Rolandelli, D. R., Wright, J. C., Huston, A. C., & Eakins, D. (1991). Children's auditory and visual processing of narrated and nonnarrated television programming. *Journal of Experimental Child Psychology, 51*, 90–122.

Rubenstein, A. J., Kalakanis, L., & Langlois, J. H. (1999). Infant preferences for attractive faces: A cognitive explanation. *Developmental Psychology, 35*, 848–855.

Schwarz, N., Wagner, D., Bannert, M., & Mathes, L. (1987). Cognitive accessibility of sex role concepts and attitudes toward political participation: The impact of sexist advertisements. *Sex Roles, 17*, 593–601.

Shriver, M. (2009). A women's nation. In H. Boushey & A. O'Leary (Eds.), *The Shriver report: A woman's nation changes everything* (pp. 1–16). Washington DC: Center for American Progress.

Signorella, M. L., Bigler, R. S., & Liben, L. S. (1993). Developmental differences in children's gender schemata about others: A meta-analytic review. *Developmental Review, 13*, 147–183.

Signorielli, N. (1989). Television and conceptions about sex roles: Maintaining conventionality and the status quo. *Sex Roles, 21*(5/6), 341–360.

Signorielli, N. (1993). Television and adolescents' perceptions about work. *Youth & Society, 24*(3), 314–341.

Signorielli, N., & Lears, M. (1992). Children, television, and conceptions about chores: Attitudes and behaviors. *Sex Roles, 27*(3/4), 157–170.

Smith, S. L. & Choueiti, M. (2010a). Study 1. In S. L. Smith's (Ed.), *Gender oppression in cinematic content? A look at females on screen & behind-the-camera in top-grossing 2007 films.* Los Angeles: Annenberg School for Communication & Journalism.

Smith, S. L., & Choueiti, M. (2010b). *Gender disparity on screen and behind the camera in family films: The executive report.* Report prepared for the Geena Davis Institute for Gender in Media, Los Angeles.

Smith, S. L., & Choueiti, M. (2011a). *Gender inequality in cinematic content? A look at females on screen & behind-the-camera in top-grossing 2008 films.* Los Angeles: Annenberg School for Communication & Journalism.

Smith, S. L., & Choueiti, M. (2011b). *Gender inequality in popular films: Examining on screen portrayals and behind-the-scenes employment patterns in motion pictures released between 2007-2009*. Los Angeles: Annenberg School for Communication & Journalism.

Smith, S. L., Choueiti, M., & Gall, S. (2012). *Asymmetrical Academy Awards®: Another look at gender in best picture nominated films from 1977 to 2010*. Los Angeles: Annenberg School for Communication & Journalism.

Smith, S. L., Choueiti, M., Granados, A., & Erickson, S. E. (2008). *Asymmetrical Academy Awards®? A look at gender imbalance in Best Picture Nominated Films from 1977 to 2006*. Los Angeles: Annenberg School for Communication & Journalism.

Smith, S. L., Choueiti, M., & Stern, J. (February, 2011a). *Occupational aspirations: What are G-rated films teaching children about the world of work?* Paper submitted to the Geena Davis Institute for Gender and Media, Los Angeles.

Smith, S. L., & Cook, C. A. (2008). *Gender stereotypes: An analysis of popular films and tv*. Report prepared for the Geena Davis Institute for Gender in Media, Los Angeles.

Smith, S. L., & Granados, A. (2009). Content patterns and effects surrounding sex-role stereotyping on television and film. In J. Bryant & M. B. Oliver (Eds.), *Media effects: Advances in theory and research* (3rd edition, pp. 342–361). New York: Routledge.

Smith, S. L., Granados, A., & Choueiti, M. (2011b). *Changing the status quo 2: Sexualization of females in animated family films*. Report prepared for the Geena Davis Institute for Gender in Media, Los Angeles.

Smith, S. L., Granados, A., Choueiti, M., Erickson, S., & Noyes, A. (2011c). *Changing the status quo: Industry leaders' perceptions of gender in family films*. Report prepared for the Geena Davis Institute for Gender in Media, Los Angeles.

Smith, S. L., Pieper, K. M., Granados, A., & Choueiti, M. (2010a). Assessing gender-related portrayals in top-grossing G-rated films. *Sex Roles, 62*, 774–786.

Smith, S. L., Weber, R., & Choueiti, M. (August, 2010b). *Female characters and financial performance: An analysis of 100 top-grossing films at the box office and DVD sales*. Paper presented at a poster session at the annual conference of the Association for Education in Journalism and Mass Communication, Denver, CO.

Smith, S. L., Pieper, K. M., & Choueiti, M. (2013). *Exploring the barriers and opportunities for independent women filmmakers*. Report prepared for Sundance Institute and Women In Film Los Angeles Women Filmmakers Initiative.

Stern, S. R. (2005). Self-absorbed, dangerous, and disengaged: What popular films tell us about teenagers. *Mass Communication & Society, 8*(1), 23–38.

Stice, E., Schupak-Nueberg, E., Shaw, H. E., & Stein, R. I. (1994). Relation of media exposure to eating disorder symptomatology: Examination of mediating mechanisms. *Journal of Abnormal Psychology, 103*(4), 836–840.

Taylor, C. B., Sharpe, T., Shisslak, C., Bryson, S., Estes, L. S., Gray, N., et al. (1998). Factors associated with weight concerns in adolescent girls. *International Journal of Eating Disorders, 24*(1), 31–42.

Thomas, D. (May, 12, 1935). Meet Hollywood's men of action. *The Ogden Standard Examiner*. Retreived on 6/25/13 from http://www.cartoonbrew.com/classic/hollywoods-men-of-action-3375.html

Thompson, J. G., & Myers, N. A. (1985). Inferences and recall at ages four and seven. *Child Development, 56*, 1134–1144.

Umphress, E. E., Smith-Crowe, K., Brief, A. P., Dietz, J., & Watkins, M. B. (2007). When birds of a feather flock together and when they do not: Status composition, social dominance orientation, and organizational attractiveness. *Journal of Applied Psychology, 92*, 396–409.

Vaughan, J. E., & Fisher, V. L. (1981). The effect of traditional and cross-sex modeling on children's sex-role attitudes and behaviors. *Journal of Psychology, 107*(2), 253–260.

Volgy, T. J., & Schwarz, J. E. (1980). TV entertainment programming and sociopolitical attitudes. *Journalism Quarterly, 57*(1), 150–155.

Wallace, W. T., Seigerman, A., & Holbrook, M. B. (1993). The role of actors and actresses in the success of films: How much is a movie star worth? *Journal of Cultural Economics, 17*, 1–27.

Wells, P. (1998). *Understanding animation*. London: Routledge.

White House Project. (2009). *The White House Project Report: Benchmarking women's leadership*. New York: Author.

Wroblewski, R., & Huston, A. C. (1987). Televised occupational stereotypes and their effects on early adolescents: Are they changing? *Journal of Early Adolescence, 7*(3), 283–297.

Wright, J., Huston, A. C., Truglio, R., Fitch, M., Smith, E., & Piemyat, S. (1995). Occupational portrayals on television: Children's role schemata, career aspirations, and perceptions of reality. *Child Development, 66*(6), 1706–1718.

Writer's Guild of America, West (2011). *Recession and regression: The 2011 Hollywood writer's report*. Los Angeles: Author.

Zohn, P. (2010). Coloring the kingdom. *Vanity Fair*. Retrieved from http://www.vanityfair.com/culture/features/2010/03/disney-animation-girls-201003

Zuckerman, D. M., Singer, D. G., & Singer, J. L. (1980). Children's television viewing, racial and sex-role attitudes. *Journal of Applied Social Psychology, 10*(4), 281–294.

Zurbriggen, E. L., Ramsey, L. R., & Jaworski, B. K. (2011). Self- and partner-objectification in romantic relationships: Associations with media consumption and relationship satisfaction. *Sex Roles, 64*(7/8), 449–462.

3

RESOLVING THE PARADOX OF FILM MUSIC THROUGH A COGNITIVE NARRATIVE APPROACH TO FILM COMPREHENSION

Annabel J. Cohen

In the cinematic context, the domain of sound is typically taken for granted and subordinated by visual information. People go to concerts to *hear* music, and they go to the cinema to *see* a film. Yet music plays an important role in the cinema. It has done so since its earliest days, when live piano accompanied silent films, initially to mask the noise of the film projector and later to serve dramatic functions (Marks, 1997). Every theater for silent film employed live musicians. At the peak of the silent film era in the late 1920s, musicians in the Western world owed their livelihood to silent film: more than 80 percent of performing musicians in the United Kingdom, for example worked in silent film theaters (Cooke, 2008, p. 46). The success of *The Jazz Singer* in 1927, the first feature film with recorded speech and music, heralded the arrival of the "talkies" and the demise of the music for silent film industry.

Music and Cinematic Narrative

New sound recording technology eventually replaced the live music accompanying silent films with recorded sound. This recording technology enabled a new type of film music industry, one employing far fewer musicians than in the days of silent film. The new film music industry took about a decade to find its way. Directors appreciated that music was important to the success of a film, but they intuited that the new mindset created by realistic sound, particularly the sound of the actors' voices, would exclude music that had no logical source in the story. Even directors like Alfred Hitchcock felt the necessity of providing plot reasons for the inclusion of music in early talking pictures (Cooke, 2008, p. 61). Directors knew that audiences liked music, but they wrongly believed that film music should be part of the drama. In the early talkies era, it seemed counterintuitive that unrealistic background music—music that would not be in the scene—could contribute to a film that featured the realistic sound of the actors' voices. This seems strange, given the long history of incidental music to plays as well as the operatic and musical theater forms; after all, music has been associated with drama for a very long time. However, the technological wonder of presenting the recorded voices of actors blinded directors into believing that such use of music was from a bygone day and would not fit the new realism that recorded sound offered.

By the early 1940s, however, music regained its special place, one that it holds to this day, a place outside the story of the film, outside the *diegesis*, as the world of the story is called (cf., Gorbman, 1987). It is generally acknowledged that this place of music outside the story assists in the telling of the story of the film. However, that there is an important role for this extradiegetic (also referred to as nondiegetic) music in film still remains counterintuitive, at least on the surface. Why is there a need for extradiegetic music to make a film work? Music adds to the compelling nature of a film, as anyone knows who has turned down the sound of a horror film. Turn up the volume again on the music, and the fear and dread return. The narrative becomes more real while becoming less real on another level (adding music to an otherwise credible scene). This paradox of film, that music, which plays no role in the film story, is needed to make the film more compelling, must reflect how the mind uses multimedia input to process stories or create stories.

A further aspect of the paradoxical nature of film music is its status with respect to consciousness. One prominent perspective is that film music creates its magic without being heard, a view captured by the title of Claudia Gorbman's (1987) influential book *Unheard Melodies: Narrative Film Music*. There, she analyzed the workings of music in several classic Hollywood films to support the idea that the music is effective without drawing attention to itself as music. But how can music play its many roles—from setting the mood, helping with the continuity, and engaging the audience (Cohen, 1999)—while being essentially unheard?

Music Perception and Cognition

To address this question, one can turn to the field of music perception and cognition. Over the past 150 years, within the broader field of experimental psychology, this field has accumulated much knowledge from psychological experiments measuring various aspects of behavior of persons who are asked to listen and respond to particular kinds of musical stimuli (Cohen, 2009). Some research has also investigated situations in which music is presented in an audiovisual context. The results of these studies and their ensuing theoretical explanations, as well as more general theories in perception, cognition, and neuroscience, can help to explain the paradox of film music: that music outside of the drama helps to make the drama more compelling. This chapter takes this cognitive approach to address this question: Why does *unreal* music make the drama more real, and how does music that is not heard contribute to the impact of a film? The question of whether the music is actually not heard will also be considered.

Music

The first step in addressing these challenging questions is to examine music. Although fleeting and ephemeral, music submits well to analysis, and, through its analysis, we can begin to understand its role in film. Music is not just one thing. Like speech and language, music can be analyzed on many levels, from the acoustic physical level of description of sounds, to the level describing relations among tones and acoustical elements, to the level of meaning and its impact on the emotions. A single note of music, for example, can entail variation on dimensions of loudness (e.g., soft to loud), pitch height (e.g., high or low), musical instrument type (e.g., clarinet or piano, which in turn depend on the strength of the harmonics of each tone), and attack (e.g., soft or harsh). Multiply this information by each note that arrives simultaneously or in succession in a musical piece. Add to that the descriptions of relations among these notes—relations that create sets of tones defining the scale or alphabet for the particular piece of music, melodic contours (up and down patterns of pitch) and harmony progressions that create tension and relaxation. The cognitive complexity mounts quickly from just a few tones. A few tones, varying in particular ways, can reliably cue emotional meanings such as happiness, sadness, suspense, fear, and surprise. For example, high versus low, ascending versus descending, fast versus slow, and major versus minor tonality all convey happiness versus sadness (cf. Cohen, 2005, 2013-a; Collier & Hubbard, 2001; Vieillard et al., 2008). Specific associations to groups of musical tones come about for an individual or a cultural group through the use of a particular group of musical tones in particular contexts, such as special days (birthday, Christmas, New Years), events (sports, weddings, funerals), cultures (American, Asian), époques (medieval, 1920s), and so on. For example, the first six notes of the familiar *Happy Birthday* song bring associations of birthdays to mind in North American and British cultures, and in many more cultures for which there are translations. Prior to the creation and popularity of this song and its use in this particular setting, the six notes would not have held this special meaning. Given all of the information processing associated with even short sequences of tones, it is no wonder that brain imaging during music listening reveals the engagement of most brain regions (Overy & Molnar-Szakacs, 2009).

Structure and Association

The analysis of music from a psychological standpoint can be simplified by thinking of it from two perspectives—that of its structure and that of the associations it brings to mind. Both of these are aspects of the meaning of music, but the former (structure) depends on relations internal to the music, and the latter (associations) depends on connections to events outside the music. The distinction applies beyond music, of course. Visual scenes, for example, have formal characteristics such as the pattern of light and shade, and the particular shapes or motions represent objects in the world. Text also has formal features, for example, the shape of the word or the letter font, and text elicits particular associations through its denotation and connotations. Similarly, patterns of sound intensity or pitch characterize speech, and the particular speech refers to objects, concepts, and ideas. Sound effects also can be characterized by their formal features that are distinguished by the objects depicted as the source of the sounds. Finally, human bodily motion can also be described with respect to its formal features, such as the visual pattern made by the joints, and with respect to its meaning, such as walking, dancing, or climbing the stairs (Troje, 2008). All of these sources of structural and associationist information may be presented by cinema, through the screen and the audio speakers, and, in rare cases, kinanesthetically through special chairs that vibrate or move.

From this array of structural and associationist information, the audience member creates a narrative. The director has arranged these sensory materials to engage the audience member in an enjoyable narrative experience, and he or she counts on the mental resources of the audience member to analyze these many channels of information. But the analysis is not sufficient to create an engaging narrative. The output of the analysis from the various media channels must be integrated into a story and, to do this, the audience member's memory of past experience is required, as well as his or her memory or knowledge about stories in general.

Memory

As decades of memory research have shown, some memories endure for only milliseconds or seconds, whereas others may be retained for life. Short-term memory

(STM) refers to the temporary storage of memories whereas working memory (WM), a term originating with Baddeley (1986), refers to a combination of storage and manipulation (Baddeley, 2012, p. 4). Baddeley (2007) distinguished between a phonological loop and a visual-spatial sketchpad that were slaves of a central executive. His research suggested that the visual and auditory memory systems were independent. Support came from studies in which auditory memory was not compromised by an ongoing visual information-processing task. Some aspects of music may be served by the phonological loop (Williamson, Baddeley, & Hitch, 2010). Baddeley has more recently referred to his working memory model as M-WM for *multicomponent model*, and he added an episodic buffer (Baddeley, 2000) that receives input from the phonological loop and visuospatial sketchpad and sends these to the central executive. The buffer was needed to integrate audio and visual information into meaningful chunks, and their retrieval from the buffer en route to the central executive "occurred through conscious awareness." The notion of the consciousness buffer resembles Baars's (1988) theory of consciousness (cf. Baddeley, 2012), which assumes "that consciousness serves as a mechanism for binding stimulus features into perceived objects." Baddeley (2012, p. 18) summarizes his concept of working memory in fairly general terms "as a complex interactive system that is able to provide an interface between cognition and action, an interface that is capable of handling information in a range of modalities and stages of processing." Although cinema audiences do not typically physically act in response to a film, the utility of working memory for handling information in a range of modalities and stages of processing seems relevant to the processing of cinema. Baddeley's particular conceptualization may be inspirational although its details often, and not surprisingly, change as new data become available.

Baddeley's early idea of working memory inspired Foley and Cohen (1984) when they were studying the mental representation of large-scale space, as in complex buildings. Their studies entailed distance estimates between pairs of locations in a large irregular megastructure that housed an entire campus. Their findings led to their proposal of the concept of a *working map* to describe the cognitive map that people generated in order to carry out real-world spatial tasks. They argued that, depending on many factors, dynamic mental representation can take many forms, depending on the problem and individual proclivities. In the case of cognitive mapping, the participants aim to create a representation of space that has width, height, and depth; in a film, the participant aims to represent a story that takes place in space and time.

Long-term memory (LTM) refers to information retained possibly forever, but that could also last only a matter of minutes—typically longer than WM, which is measured in seconds. Three kinds of LTM and their associated underlying systems have been differentiated: memory for facts (semantic memory),

memory for action procedures like riding a bicycle (procedural memory), and memory for what happened (episodic or autobiographical memory) (Tulving, 1983). Knowledge of the rules of grammar have been regarded as an aspect of procedural memory by Ullman's (2001) influential *declarative procedural model of lexicon and grammar*. Here, the lexicon (containing all known words and their meaning) is relegated to semantic memory, which, along with episodic memory, is regarded as part of *declarative memory*. The same breakdown into procedural and semantic memory can be proposed for music grammar (rules of musical grammar generation applied to notes) and story grammar (rules of stories applied to story elements—the characters, actions, emotions). Although there is debate about the origins of these grammars (i.e., the extent to which they are available at birth), it is clear that experience is required to establish specific language and music grammars (Patel, 2008), and only after several years of life does a child grasp the concept of a story with a beginning, middle, and end (Nelson, 2005). Explanation of film and film music needs to account for memory representations of the visual but also of language and music.

The director provides the audience with sequential multimedia information and implicitly assumes that the audience will create a narrative from it. There is no guarantee that every audience member will interpret the film in the same way; the narrative of a film is fashioned by the audience member from his or her general knowledge of stories (which we can refer to as story grammar; e.g., most stories have a beginning, middle, and end) and long-term memories from which expectations can arise about what will happen next. The audience may be understood as engaged in deciphering the meaning of the lower level analysis of the sensory information received visually and through hearing. The sensory analysis works at two speeds and respective resolutions, and I have proposed that this dual-speed/dual-resolution system is essential for making sense of film (Cohen, 2010; 2013a; 2013b). The fast speed/lower resolution analysis can quickly send clues "up" to LTM, so that hypotheses can be generated about what the stimuli from the cinema screen and audio speakers might mean. These hypotheses can then be compared against the more refined analysis that is slower paced and of higher resolution. The best match between the multiple top-down hypotheses from the LTM and the information from the slower bottom-up analysis is what I refer to as the *working narrative*—the brain's best inference about moment-to-moment cinema action—the conscious experience of the film. Figure 3.1 represents the bottom-up analytic processes and the top-down expectancies converging on the working narrative.

Figure 3.1 represents your brain at the movies carrying out an analysis on six hierarchically organized channels of information beginning at A. These channels are referred to as text, speech, visual scenes, music, sound effects, and bodily

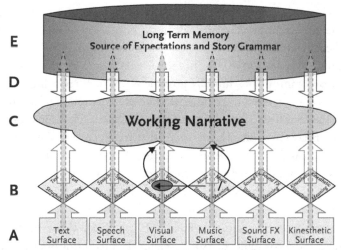

FIGURE 3.1 Congruence-Association model with the working narrative (CAM-WN). Reproduced from Cohen, A. J. (2013a). Film music from the perspective of cognitive science. In Neumeyer, D. (Ed.), *Oxford handbook of music in film and visual media* © Oxford University Press with permission. See also Cohen (2013b).

kinesthetic surfaces. The term *surface* implies a representation of detailed sensory information and has prior use, for example, by Krumhansl (1991) in the discussion of memory for detailed acoustical information of music. The term *surface* also is used to refer to the first level of models of representation of oral and written discourse (e.g., Graesser & McNamara, 2011), a level that includes detailed sensory information, although it also carries out analysis (e.g., identification of nouns and verbs) that is not implied in Figure 3.1.

The first five of these domains (i.e., text, speech, visual scenes, music, and sound effects) stem from film theorist Christian Metz (1974), who identified these as the channels of information that comprise film. His system, in comparison to that of other film theorists, is notable for its inclusion of music. The sixth channel arises from more recent grounds. Technology has developed such that motion effects and vibrations can be digitally encoded into the movie frame-by-frame for the purpose of controlling the motion of a theater chair that is designed to respond to the code, thus providing a new kinesthetic dimension of sensation. For the past few years, some theater have provided bodily kinesthetic information through such specially constructed theater seating. This capacity was generally unavailable in the time of Metz. Regardless of whether this kinesthetic novelty catches on, a recent psychological theory postulates a mirror neuron system in the brain (Rizzolatti & Craighero, 2004) that would make use of information in the kinesthetic channel. The proposed mirror neuron system in humans follows from a discovery of mirror neurons in the macaque monkey. These neurons were activated when the primate either performed an action, like grasping a peanut, or saw another animal or human carry out the same activity. Similar findings have been replicated with primates, although comparable studies with humans cannot typically be carried out in that they involve recording directly from neurons in the human brain. It is technically possible to do such recording in humans, but, for ethical reasons, such recordings cannot be attempted unless they are of medical value. (Similarly, it would be technically possible to obtain more primate data, but there are few primate laboratories, due in part to the animal rights activism with concerns about invasive animal research). Several rare human single-cell recordings have been carried out in conjunction with medical goals, revealing that some neurons in the motor cortex are sensitive to *perceived* actions performed by others and that some neurons in the sensory cortex are sensitive to *self-performed* actions (Mukamel & Fried, 2012, p. 526). This evidence is sufficient to suggest the possibility of a special channel representing bodily kinesthetic motion whether perceived or executed by the self. In other words, if someone watches an actor depicted walking on the screen, part of the mirror neuron system involving motor cortex would be activated, even though the viewer is only watching someone else walk. It should be pointed out that the notion of channels and reference to particular regions of the brain is not to suggest a simple neural anatomical circuitry defined for each channel. The notion is more functional than structural. Each of the six channels represents a job to be done by constellations of neurons. Although some brain areas are specialized for certain tasks (e.g., the retinal ganglia respond to light energy, the auditory nerve reflects sound transduced by the hair cells in the cochlea), the general interconnectedness of neurons through multiple dendrites associated with every neuron and the possibility of influence of neural firing at a distance destroys the possibility of distinct anatomical pathways for each channel on all but the peripheral (surface) level.

The next level in Figure 3.1, B, represents an analysis of the information of each of these channels into formal features (labeled *structure*) and into associations; that is, the meanings brought to mind (labeled *meaning*). As previously described, all six types of surface information are amenable to formal structural and associative meaning analysis. The activity within different channels may be correlated across some channels. For example, if an actor is speaking, the timing of the lip motion (represented in the visual and kinesthetic channels) matches the dynamic pattern of the speech sounds (represented in the speech channel). Thus, similar outcomes of structural analysis would arise in three different channels— the speech channel, the visual channel, and the bodily kinesthetic channel. This redundancy could alert attention: Similar information from three different sources means "pay attention." As another example, if the beat of music is synchronized with the steps of one of several individual runners depicted on the screen, the formal analysis of the music would coincide with the formal analysis of the visual representation of one, but not all, of the runners. The horizontal black arrow in Figure 3.1 represents such a situation in which the structure of the music parallels the structure of part of the visual scene represented in the dark shaded oval. The dark area represents the principle that shared structure between one channel of information and visual scene information directs attention to that part of the visual scene that is correlated with this other modality. Note that this is not specific to music. In an example of a ventriloquist with a puppet, speech dynamics do not match the movement of the actual speaker (who speaks without obvious articulatory motion) but rather with the movement of the puppet (be it the mouth area, or head or body motion). Attention is directed to the face of the "speaking" puppet. Although, in general, there is an asymmetry proposed, typically referred to as *visual dominance*, certain media types, such as music videos, may operate with the opposite asymmetry, in which the music is the focus and is potentially modified by information from other modalities (cf. Boltz, 2013; Boltz, Ebendorf, & Field, 2009). Recognizing that the amount of information presented by a film exceeds the moment-to-moment processing capacity of the human brain, the model postulates that structural congruencies control attention to part of the screen or (in the case of music videos) to the music, allowing for efficient coding of the most likely salient information.

Different channels may generate redundant associations. For example, the meaning of music playing at the same time as a character is speaking, although asynchronous with the articulation motion, might overlap with the meaning of the speech—for example, perhaps a sad topic discussed with background music in a minor key or reminiscent of music played at funerals. Again, this redundancy can serve to identify this information as important. Boltz, Schulkind, and Kantra (1991) showed that when music and film meaning coincided, subsequent memory for the film clip was heightened as compared to a condition in which there was no music or the music was inconsistent with the visual scene. The CAM-WN model suggests that important associations are allowed safe passage to the next level, as the ascending black arrow from music in Figure 3.1 indicates.

As mentioned earlier, the analysis of the sensory materials provided by the film takes place on two time spans: rough, fast preprocessing and a slower, higher resolution detailed processing. In Figure 3.1, the fast preprocessing is represented by the dashed elongated arrows beginning in all six surfaces at A and ending in the reservoir of LTM at E. The preprocessing is initially all that the brain, specifically LTM, has to go on regarding the interpretation of the sensory information provided. Based on these early cues, expectations or hypotheses can be generated from the combination of prior experience with both similar information and the nature of narrative (the story grammar). The hypotheses and expectations or schemas that make up the potential story of the film are represented by the descending arrows at D in Figure 3.1. The descending information at D and the ascending information at B are both related to the audience member's goal of enjoying a story provided by the cinema experience. The satisfaction of this goal, by the conscious representation of a multimodal narrative, arises as the best match between information from D and B. This process takes place at C, and the conscious outcome is referred to as the *working narrative*. The working narrative is the conscious experience of the film. Information from the working narrative can travel back to LTM at level E to become memories of the film and, recursively, add to the knowledge on which the audience member can draw for interpretation of the present film and future ones, or future experience in general.

On Not Hearing Film Music: The Paradox

Music typically takes its place in the film soundtrack along with sound effects and speech. It is an interesting psychological problem in itself to explain how the audience can make sense of this complex of acoustical streams. In real life, although there may be three streams, the music stream can always be categorized as coming from a live source. In film, this happens only when music is available to (is presumably heard by) the characters, for example, in a car with the radio on, at a wedding party, in a dance club. For many if not most scenes, there would be no music, but in film there is often a great deal of music when none would be present in the scene.

In the extreme case, the director includes *only* music on the soundtrack in a scene that would normally have speech and sound effects and would not have any music. An example about which I have previously written (Cohen, MacMillan, & Drew, 2006) comes from a key moment in the film *Witness* (Feldman & Weir, 1985) when the young Amish boy, Samuel, who has recently witnessed a crime, is brought to the police station to report what he knows (see Figure 3.2). While there, Samuel notices a photograph that honors a police officer and, to Samuel's horror, that police officer is the man he saw commit the crime.

Why, at this particular critical moment in the film, do all sound effects and speech cut out, leaving only the music score of composer Maurice Jarre? By removing the realistic sounds, does the music in some way add to the realism? To address these questions, we created two additional soundtracks, one that was solely of speech characteristic of the police station and also included the spoken

FIGURE 3.2 Frames from the critical scene in *Witness* (Feldman & Weir, 1985).

thoughts of Samuel. The other was solely of sound effects that would be heard in the police station of that day, such as phones ringing, typewriters, and sirens in the background. Three different groups participated in the study. Each group was presented with the film clip and with one of these three audio backgrounds. The plot was described to them, up to the point when the clip began. They were asked to rate on a 5-point scale their level of absorption in the film, their judged sense of reality conveyed by the film, and the professional quality of this segment of the film. The results indicated that the music soundtrack led to the highest level of absorption in the film. The sense of realism was judged the same for all three conditions. Thus, the music-only condition did not destroy the sense of realism of the film and led to the most absorbing clip. The professional quality of the music soundtrack was also rated more highly than the other two soundtracks, which may have reflected that the speech and sound effects tracks had not been created by film sound professionals. Nevertheless, it was the choice of the director to use only music here, and it might be argued that even if the speech track and sound effects track had been professionally created, the music track by itself would still lead to the most compelling scene. The CAM-WN model explains that the emotional meaning of the music arising from the bottom-up analysis is matched by the expectancies descending in the top-down analysis, and, through the matching process, this meaning becomes part of the working narrative. There are no expectations descending from D to match the musical acoustical information arising from B, and hence the sound of the music itself does not appear in the working narrative, at least not to any great extent.

Babel

More recent examples of this *exclusionary music* (a soundtrack that excludes all sounds but music, although dialogue and sound effects would more appropriately characterize the reality of the scene), a term coined by Martin Marks (personal communication), are found in the film *Babel* (Golin, Kilik, & Iñárritu, 2006). The film received an Academy Award for the music soundtrack composed by Guastavo Santaolalla. There are several key scenes that lack sound effects and speech but have music. It is noteworthy that director Alejandro González Iñárritu has a special sensitivity to film music, having himself scored six Mexican feature films in the late 1980s, prior to becoming professionally involved in film.

The title *Babel* brings to mind the biblical story of the city of Babel, in which confusion arose when its people changed from having one language to having different languages. The theme of failed communication underlies the film, which tells four strangely interrelated stories that take place in Morocco, Japan, the United States, and Mexico. Two Moroccan peasant boys do not listen to their father and instead test the range of his newly acquired secondhand (actually thirdhand) gun by shooting at a distant tourist bus rather than at the nearby jackals that threaten their goat herd. The bullet tragically lodges in the shoulder of an American tourist, Susan, traveling with her husband on the bus. Their children are home in California, but, due to the delayed return of the parents, the children are driven to Mexico by their Mexican caregiver, who needs to attend her son's wedding and cannot find anyone else to take care of the children. The gun is traced to its original owner, a businessman in Japan, who gave it to a native guide in Morocco employed on a recent hunting vacation. The businessman has an angry deaf daughter, Chieko, who, as part of the theme of communication failure, cannot hear him, even if she were able to hear. He has been under suspicion for the suicide of his wife; the gun traced to him places him further in harm's way. Chieko does not care and seeks love of some kind (from her dentist, boys who she does not know, a police inspector).

The film *The Artist* (Langmann & Hazanavicius, 2011) won the Academy Award for best picture and best soundtrack for 2011 and was overtly a silent film; *Babel,* which won the Oscar for the best original score in 2006, operates like a silent film in several key places. Although sparse, the music works hard to enable audience engagement in the complex narrative of the film. There is much less emphasis on speech in this film than there is in traditional Hollywood movies. First, subtitles are used when the language spoken is not English. This happens frequently because so much of the film takes place with Japanese, Moroccan, and Mexican protagonists. Second, long segments of the film are without speech. Third, in some scenes, music is the only sound presented, as in a silent film. Finally, in some scenes, extradiegetic music is so loud as to drown out voices. In the majority of scenes, as in the majority of films, the music is not part of the scene; that is, it is extradiegetic. In these extradiegetic cases, the meaning of the music is seeking an object, a concept introduced by musicologist Nicholas Cook (1998), and which I interpret in this instance as the music playing the role as an adjective might modify a noun or an adverb a verb. The music gives rise to ideas that become part of the narrative. Primarily, these are ideas about how the characters are feeling. The emotion expressed by the music becomes connected to the protagonist. The audience then understands how the protagonist feels, and, consequently, the audience responds emotionally. But the music does more than this.

The examples to be described here come from the DVD recording of *Babel*. Most films begin with music during the opening credits, establishing a context for the film. However, *Babel* (DVD) is an exception. In fact, music in *Babel* is absent in the entire first "chapter" of the film (approximately 8 minutes) that introduces the tragic shooting at the tourist bus by the Moroccan boy. As the two brothers run off in terror when they realize their bullet has actually hit and stopped the tourist bus, another young boy in America is running in much more affluent and seemingly playful circumstances, innocent of the fact that his mother has just been shot. The action of running in America mirrors that of the boys running in Morocco, a case of structural similarity that would be picked up at B in the structure analysis of the visual scene, or possibly also in the kinesthetic analysis, assuming the mirror neuron system is activated by watching the running. It is only when the American children are put to bed by Amelia, their Mexican nanny, that a melody is presented, performed on an oud, a Middle Eastern lute-like instrument. This Middle Eastern (Moroccan) music becomes associated with the American children and foreshadows their connection to the story unfolding in Morocco (see Figure 3.3).

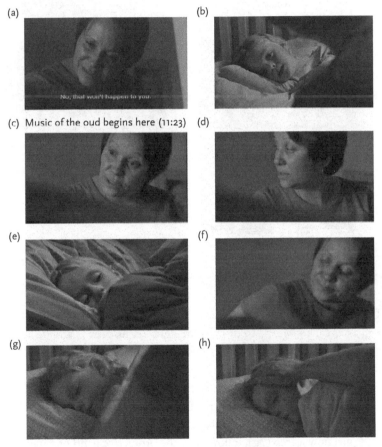

FIGURE 3.3 Frames from *Babel* during which background music is presented. The children in California are going sleep. The music is performed on the oud, an instrument common in Morocco, where their parents are visiting and in crisis. Chapter 2, 11:23–12:04 on the DVD of *Babel*, directed by Alejandro González Iñárritu (Los Angeles: Paramount Vantage, 2006).

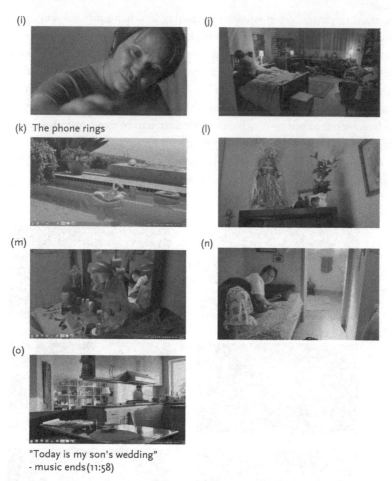

(i)

(j)

(k) The phone rings

(l)

(m)

(n)

(o)

"Today is my son's wedding"
- music ends (11:58)

FIGURE 3.3 Continued.

Figure 3.3 shows two shots prior to the introduction of the music cue. The little girl has called Amelia to turn on the light because she is afraid she will die (of sudden infant death) like her baby brother. Amelia (3a), speaking in Spanish (with subtitles), tells her "that won't happen to you." The next shot (3b) is of the little girl, followed by Amelia (3c) at the same time as the simple oud melody begins (11 minutes, 23 seconds into the DVD). Amelia (3d) then directs her gaze to the little boy seen in the next shot (3e). Then back to Amelia (3f) and then to the little girl now asleep (3g), followed by the protective hand of Amelia on the little girl's head (3h). All of these shots are close-ups on only one character. The situation is similar to a melody that presents related notes one after the other and that the mind makes sense of. Hugo Münsterberg (1916/1970), the first psychologist to write about film in his book *The Photoplay,* describes this capacity of film to juxtapose concepts, bringing them into relations like the three notes of a musical triad. He gave the example of the juxtaposition of a triad of scenes: a working woman at the end of her day cavorting with her boss, her parents at home anxiously waiting for her to return, and, finally, the boss's wife at home awaiting his return. "It is as if we saw one through another, as if three tones blended into one chord" (p. 105; see further Cohen, 2002, p. 216).

In this scene in *Babel*, the three characters shown in separate shots become more closely related, perhaps because the audience has to work to keep them together, and the music, note by note, helps to construct this unity. At the same time, the music of the oud is not the music of either the children or Amelia. The children, in fact, don't share the music of Amelia. Her music is Mexican; their music is from cartoons. The background Middle Eastern music of the oud is associated with the scene from Morocco, almost impossibly related to these children's bedtime scene in America. Considerable research in the past two decades shows how associations of music can rather straightforwardly influence the interpretation of ambiguous scenes (e.g., Bolivar, Cohen, & Fentress, 1994; Cohen, 1993; Shevy, 2007; Tan, Spackman, & Bezdek, 2007; Van den Stock, Peretz, Grèzes, & van Gelder, 2009), although there can also be more complex influences. It is reasonable to assume that the associations of the oud music link Morocco to the children. Research by Boltz (2004) affirms that connections between music and visual images are formed such that the music consistent with a narrative later serves as a retrieval cue.

With the children in bed for the night, the Middle Eastern music continues through another series of shots. The music (sounding foreboding) is consistent with Amelia worrying in her room. A cut to (k) doubly surprises with daylight and a shot of the exterior of the house, including a lap pool and a sandbox, an ironic contrast to the Moroccan desert scene. The phone rings during this shot and continues to ring through a further interior shot (l) showing a (Mexican) doll with a bow on top, presumably a gift. A shot (m) of the same doll from a new angle reveals Amelia in a mirror, awakened by the phone. At (n), the focus is now on Amelia scrambling from bed to answer the phone, and, at (o), on the phone she exclaims that she must attend her son's wedding in Mexico. The voice on the phone (the children's father in Morocco) orders her to change her plans in order to stay with the children; he will pay for a better wedding later. The extradiegetic oud music ends, having covered numerous shots in just over 30 seconds.

Two short examples of diegetic music soon follow. First (at 12:31), it is 20 seconds of music from a Mighty Mouse cartoon, part of the diegesis of the children absorbed in television as Amelia tries to find another person to take care of them. With no solution to the problem, Amelia's nephew drives up in his car blaring Mexican music from the radio (at 13:27). The music abruptly stops after 5 seconds as he turns the key in his car and jumps out to see his aunt. The departure of the foursome in the car is punctuated by the loud Mexican music from the car's radio that again stops abruptly after just 2 seconds, this time with a cut to tourists in a Middle Eastern market and cafe area.

What needs comment here is the ease with which the mind encodes both the music that essentially has no physical place in the scene (the music of the oud) and the music that plays a part in it (the cartoon music and the Mexican music from the car). The music of the oud, which says "Middle Eastern culture" raises the question of how this situation in California can be linked to the boys in Morocco. The simple melodic line of the oud also serves the purpose of linking the disparate and fast cuts from the children's bedroom, to Amelia's bedroom, to the outdoor swimming pool in daylight, to the interior shots of a doll, a mirror, and Amelia scrambling to get the phone, and finally ending in the kitchen. Throughout this chaotic montage is the continuous melodic structure arising from the enduring tones of the oud. The CAM-WN model directs attention to the structural relations of the music, allowing this to serve a continuity function distinct from the associations of the music, which have significance in another way, saying that this scene somehow connects to Morocco.

In nonlinear fashion, the film switches back in time and place and introduces the parents of the American children, Susan and Richard, traveling in Morocco. We meet them first in an outdoor cafe (see Figure 3.4). An establishing shot (14:33) reveals them at their table, physically separated in the frame by the caftan of their server (a). Other than this image, there is never a shot of both of them in the same frame. From then on, the shots are all close-ups of one or the other of the pair, for example Richard at (b). In fact, there are 11 pairs of alternating close-ups of Richard and Susan in just over the next 2 minutes. This disjunction represents their relation at this point. Susan is in a bitter, angry, and disgruntled mood, and asks "Why did we come here?" Richard's incoherent answer characterizes the entire conversation that exemplifies failure to communicate, like two computers echoing a few words from each other's sentences without fully processing meaning, or like two inhabitants of a city of Babel. After Susan's final words in this conversation "just tell me when you are ready to argue; tell me you're not going to run away again," the music of the oud begins a simple melody, an ascending interval of a fourth depicted as the notes B to E in the Western music system in Figure 3.4(c). (See also Figure 3.6 that provides an acoustic representation and music notation.) A shot of the desert landscape at (d) is accompanied by another pair of notes, descending from the previous ascending B E interval to D and then up a third to F sharp. The next shot (e) of a cyclist on the road repeats this four-note theme (a *maqam*, in Arabic music terminology). The next shot (f) is

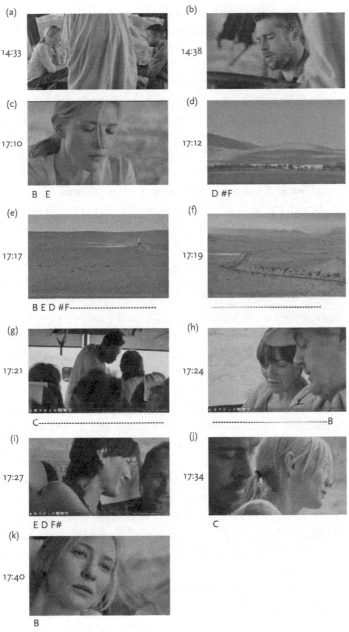

FIGURE 3.4A–K Frames from *Babel* during which the music (a repeated four-note ascending motif) is the only sound presented (i.e., no speech, or sound effects) for a large segment of the clip (4c–k); Chapter 3, 14:33–17:40 on the DVD of *Babel*, dir. Alejandro González Iñárritu (Los Angeles: Paramount Vantage, 2006). Times shown in minutes and seconds were obtained during playback using VLC media player software. Letters below images are musical note names (e.g., A, A#, B, C…etc).

a long shot of a bus followed by (g) inside the bus with the driver speaking to a tourist—speaking but not speaking because the scene has changed from being acoustically realistic in the conversation between Susan and Richard, to now one that is acoustically unrealistic; music is the exclusive sound. The sound effects are gone and instead the extradiegetic music takes over. I would argue, based on our findings from *Witness* (Cohen et al., 2006), that the audience does not notice a change in the sense of reality of the film, unless it is to render the film world even more compelling. The bus driver is soundlessly in conversation with the board-ing passengers; couples engage in normal conversations (h) and laughter (i), but there is only the melody of the oud in the background—a new note C drones on during (g), while the previous *maqam* begins with a focus on the first couple (h) and ends with the second laughing couple (i). The same *maqam* has played three times, serving a structural role in binding these disparate shots into a coher-ent whole. The camera then focuses on Richard and Susan (j) who, in contrast to the two previous couples depicted, engage in neither couple-talk nor laughter. At (k), during a new sustained note, Susan gazes out the window, deep in thought it seems.

As shown in Figure 3.5 (see also Figure 3.6 for the acoustic representation and music notation), the oud music continues but changes to a descending pattern. The melody is again four notes, easily interpreted by Western ears as the first four notes of the descending harmonic minor scale (e.g., E D sharp C B). In the first presentation of this theme, which is from Susan's perspective looking out the win-dow, each note accompanies a different shot. The first two are of women in hijabs (a and b), and the second two are of Susan's face (c and d). The melody repeats, with again two shots of Susan's face, then a shot of her hand on her lap, and finally a shot where she has placed her hand on Richard's. The closure of the melodic motif and the movement of the hand represent congruent structures— although not perfectly aligned, still serving in the CAM-WN model to draw attention to this action. A softer note enters with eerie overtones, potentially symbolizing that the holding of hands is not for long. She ultimately removes her hand. Yet a fourth time the minor four-note motif descends, with the first two notes on Richard's pensive face (j); the third on Susan, her eyes open on (k); and the fourth with her eyes closing (l). Here the closure of the motif coincides with the closing of the eyes, and, following research by Thompson, Sinclair, and Russo (1994) that examined the role of closure, it is fair to say that the parallel music-visual struc-tural closure gives a sense of completion. For a final repetition of this four-note motif, each tone accompanies a different shot, first a long shot (m) of the bus. Here, for the first time, realistic sound creeps back surreptitiously into the drama. The noise of the road is introduced on the first note, and this noise continues and strengthens in a close-up (n) of the wheels of the bus turning a corner, locking the

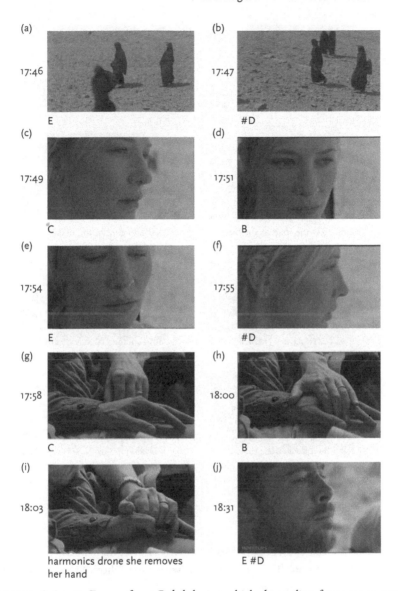

FIGURE 3.5A–R Frames from *Babel* during which descending four-note sequence is repeated four times, the last during which the realistic sound of the bus resumes, followed by the sound of a page turning, and the background noise of the vehicle's motor. To the realistic sound effects is suddenly added that of a bullet piercing the window glass. Chapter 3, 17:46–19:02 on the DVD of *Babel*, dir. Alejandro González Iñárritu (Los Angeles: Paramount Vantage, 2006). Times shown in minutes and seconds are approximate.

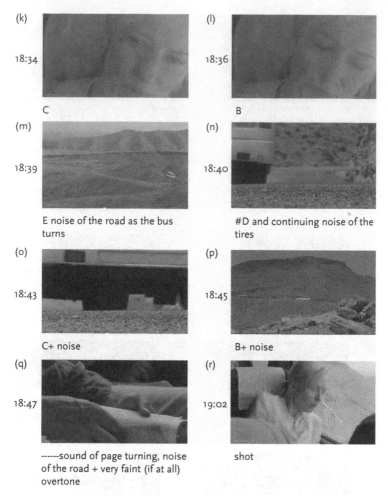

FIGURE 3.5 Continued.

audience now into the diegetic sound. A further shot of the wheels (o) is accompanied by the next note. The sequence ends with a long shot of the bus (p), with appropriate sound effects remaining.

I believe that the music makes the audience more at one with the thoughts of the characters as the camera focuses directly on the heads (minds) of Richard and Susan, first one, then the other, then both, and then on their hands. The same instrument, the oud, played when their children are going to bed, can serve to tie thoughts about the children left alone to the parents' minds (or, at least, to Susan's mind). The music also speaks of emotion that can be interpreted as love between the couple and for their children, but also despair on the part of Susan and Richard in their separateness from each other. The acoustics of the oud itself

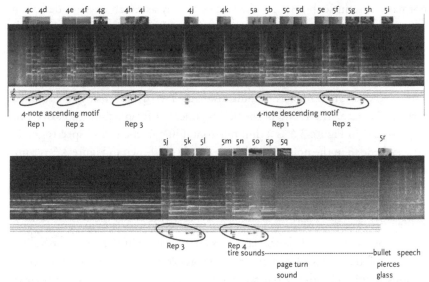

FIGURE 3.6 Acoustic spectrographic representation of the soundtrack accompanying the frames of Figures 3.4 and 3.5. Time is represented along the horizontal axis and frequency (0–15,000 Hz) along the vertical axis. The music staff line shows the corresponding music notation of the oud, which is mirrored by the acoustic representation of the notes. For each note of the oud, the lowest horizontal bar represents the lowest frequency (the fundamental), and higher horizontal bars represent the overtones (or harmonics, which are frequencies at whole-integer multiples of the fundamental frequency, usually sounding at a lower intensity level). The natural sounds of the oud had been supplemented in the original soundtrack by digital editing, such that certain overtones could be emphasized. As the acoustic representation shows, at no time is the music absent, until 5q (page turn). The first four-note ascending motif is shown repeating three times, followed by four repetitions of the second (descending) motif. The return of the diegetic sound (5m) occurs at the noise of the wheels of the bus, shown as haze across the entire frequency range that continues throughout the rest of the clip including the page turn (5q, which appears as fine vertical lines in the high-frequency range on the graph), and the final sound of the gunshot through the bus window (5r, a prominent vertical noise band representing all frequencies at once for a brief instant).

has no place in this story reality, but the emotion conveyed by the music and the associations it brings of Morocco and the children mean much to the story. The expectations from level D of the CAM-WN model match the information at level B arising from the meaning analysis of the music, but there is nothing in terms of expectations from D to match the acoustic information from the music and hence the acoustical aspect of the music does not become part of the working narrative. The CAM-WN model therefore helps to explain why this extradiegetic music works in the scene, not only for the sake of the music itself, but for its exclusion of the real sounds—the speech and sound effects—that would normally arise in such a scene. The visuals convey as much as is needed about how the other couples on the bus are interacting. The acoustic information of the other conversations on the bus is not important. For both the audience and Susan and Richard, the people on the bus are there only at a remote level.

The real sounds surreptitiously return with the sound of the noise of the bus wheels. The return to Richard reading inside the bus (q) now brings the sound of turning the page. The sound of the oud is gone, but for possibly a soft overtone (represented in Figure 3.6 as a thin horizontal line in the sound spectrograph), now embedded in the noise of the bus or the wind (shown in Figure 3.6 as a uniform haze on the spectrograph). The noise continues through an image of Susan sleeping and then, at (r), a bullet shot pierces the glass (and Susan's shoulder) making the gunshot/glass-piercing sound one would expect (shown in Figure 3.6 as the bright vertical bar).

The music, now ended, has served its dual purpose in the words of Kalinak (1992) "of both articulator of screen expression and initiator of spectator response [which] binds the spectator to the screen by resonating affect between them" (p. 87; see also Cohen, 2010). The repetition of both the ascending and descending musical scale motifs have made for easy perceptual analysis and have enabled the music to serve a structural function in the film. The associations of the minor mode, the Middle Eastern theme, the acquired connection to the children, all play their part in establishing context for the climactic, catastrophic shooting. The expectations from level E and D of CAM-WN have no doubt been working overtime in trying to answer the narrative question "what will happen next?" as information, including that of the music, becomes available through the bottom-up processing at A and B.

The frames of the film, the notes of the accompanying music, and acoustical analysis are rich sources of information. For reasons of space, it is not possible to describe in full detail all the nuances associated with the film music. Moreover, the description and interpretation is mine, and although based on past research on film music and adherence to the acoustical representation, empirical behavioral studies with this particular material have not been carried out to show what the "average" audience member perceives or remembers. We need to find out what audiences actually hear, see, and conjecture. Indeed, whereas I have focused on the music and the significance of the sound that accompanies this portion of *Babel*, film score theorist Kulezic-Wilson (2009) has focused on a discussion of *silence* in films, using frames from *Babel* from the ending shots of Figure 3.4 and continuing through to frame 5(i). She says:

> [T]he melancholytheme played on oud, which starts at the beginning of the scene accompanying images of the desert and occasional passersby, is

actually removed at the instant when the wife reaches for her husband's hand, leaving only a barely audible accompaniment made of electronically sustained sounds. Iñárritu deliberately leaves that moment "dry," allowing the audience to read the emotional weight of silence and the tiniest gestures themselves rather than trying to interpret them through music. On the other hand, the withdrawal of the musical theme at the crucial moment should not be understood only as a simple refusal to comply with the conventions of "emotional" scoring but also as an acknowledgment of the insurmountable gap between the husband and wife at that point in their relationship.

Her interpretation differs from the one presented here, which is more closely tied to the acoustical information as revealed in Figure 3.6, showing perhaps more acoustical information than Kulezic-Wilson's analysis suggests. The difference in these descriptions, in addition to emphasizing the need for psychological research, serves also to show the richness of musical information even in scores that consist of but a few notes.

Award-Winning Scores

Babel won the 2006 Oscar for the best original score and was nominated for six other Oscars, including best picture. It received the Golden Globe award for best film and received several other awards for its score and direction. The connection between the film score and the film's success as measured by awards and box office is not anomalous. Dean Keith Simonton (2007; 2011) has noted an association between award-winning film scores and chances of obtaining other awards for a film, but an award-winning song in a film does not have the same impact. The analysis provided by the CAM-WN model helps to confirm Simonton's conjecture that the award-winning song distracts the audience, whereas the award-winning soundtrack engages the audience member in a compelling narrative. The analysis of parts of the score of *Babel* by Guastavo Santaolalla has revealed many contributions from minimal music resources: a monophonic melody from a single instrument and the repetition of short motifs of four notes. Yet these motifs contain the elements of musical structure. Each motif produces a pattern of relaxation and tension, and repetition of the motif produces higher order tension/relaxation patterns. Tension/relaxation supports emotional meaning, an ingredient of narrative that, rather than dictating how to feel, allows the audience member to feel (although this is a matter of debate among film theorists as to whether the audience becomes controlled by the music rather than allowed to interpret the film independently). Because what one is conscious of represents only a fraction of brain activity, it is not surprising that the musical packaging (i.e., the acoustics) is unattended to while the package contents of structure and emotional and contextual meaning facilitate the creation of the working narrative.

Conclusion

This chapter has introduced some of the research on the psychology of film music that can be called on to understand how film music works. Specifically, the focus is on what I have referred to as the paradox of film music—how music that has no place in the drama makes the drama more compelling. The CAM-WN model was presented as a way to consider the bottom-up and top-down mental processes that might account for the conscious experience (or rather creation) of the film in the working narrative. A shot-by-shot analysis of a small but critical portion of the film *Babel*, along with a note-by-note analysis of its score and its acoustical representation, were offered to depict both the complexity and the simplicity of music and visual relations and to show how their functioning could be understood by means of the CAM-WN framework. The opportunities for research in this domain are abundant, with potential outcomes explaining not only how music works in cinema, but how the mind processes multimodal information in real life in the absence of a musical soundtrack.

Acknowledgments

The support of the Social Sciences and Humanities Research Council of Canada is gratefully acknowledged for this program of research beginning in 1987. Robert Drew kindly assisted with the score notation of the oud and synchronization with the spectrographic representation and film frames in Figure 3.6.

References

Baars, B. J. (1988). *A cognitive theory of consciousness.* Cambridge: Cambridge University Press.

Baddeley, A. D. (1986). *Working memory.* Oxford: Oxford University Press.

Baddeley, A. D. (2000). The episodic buffer: A new component for working memory? *Trends in Cognitive Science, 4,* 417–423.

Baddeley A. D. (2007). *Working Memory, Thought and Action.* Oxford, UK: Oxford Univ. Press.

Baddeley, A. (2012). Working memory: Theories, models, and controversies. *Annual Review of Psychology, 63,* 1–29.

Bolivar, V. J., Cohen, A. J., & Fentress, J. C. (1994). Semantic and formal congruency in music and motion pictures: Effects on the interpretation of visual action. *Psychomusicology*, *13*, 28–59.

Boltz, M. G. (2004). The cognitive processing of film and musical soundtracks. *Memory & Cognition*, *32*, 1194–1205.

Boltz, M. G. (2013). Music videos and visual influences on music perception and appreciation: Should you want your MTV? In S. –L. Tan, A. J. Cohen, S. Lipscomb, & R. Kendall, R. (Eds.), *The psychology of musical multimedia* (pp. 213–230). Oxford: Oxford University Press.

Boltz, M. G., Ebendorf, B., & Field, B. (2009). Audiovisual interactions: The impact of visual information on music perception and memory. *Music Perception*, *27*, 43–59.

Boltz, M., Schulkind, M., & Kantra, S. (1991). Effects of background music on remembering of filmed events. *Memory and Cognition*, *19*, 595–606.

Cohen, A. J. (1993). Associationism and musical soundtrack phenomena. *Contemporary Music Review*, *9*, 163–178.

Cohen, A. J. (1999). Functions of music in multimedia: A cognitive approach. In S. W. Yi (Ed.), *Music, mind science* (pp.40–68). Seoul: Seoul University Press.

Cohen, A. J. (2002). Music cognition and the cognitive psychology of film structure. *Canadian Psychology*, *43*, 215–232.

Cohen, A. J. (2005). How music influences the interpretation of film and video: Approaches from experimental psychology. In R. A. Kendall & R. W. Savage (Eds.), *Reports in ethnomusicology: Perspectives in systematic musicology* (vol. 12, pp. 15–36). Los Angeles: University of California Press.

Cohen, A. J. (2009). Music in performance arts: Film, theatre and dance. In S. Hallam, I. Cross, & M. Thaut (Eds.), *The Oxford handbook of music psychology* (pp. 441–451). New York: Oxford University Press.

Cohen, A. J. (2010). Music as a source of emotion in film. In P. Juslin & J. Sloboda (Eds.), *Handbook of music and emotion*. (pp. 879–908). Oxford: Oxford University Press.

Cohen, A. J. (2013a). Film music from the perspective of cognitive science. In D. Neumeyer (Ed.), *The Oxford handbook of music in film and visual media*. New York: Oxford University Press.

Cohen, A. J. (2013b). Film music and the unfolding narrative. In M. Arbib (Ed.), *Language, music, and the brain: A mysterious relationship* (pp. 173–201). Cambridge, MA: MIT Press.

Cohen, A. J., MacMillan, K. A., & Drew, R. (2006). The role of music, sound effects & speech on absorption in a film: The congruence-associationist model of media cognition. *Canadian Acoustics*, *34*, 40–41.

Collier, W. G., & Hubbard, T. (2001). Judgments of happiness, brightness, speed and tempo change of auditory stimuli varying in pitch and tempo. *Psychomusicology*, *17*, 36–55.

Cook, N. (1998). *Analyzing musical multimedia*. Oxford: Oxford University Press.

Cooke, M. (2008). *A history of film music.* Cambridge: Cambridge University Press.

Feldman, E. S. (Producer), & Weir, P. (Director). (1985). *Witness.* Paramount Pictures, United States.

Foley, J. E., & Cohen, A. J. (1984). Working mental representations of the environment. *Environment and Behavior, 16,* 713–729.

Golin, S., Kilik, J., & Iñárritu, A. G. (Producers), & Iñárritu, A. (Director). (2006). *Babel.* Central Films Studio (France) and Media Rights Capital Studio, USA.

Gorbman, C. (1987). *Unheard melodies: Narrative film music.* Bloomington: Indiana University Press.

Graesser, A. C., & McNamara, D. S. (2011). Computational analyses of multilevel discourse *Comprehension Topics in Cognitive Science, 3,* 371–398.

Krumhansl, C. L. (1991). Memory for musical surface. *Memory & Cognition, 19,* 401–411.

Kulezic-Wilson, D. (2009). The music of film silence. *Music and the Moving Image, 2,* 1–10.

Langmann, T. (Producer), & Hazanavicius, M. (Director). (2011). *The artist.* [Motion picture]. US: The Weinstein Co.

Marks, M. M. (1997). *Music and the silent film.* New York: Oxford University Press.

Metz, C. (1974). *Film language: A semiotics of the cinema* (M. Taylor, Trans.). New York: Oxford University Press.

Mukamel, R., & Fried, I. (2012). Human intracranial recordings and cognitive neuroscience. *Annual Review of Psychology, 63,* 511–537.

Münsterberg, H. (1970). *The photoplay: A psychological study.* New York: Arno. (Original work published 1916)

Nelson, K. (2005). Emerging levels of consciousness in early human development. In H. S. Terrace & J. Metcalfe (Eds.), *The missing link in cognition: Origins of self-reflective consciousness* (pp. 116–145). New York: Oxford University Press.

Neumeyer, D. (Ed.), (2013). *Oxford handbook of music in film and visual media.*

Patel, A. D. (2008). *Music, language, and the brain.* New York: Oxford University Press.

Overy, K., & Molnar-Szakacs, I. (2009). Being together in time: Musical experience and the mirror neuron system. *Music Perception, 26,* 489–504.

Rizzolatti, G., & Craighero, L. (2004). The mirror-neuron system. *Annual Review of Neuroscience, 27,* 169–192.

Shevy, M. (2007). The mood of rock music affects evaluation of video elements differing in valence and dominance. *Psychomusicology, 19,* 57–78.

Simonton, D. K. (2007). Film music: Are award-winning scores and songs heard in successful motion pictures? *Psychology of Aesthetics, Creativity, and the Arts, 1,* 53–60.

Simonton, D. K. (2011). *Great flicks: Scientific studies of cinematic creativity and aesthetics.* Oxford: Oxford University Press.

Tan, S.-L., Spackman, M. P., & Bezdek, M. A. (2007). Viewers' interpretation of film characters' emotions: Effects of presenting film music before or after a character is shown. *Music Perception, 25,* 135–152.

Thompson, W. F., Russo, F. A., & Sinclair, D. (1994). Effects of underscoring on the perception of closure in filmed events. *Psychomusicology, 13*, 9–27.

Troje, N. F. (2008). Retrieving information from human movement patterns. In T. F. Shipley, & J. M. Zack (Eds.), *Understanding events: How humans see, represent, and act on events* (pp. 308–334). New York: Oxford University Press,.

Tulving, E. (1983). *Elements of episodic memory*. New York: Oxford University Press.

Ullman, M. T. (2001). The declarative /procedural model of lexicon and grammar. *Journal of Psycholinguisitic Research, 30*, 37–39.

Vieillard, S., Peretz, I., Gosselin, N., Khalfa, S., Gagnon, L., & Bouchard, B. (2008). Happy, sad, scary and peaceful musical excerpts for research on emotions. *Cognition and Emotion, 22*, 720–752.

Van den Stock, J., Peretz, I., Grèzes, J., & de Gelder, B. (2009). Instrumental music influences recognition of emotional body language. *Brain Topography, 21,* 216–220.

Weiss, M. W., Trehub, S. E., & Schellenberg, E. G. (2012). Something in the way she sings: Enhanced memory for vocal melodies. *Psychological Science, 23*, 1074–1078.

Williamson, V., Baddeley, A., & Hitch, G. (2010). Musicians' and nonmusicians' short-term memory for verbal and musical sequences: comparing phonological similarity and pitch proximity. *Memory and Cognition, 38*, 163–175.

II   THE AUDIENCE

4 WHAT TYPE OF MOVIE PERSON ARE YOU?

UNDERSTANDING INDIVIDUAL DIFFERENCES IN FILM PREFERENCES AND USES: A PSYCHOGRAPHIC APPROACH

Tomas Chamorro-Premuzic, Andrea Kallias, and Anne Hsu

Motion pictures[1] play a major role in contemporary society, providing us with glimpses into worlds and lives we ordinarily do not have access to (Anderson & Iannaco, 2010). Although it is difficult to calculate precisely how much time the average person spends watching movies, related figures are indicative of the importance of film watching in everyday life. For instance, people in the United States devote almost half of their leisure time to watching TV. Thus, on a typical day, the average American will watch at least 4 hours of TV: the equivalent of 2 months per year or 13 years in an average lifetime.

Of course, TV consists of more than just movies, but people also watch movies through other means. In 2010, worldwide box office revenues exceeded $30 billion and more than 80 percent of the US population watched videos over the internet, bringing the total number of videos watched online to a record 20 billion per year. Pay-monthly film rentals, which offer a wide range of movies online, are growing fast, too. Netflix, a service that allows subscribers to stream movies online for a fixed monthly fee (around $8), counts more than 20 million members in the United States and Canada, and Amazon-owned Lovefilm provides a similar service to 1.5 million members in the United Kingdom and Europe.

Despite the widespread popularity of movies, there are clear individual differences in movie preferences and choices, which most people will have experienced firsthand. Open databases, such as the International Movie Data Base (IMDB), provide compelling evidence for the diversity of opinions a movie can generate (see Figure 4.1). For example, preference ratings for *Dick Tracy* by 26,183 viewers produce an average rating of 6/10 and are normally distributed, but even top-rated movies, such as *Inception* (the eighth most highly rated movie of all time), polarize opinions. Although more than half of the voters in a sample of more than 300,000 gave it a rating of 10, there were almost 6,000 people who gave it a rating of 1. Thus, one reviewer deemed *Inception* "a cinematic experience so audacious, so incredible, and in the end so gratifying, that it will remain a benchmark for many filmmakers in years to come," whereas others thought it was "a 'fake thinking person's' movie," or a "pretentious, incomprehensible piece of garbage."

The increase in digital movie consumption enables film providers to identify individual film preferences and develop formulas or "algorithms" to make movie recommendations to individual users based on their particular profile of preferences. The two best-known examples are Amazon (owner of IMDB) and e-Bay, which use individual-level data on past choices to recommend items with similar characteristics. For example, if you buy a Robert De Niro film, you will be recommended other films by the same actor; if you buy a movie on World War II, you will be recommended other war movies, and so on. Although recommendations may be based on a wide range of variables, the underlying logic is based

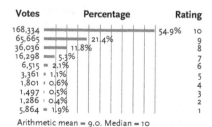

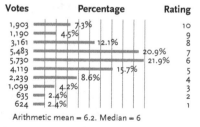

retrieved from www.imdb.com on Feb 22nd 2011

FIGURE 4.1 Reproduced with permission from the International Movie Data Base (IMDB).

on two intuitive principles: (1) identifying similarities between a chosen movie and other (not yet chosen) movies; (2) recommending similar movies to similar consumers. The first step may be determined a priori—for example, by using predefined product categories, such as genre, actor, director, and the like to profile movies—or ad hoc, by analyzing the choices of other consumers who have made similar choices. For example, if people who ordered Robert De Niro films have also ordered Al Pacino films, then the engine will recommend De Niro films to anyone who orders a Pacino film, and so on.

In that sense (see section "The Matching Process: From Collaborative Filtering to Personality and Uses"), recommendation engines act like a trustworthy friend who is aware of our choices and other people's choices and translates knowledge of our film choices into recommendations of allegedly similar movies: "if you liked *x* film you should check out *y because x and y are similar,*" or "if you liked *x* film you should check out *y because other people who liked x tended to also like y*" (which makes x and y similar). The main caveat, however, is that even if we dislike some of the movies we order, the system will still assume that we liked them and recommend similar movies to our friends and ourselves. This problem is akin to the issue of text-based behavioral targeting (commonly used by Googlemail and Facebook), in which a product or brand is assumed to be liked just because it is mentioned (and detected) in an e-mail text, even if the reasons for mentioning it may, in fact, be completely unrelated to the level of preference. Tell a friend that you dislike your new Ray-Ban sunglasses, and you will be bombarded with pop-up ads for Ray-Bans the next time you log in to your e-mail or Facebook account. Furthermore, because recommendation engines can only "learn" from our past behaviors, they cannot generate truly novel recommendations, thus making any recommendation as good (or bad) as our previous choices.

Despite the wealth of available data and the clear benefits of profiling consumer preferences, understanding the key drivers of individual differences in movie preferences is a largely unaccomplished mission, not least because "what is missing is a concern with choices expressed by consumers" (Kerrigan, 2010, p. 103). However, if individual differences in film preferences reflect any meaningful characteristics of an individual's psychological profile, psychologists should be able to predict and explain a person's movie preferences and choices. In this chapter, we provide some theoretical and methodological foundations to advance the scientific understanding of the psychological determinants of individual differences in film preferences. We begin by providing some background on the science of personality assessment, a robust branch of academic and professional psychology with a long-standing theoretical and empirical history and state-of-the-art statistical methods. Next, we review the salient evidence for the relationship between movie preferences and psychographic variables, notably personality and motives. We then provide conceptual and mathematical models examining the psychographic determinants of individual differences in movie preferences. Our conclusion is that people's film preferences are likely to be a function of important psychological needs, which are influenced by broad, stable psychological tendencies, namely, personality traits.

The Science of Personality and Personality Assessment

Personality concerns the nature of human nature (Hogan, 2007). In mainstream personality research, personality is broadly conceptualized in terms of largely stable and biologically influenced individual differences that characterize an individual's typical patterns of behavior across different situations. Personality can therefore be defined as a person's probability to do x. For instance, the personality trait *impulsivity* determines a person's likelihood of smoking, drinking, or dying younger (Kern & Friedman, 2011); the personality trait *neuroticism* determines a person's likelihood of being depressed, unhappy, underperforming on an exam (Chamorro-Premuzic & Furnham, 2005); the personality trait *conscientiousness* determines a person's likelihood of doing well at school, university, or work (von Stumm, Hell, & Chamorro-Premuzic, 2011).

The most widely used schema for describing major differences between normal people (i.e., those who do not suffer from clinically diagnosed symptoms) is the so-called Five-Factor Model.[2] According to this model, there are five main personality traits that explain individual differences between people; namely, *Neuroticism, Extraversion, Openness, Agreeableness,* and *Conscientiousness.* *Neuroticism,* or low emotional stability, refers to a person's propensity to experience negative emotions, worry, and stress. Highly neurotic people are anxious, pessimistic, and moody; they have a gloomy take on life and are irritable and insecure. Conversely, highly emotionally stable people remain calm even in difficult times and tend not to experience anxiety and negative emotions unless bad things really happen. *Extraversion* refers to a person's propensity to seek interpersonal contact and be socially dominant and outgoing. Highly extraverted people are confident, talkative, and love being the center of attention; they are also more likely to be leaders and tend to experience lots of positive emotions. Conversely, highly introverted people are socially passive, reserved, and shy; they prefer to be alone or in the company of a few intimate friends and are quiet and low-key. *Openness* (also called *openness to experience, intellect, or culture*) refers to individual differences in aesthetic sensitivity, novelty-seeking, intellectual curiosity, and creativity. Highly open people are creative, liberal, intellectual, and have a vivid imagination; they love trying out new things and are more open-minded than the average person. People low in Openness tend to be concrete thinkers and rarely think outside the box; they are more conservative and authoritarian and less interested in culture and the arts than the average person. *Agreeableness* describes how friendly, altruistic, and modest someone is. People high in Agreeableness are polite and modest and try not to hurt other people's feelings. Disagreeable people, on the other hand, are straight-talking, arrogant, and have little time for others. The final trait, *Conscientiousness*, assesses a person's level of responsibility, ambition, and self-control. Highly conscientious people are good at self-management and well-organized; they are responsible and reliable and try to excel in their careers. People low in Conscientiousness tend to lack self-control and are disorganized; they hate routine and are less career-focused than the average person (see Chamorro-Premuzic [2011] for an overview of the these "Big Five").

Although many psychological tests are available to assess the "Big Five" personality traits, the most valid method consists of self-report inventories. Such tests simply ask respondents to rate the degree to which they agree or disagree with a number of statements (typically ten for each "Big-Five" trait). For instance, a statement about Extraversion could be "I am the soul and life of a party," and a statement about Openness could be "People think of me as highly creative"—with the answers being recorded on a 5- or 7-point Likert-type scale, ranging from "strongly agree" to "strongly disagree." This implies that there are two basic assumptions made by personality inventories, namely: (a) people are able to provide accurate information about their own past behaviors, particularly in relation to the behavior they observe in others; and (b) past behavior is a good predictor of future behavior (people are consistent and predictable in their behaviors). In line with these assumptions, the validity of personality inventories is determined by the degree to which test scores (obtained by aggregating the individual responses for each trait) predict the outcomes the test was designed to predict. Thus, the higher the correlation between a test score and an outcome, the more valid the test is. Typical validities for established personality tests range from 0.2 to 0.3 (Chamorro-Premuzic, 2007). If one divides these coefficients by 2 and adds the remaining to 50 percent, one obtains a binomial effect size (Randolph & Edmondson, 2005), which is a much clearer index to use for assessing how accurate or better than chance our prediction will be. For example (see Figure 4.2), the validity for Openness scores in the prediction of aggressive behavior is reportedly $r = 0.0$ (Egan, 2011), implying that a person high in openness will be as likely to act aggressively as someone low in openness. The validity of Extraversion scores as predictors of job satisfaction is around $r = 0.2$ (Chamorro-Premuzic & Furnham, 2010), which implies that an extraverted person will be 10 percent more likely than the average person (and 20 percent more than an introverted one) to like his or her job. The validity

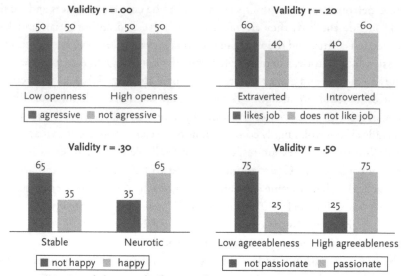

FIGURE 4.2 Sample binomial effect sizes for personality.

of Neuroticism scores in the prediction of subsequent happiness levels (around $r = 0.3$; Chamorro-Premuzic, 2007) suggests that an emotionally stable person will be 30 percent more likely to be happy than a highly neurotic person. The effect size for Agreeableness as a predictor of passionate relationship style ($r = 0.5$ in Ahmetoglu, Swami, & Chamorro-Premuzic, 2009) suggests that highly agreeable people will be 50 percent more likely to be passionate with their sexual partners than their disagreeable counterparts would.

Personality Predictors of Movie Preferences

Movie preferences are typically operationalized as the evaluative judgments consumers make of the satisfaction they obtain from the consumption of specific movies (Palmgreen, 1984). This satisfaction can be retrospective (past experiences), prospective (expected), or current (present experiences), and it varies not only between movies, but also between people. A great deal of psychological research has been devoted to investigate the content of movies, including their characters' personality (Gilpatric, 2010; Hesse et al., 2005; Hoffman, 2006; Schulz, 2002), the portrayal of gender roles (Welsh, 2010; Benton, Czechanski et al., 1993; Kalisch, Kalisch et al., 1982), national stereotypes (Kracauer, 1949), and even film reviewers (Hughey, 2010), as well as their effects, including alcohol consumption (Tanski, Cin et al., 2010), attitude change (Baumert, Hofmann et al., 2008), and empathy (Shapiro & Rucker, 2004).

In contrast, with the exception of violent and scary movies, studies on the personality correlates of movie preferences are limited. Indeed, there is substantially more research into the personality correlates of other media preferences, such as music (Chamorro-Premuzic & Furnham, 2007; Chamorro-Premuzic, Swami, & Cermakova, 2012) and visual arts (Chamorro-Premuzic, Burke, & Swami, 2011a). Given the popularity of movies, this seems surprising—although one of the practical drawbacks to examining movie preferences is the inability to show a large group of subjects (such as those required in personality research) a full-length movie. Thus, researchers typically prefer showing movie clips—which enables them to overcome the problem of familiarity with the film—or asking people to rate a movie description; that is, the synopsis of a full film or movie scene (see Weaver, Brosius et al., 1993). The next section summarizes the findings on the personality correlates of preference for violent and scary movies (the two most researched movie types), as well as preference for disgusting, sad, funny, or sexual movies. Rather than providing an explanation for these associations, the goal in this section is to simply identify the relationships between measures of personality and individual differences in movie preference.

Personality and Preferences for Violent Movies

One of the earliest and most explored areas of research in personality and film preference concerns the examination of individual differences in preference for violent or aggressive film content (Johnson, 1980). Although psychologists were initially focused on the effects of violent media exposure on aggression (Bandura & Walters, 1963; Lovaas, 1961), it soon became apparent that there are individual differences in preferences for, and reactions to, violent media content (Speisman, Lazarus et al., 1964). These individual differences are best conceptualized in the term Agreeableness. In particular, individuals lower in Agreeableness would be less likely to empathize with the victims of violence, which would enable them to enjoy violent scenes more. Conversely, people high in Agreeableness would be more likely to show altruistic concerns and empathic feelings for the targets of violence in films, which would make violent scenes less appealing.

In line, studies report that individuals higher in Psychoticism—a strong negative correlate of Agreeableness—tend to prefer movies with explicit violence (Weaver, 1991) and find harmful violence to be less violent and more humorous (Gunter, 1985) compared to lower Psychoticism (higher Agreeableness) individuals. In a cross-cultural study conducted with US and German participants, higher Psychoticism was linked to stronger preference for deviant and graphic violence movie content (Weaver et al., 1993). More recent studies also show that individuals lower in trait sympathy—a proxy for Agreeableness—tended to be more indifferent about movie clips of abused dogs (Lee, Gibbons, & Stephen, 2010). Likewise, Fabregat (2000) found that schoolboys who watch violent movies are typically rated as more aggressive by their teachers.

Some studies (Gunter, 1985; Lee et al., 2010) also report negative correlations between Neuroticism and preference for violent movie clips. This pattern is in line with a well-established sex difference in personality: women tend to score higher in Neuroticism and anxiety-related traits (Feingold, 1994), whereas men tend to score higher in Psychoticism and psychopathic traits (Egan, 2011). It is therefore plausible that personality accounts for some of the sex differences in preferences for violent movies, although the relationship among sex, personality, and violent movie preferences is likely to be more complex. Indeed, it would appear that sex moderates the effects of violent movie clips on physiological measures of stress, such as sweat gland activity and skin conductance response (Gilbert & Gilbert, 1991; see also Bruggemann & Barry, 2002). This suggests that sex and personality differences in violent movie preferences are, at least in part, biologically determined. Accordingly, Hirschman (1987) argued that individuals use violent movies to increase their levels of physiological arousals to an optimum (see the later section on horror films). Finally, Schierman and Rowland (1985) found that sensation seekers of both genders were more likely to spend more of their movie-watching time on the consumption of action movies.

Personality and Preferences for Scary Movies

Another relatively well-explored research area in the study of individual differences in movie preferences concerns the identification of personality correlates of preferences for frightful or fear-evoking films, notably horror movies. Just as a preference for violent movies is primarily explained by the personality traits of Agreeableness and Psychoticism, individual differences in preference for scary films is primarily explained in terms of (low) Neuroticism and (high) Sensation Seeking—the latter was conceptualized by Zuckerman (1979) as the tendency to seek novel and exciting experiences and is represented by the Big-Five traits of Openness and Extraversion.

For instance, studies report that individual differences in secure attachment style (an antecedent of high emotional stability/low Neuroticism) explain variability in responses to fear-evoking movie clips in children as young as 4–7 years old (Gilissen, Bakermans-Kranenburg et al., 2008) whereas trait fearfulness—a proxy of Neuroticism—has been found to interact with parent–child relationship quality to moderate the effect of fearful film clips on physiologically measured emotional responses (Gilissen, Koolstra et al., 2007).

Evidence for the importance of Sensation Seeking as a determinant of preference for scary movies was first highlighted by Zuckerman and Litle (1986), who found the trait to be positively associated with preference for erotic, violent, and fear-provoking films. The authors concluded that sensation seekers have a generic preference for media that are novel and arousing, regardless of genre or content. Likewise, Tamborini and Stiff (1987) reported that individuals attending a horror movie tended to have a high desire for destruction and higher-than-average Sensation Seeking scores and that the film was enjoyed more by younger people. Given that Sensation Seeking decreases with age (Steinberg, Albert, Cauffman, Banich, Graham, & Woolard, 2008), these results suggest that the trait may explain some of the age differences in preference for scary movies. In addition, stronger preferences for horror films have been associated with higher scores on *machiavellianism*, a trait that assesses the propensity to manipulate and hurt others (and is positively linked to psychopathy) and preferences for pornography in males (Tamborni, Stiff et al., 1987).

Subsequent studies tended to replicate this pattern of results (Potts, Dedmon, & Halford, 1996; Schierman & Rowland, 1985). In fact, a recent study by Trice (2010) showed that the effect is found even in second-grade schoolchildren. The author asked participants to choose a video about "scary sharks" or "bunnies" and found that sensation seekers were more likely to choose and prefer the scary sharks, as well as the more arousing versions of the two clips of sharks.

Some scholars see horror films as a way of exploring "beyondness" (Hutchings, 2004, p. 105), that is, the experience of speculative and unexpected experiences, akin to the Jungian notion of *the shadow*. Such experiences would increase levels of physiological arousal to an optimum only in individuals high in Sensation Seeking but overarouse those low in Sensation Seeking or high in Neuroticism. This relates to a famous psychophysiological effect called the *Yerkes-Dodson law* (1908), which describes the relationship between performance and arousal. The law states that there is a curvilinear relationship between performance and electrocortical arousal (the level of brain activity). As shown in Figure 4.3, people perform best when they are moderately aroused. Although arousal is influenced by external stimulation, such as media exposure, there are individual differences in people's optimal level of arousal, and these overlap with Extraversion, Neuroticism, and Sensation Seeking. Thus, sensation seekers need more external stimulation to compensate for their lower baseline levels of cortical arousal: violent, scary, or sexual media seem to provide this stimulation.

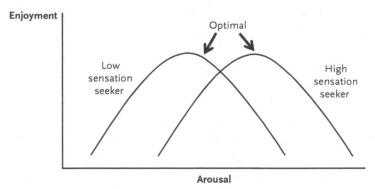

FIGURE 4.3 Sensation seeking, arousal, and enjoyment.

Personality and Preference for Disgusting, Funny, Sad, and Sexual Movies

Despite not being considered an actual genre, disgusting scenes feature prominently among some horror, comedy, and science fiction films (e.g., *Zombie Flesh Eaters, Bruno,* or *War of the Worlds*). Similarly to horror films, one would expect individuals higher in Sensation Seeking to show stronger preference levels for disgusting movie clips (Zuckerman & Litle, 1986). That said, the most relevant personality trait for understanding individual differences in preference for disgusting movie clips is *disgust sensitivity*. For instance, a recent study showed that the disgust sensitivity scale predicted self-reported physiological responses to disgusting movie clips even after controlling for other relevant predictors (Valentiner, Hood et al., 2005). This association has been replicated by brain imaging studies. For example, Stark and colleagues (Stark, Schienle et al., 2005) found a positive correlation between overall disgust sensitivity and prefrontal cortex activation during exposure to disgusting images, such as a cockroach invasion. Moreover, the authors reported a substantial correlation ($r = .76$) between one of the subscales of disgust sensitivity (spoilage/decay) and activation levels of the amygdala, an area of the brain responsible for the spontaneous and preconscious processing of threatening stimuli.

Research has also identified some personality correlates of individual differences in preferences for funny or comedic films. In an analysis of TV preferences, Weaver (1991) found that individuals scoring high on Psychoticism tended to dislike comedy compared to people scoring low on Psychoticism. In line, a psychophysiological study that matched higher and lower Psychoticism scorers (from a wide age range) on Extraversion, Neuroticism, and sex, found that individuals high in Psychoticism showed a stronger preference for violent than comedic films and perceived comedic films as less comical and enjoyable than violent ones. In addition, measures of skin conductance showed that people higher in Psychoticism quickly habituate to violence compared to individuals low in Psychoticism (Bruggemann & Barry, 2002).

Although research in the area of individual differences in preferences for sad movies is limited, some studies have identified certain logical associations between personality traits and sad film preferences. Most notably, a study with 114 students found that a wide range of personality variables (e.g., empathy, Extraversion, femininity, stress propensity, and ego strength) were associated with crying and sadness following exposure to sad movies (Choti, Marston et al., 1987).

Finally, studies examining a preference for erotic, pornographic, or sexual films indicate that individuals who evaluate sexual movies as relatively nonpornographic tend to have less inhibited sexual lives than do individuals who condemn those same movies as pornographic. Thus, individuals higher in deinhibition (who would be lower on Conscientiousness and Neuroticism and higher on Openness) tend to respond more favorably to images of sexual content (Fisher & Byrne, 1978). Preferences for sexual media have also been linked to cognitive abilities (Bogaert, 2001), suggesting that men with lower IQ scores and higher trait aggressiveness have stronger preference for violent sexual media—e.g., pornography—than do their less aggressive and more intelligent counterparts. In a study of wider media preferences, Schierman and Rowland (1985) found that males and females higher in Sensation Seeking tended to prefer media with more explicit sexual content, whereas Sparks (1986) and Zuckerman and Litle (1986) found that those, regardless of sex, with higher levels of Sensation Seeking reported higher levels of enjoyment of X-rated movies and horror films (see also Zuckerman, 1994).

Movie-Watching Motives: Psychological Dimensions of Film Uses

The fact that "consumers of film are motivated by different wants and needs" (Kerrigan, 2010, p. 104) is well-established. Indeed, one of the first studies to empirically assess attitudes focused on film-related attitudes (Thurstone, 1930). Although personality predicts film preferences, personality inventories were not designed for that purpose—personality traits are descriptors of much wider individual differences than of specific movie choices. In addition, theories of motivation suggest that personality affects behavior via specific goals or motives (Diefendorff & Chandler, 2010), which begs the question of what specific motives can be satisfied by watching movies. This is consistent with a long tradition in

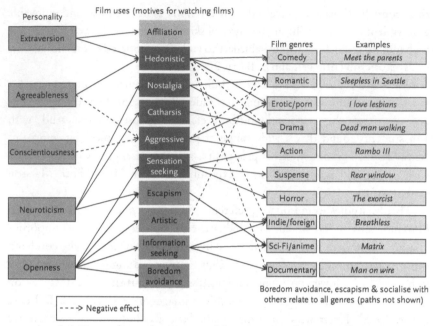

FIGURE 4.4 Personality and motivational determinants of movie preferences.

media psychology of understanding how media can enable consumers to attain some basic psychological needs, uses, and gratifications (Blumler & Katz, 1974; Bartsch & Viehoff, 2010; Rosengren & Windhal, 1977; Rubin, 1983). Thus, people consume films for a variety of reasons (Holbrook, 1999), and these can be expected to differ among people and situations. In this section, we identify the main dimensions of film uses, that is, the major psychological motives or goals individuals seek to attain when they consume movies. Given the limited research evidence in this area, it is necessary to also review the literature on other media uses, especially TV (Potts et al., 1996), to conceptualize a comprehensive catalogue of film uses. In our search, we identified ten main dimensions or uses of film (see Figure 4.4); in turn, these can be grouped into three types of uses: emotional, cognitive, and social. This is consistent with research on motives for using music (Chamorro-Premuzic & Furnham, 2007; Chamorro-Premuzic et al., 2011b), which identified the same three types of uses.

Emotional Uses of Film

A well-established literature on media-related mood regulation suggests that people consume media to achieve specific emotional states (Greenwood, 2008). Perhaps the most salient body of empirical work relates to Zillmann's (1988; 2000) mood-management theory, an explicit model for understanding the role of emotions in media consumption. An important aspect of this theory is the adaptation of the Yerkes-Dodson law (1908) (discussed earlier) to the notion of enjoyment. That is, Zillmann's model posits that an intermediate level of arousal is experienced as more pleasurable, leading bored and understimulated individuals to prefer arousing movies whereas overstimulated individuals will tend to prefer soothing media. There are five types of emotional or affective reasons for watching movies: hedonistic, nostalgic, cathartic, aggressive, and sensation seeking. These are described here (see also Figure 4.4).

Hedonism. One of the simplest and most obvious of reasons for watching a movie is pleasure (Bartsch, 2010). Thurstone's (1930) early study on film attitudes showed that people evaluate movies in terms of their value for leisure-time pursuit. Indeed, there is compelling empirical evidence for the importance of pleasure-based or "hedonic" consumption as a driver of media preferences. Unsurprisingly, there is a great deal of appetite for the consumption of "uplifting" movies (Kerrigan, 2010). Although research has yet to examine how intra- and interindividual differences in hedonic film use affect movie preferences, one would expect positive associations between this film use and preference for comedy (including romantic comedies) and sexual films and negative associations with drama, documentaries, and indie/foreign films (which tend to require more concentration and intellectual engagement). People higher in Extraversion and Agreeableness may be expected to watch films more for hedonic purposes because they are generally more likely (than individuals low in those traits) to experience positive emotions. Given that personality predisposes individuals to select mood-congruent media (Chamorro-Premuzic et al., 2011a), a "feel-good" personality should propel individuals to maintain positive emotions via the consumption of fun, happy, and pleasurable movies. In line, studies have found that Neuroticism is negatively correlated with preferences for comedy TV shows (Weaver, 1991).

Catharsis. Just as people may choose to watch a film for hedonistic or pleasure-seeking purposes, they may also do it to experience negative emotions—thus, the cathartic movie-watching motive is the opposite of the hedonistic motive just described. Indeed, individuals may choose media that mirror and validate their unhappy mood states (Knobloch & Zillmann, 2002). Kerrigan (2010, p. 103) defined catharsis as the opposite of uplifting. The concept dates back thousands of years, to Aristotle, who first defined it as a major explanatory cause for people's enjoyment of dramatic art (Feshbach & Singer, 1971). Thus, catharsis enables people to "cleanse the soul" by empathically experiencing the suffering of others (the actors). Typically, this involves downward social comparisons, whereby individuals who are feeling down are cheered by consuming movies featuring others who are worse off than themselves. In line, Mares and Cantor

(1992) found that elderly participants who felt lonely tended to prefer portrayals of lonely old people. In a similar vein, Knobloch and Zillmann (2002) found that young people who are lonely or lovelorn preferred love-lamenting pop songs over love-celebrating ones. This indicates that motion pictures featuring others with problems similar to our own can help us cope with our own misfortunes and shortcomings. Some scholars (Bartsch & Viehoff, 2010) have suggested that coping with media-induced emotions is a skill-demanding activity that can lead to feelings of success and competence if the person manages to cope—for instance, if one manages to cope with the emotional challenges of an intense drama.

Recent research suggests that cathartic experiences generate a high level of absorption, which serves to distract people from their everyday problems and negative thoughts (Knobloch-Westerwick & Alter, 2006; Zillmann, 1988, 2000). Thus, Bartsch and Viehoff (2010) pointed out that one of the main functions of media is "acting out emotions that have no room in everyday life" (p. 2252). Because individuals higher in Neuroticism are more likely to experience negative affect (Chamorro-Premuzic, 2011), and given that individuals tend to prefer the consumption of media that match their mood states (Chamorro-Premuzic, Fagan, & Furnham, 2010), one would expect Neuroticism to be positively correlated with the cathartic use of film. Moreover, both variables should be positively related to a preference for drama movies. In line, Davis and colleagues (1987) found that individual differences in cognitive and emotional empathy moderated the effects of dramatic film scenes on preferences.

Nostalgia. Another mood-related motive for watching movies is *nostalgia*, broadly defined as the emotional experience of past experiences. Thus, individuals motivated by nostalgia will seek movies that transport them to the past, enabling them to relive treasured moments. Holbrook (1999) noted that consistent individual differences in the psychographic variable of nostalgia proneness moderate the effect of nostalgic movies on individuals (see also Schindler & Holbrook, 2003). Although research has yet to examine the Big-Five personality correlates of nostalgic film use, one would expect this melancholic, emotionally intense, quasi-dramatic use of film to be positively correlated to Neuroticism.

Aggression Release. People also watch movies to release aggression. This "aggressive" use of film has been documented primarily in terms of the effects of watching violent media. For instance, Leyens and colleagues (1975) found that violent movies were more likely to increase aggression levels in those individuals who are naturally more aggressive. Given that aggression is also a personality characteristic—trait aggressiveness—one would expect steady individual differences in personality to overlap with both a preference for aggressive films and a tendency to consume movies to release aggressive tendencies. Agreeableness and

Conscientiousness (two negative markers of trait aggression) should therefore be negatively correlated with the aggressive use of film.

Sensation Seeking. Although sensation seeking is a major personality trait (Chamorro-Premuzic, 2007; Zuckerman, 1979), it is also a movie-watching motive (we use the lower case term to refer to the latter). Thus, individuals differ in their typical levels of desire for experiencing intense, arousing, and exciting emotions, and, at the same time, they do not always experience the same thirst for sensations (implying intraindividual differences). In their analyses of TV-watching motives, Weaver (2003) identified "stimulation" and "relaxation" as two key motives for watching TV—these are positively and negatively related to sensation seeking, respectively. As described in the section "Personality of Movie Preferences," arousal is affected by both personality and media exposure, such that it increases with Introversion, Neuroticism, and novel media content, but decreases with Sensation Seeking and Psychoticism. In addition, Hirschman (1987) identified sensual/sensory arousal as one of the main media uses, characterized mainly by preferences for violent, sexual, or exciting content. In line, sensation seekers have been found to prefer violent and horror films (Hoffner & Levine, 2005), supporting the notion that emotionally intense media stimuli can help consumers attain their preferred levels of excitement and stimulation (Zuckerman, 1983). Zillmann's (1996) concept of *excitation transfer* is helpful to understand how intense negative emotions evoked by a movie can eventually produce positive emotional reactions—when spectators are made to believe that bad outcomes will follow, they first experience fear, but this empathic distress can spill over and be reframed as positive emotions and thoughts once the tension is resolved by a happy ending. It is, however, noteworthy that the arousal-based explanation of sensation-seeking movie use does not distinguish between positive and negative affect, postulating instead that novel, complex, and intense sensations will be experienced as gratifying in their own right (Zaleski, 1984). Given that sensation seeking is positively related to Openness, we would expect higher Openness to be associated with a tendency to consume movies for the purpose of sensation seeking.

Cognitive Uses of Film

Motives for using movies include not only emotional but also cognitive factors; these are described here.

Boredom Avoidance. One of the most intuitive reasons for watching movies is boredom avoidance or the consumption of movies for the mere purpose of passing time. This motive mirrors one of the major TV-viewing motives (see Weaver, 2003) and can be seen as the cognitive equivalent of the sensation seeking use of film. Thus, boredom avoidance—or pass-time movie use (Potts et al., 1996)—is closely linked to the arousal theory of media consumption, although to a less extreme version. In line, Rowland, Fouts, and Heatherton (1989) found that sensation seekers were more likely to use TV while working or studying. This is consistent with studies on music uses, which revealed that Extraversion—a positive correlate of Sensation Seeking—increases an individual's probability to use music as a background to other activities (Chamorro-Premuzic & Furnham, 2007). Although boredom avoidance is clearly linked to the sensation seeking use of film, the former emphasizes the cognitive aspects of arousal, whereas the latter emphasizes the emotional ones. Some scholars (see, e.g., Greenwood, 2008) argued that boredom-based media consumption may be used to buffer unpleasant ruminations that would be heightened under boredom, although it is yet to be determined "whether such a strategy is in fact adaptive or whether turning to media when bored ultimately postpones, rather than resolves, a tendency to focus on negative thoughts and events" (p. 616). In that sense, boredom avoidance also overlaps with the escapism use of film (see later section) and should be higher in more highly open individuals.

Information Seeking. As Potts et al. (1996) and Weaver (2003) pointed out in their studies of TV-watching motives, one of the major uses of films is *information seeking*. This use of film was already documented by Thurstone's (1930) early study on movie attitudes, in which "educational evaluations" emerged as a distinct category. More recently, Bartsch & Viehoff (2010) noted that one of the key functions of media is to facilitate "thought-provoking experiences" (p. 2252). Indeed, films give people access to a wide range of languages, culture, and geographies, educating them about remote historical times, the biographies of illustrious people, environmental and political issues (Kerrigan, 2010), and helping them to understand human nature (Potts et al., 1996). The information seeking use of film is most compatible with documentaries, films based on "true stories," and films that provide factually correct information—these movies should be very realistic, and they tend to require high levels of concentration and a "hungry mind" (von Stumm et al., 2011). The personality trait that most clearly encompasses these characteristics is Openness to New Experience. Open individuals prefer imaginative (rather than conventional) forms of entertainment (Dollinger, Orf, & Robinson, 1991) and enjoy "richer" or more complex film experiences (Palmgreen, Cook, Harvill, & Helm, 1988). In addition, studies have found that higher Neuroticism scores are associated with higher levels of preference for information/news television (Weaver, 1991) and more common use of the internet for information (Amiel & Sargent, 2004).

A related concept to the information seeking use of movie is the notion of *eudaemonic motivation* (Oliver, 2008; Oliver & Raney, 2008), which refers to a propensity to use of media, including movies, to search for deeper insights, meaning, and purpose in life. For example, Katz, Gurevitch, and Haas (1973) found that individuals used media not only for sheer entertainment but also as a means of experiencing beauty and raising morale. Likewise, Tesser, Millar, and Wu's (1988) research on movie gratifications has identified a motivational factor, namely, "self-development," driven by consumers' desire to use media to understand how others think and feel. In a similar vein, Cupchik (1995) differentiated between "reactive" aesthetic experience, which is based on rewarding-feeling states of positive valence and arousal, and "reflective" aesthetic experience, which is characterized by the experience of profound and meaningful self-reflection and insight. Thus, Oliver and Bartsch (2010) conceptualized "appreciation" as "the perception of deeper meaning, the feeling of being moved, and the motivation to elaborate on thoughts and feelings inspired by the experience" (Oliver & Bartsch, 2010, p. 76). Again, people higher in Openness should be higher on the information seeking dimensions of film uses.

Escapism. Movies enable people to abandon the hum-drum of everyday life and be transported to fantastic worlds (Holbrook & Hirschman, 1982). In accordance, Potts et al. (1996) found that one of the main uses of TV was to escape from everyday problems. Thus, screened fiction has the potential to engage our minds and produce altered states of consciousness, an idea put forward by Jung's concept of "active imagination" (Izod, 2000). People use movies to temporarily "switch-off" and forget their current concerns and worries. This *escapism* use of film was one of the first movie uses ever identified and has been replicated widely. For example, Lehman and Witty (1928) noted that watching films provides an enjoyable escape mechanism, whereas Hirschman's (1987) study on TV-watching motives identified escape from reality as a major motive (more common in males than females). In a similar vein, Suckfüll (2004) noted that there are different types and levels of movie involvement. *Diegetic involvement* refers to the act of getting fully absorbed by the fictional worlds portrayed in movies, *socio-involvement* refers to consumers' identification with movie characters, and *ego involvement* refers to the act of establishing a connection between different aspects of the movie and one's own personal life. It would seem that these different forms of escapism would help to protect people's self-esteem by reducing the gap between the ideal and actual self and to escape negative self-related feelings (Moskalenko & Heine, 2003). Neuroticism and Openness both seem conceptually related to higher escapism use of film.

Artistic. Another cognitive use of film, one that overlaps with some aspects of escapism, sensation seeking, and information seeking, is artistic film use. This movie-watching motive refers to someone's consumption of movies for the purpose of aesthetic appreciation, and it is strongly related to individual differences in Openness to Experience (Chamorro-Premuzic, 2011). Thus, individuals sometimes watch films to feel creatively empowered and to have an "artistic experience," and some individuals—those higher in Openness—are much more prone to this use than others.

Social Use of Film

Research on media uses clearly suggests that media can help individuals attain interpersonal goals, such as bonding or connecting with others (Lull, 1990; Rubin, 1983). In line, Potts et al. (1996) found that one of the main uses of TV was sharing time and having something to discuss with people. Thus, movies provide people with a good excuse for relating to others—for example, watching films in the company of others, discussing movies with others, and so on. As Bartsch and Viehoff (2010) recently noted, movies facilitate communication, affiliation, social learning, and role enactment. With regard to the latter, scholars from various research traditions have pointed out that movies enable viewers to establish a close psychological connection with the characters, persons, or avatars they see on-screen (Giles, 2002). Studies on TV-watching motives show that one of the main reasons for watching TV is affiliation or bonding with others (Weaver, 2003). This is in line with broader views on motivation, such as the universal needs theories of McClelland (1985) and Hogan (2007), which highlight "getting along" as a fundamental human motive. At the same time, there are clear individual differences in people's propensity to get along, which can be conceptualized in terms of Agreeableness and Extraversion. In line, this *social* or interpersonal use of film can be expected to be more common in individuals with higher Agreeableness and Extraversion scores. However, Weaver (2003) reported that introverts and more neurotic individuals were more likely to report watching TV for social or interpersonal reasons ("companionship").

Using Movie Uses to Profile Movie Preferences

Despite the compelling evidence for the fact that people watch movies to satisfy specific psychological needs, there is still insufficient research on the relationship among different movie uses, personality traits, and film preferences—Figure 4.4 provides a conceptual model for integrating these variables. One limitation of past studies is that they have tended to classify movie preferences in terms of predefined aesthetic categories, such as film genre, which may not be related to specific movie uses or relate to multiple uses in tandem. In line, Bartsch and Viehoff (2010) proposed the notion of "meta-emotion" to account for the simultaneous gratification of multiple psychological needs that should not be seen as mutually exclusive. Rather, people may satisfy several film-watching motives simultaneously, and some uses (e.g., boredom avoidance, sensation seeking, catharsis) are more clearly intertwined than others (e.g., information seeking, aggression release, and nostalgia). In fact, some scholars have conceptualized different umbrella terms or meta-motives to highlight the broader psychological functions of movie consumption. Thus, Wilschinsky (2006) noted that film consumption, in its variety of uses, stimulates individuals' personal growth by increasing their self-awareness levels. He notes that personal growth may include "re-examining one's understanding of one's personality, one's relationship to family, to friends and others, and to the world at large as well as one's opinions about the political and social state of the world" (p. 67).

As noted earlier, movie consumption elicits the experience of a wide range of emotions and psychological responses, ranging from simple hedonistic gratification, such as pleasure, to more abstract, intellectual, or complex gratifications, such as the satisfaction of social and cognitive needs (Bartsch & Viehoff, 2010, p. 2247). Because personality traits influence behaviors via goals (Diefendorff and Chandler, 2010), one may expect different uses of films to mediate the effects of personality on movie preferences. For instance, individuals' personalities will affect their optimal levels of arousal, intellectual curiosity, and propensity to experience positive and negative mood states. In turn, these variables will determine the extent to which the consumption of a movie will satisfy an individual's needs—if it does, the individual will probably categorize that movie as good, and vice-versa. Thus, individuals with a tendency to experience positive affect—those with high Extraversion scores, for example—will gravitate toward movies that improve or maintain their good moods (Knobloch & Zillmann, 2002), which should be reflected in their higher levels of liking for uplifting, fun-evoking movies. Although these films may be classified as comedies, the main relevance of a genre denomination is the psychological message it carries for the consumer: "if you watch this film, you will experience happiness" (in the case of comedy), "if you watch this film, you will experience sadness" (in the case of drama). The implication is that genre denominations set out expectations for the consumer about certain needs that the movie may help him or her satisfy. As pointed out by Greenwood and Lippman (2010, p. 616), "clarifying who uses which media in what kind of mood state is a first crucial step toward understanding whether media use may serve a therapeutic or self-defeating function for those with increased difficulty managing their moods and emotions."

The Matching Process: From Collaborative Filtering to Personality and Uses

The overwhelming amount of online movies and users has enabled web portals like Amazon and Netflix to develop recommender systems to improve consumers' choices. The most common method, collaborative filtering (CF), is based on the idea that preferences across a wide range of users can be used in "collaboration" to "filter" out those options that would be of most interest to a given individual (Goldberg, Nichols, Oki, & Terry, 1992; Goldberg, Roeder, Gupta, & Perkins, 2001; Miller, Konstan, & Riedl, 2004; Resnick & Varian, 1997). The fundamental assumption of collaborative filtering techniques is that an individual will like movies that are (a) liked by other people who have shared the individual's opinion on other movies and (b) similar to other movies that the individual has liked in the past. The basic CF algorithm uses a list of movie ratings by different users (the "user-item database") to predict how much a particular user (the "active user") will like a given movie. Similarly, CF algorithms can also be used to come up with a list of the top N recommended movies for the active user. Here, we provide an overview of how a variety of CF algorithms work and discuss how CF can be integrated with personality and uses of films to improve both the recommendations and our understanding of individual differences underlying movie preferences.[3]

Collaborative Filtering: The Basics

The most straightforward approach to CF uses memory-based algorithms (Resnick et al.; Sarwar, Karypis, Konstan, & Riedl, 2001), such as those used by Amazon (Linden, Smith, & York, 2003). These algorithms function as follows: Suppose that you are faced with the problem of deciding whether you would like to see a movie M. We assume, for now, that you have no information about the movie content. However, you do have a list of movie titles, including movie M, along with your friends' ratings of how much they liked each movie on the list. These ratings could be binary (e.g., like/dislike; or numerical, e.g. on a scale of 1–5). This list also contains *your* ratings for the movies you have already seen. We can also assume you have a very bad memory for movies and that you can neither remember anything about the content of the movies you have seen, nor identify the movies you haven't seen. You must therefore speculate about whether you may like movie M based only on the list of movies and your friends' ratings. In CF terminology, your list is your user-item database, and you are the active user. In determining your preference from your friends' ratings, you need to figure out how similar your preferences are to each of your friends'. You will want to weight the opinions of friends whose movie preferences most closely match yours and ignore those friends who have dissimilar preferences. To achieve this, you assign "weights" to each of your friends, giving the largest weight to the friend whose movie preference pattern—or movie profile—is most similar to yours and the smallest weight to the friend whose movie profile is least similar to yours. You then predict how much you will like movie M by considering the ratings of movie

M given by all your friends, giving more weight to the opinions of those friends whom you've determined to have movie tastes that are most similar to yours (see Figure 4.5).

In addition, you can try to figure out which of the movies you have seen is most similar to movie *M*. You can then extrapolate how much you will like movie *M* based on your own judgments of the movies you have seen that are most similar to movie *M*. Assuming, as we did, that you have no information about the movie's content, you would now have to assess movie similarity based on your list of movies and your friends' ratings. To this end, you could characterize each movie based on how it divides public opinion. For example, some movies may tend to elicit differing opinions based on gender (e.g., action films are rated more highly by males; artistic films tend to be rated more highly by creative/artistic people, etc.). You can then characterize movie *M* by how it tends to divide opinions among your friends and then find other movies that tend to divide opinions most similarly to movie *M*. In the same manner in which you weighted friends according to the degree to which their movie preference patterns matched yours, you can also assign weights to movies according to how similar each movie's friend-preference patterns are to movie *M*. You then look over your own previous ratings for movies that you've weighted as similar to *M* to predict how much you will enjoy movie *M* (notice the perfect symmetry between the methods for using most similar friends

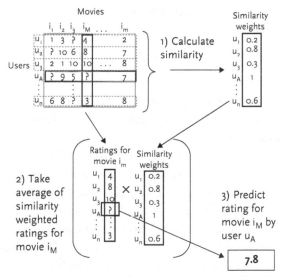

Schematic shows process for memory based CF algorithm using user-based similarity. To predict rating of movie i_M by user u_A. 1) Begin with user-item data base and calculate similarity between all rows and active user u_A. 2) Use ratings of movie u_M for all other users weighted by the users' similarity with the active user to give 3) a predicted movie rating.

FIGURE 4.5 Computation of a memory-based collaborative filtering algorithm (example).

and most similar movies). Although you and your friends may not have seen all the listed movies, calculations can be based only on the movie ratings that are jointly available, or average ratings could be used to replace missing values.

In addition, user-based (using similar friends) and item-based (using similar movies) algorithms can also be combined. More sophisticated strategies include building a model for either finding similar clusters of users or movies and for making predictions. Also, hybrid CF algorithms can incorporate content, such as texts associated with each movie, to aid recommendations (see section "Putting It All Together: A Psychographic Science of Movie Preferences").

Mathematical Basis of Memory-Based Collaborative Filtering

Memory-based CF algorithms are designed to quantify similarity between users (based on each user's pattern of movie ratings) or movies (based on each movie's pattern of user ratings)—the formula is essentially the same. Two main ways of assessing similarity are *correlation-based* and *vector cosine-based* similarity. The similarity computation may be performed between user pairs (evaluated based on movies that have been rated by both users) or between movie pairs (evaluated based on the users who have rated both movies). This measure of similarity between every pair of users (for user-based CF) or movies (for item-based CF) is then transformed into a predicted rating for the active user A for a particular movie M. (See Appendix for further details.)

Model-Based and Hybrid Collaborative Filtering

In an attempt to improve the limitations of memory-based CF, algorithms have been developed that form computational models of user preferences and movie characteristics to make predictions (Linden et al., 2003; Sarwar et al., 2001). This technique has met with varying degrees of success over simpler memory-based CF algorithms. Some CF models may cluster users and/or movies into particular "similar" subgroups (Sarwar et al., 2002). The active user is then assigned to the most appropriate subgroup (or a weighted probability of belonging to each subgroup), and the movie being considered is assigned to the appropriate movie subgroup (or using a weighted probability over all movie subgroups). A prediction is then made based on a model of how much the relevant subgroup of users may like the relevant subgroup of movies. Other classification models may learn to recognize complex patterns (more complicated than just cosine or correlation similarity) in the user-item database and use these patterns to predict user preference. Hybrid algorithms expand on the item-user database by incorporating more information about movie content into ratings predictions (Melville, Mooney, &

Nagarajan, 2002). Movie content information is usually represented textually (i.e., in words describing either viewer reactions or movie themes).

One particularly common problem in CF algorithms is that the user-item database is usually very sparse—most users only have seen and rated a very small proportion of movies in the database. Thus, many modeling techniques will aim to find a reduced representation of the user-item database using dimensionality reduction techniques. The most common versions include singular value decomposition (SVD) (Canny, 2002; Sarwar et al., 2002), which is a method for reducing high-dimensional data (such as user-item databases) into a simpler representation. The chosen representation will be the one that most effectively describes the variance in the data (i.e., predicting most of the variability in movie ratings). An intuitive explanation for dimensionality reduction for movie ratings would be as follows: Suppose one is considering a user-item database that contains only four movies, W, X, Y, and Z. The original representation contains ratings for each movie separately. However, suppose that if people liked movie X, they also tended to like movie Y; and if they liked movie W, they also tended to like movie Z. This database can then be represented in a different way, with just two "movie components": component X-Y and component Y-Z. Singular value decomposition takes large dimensional datasets (such as a user-item database with vast numbers of movies and users) and finds a more compact representation for the dataset based on those "components" that vary together. In practice, these components are not just simple combinations of a few items, as in our example, but rather a combination of weights over all the items. For example 2^*W, 3^*X, 0^*Y, and 6^*Z might be a "movie component" that describes much of the variability in ratings (2, 3, and 6 are the weights). In the simplest world, if this one component was predictive of all the ratings in the database (known as describing all the variance in the dataset), it would mean that, for all users, if a user gave movie W a rating of 2 and movie X a rating of 3, they would predictably rate movie Z a 6. In practice, a dataset of 1,000 movies may perhaps be reduced to fifty crucial movie components that are most useful for predicting movie ratings. Movie components can be ranked according to their importance (i.e., in how much predictive power they lend to predicting user-movie ratings). This dimensionality reduction tool thus makes large user-item databases more tractable for model building.

Putting It All Together: A Psychographic Science of Movie Preferences

Collaborative filtering algorithms can be used as a quantitative tool for understanding how personality affects movie preferences. One possibility is to see if people who show similar preference patterns over movies also share the same personality traits (see the section "Personality Predictors of Movie Preference") or film uses (see the section "Movie-Watching Motives: Psychological Dimensions of Film Uses"). This can be done by implementing a user-item memory-based CF algorithm to find users with the highest similarity in weightings for a given active user. Assuming that all users in the database could also be asked to answer some questionnaires diagnostic of personality traits or film uses, the users with highest similarities could then be examined for similarities in personality or film-watching motives. More sophisticated model-based CF methods can also be used to find clusters of similar users. These clusters can then be examined for how well they correlate with particular personality traits or film uses. Thus, we could find which personality traits or film uses are most predictive of similarity in movie preferences.

Model-based CF computations, such as the use of SVD described earlier, can be used to uncover relevant "movie uses" and "movie personality traits" or even to define both. In the most basic implementation, one could find the crucial movie components obtained from applying SVD to a large user-item database and use the movies that feature strongly in these movie components to define movies that then become benchmarks for diagnosing movie personality or uses. For example, SVD might find that *Sound of Music* happens to have a large weighting in a very important movie component. Thus, *Sound of Music* could become a movie-personality trait, as in "how much of a *Sound of Music* type person are you?" More sophisticated implementations of this idea can come from hybrid-based CF algorithms that associate movies with texts (i.e., words relating to a movie's descriptions, themes, or user reactions). Thus, when SVD is used to isolate an important movie component from a large user-item database, the textual descriptions associated with this movie component can be used to define the "movie personality" trait. For example, a movie component could feature movies that are associated with the set of words *adventure, epic, historical.* Such an SVD method is, in fact, how the commonly used Five-Factor personality traits were found, by taking a large database of personality descriptions and finding the groupings of descriptions that formed the personality components that most powerfully described the variety of personality types seen across people.

Finally, although CF algorithms can be used in a variety of ways to provide more insight into our understanding of the link between personality and movie preferences, personality information can also, in turn, be used to help CF recommendations. A very straightforward application would be to include personality trait values along with movie ratings, expanding the typical user-item database into a user-item-and-personality database (and the same applies to movie uses). The incremental predictive power would justify having users of a movie website answer a few movie personality questions that are crafted to be diagnostic of some well-picked movie personality trait or uses that have been found to be useful in predicting movie preferences (perhaps found by the SVD method).

In our view, the inclusion of individual differences data (personality and movie uses) within CF-based algorithms will improve the accuracy of recommendations for several reasons. First, personality has been shown to be predictive of movie preferences (see the section "Movie-Watching Motives: Psychological Dimensions of Film Uses"). Second, there are clear individual differences in people's motives for using movies (see the section "The Matching Process: From Collaborative Filtering to Personality and Uses"). Thus, the inclusion of personality and motives measures will refine similarity measures by offering more preference-relevant information about each user. This is likely to lead to a substantial improvement in recommendation accuracy. Third, the inclusion of personality and film-use data will greatly facilitate two main problems that have traditionally plagued CF algorithms: the sparsity problem and the start-up problem. The sparsity problem occurs when there are a lot of missing entries for the particular user-movie combination. The start-up problem occurs when a new user has joined, one who has rated few or no other movies. Thus, the inclusion of a few key measures of individual differences that give information about a user's "movie personality" may significantly facilitate recommendations in situations in which there is limited rating information.

Implications and Applications

Movie consumption is an important human activity, but people differ in their movie preferences. Understanding the determinants of these differences is important for several reasons. First, films are a powerful tool for experimental research, in particular mood-induction studies (Gilissen, Bakermans-Kranenburg, et al. 2008; Kaviani, Kumari et al., 2010; Isen & Gorgoglione, 1983); yet there are salient individual differences in how viewers respond to movies. Second, films are used for clinical interventions, as in cinematherapy; hence, knowledge of how to match movies to individual preferences will translate into more positive therapeutic effects (Knickerbocker, 2010). Third, films are used for educational purposes (Snow, Tiffin et al., 1965), as in children's learning programs; thus, understanding consumer preferences and motives should improve the selection of movies (which could be tailored to address different psychological needs). Fourth, movie preferences are an important ingredient of interpersonal etiquette, providing a topic of conversation, as well as a vehicle for assessing others' attitudes and interpersonal compatibility. For instance, people discuss film preferences in social networking and online dating sites to decide whether their views are shared by others—this has important relationship implications and relates to individuals' social identity and self-concept.

Last, but not least, the identification of consistent links between individual differences in personality, film use, and movie preferences can undoubtedly improve both our understanding and the prediction of consumer choices. It is noteworthy that although our focus here is on movie preferences, the same methodology could be applied to other product-categories, too.

Conclusion

Marked individual differences in movie preferences can be explained in terms of stable personality characteristics, like the Big Five, by and specific movie uses— that is, motives for consuming motion pictures (e.g., information seeking, boredom avoidance, catharsis, etc.). In line, people watch movies to satisfy different psychological needs, and individual differences in personality partly explain why some people are more likely to seek the satisfaction of some needs over others. For example, consumers motivated primarily by the pleasure-seeking motive will gravitate toward "feel-good," fun, comedic films—although any person may pursue this goal at some point, some individuals will do it more often than others (and the personality trait of Extraversion should predict these differences). Conversely, consumers may be motivated by an intellectual experience and choose to watch movies that provide them with a learning opportunity. Any person may feel such a need at some point, but the movie choices of some individuals will be much more influenced by this information-seeking use of film than others (and the personality trait of Openness to Experience should predict these differences). Thus, personality explains someone's tendency to like thought- or fun-provoking movies, which, in turn, will determine how much someone will like a given movie. As noted, these are just two of the uses of film or movie-watching motives, and there are connections with other personality traits and genres, too.

The explosion of internet-based movie consumption (e.g., online retailers, streaming, downloading, etc.) has inspired empirical research on the relationship between movie preferences and consumer profiles. Although most of the research has so far been commercial rather than academic, it is usually motivated by the same goal; namely, to predict and understand consumer choices in movies. The CF algorithms we discussed provide some examples of how individual-level data can be extrapolated to make a wider range of predictions or recommendations. It is, however, noteworthy that such algorithms can provide only a limited understanding of consumer movie preferences because they are focused on individuals' behaviors, rather than on their motives or traits. We believe that to fully understand the psychology of movie preferences and improve the accuracy of film recommendation engines, information on consumers' personality traits and movie-watching motives should also be examined. Moreover, classifying movies according to their ability to satisfy consumer's psychological needs, rather than merely based on traditional genres, is likely to improve matching algorithms and recommendation engines. This will enable us to predict a much wider range of movie preferences and understand their underlying causes.

Notes

1. Throughout this chapter, we will use "motion pictures," "films," and "movies" as interchangeable terms.
2. Despite the dominance of this model in mainstream personality research, critics have highlighted several limitations to the Five-Factor Model, which we will not discuss here (but see Fergusson, Chamorro-Premuzic, Pickering, and Weiss [2011] and Hogan [2007]).
3. Due to space constraints, we only present mathematical details of memory-based CF algorithms here, with the purpose of explaining the basic principles of CF. Readers interested in a more comprehensive review of CF algorithms should consult Su and Khoshgoftaar (2009).

References

Ahmetoglu, G., Swami, V., & Chamorro-Premuzic, T. (2009). The relationship between dimensions of love, personality, and relationship length. *Archives of Sexual Behavior, 39*,1181–1190.

Amiel, T., & Sargent, S. L. (2004). Individual differences in Internet usage motives. *Computers in Human Behavior, 20*, 711–726

Anderson, D., & Iannaco, G. (2010). Love and hate in dementia: The depressive position in the film Iris. *The International Journal of Psychoanalysis, 91*, 1289–1297.

Bandura, A., & Walters, R. H. (1963). *Social learning and personality development.* New York: Holt, Rinehart, & Winston.

Bartsch, A. (2010). Vivid abstractions: On the role of emotion metaphors in film viewers' search for deeper insight and meaning. *Midwest Studies in Philosophy, 34*, 240–260.

Bartsch, A., & Viehoff, R. (2010). The use of media entertainment and emotional gratification. *Procedia Social and Behavorial Sciences, 5*, 2247–2255.

Baumert, A., Hofmann, W., & Blum, G. (2008). Laughing about Hitler? Evaluation of the movie "My Fuehrer"—The truly truest truth about Adolf Hitler. *Journal of Media Psychology: Theories, Methods, and Applications, 20*, 43–56.

Benton, R., Czechanski, B., et al. (1993). Breaking the law, a metaphor for female empowerment through aggression: Women in film. *Journal of the American Academy of Psychoanalysis, 21*, 133–147.

Blumler, J. G., & Katz, E. (Eds.) (1974). *The uses of mass communication: Current perspectives on gratifications research* (pp. 19–32). Beverly Hills, CA: Sage.

Bogaert, F. A. (2001). Personality, individual differences and preferences for the sexual media. *Archives of Sexual Behavior, 30*(1), 29–53.

Bruggemann, J. M., & Barry, R. J. (2002). Eysenck's P as a modulator of affective and electrodermal responses to violent and comic film. *Personality and Individual Differences, 32*, 1029–1048.

Canny, I. (2002). Collaborative filtering with privacy via factor analysis. *Proceedings of the 25th Annual International ACM SIGIR Conference on Research and Development in Information Retrieval, 25*, 238–245.

Chamorro-Premuzic, T. (2007). *Personality and individual differences*. Oxford: Blackwell-Wiley.

Chamorro-Premuzic, T. (2011). *Personality and individual differences* (2nd ed.). Oxford: Wiley.

Chamorro-Premuzic, T., Burke, C., & Swami, V. (2011a). Personality predictors of artistic preferences as a function of the emotional valence and perceived complexity of paintings. *Psychology of Aesthetics, Creativity and the Arts, 4*, 196–204.

Chamorro-Premuzic, T., Fagan, P., & Furnham, A. (2010). Personality and Uses of Music as Predictors of Preferences for Music Consensually Classified as Happy, Sad, Complex, and Social. *Psychology of Aesthetics, Creativity and the Arts, Vol. 4, No. 4*, 205–213.

Chamorro-Premuzic, T., & Furnham, A. (2005). *Personality and intellectual competence*. Mahwah, NJ: Lawrence Erlbaum Associates.

Chamorro-Premuzic, T., & Furnham, A. (2007). Personality and music: Can traits explain why people listen to music? *British Journal of Psychology, 98*, 175–185.

Chamorro-Premuzic, T., & Furnham, A. (2010). *The psychology of personnel selection*. Cambridge: Cambridge University Press.

Chamorro-Premuzic, T., Swami, V., & Cermakova, B. (2012). Individual differences in music consumption are predicted by uses of music and age rather than emotional intelligence, neuroticism, extraversion or openness, *40*, 285–300.

Choti, S. E., Marston, A. R., et al. (1987). Gender and personality variables in film-induced sadness and crying. *Journal of Social and Clinical Psychology, 5*, 535–544.

Cupchik, G. C. (1995). Emotion in aesthetics: Reactive and reflective models. *Poetics, 23*, 177–188.

Davis, M. H., Hull, J. G., Young, R. D., & Warren, G. G. (1987). Emotional reactions to dramatic film stimuli: The influence of cognitive and emotional empathy. *Journal of Personality and Social Psychology, 52*, 126–133.

Diefendorff, J. M., & Chandler, M. M. (2010). Motivating employees. In S. Zedeck (Ed.), *Handbook of industrial and organizational psychology*. Washington, DC: American Psychological Association, viii, 960 pp.

Dollinger, S. J., Orf, L., & Robinson, A. (1991). Personality and campus controversies: Preferred boundaries as a function of openness to experience. *Journal of Psychology, 125*, 399–406.

Egan, V. (2011). Personality and antisocial behavior. In T. Chamorro-Premuzic, S. von Stumm, & A. Furnham (Eds.), *Handbook of individual differences*. Oxford: Wiley.

Fabregat, A. (2000). Personality and curiosity about TV and films violence in adolescents. *Personality and Individual Differences, 29*, 379–392.

Feingold, A. (1994). Gender differences in personality: A meta-analysis. *Psychological Bulletin, 116*, 429–456.

Fergusson, E., Chamorro-Premuzic, T., Pickering, A., & Weiss, A. (2011). Five into one does not go: Critique of the general factor of personality theory. In T. Chamorro-Premuzic, S. von Stumm, & A. Furnham (Eds.), *Handbook of individual differences* (pp. 162–187). Oxford: Wiley.

Feshbach, S., & Singer, R. D. (1971). Television and Aggression: An experimental field study. *San Francisco. Jossey-Bass*

Fisher, W. A., & Byrne, D. (1978). Individual differences in affective, evaluative, and behavioral responses to an erotic film. *Journal of Applied Social Psychology, 8*, 355–365.

Gilbert, B. O., & Gilbert, D. G. (1991). Electrodermal responses to movie-induced stress as a function of EPI and MMPI scale scores. *Journal of Social Behavior & Personality, 6*, 903–914.

Giles, D. C. (2002). Parasocial interaction: A review of the literature and a model for future research. *Media Psychology, 4*, 279–305.

Gilissen, R., Bakermans-Kranenburg, M. J., et al. (2008). Parent-child relationship, temperament, and physiological reactions to fear-inducing film clips: Further evidence for differential susceptibility. *Journal of Experimental Child Psychology, 99*, 182–195.

Gilissen, R., Koolstra, C. M., et al. (2007). Physiological reactions of preschoolers to fear-inducing film clips: Effects of temperamental fearfulness and quality of the parent-child relationship. *Developmental Psychobiology, 49*, 187–195.

Gilpatric, K. (2010). Violent female action characters in contemporary American cinema. *Sex Roles, 62*, 734–746.

Goldberg, D., Nichols, D., Oki, B. M., & Terry, D. (1992). Using collaborative filtering to weave an information tapestry. *Communications of ACM, 35*, 61–70.

Goldberg, K., Roeder, T., Gupta, D., & Perkins, C. (2001). Eigentaste: A constant time collaborative filtering algorithm. *Information Retrieval, 4*, 133–151.

Greenwood, D. N. (2008). Television as escape from self: Psychological predictors of media involvement. *Personality and Individual Differences, 44*, 414–424.

Greenwood, D. N., & Lippman, J. R. (2010). Gender, media use and impact. In J. Chrisler & D. McCreary (Eds.), *Handbook of gender research in psychology* (vol. 2, pp. 643–669). New York: Springer.

Gunter, B. (1985). *Dimensions of television violence*. Aldershot, UK: Gower Press.

Rowland, G., Fouts, G., & Heatherton, T. (1989). Television viewing and sensation seeking: Uses, preferences and attitudes. *Personality and Individual Differences, 10*, 1003–1006.

Hesse, M., Schliewe, S., et al. (2005). Rating of personality disorder features in popular movie characters. *BMC Psychiatry, 5*, 45.

Hirschman, E. C. (1987). Consumer preferences in literature, motion pictures, and television programs. *Empirical Studies of the Arts, 5*, 31–46.

Hoffman, T. (2006). Hysteria in wine country: Movie review: "Sideways". (2004). *Psychoanalytic Psychology, 23*, 667–674.

Hoffner, C. A., & Levine K. J. (2005). Enjoyment of mediated horror and violence: A meta-analysis. *Media Psychology, 7*, 207–237.

Hogan, R. (2007). *Personality and the fate of organizations*. Mahwah, NJ: Lawrence Erlbaum Associates.

Holbrook, M. B. (1999). Popular appeal versus expert judgments of motion pictures. *Journal of Consumer Research, 26*, 144–155.

Holbrook, M. B., & Hirschman, E. C. (1982). The experiential aspects of consumption: Consumer fantasies, feelings, and fun. *Journal of Consumer Research, 9*(2), 132.

Hughey, M. W. (2010). The white savior film and reviewers' reception. *Symbolic Interaction, 33*, 475–496.

Hutchings, P. (2004). *The horror film*. London: Longman.

Isen, A. M., & Gorgoglione, J. M. (1983). Some specific effects of four affect-induction procedures. *Personality and Social Psychology Bulletin, 9*, 136–143.

Izod, J. (2000). Active imagination and the analysis of film. *The Journal of Analytical Psychology, 45*, 267–285.

Johnson, B. R. (1980). General occurrence of stressful reactions to commercial motion pictures and elements in films subjectively identified as stressors. *Psychological Reports, 47*, 775–786.

Kalisch, B. J., Kalisch, P. A., et al. (1982). The nurse as a sex object in motion pictures, 1930 to 1980. *Research in Nursing & Health, 5*, 147–154.

Kaviani, H., Kumari, V., et al. (2010). A psychophysiological investigation of laterality in human emotion elicited by pleasant and unpleasant film clips. *Annals of General Psychiatry, 9*, 25.

Katz, E., & Gurevitch, M., & Haas, H. (1973). On the use of mass media as an escape: Clarification of a concept. *Public Opinion Quarterly, 26*, 377–388.

Kern, M. L., & Friedman, H. S. (2011). Personality and differences in health and longevity. In Chamorro-Premuzic, T., von Stumm, S., & Furnham, A. (Eds.), *Handbook of individual differences*. Oxford: Wiley.

Kerrigan, F. (2010). *Film marketing*. Butterworth-Heinemann. Time: 1 edition. Oxford.

Knickerbocker, J. F., Jr. (2010). Toward improving the film selection process in cinematherapy. *Dissertation Abstracts International: Section B: The Sciences and Engineering, 70*, 5169.

Knobloch, S., & Zillmann, D. (2002). Mood management via the digital jukebox. *Journal of Communication, 52*(2), 351–366.

Knobloch-Westerwick, S., & Alter, S. (2006). Mood adjustment to social situations through mass media use: How men ruminate and women dissipate angry moods. *Human Communication Research, 32*, 58–73.

Kracauer, S. (1949). National types as Hollywood presents them. *Public Opinion Quarterly, 13*, 53–72.

Lee, S. A., Gibbons, J. A., & Stephen (2010). Sympathetic reactions to the bait dog in a film of dog fighting: The influence of personality and gender. *Society & Animals: Journal of Human-Animal Studies*.

Lehman, H. C., & Witty, P. A. (1928). A study of play in relation to intelligence. *Journal of Applied Psychology, 12*, 369–397.

Leyens, J. P., Camino, L., Parke, R. D., & Berkowitz, L. (1975). Effects of movie violence on aggression in a field setting as a function of group dominance. *Journal of Personality and Social Psychology, 32*, 346–360.

Linden, G., Smith, B., & York, J. (2003). Amazon.com recommendations: Item-to-item collaborative filtering. *IEEE Internet Computing, 7*, 76–80.

Lovaas, O. I. (1961). Effect of exposure to symbolic aggression on aggressive behavior. *Child Development, 32*, 37–44.

Lull, J. (1990). *Inside family viewing: Ethnographic research on television's audience*. London: Routledge.

Mares, M. L., & Cantor, J. (1992). Elderly viewers' responses to televised portrayals of old age: Empathy and mood management vs. social comparison. *Communication Research, 19*, 459–478.

Moskalenko, S., & Heine, S. J. (2003). Watching your troubles away: Television viewing as a stimulus for subjective self-awareness. *Personality and Social Psychology Bulletin, 29*, 76–85.

McClelland, D. (1985). *Human motivation*. New York: Scott, Foresman.

Melville, P., Mooney, R. J., & Nagarajan, R. (2002). Content-boosted collaborative filtering for improved recommendations. *Proceedings of the 18th National Conference on Artificial Intelligence, 18*, 187–182.

Miller, B. N., Konstan, J. A., & Riedl, J. (2004). PocketLens: Toward a personal recommender system. *ACM Transactions on Information Systems, 22*, 437–476.

Oliver, M. B. (2008). Tender affective states as predictors of entertainment preference. *Journal of Communication, 58*, 40–61.

Oliver, M. B., & Bartsch, A. (2010). Appreciation as audience response: Exploring entertainment gratifications beyond hedonism. *Human Communication Research, 36*, 53–81.

Oliver, M. B., & Raney, A. A. (2008). *Development of hedonic and eduaimonic measures of entertainment motivations: The role of affective and cognitive gratifications.* Paper presented at the annual convention of the International Communication Association, Montreal, Canada.

Palmgreen, P. (1984). Uses and gratifications: A theoretical perspective. In R. N. Bostrom (Ed.), *Communication yearbook 8* (pp. 20–55). Beverly Hills, CA: Sage.

Palmgreen, P., Cook, P. L. Harvill, J. G., & Helm, D. M. (1988). The motivational framework of moviegoing: Uses and avoidances of theatrical films. In B. A. Austin (Ed.), *Current research in films: Audiences, economics, and law* (Vol. 4). Norwood, NJ: Ablex.

Potts, R., Dedmon, A., & Halford, J. (1996). Sensation seeking, television viewing motives, and home television viewing patterns. *Personality and Individual Differences, 21*, 1081–1084.

Randolph, J. J., & Edmondson, R. S. (2005). Using the binomial effect size display (BESD) to present the magnitude of effect sizes to the evaluation audience. *Practical Assessment Research and Evaluation, 10*, 1–7.

Resnick, P., & Varian, H. R. (1997). Recommender systems. *Communications of the ACM, 40*, 56–58.

Rosengren, K. E., & Windahl, S. (1977). Mass media Use: Causes and effects. *Communications: International Journal of Communication Research, 3*, 336–351.

Rubin, A. M. (1983). Television uses and gratifications: the interactions of viewing patterns and motivations. *Journal of Broadcasting, 27*, 37–51.

Sarwar, B. M., Karypis, G., Konstan, J., & Riedl, J. (2001). Item based collaborative filtering recommendation algorithms. In *Proceedings of the 10th International Conference on World Wide Web* (pp. 285–295).

Sarwar, B. M., Karypis, G., Konstan, J., & Riedl, J. (2002). Incremental SVD-based algorithms for highly scaleable recommender systems. In *Proceedings of the 5th International Conference on Computer and Information Technology* (pp. 1–36). Berlin, Heidelberg: Springer-Verlag.

Schierman, M. J., & Rowland, G. L. (1985). Sensation seeking and selection of entertainment. *Personality and Individual Differences, 6*, 599–603.

Schindler, R. M., & Holbrook, M. B. (2003). Nostalgia for early experience as a determinant of consumer preferences. *Psychology & Marketing, 20*, 275–302.

Schulz, G. A. (2002). The iconic 1960's English film "Darling": Portrait of the contemporary empty self. *Progress in Self Psychology, 18*, 217–242.

Shapiro, J., & Rucker, L. (2004). The Don Quixote effect: Why going to the movies can help develop empathy and altruism in medical students and residents. *Families, Systems, & Health, 22*, 445–452.

Snow, R. E., Tiffin, J., et al. (1965). Individual differences and instructional film effects. *Journal of Educational Psychology, 56,* 315–326.

Sparks, G. G. (1986). Developing a scale to assess cognitive responses to frightening films. *Journal of Broadcasting and Electronic Media, 30,* 65–73.

Speisman, J. C., Lazarus, R. S., et al. (1964). Experimental analysis of a film used as a threatening stimulus. *Journal of Consulting Psychology, 28,* 23–33.

Stark, R., Schienle, A., et al. (2005). Influences of disgust sensitivity on hemodynamic responses towards a disgust-inducing film clip. *International Journal of Psychophysiology. Special Issue: Neurobiology of Fear and Disgust, 57,* 61–67.

Steinberg, L., Albert, D., Cauffman, E., Banich, M., Graham, S., & Woolard, J. (2008). Age differences in sensation seeking and impulsivity as indexed by behavior and self-report: Evidence for a dual systems model. *Developmental Psychology, 44,* 1764–1777.

Su, X., & Khoshgoftaar, M. (2009). A survey of collaborative filtering techniques. *Advances in Artificial Intelligence, 2009,* 1–19.

Suckfüll, M. (2004). *Rezeptionsmodalitaeten. Ein integratives Konstrukt fuir die Medienwirkungsforshcung.* Munich: Reinhard Fischer.

Tamborni, R., Stiff, J., et al. (1987). Preference for graphic horror featuring male versus female victimization: Personality and past film viewing experiences. *Human Communication Research, 13,* 529–552.

Tanski, S. E., Cin, S. D., et al. (2010). Parental R-rated movie restriction and early-onset alcohol use. *Journal of Studies on Alcohol and Drugs, 71,* 452–459.

Tesser, A., Millar, K., & Wu, C. H. (1988). On the perceived functions of movies. *Journal of Psychology, 122,* 441–449.

Thurstone, L. L. (1930). A scale for measuring attitude toward the movies. *Journal of Educational Research, 22,* 84–89.

Trice, A. (2010). Sensation-seeking and video choice in second grade children. *Personality and Individual Differences, 49,* 1007–1010.

Valentiner, D. P., Hood, J., et al. (2005). Fainting history, disgust sensitivity, and reactions to disgust-eliciting film stimuli. *Personality and Individual Differences, 38,* 1329–1339.

von Stumm, S., Hell, B., & Chamorro-Premuzic, T. (2011). Intellectual curiosity as a third pillar of intellectual competence: importance of the "hungry mind." *Perspectives of Psychological Science, 6,* 574–588.

Vrugt, A., Jacobs, M., et al. (2010). Reductie van negatieve stereotypen over Marokkanen door een speelfilm. (Reduction of negative stereotypes about Moroccans through a movie) *Gedrag en Organisatie, 23,* 19–27.

Weaver, J. B. (1991). Exploring the links between personality and media preferences. *Personality and Individual Differences, 12,* 1293–1299.

Weaver, B. J. III. (2003). Individual differences in television viewing motives. *Personality and Individual Differences, 35,* 1427–1437.

Weaver, J. B., Brosius, H.-B., et al. (1993). Personality and movie preferences: A comparison of American and German audiences. *Personality and Individual Differences, 14,* 307–315.

Welsh, A. (2010). On the perils of living dangerously in the Slasher horror film: Gender differences in the association between sexual activity and survival. *Sex Roles, 62,* 762–773.

Wilschinsky, T. (2006). Experiencing and reflecting on cinema as a modality for personal growth. *Dissertation Abstracts International Section A: Humanities and Social Sciences, 67.*

Yerkes, R. M., & Dodson, J. D. (1908). The relation of strengths of stimulus to rapidity of habit-formation. *Journal of Comparative Neurology and Psychology, 18,* 459–484.

Zaleski, Z. (1984). Sensation seeking and risk taking behaviour. *Personality and Individual Differences, 5,* 607–608.

Zillmann, D. (1988). Mood management through communication choices. *American Behavioral Scientist, 31,* 327–340.

Zillmann, D. (1996). The psychology of suspense in dramatic exposition. In P. Vorderer, H. J. Wulff, & M. Friedrichsen (Eds.), *Suspense: Conceptualizations, theoretical analyses, and empirical explorations* (pp. 199–231). Mahwah, NJ: Lawrence Erlbaum Associates.

Zillmann, D. (2000). Mood management in the context of selective exposure theory. In M. F. Roloff (Ed.), *Communication yearbook 23* (pp. 103–123). Thousand Oaks, CA: Sage.

Zuckerman, M. (1983), Sensation seeking and sports. *Personality and Individual Differences, 4,* 285–292.

Zuckerman, M. (1979). *Sensation seeking: Beyond the optimal level of arousal.* Hillsdale, NJ: Lawrence Erlbaum.

Zuckerman, M. (1994). *Behavioral expressions and biosocial bases of sensation seeking.* New York: Cambridge University Press.

Zuckerman, M., & Litle, P. (1986). Personality and curiosity about morbid and sexual events. *Personality and Individual Differences, 7,* 49–56.

Appendix: Mathematical Details for Basic Collaborative Filtering Algorithm

Correlation-based similarity measures most commonly use Pearson's correlation and are measured as follows: the similarity $s_{u,v}$ between the pair u and v is

$$s_{u,v} = \frac{\sum_{i \in I}(r_{u,i} - \bar{r}_u)(r_{v,i} - \bar{r}_v)}{\sqrt{\sum_{i \in I}(r_{u,i} - \bar{r})^2}\sqrt{\sum_{i \in I}(r_{vu,i} - \bar{r}_v)^2}}. \tag{1}$$

For user-based similarity, u and v are two different users, i ∈ I are all items that have been rated by both user u and v, and $\bar{r}_v$ is the average rating by user u over these items. For item-based similarity, u and v are two different movies, $i \in I$ are all users who have rated both movies u and v, and $\bar{r}_v$ is the average rating of movie v over all the common users.

Vector cosine similarity computes the similarity ratings as the cosine between angles formed by two frequency vectors that are formed from each user or item pair's ratings. Specifically, the user-item database can be written as an $m \times n$ matrix D, where the rows correspond to the m users and columns correspond to the n items (i.e., movies). The vector cosine similarity between a pair i and j is:

$$w_{i,j} = \cos\left(\vec{i} \cdot \vec{j}\right) = \frac{\vec{i} \cdot \vec{j}}{\|\vec{i}\| * \|\vec{j}\|}. \tag{2}$$

where • indicates the dot product between two vectors. For user-based similarity, $\vec{i}$ and $\vec{j}$ consist of vectors formed from the ratings of user i and j for all the movies that both have rated. For item-based similarity, these vectors consist of the ratings of movies i and j by all users who have rated both movies. Cosine similarity does not inherently take into account possible individual differences in rating scales among users (e.g., a rating of 10 out of 10 from a user who readily gave extremely high ratings might be equivalent to another user's 7 out of 10). Thus, adjustments can be made to cosine similarity by subtracting out a user's average over a given movie pair. Theoretically, adjustments could also be made by subtracting out a movie's average over two user pairs, but this is usually not done because any differences in ratings between movies are not obviously affected by internal scale differences within people and thus are assumed to reflect real preference differences. Note that although correlation similarity may be negative, cosine similarity is always positive.

Once the similarity has been quantified between every pair of users (for user-based CF) or movies (for item-based CF), these need to be transformed into a predicted rating for the active user A for a particular movie M. For user-based CF, the mean-adjusted ratings of all other users for movie M (i.e., the difference between rating of movie M for each user from the user's average rating over all other movies) is weighted by the users' similarity with the active user A. These weighted-difference ratings are averaged to form a prediction of how different this user A's rating of movie M will differ from user A's average ratings. This predicted difference is then added to user A's average ratings to give $P_{A,M}$, the predicted value of user A for movie M. This is exemplified by the following formula:

$$P_{A,M} = \bar{r}_A + \frac{\sum_{u \in U} \left(r_{u,M} - \bar{r}_u\right) * s_{A,u}}{\sum_{u \in U} \left|s_{A,u}\right|}. \tag{3}$$

where $\bar{r}_A$ and $\bar{r}_u$ are the average ratings for user A and u on all other movies, and $S_{A,u}$ is the similarity between user A and u. The summations are over all users $u \in U$ who have rated movie M. For item-based CF, the direct weighted average can be used (no differences in individual user scales need be taken into account).

$$P_{A,M} = \frac{\sum_{i \in I} \left(r_{i,M} \right) * s_{A,i}}{\sum_{i \in I} \left| s_{A,i} \right|}. \tag{4}$$

The summation $i \in I$ is over all items (movies) i that have been rated by active user A.

5

FILM THROUGH THE HUMAN VISUAL SYSTEM

FINDING PATTERNS AND LIMITS

Jordan E. DeLong, Kaitlin L. Brunick,
and James E. Cutting

You would be hard-pressed to find someone who does not watch film. Cultures around the globe have embraced the art of the moving image and run with it, creating so many movies that no one person can hope to watch even a majority of them in his or her lifetime. Cinema has become such a fixture in our lives that the average American watches five films in theaters every year, as shown in Figure 5.1. Cinema's prominent place in society makes it easy to forget that film (in a form we would recognize) has only existed for roughly 100 years. Film has progressed from a technical curiosity to a large-scale form of entertainment that engages viewers from all walks and stages of life. Filmmakers have constantly changed and updated their craft, using trial and error to map out some of the "rules" needed to interface film effectively with the human mind. Several of these rules include matching action, eye gaze, and spatial layout between shots. Determining the bounds of what makes sense to viewers was only the beginning; knowing how to transition effectively between shots is a complex process under constant revision by a community of skilled filmmakers.

Although some people might describe today's films as "uniform" and "formulaic," films continue to evolve. This long-ranging and systematic reimagination of films can afford us insight into elements of the human visual system. In other words, movies have the potential to

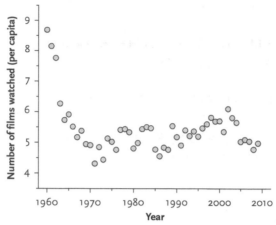

FIGURE 5.1 After the introduction of television, the average number of films viewed in theaters by US citizens leveled off at roughly five films per year. Data were compiled by comparing yearly ticket sales from an online database (boxofficemojo.com) with population data from the US Census Bureau for citizens over 5 years of age.

give us insight into the structures and statistics required to process the oppressive deluge of optical information that constantly flows into our brains from a relentlessly changing world. This insight is valuable and welcome; psychologists studying vision have yet to understand in full how the brain continuously extracts meaning from a series of changing, moving, shifting patterns of actions and events. Filmmakers have been playing with the same perceptual puzzles, searching for new and better ways to engage and entertain people across the world. Hollywood's widely successful creations haven't explained how our brains process this vast amount of visual information, but the changing structure of film shows a number of interesting patterns that can provide new insight into how our brains encode information from the visual world.

This exchange of insight can go in both directions. Work done by psychologists can also predict and explain the future of film, given what we do know about the abilities of human perception. Film scholars such as Joseph Anderson (1998) and David Bordwell and Noël Carroll (1996) have shown an interest in the process of how humans perceive film, and they are classified as cognitivists. Looking at film through the lens of cognition is a viewpoint in opposition to other film theories that interpret cinema from feminist, Marxist, or psychoanalytic perspectives. The friction between cognitive film scholars and their peers hinges on the fact that cognitivists reject forms of ideological interpretation (such as Freudian psychoanalysis) that have driven most film theory in the past decades. Instead, the cognitivist study of film attempts to evaluate filmmaking using findings and theories from fields within the loose confederation of the cognitive sciences, such as psychology, philosophy, computer science, and linguistics.

It is important to note that this chapter is written from a perspective even more radical than most cognitive film theorists would adopt. As researchers with a cognitive psychological viewpoint, we see film as a stimulus with a number of fascinating properties, many of which have not been examined quantitatively. The types of analysis presented in this chapter are agnostic to the types of interpretation found in most film studies; the data produced by our analysis are largely quantitative. Our methodology conspicuously ignores aspects of film like character development, set design, critical review, cultural relevance, director's intent, and most aspects of cinematography. Our data do not describe whether a single film is "good" or not, but instead track a number of low-level, slow-changing statistics of popular films. Other film researchers have also been interested in this type of data, extracting comparison statistics from films released throughout the last century.

For our sample, we chose films from every 5 years, starting in 1935 and ending in 2005. The films were selected based on a number of criteria such as box office gross, coarse genre type, and viewer rating in the Internet Movie Database (IMDB). Digital versions of these films were converted into a series of 256 × 256 grayscale images. This collection of movies makes up the dataset that we use throughout the different types of analysis in this chapter. A selection of films included in our database includes *The 39 Steps* (1935), *Back to the Future* (1985), and *Star Wars Episode III: The Revenge of the Sith* (2005). A complete list of the films can be found in the supplementary materials of Cutting, DeLong, and Nothelfer (2010).

Our first analysis involved finding the boundaries between shots in the visual sequence. In film, a "shot" is continuous footage from the same camera. Shots are then pieced together using a number of different transitions, such as the *straight cut* (the vast majority of modern transitions), *dissolves, fades,* and *wipes.*

Detecting transitions between shots may appear to be a trivial task, but editors do their best to "hide" these discontinuities; in particular, some *jump cuts* (cuts that bind two shots with little perspective change) are regularly missed by human observers (Smith & Henderson, 2008). In addition, the rules for continuity editing have become so commonplace in popular film that viewers regularly miss cuts that follow these continuity rules (Smith & Henderson, 2008). Although many computer algorithms are somewhat adept at detecting straight cuts, slowly changing dissolves are difficult for them to detect. To raise accuracy in our analyses, human observers also viewed the films to supplement the results of our computerized analysis. After this process, we were left with a series of precise lengths for every shot within in the 150-film sample.

Changing Shot Lengths

The most popular type of quantitative film data to examine is average shot length (ASL), a metric of how long a shot is on-screen before transitioning to a new shot. David Bordwell noted that ASLs have been getting shorter than those during the "studio era" of Hollywood (Bordwell, 2002). This result may not be surprising if Bordwell was simply looking at the earliest of films, but data from more than 13,000 films have shown that ASL is still decreasing today (Salt, 2006). Our database of 150 films supports these findings, showing a decrease in shot length beginning at the end of the 1960s. An overview of these data is presented in Figure 5.2.

One common method for detecting ASL is to simply count how many cuts a film contains and then divide that number by the length of the film, a tedious enough task. However, cuts may frequently pass without the viewer noticing, requiring that researchers looking for these boundaries be either highly skilled at detecting subtle changes in real time or examine the film at an arduously slow pace. Our analysis utilized custom video-processing software to look for the statistical changes that accompany a transition in film, as well as confirmation by human observers (Cutting, Delong, & Nothelfer, 2010). After verifying the location of each cut throughout the film, we were able to compute the length of every shot. Despite being the popular metric, ASL may be inappropriate because

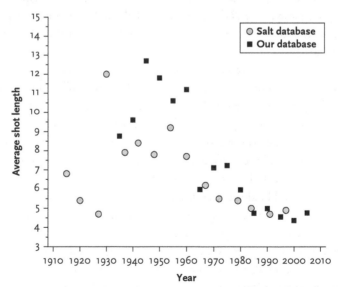

FIGURE 5.2 Average shot lengths (in seconds) increased with the advent of sound films in the late 1920s, but have been experiencing a steady decrease since 1960 (adapted from Cutting, DeLong, and Brunick, in press).

the distribution of shot lengths does not follow a normal bell curve, but is rather a highly skewed, approximately log-normal distribution. Thus, although most shots are short, a small number of remarkably long shots inflate the mean. The large majority of shots in a film are actually below average in length, leading to systematic overestimation of an individual film's shot length. A better estimate is a film's median shot length, a metric that shows the same decrease in shot length over time but provides a better estimate of shot length, as shown in Figure 5.3. Regardless of metric used, however, it's clear that shot lengths in film have been decreasing over time.

The most common explanations for the decrease in shot length usually revolve around technology or cultural factors. The argument from technology claims that cheaper film and the rise of digital editing give directors and editors the ability to cut at a pace that earlier generations would have done if given the chance. Others explain decreasing shot length as an effect of culture, of the younger generation's lowered attention span or rises in attention-deficit hyperactivity disorder; in the 1980s, this change was blamed on the fast cutting and short duration of music videos that catered to the "MTV Generation" (Postman, 1985). Recent literature warns that the next generation's attention span is being damaged by video games (Swing, Gentile, Anderson, & Walsh, 2010), the internet (Carr, 2010), and Twitter (Ebert, 2010). This isn't the first

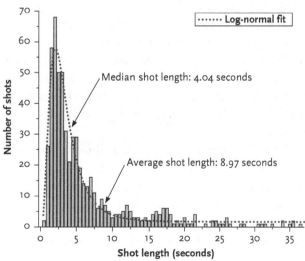

FIGURE 5.3 A plot of shot lengths in seconds by how common shots of those lengths are in the film *A Night at the Opera* (1935). Because the distribution has a heavy positive skew, median shot length can be seen as a more accurate description than average shot length for shots in a film.

time youth culture has been vilified, however; Frank Sinatra once claimed that the music of Elvis Presley "fosters almost totally negative and destructive reactions in young people" (Shapiro, 1981, p. 305).

Both arguments from culture and technology can be countered by a simple fact; Salt's data, shown in Figure 5.2, show us that films in the late silent era (1920s–1930s) exhibited editing that was essentially as fast-paced as today. Critics of modern culture would be reticent to say that the pace of life in the late 1920s was equivalent to today. We can also rule out a purely technological explanation for the decrease in ASL because editing equipment in the 1920s would be considered primitive even by 1960s' standards.

A more satisfying explanation for the equivalence between ASLs in the late 1920s and 1990s lies in the introduction of sound. Incorporating dialogue and a set soundtrack changed a number of ways that films were made. These changes promoted increased use of techniques such as *shot/reverse-shot* that are often the backbone of contemporary films. As the narratives within sound films became increasingly complex, shot length also increased. Near the conclusion of Hollywood's studio era, many filmmakers felt that film needed to compete with television to combat falling viewership (shown in Figure 5.1). The resulting push created larger, event-centered films like *Tora! Tora! Tora!* (1970), a film considered to be a commercial failure at the time. Filmmakers were struck with a problem: How do you create complex storylines while keeping audiences interested?

A number of films in this era exhibited a different way of presenting a narrative, one that was inspired by foreign styles of editing, such as French New Wave; this was quickly adopted and modified by a new generation of filmmakers. One often-examined film from within this era is *Easy Rider,* a 1969 film directed by a violent and cocaine-addicted Dennis Hopper. The original cut for *Easy Rider* was more than 4.5 hours in length but was pared down to a palatable 90 minutes by adopting a number of quick cuts out of necessity, as well as for the sake of being stylistically different.

Bordwell (2002) highlighted a number of stylistic changes that have taken place since the 1960s that have led to more condensed and intense narratives. These films were made using a fast cutting pace and different lens types, including close-up shots in dialogue and free-ranging cameras that move around an otherwise static scene. It's also worth pointing out that films from the 1960s weren't just changing thematically, but also show increasingly different structure as well.

The quick-cutting style that has become more commonplace in film may also have benefits outside of simply compressing the narrative. In recent work, Pronin and Wegner (2006) found that quicker "thought speed" generates a more positive affect in an individual. The speed of thought can be induced by external sources, including the speed of shots in a film clip; people who were shown clips with a rapidly moving shot pace reported a more positive mood than did those shown similar clips with slower moving shots (Pronin & Jacobs, 2008).

Although the speed of cut sequences no doubt influences perceptual and emotional elements in the viewer, cut speed is not the only variable responsible for the perception of newer films as more "fast paced." The increased prominence of the action genre has coupled quick cutting with increased motion (optical change resulting from objects in the environment) and movement (the camera itself changing position). We chose to conduct analysis on this other type of "speed" in film, the speed with which activity occurs on-screen.

Motion and Movement on Film

There is little doubt that the tools filmmakers use to shoot and edit films have changed dramatically since the 1930s. Cameras have continually become smaller, lighter, and higher in quality in nearly every decade (Salt, 2006). Regardless of these changes, Hollywood has practiced conservative camerawork from the beginning, when filmmakers feared that *any* amount of camera motion would confuse and disorient their viewers (Bottomore, 1990). These fears were eventually dampened; films today often have subtle camera motion that viewers don't even notice. Today, we know that *some* degree of camera motion can be tolerated, but how much can we deal with?

A number of recent films have pushed the envelope of camera motion, leaving some viewers to question whether these "queasy-cam" films are hitting a limit (Ebert, 2007). One of these films is J. J. Abram's *Cloverfield* (2008), a romp through monster-ravaged New York City filmed from the perspective of a hand-held camera. The deliberately unsteady camera work was so extreme that several theaters were forced to put up warnings so that they weren't liable for any ill-effects related to induced seizures or motion sickness. Not all films feature the same level of continuous movement as *Cloverfield*; other action films, like *The Bourne Ultimatum* (2007) and *Quantum of Solace* (2008), feature sequences with very fast cuts and extreme camera movement as a means of giving the viewer a chaotic interpretation of events.

Moviegoers who watch these films walk away with an understanding that the films feature a different type of editing, but how can we quantify this change? How can we place the films of the 1940s on a scale of zero to *Cloverfield*? The simplest way to investigate this relationship is to compare how much change occurs between two sequential still frames. This can be done by using a two-dimensional Pearson correlation, a technique that compares every pixel in an image to that of a second image. For the films in our database this required comparing 65,536 pairs of pixels for each of the roughly 165,000 image pairs in a typical Hollywood film. At the turn of the millennium, this technique would have required considerable processing power, storage resources, and months of processing time. It can currently be accomplished within a feasible timeframe on a basic laptop computer. To make our results more intuitive, we calculated the effects of camera motion and scene movement into a single metric, the Visual Activity Index (VAI), which can be described as 1 minus the median interframe correlation.

It is clear that visual activity has been increasing over time, a trend shown in Figure 5.4, with action films leading the way (Cutting, DeLong, & Brunick, 2011). The motion and movement in film is becoming more pronounced, but where will this trend stop? Research in the area of visual perception has shown us that a series of images can be recognized even when they are presented every 100 milliseconds, a methodology known as rapid serial visual presentation (RSVP; Potter, 1976). It seems clear that our visual system limits how dissimilar frames can be in a feature film; interpreting a disconnected series of images is difficult for more than a couple seconds at a time. Average RSVP sequences have a VAI of roughly 0.80, but also depend on the images being displayed. *Cloverfield*'s VAI for the entire film is only 0.24. This places it well short of being a random sequence of images, but with a vastly higher amount of motion and movement than films like *All About Eve* (1950), which has a VAI of 0.012.

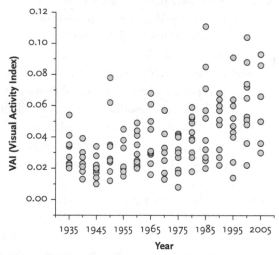

FIGURE 5.4 Visual activity (described as 1 minus the median interframe correlation for each pair of frames in a film) has been slowly increasing with time (adapted from Cutting, DeLong, and Brunick, in press).

Motion and movement have developed a distinct relationship to stimulus duration in recent years. Figure 5.5 shows the relationship between the duration of presentation (either of a shot, series of shots, or image in a rapid serial visual presentation sequence) and visual activity. When considering a whole film, a relatively low level of visual activity is present, even in films considered distinct in their levels of visual activity (for example, *The Bourne Ultimatum* and *Cloverfield*). However, when sequences are extracted from a film, a trend emerges that suggests more activity can be tolerated as long as it occurs over a shorter period of time. For example, a segment of the escape from the burning hotel in *Quantum of Solace* lasting for about 10 seconds exhibits a higher overall VAI than a 1-minute segment of the tunnel car chase sequence at the beginning of the film.

It appears as if the amount of camera movement and object motion that will be tolerated in a film isn't a constant rate, but rather a dynamic saturation point we reach when we've simply processed too much variation for too long. Highly noncorrelated sequences in film exhibit a high amount of visual activity, but can only persist with that level of activity for a certain amount of time before having

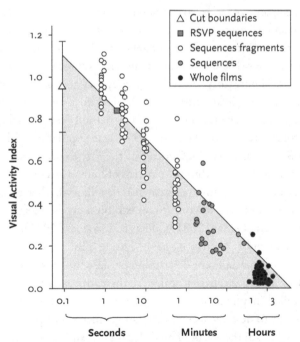

FIGURE 5.5 The amount of visual activity in different types of media appear to fall on the same line. Rapid serial visual presentation sequences (images shown in quick succession) can be viewed for a few seconds at a time, but would not be tolerated at longer timescales (adapted from Cutting, DeLong, and Brunick, in press).

to back off and retreat to baseline. This finding makes sense intuitively; however, psychological experiments rarely take into account how our perceptual abilities may fluctuate over timescales longer than 3 seconds. This fluctuation not only has consequences for the use of visual activity, but also for how shots are distributed. It begs the question as to whether shot lengths are catered to these fluctuations in the same way visual activity is; however, these fluctuations are likely linked to attentional systems rather than perceptual systems.

Shot Structure: Evolving Patterns

Although ASL and visual activity give us a good metric of how films are changing over the decades, they aren't very descriptive about the structural components of an individual film. As sequences of shots in film become more standardized, the length of an individual shot isn't independent from its position in the film. To numerically determine the presence of these types of patterns, we borrowed a technique from David Gilden, an astrophysicist-turned-psychologist who has studied hidden structure within human reaction time data.

Many experiments in the field of psychology utilize reaction time, a metric in which participants are asked to respond quickly to a particular target stimulus and inhibit responses to the nontarget stimuli. Individuals performing this type of task perform individual trials at different speeds even when performing the same task repetitively. These variations are usually averaged out and "relegated to a kind of statistical purgatory" even though they may actually hold some kind of structure within them (Gilden, 2001, p. 33). Mathematical tools have uncovered similar patterns in other phenomena, such as natural scenes (Field, 1987), the presence of solar flares (Lu & Hamilton, 1991), the population of different cities across the US (Newman, 2005). Gilden was the first to use these techniques to characterize this structure within the patterns of human attention.

When performing cognitive tasks (such as deciding whether a string of letters makes up a word), human reaction times exhibit a type of temporal structure called a $1/f$ pattern (Gilden, 2001; Gilden & Hancock, 2007). This pattern is also known by a number of other names including "pink noise" or "fractal noise." Fractal noise is an especially apt description because the presence of this pattern suggests self-similarity at different scales. Mathematicians have known these patterns, often called "mathematical monsters," for centuries. They are characterized as being difficult to describe using Euclidian geometry, but pioneering work by Benoit Mandelbrot in the 1970s offered elegant explanations for these patterns.

Finding a $1/f$ pattern within the context of reaction times suggests that our bodies and brains have a number of different mechanisms that contribute to the completion of a reaction time task. The time in which these mechanisms complete the task isn't necessarily constant and varies based on whether these mechanisms are in sync. It is also important to note that the magnitude of the influence of these mechanisms varies *proportionally* with the amount of time it takes for these fluctuations to occur.[1]

To test if the pattern of shot lengths in Hollywood films follows a similar pattern, we analyzed our previous data, using cut boundaries to calculate a series of shot lengths for an entire film. We then used Gilden's technique to calculate the power spectra for each of the 150 films, using the sequence of shot lengths as a time series. This technique allowed us to estimate the slope of the power spectra, a diagnostic metric of self-similarity. If the slope of the power spectrum is equal to 0 (known as a "flat spectrum"), then all frequencies are equally likely in the signal, meaning that there is no way to predict the next value, and no temporal structure exists within the signal. A slope of −2 means that the process can be modeled as a *random walk*, commonly described as a mathematical abstraction in which something moves by simply choosing a sequence of random steps. A slope of −1 lies directly between these types and is indicative of a $1/f$ pattern.

Our data show that after the 1960s (roughly the beginning of shot length's most recent decrease), films increasingly adhere to a $1/f$ pattern in their shot lengths (Cutting, DeLong, & Nothelfer, 2010). There is no clear reason why this change would occur at the same time as decreasing shot lengths; computing the slope of the power spectra isn't affected by the average value, but rather by the relationships between values. Fluctuations in human attention that follow a $1/f$ pattern tend to mirror the same type of pattern found in the shot lengths of Hollywood films. These similarities lead us to believe that film may be evolving; the characteristics of films may have changed over time to better serve cognitive mechanisms such as attention (see Figure 5.6).

Filmmakers clearly haven't been consciously attempting to replicate a $1/f$ pattern while editing the next big blockbuster, so why is this pattern becoming more common in Hollywood films? Filmmakers are trained to use their own intuition to use cuts, camera work, and various other techniques to create something that simply *feels right*. This process of trial and error started when early filmmakers like Georges Méliès had to invent strategies to string multiple events together in a single film. This system of trial and error is still alive today; a pioneering filmmaker introduces a new technique or style that is remembered, reused, and refined. It's not difficult to see how this process acts like a genetic algorithm in which the most successful techniques are remembered and copied, and the failed experiments languish in obscurity. Over time, filmmakers settle on methods that

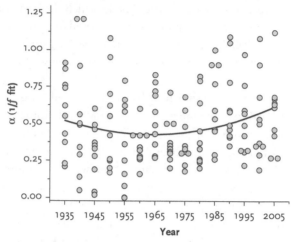

FIGURE 5.6 Films from 1960 onward follow a significantly increasing $1/f$ pattern, suggesting greater self-similarity in the pattern of cuts (adapted from Cutting, DeLong, and Nothelfer, 2010).

simply look and feel right, emerging with an intuitive understanding of how the brain understands film.

The fact that Hollywood film is a good modulator of attention appears obvious; presenting a film distracts and pacifies both unruly children and airline passengers. Exciting research shows that this effect can also be seen in our neuroanatomy. Researchers have found that some films can "exert considerable control over brain activity and eye movements" when subjects were shown different types of film while undergoing a functional magnetic resonance imaging (fMRI scan) (Hasson et al., 2008, p. 1). The results of the scan showed that when a group of viewers watched a highly structured film like Sergio Leone's *The Good, the Bad, and the Ugly* (1966), the number of brain regions that showed synchronous activity between subjects was ten times larger than when subjects watched unedited footage of a public park.

Film is not only becoming better at modulating our attention, but it can also provide researchers insight into the inner workings of the human visual system. Ongoing work aims to continue this exchange and extend our dialog beyond the mechanisms of attention to other important topics such as event segmentation, emotion, and narrative. Although our work has only scratched the surface, we hope to help introduce a fine-grained perspective into the cognitivist approach to film studies; not simply focusing on a philosophical interpretation of a single film, but also exploring how the smallest parts of a film (cuts, shots, movement) combine to construct meaning from moving pictures.

Glossary

1/*f* distribution   Representing 1 over frequency, this type of pattern can be characterized as the output of a system that is halfway between random and rigid. This distribution is found in many places in nature and is thought to signify self-similarity at multiple scales, as shown in fractal patterns.

ASL   Average Shot Length. The measure of how often a filmmaker cuts during a movie. Over the past few decades, the rate of cutting has increased and ASL has decreased as a direct result.

VAI   Visual Activity Index. A metric designed to approximate visual motion and movement present within part of a film. This metric can be characterized as a two-dimensional Pearson correlation that is subtracted from 1. Higher values denote more visual activity.

Note

1. It's worth noting, however, that $1/f$ patterns aren't *only* found in the fluctuations of human attention but in a number of varied phenomena across the earth and in space. The patterns of change found when measuring the height of the Nile River, the diameter of asteroid impacts on the moon, and the size and position of leaves on branching plants all follow the same type of pattern, yet we wouldn't dare make a claim about how they are related to Hollywood films. "Patterns of attention" merely seems like the best current explanation, but future research may show that film's gradual movement toward a $1/f$ temporal pattern may be catering to something different entirely.

References

Anderson, J. (1998). *The reality of illusion: An ecological approach to cognitive film theory*. Carbondale: Southern Illinois University Press.

Bordwell, D. (2002). Intensified continuity visual style in contemporary American film. *Film Quarterly, 55*(3), 16–28.

Bordwell, D., & Carroll, N. (1996). *Post-theory: Reconstructing film studies*. Madison: The University of Wisconsin Press.

Bottomore, S. (1990). Shots in the dark: The real history of film editing. In T. Elsaesser, & A. Barker (Eds.), *Early cinema: Space, frame, narrative* (pp. 104–113). London: BFI Publishing.

Carr, N. (2010). *The shallows: What the internet is doing to our brains*. New York: W. W. Norton and Co.

Cutting, J. E., DeLong, J. E., & Brunick, K. L. (2011). Visual activity in Hollywood film: 1935 to 2005 and beyond. *Psychology of Aesthetics, Creativity and the Arts, 5*, 115–125.

Cutting, J. E., DeLong, J. E., & Nothelfer, C. E. (2010). Attention and the evolution of Hollywood film. *Psychological Science, 21*, 440–447.

Ebert, R. (2007, August 16). Shake, rattle, and Bourne. [Web log post]. Retrieved from http://rogerebert.suntimes.com/apps/pbcs.dll/article?aid/20070816/commentary/7081600

Ebert, R. (2010, May 29). The quest for *frission*. [Web log post]. *The Chicago Sun Times.* Retrieved from http://blogs.suntimes.com/ebert/2010/05/the_french_word_frisson_descri.html

Field, D. J. (1987). Relations between the statistics of natural images and the response properties of cortical cells. *Journal of the Optical Society of America A, 4*, 2379–2394.

Gilden, D. L. (2001). Cognitive emission of 1/f noise. *Psychological Review, 108*, 33–56.

Gilden, D. L., & Hancock, H. (2007). Response variability in attention deficit disorders. *Psychological Science, 18*, 796–802.

Hasson, U., Landesman, O., Knappmeyer, B., Vallines, I., Rubin, N., & Heeger, D. J. (2008). Neurocinematics: the neuroscience of film. *Projections, 2*, 26.

Lu, E. T., Hamilton, R. J. (1991). Avalanches and the distribution of solar flares. *The Astrophysical Journal, 380*, L89–L92.

Newman, M. E. J. (2005). Power laws, Pareto distributions and Zipf's law. *Contemporary Physics, 46*, 323–351.

Postman, N. (1985). *Amusing ourselves to death: Public discourse in the age of show business*. New York: Penguin Group.

Potter, M. C. (1976). Short-term conceptual memory for pictures. *Journal of Experimental Psychology: Human Learning and Memory, 2*, 509–522.

Pronin, E., & Jacobs, E. (2008). Thought speed, mood and the experience of emotion. *Perspectives on Psychological Science, 3*(1), 461–485.

Pronin, E., & Wegner, D. M. (2006). Manic thinking: independent effects of thought speed and thought content on mood. *Psychological Science, 17*(9), 807–813.

Salt, B. (2006). *Moving into pictures: more on film, style and analysis*. London: Starword.

Smith, T. J., & Henderson, J. M. (2008). Edit blindness: the relationship between attention and global change blindness in dynamic scenes. *Journal of Eye Movement Research, 2*(2),6, 1–17.

Swing, E. L., Gentile, D. A., Anderson, C. A., & Walsh, D. A. (2010). Television and video game exposure and the development of attention problems. *Pediatrics, 126*(2), 214–221.

FILMOGRAPHY

Database Films

Balcon, M. (Producer), Montagu, I. (Producer), & Hitchcock, A. (Director). (1935). *The 39 Steps* [Motion picture]. UK: Gaumont British.

Canton, N. (Producer), Gale, B. (Producer), & Zemeckis, R. (Director). (1985). *Back to the future* [Motion picture]. USA: Amblin Entertainment.

Fleischer, R. (Producer & Director). (1970). *Tora! Tora! Tora!* [Motion Picture]. USA: 20th Century Fox.

McCallum, M. (Producer), & Lucas, G. (Director). (2005). *Star wars: Episode III- Revenge of the sith* [Motion picture]. USA: Lucasfilm.

Thalberg, I. (Producer), & Wood, S. (Director). (1935). *A night at the opera* [Motion picture]. USA: MGM.

Zanuck, D. F. (Producer), & Mankiewicz, J. L. (Director). (1950). *All about Eve* [Motion picture]. USA: 20th Century Fox.

Other Films

Abrams, J. J. (Producer), Burk, B. (Producer), & Reeves, M. (Director). (2008). *Cloverfield* [Motion picture]. USA: Bad Robot Productions.

Fonda, P. (Producer), & Hopper, D. (Director). (1969). *Easy rider* [Motion picture]. USA: Columbia Pictures.

Grimaldi, A. (Producer), & Leone, S. (Director). (1966). *The good, the bad, and the ugly* [Motion picture]. Italy: United Artists.

Marshall, F. (Producer), Crowley, P. (Producer), Sandberg, P. L. (Producer), & Greengrass, P. (Director). (2007). *The Bourne ultimatum* [Motion picture]. USA: Kennedy/Marshall.

Wilson, M. G. (Producer), Broccoli, B. (Producer), & Forster, M. (Director). (2008). *Quantum of solace* [Motion picture]. UK/USA: Columbia Pictures.

6 SELF AND THE CINEMATIC EXPERIENCE IN THE AGE OF ELECTRONIC TRANSMISSION

Gerald C. Cupchik and Michelle C. Hilscher

The self as a concept has been a part of Western European discourse since the Enlightenment of the eighteenth century, when John Locke (1997/1690) defined the self as "that conscious thinking thing…which is sensible, or conscious of pleasure and pain, capable of happiness or misery, and so is concerned for itself" (p. 307); it is both self-aware and self-reflective. The philosopher David Hume was sceptical regarding this idea because the self cannot be observed as such. From its earliest conception, we can see that the very notion the self is complex, challenging, and multidimensional. The rational and emotional facets of the self, which are present in dynamic equilibrium, were described by the Enlightenment and Romanticism, respectively (Cupchik, 2002). The rational self is realistic, addressing needs and goals with practical planning. The emotional self is rich in experience and expression that feed our imagination. Societies can favor rationality over emotionality or vice-versa, and the same might be said for different individuals, some of whom are extremely logical whereas others are more emotional. Regardless of which viewpoint or mode one adopts, the multidimensional self hovers between continuity and discontinuity, between coherence and potential ego despair (Erikson, 1950).

The problem of continuity and discontinuity applies equally well to societies as a whole. The Middle Ages in Europe offered absolute continuity, at least for those absorbed in the Judeo-Christian view of a fixed world. But with the weakening of the Church during the Reformation and Counter-Reformation and the emergence of nation states along with the Industrial Revolution in the nineteenth century, the stable roles ascribed to people began to evaporate. The promise of an existential self, which faces dilemmas regarding the meaning of life and is defined by actions, appeared in realist novels of the early nineteenth century. Similarly, painters were in the forefront of this new individualism, liberating themselves from the constraints of classical imagery. Some went outdoors to paint "impressions" of "fleeting moments," artworks that, at first, were rejected by art critics and the Parisian bourgeoisie as too sketch-like and lacking in proper subject matter. Indeed, artists found themselves in a world filled with fleeting discontinuities, rushing faster and faster into twentieth-century "modernism," with its attendant fragmentation both of self and of art.

Charney (1995) has discussed this contrast between momentary sensations that absorb the individual and the onrushing discontinuities of modern life. He cited Georg Simmel's (1950) observation that modernity is characterized by "the rapid crowding of changing images, the sharp discontinuity in the grasp of a single glance, and the unexpectedness of onrushing sensations" (p. 410). Walter Benjamin (1969/1936) described modernity's impact that effected "a change in the structure of...experience" (p. 156) in late nineteenth-century Paris "in the direction of the momentary and fragmentary" (cited in Charney, 1995, p. 282). Benjamin saw "the experience of modernity as filled with anarchic juxtapositions, random encounters, multiple sensations, and uncontrollable meanings" (Charney, 1995, p. 283). This echoed Beaudelaire's account of the "fleeting quality of the instant" (Walsh, 2008): "By 'modernity' I mean the ephemeral, the fugitive, the contingent, the half of art whose other half is the eternal and immutable" (Beaudelaire, 1964, p. 37).

Celluloid film (which appeared around 1895) embodied this dilemma of continuity and discontinuity in a literal manner. The potential for discontinuity between frames is a metaphor for the challenges we face in trying to maintain a coherent sense of self in a rapidly changing society. The process of film creation, involving different ways for directors to frame the unfolding action and cobble together a montage of individual shots and frames, goes right to the heart of the continuity-discontinuity process. Walsh (2008) describes how Sergei Eisenstein used juxtaposed frames to shock audiences into searching for meaningful relations between them. Montage was similarly explored by Lev Kuleshov and Pudovkin (see Pudovkin, 1958) who juxtaposed a close-up of an actor, whose face showed no expression, with three different shots (a bowl of soup, a dead woman in a coffin, and a child playing) to see how audiences would be affected. Ferri (2007) interprets this process in relation to Iser's (1978) ideas about "blanks" in texts that stimulate a search for meaningful connection, and Bartlett (1932) referred to this process, generally speaking, as an "effort after meaning."

Walsh (2008) has contrasted the treatment of montage by Hollywood and the avant garde. Continuity is essential for "Hollywood" films, in which a problem is posed and the resolution unfolds with narrative continuity before a passively receptive audience. In *Aesthetics and Psychology in the Cinema*, Mitry (1997) lays out the foundations of continuity. In cinema, "space is presented...in its 'existential' entirety" and "setting is presented as a concrete reality" (p. 57). The structure of the film incorporates "dramatic composition" (i.e., represented reality) that is organized in space and time and "aesthetic" or "plastic composition" organized within the boundaries of the frame. The feeling of continuity across shots and sequences requires logical coherence in the script but is achieved through montage, when shots in a sequence are interrelated to lend meaning to the narrative. The film image that is "objectively present...like the mental image,...is the image of an absent reality, a past reality...." (p. 83). Indeed, it "serves as a substitute for reality in exactly the same way as the mental image when we dream" (p. 83). In this context, identification enables a person to imagine being involved "in an adventure experienced by someone else...as though I am *experiencing* it myself....*risk-free*...from which I can voluntarily withdraw..." (p. 86).

Hochberg and Brooks (1996) treated this experience of continuity within a cognitive framework based on expectations, hypotheses, and construal in accordance with structured plans. This emphasis on inferences about the unfolding narrative is analogous to visual exploration and related momentum. Bordwell (2006) has demonstrated a progression to shorter average shot lengths in Hollywood films since 1960, which Cutting, DeLong, and Nothelfer (2010) argue can facilitate attention to the film's narrative. Thus, the contrast between Mitry's phenomenological description of the process of cinematic engagement and Hochberg and Brooks' cognitive account, which treats film reception as an extension of everyday perception/cognition, recapitulates the differences between Romanticism's emotional and the Enlightenment's rational treatment of aesthetic experience, respectively.

Discontinuity is the principle of the avant garde, which chooses to pose shocking transitions (as did Kuleshov and Pudovkin) that force people to reflect on the meaning of the sudden juxtaposition. For Walter Benjamin, the sudden shock of change in film and in modern life reawakens the person to the present (Charney, 1995). Jean Epstein offered a similar viewpoint in the 1920s, when he coined the concept of "*photogenie*" as "fleeting fragments of experience that provide pleasure in ways that the viewer cannot describe verbally or rationalize cognitively" (Charney, 1995, p. 285). "*Photogenie* is for cinema what color is for painting, volume for sculpture" (cited in Charney, 1995, p. 285). Cinema is about movement, and *photogenie* "varies simultaneously in space and time" (Charney, 1995, p. 287), thereby providing pleasure and insight at the same moment.

Charney noted a parallel with Victor Shklovsky's (1988) description of "defamiliarization" in art, the goal of which is "to impart the sensation of things as they are perceived and not as they are known" (p. 20). This is the goal of film, according to Fredric Jameson (1972), "allowing us to be reborn to the world in its existential freshness and horror," (p. 51) and is what the early "cinema of attractions" tried to do (before 1908) by presenting viewers with brief and shocking images (e.g., of an elephant being electrocuted). Once films incorporated complete stories, such a visual "presence" could be elaborated to include an "effort after meaning" (Bartlett, 1932). As Charney (1995) quotes and translates Epstein, "Discontinuity became continuity only after penetrating the spectator. It is a purely interior phenomenon" (p. 293). This is precisely how Arnheim (1957) treated the film experience, as an unfolding gestalt wherein the principles of montage are synthesized within the viewer to create meanings and feelings.

The Cinematic Situation

Now we can see the challenge posed by this chapter, one that revolves around the problem of continuity and discontinuity in the self, society, and film. Here, the focus will be on the person's relation to film, with social factors in the background. This relationship has changed over the course of the twentieth century and into the twenty-first, in accordance with the shift between analog and digital film production, storage, and presentation. In the analog world, a film at least purports an imagined relation to everyday life, whereas, in the digital world, all manner of syncretic juxtapositions are available, and viewers, as "hyperspectators" (Cohen, 2001), have the freedom to manipulate the experience at will. A theoretical goal of this chapter is to characterize the changing "cinematic situation" (Mauerhofer, 1949) in which viewers relate to films during different eras and the effects of these changes on their experiences.

Changing experiences in the "cinematic situation" lie precisely within the province of psychology. Hugo Münsterberg's (1970) book, *The Photoplay: A Psychological Study*, emphasized the rational and active role played by viewers in their imaginative engagement with a silent, black-and-white 35mm screen. His implicit gestalt viewpoint holds that "the idea of motion is to a high degree the product of our own reaction. *Depth and movement alike come to us in the moving picture world, not as hard facts but as a mixture of fact and symbol. They are present and yet they are not in the things. We invest the impressions with them*" (p. 30). His goal was to describe the "entirely new mental life conditions" entailed in experiencing this new art form. Münsterberg used the term "photoplay" to refer to this unfolding visual depiction of theatrical events. Unique to this art form is the close-up, which "has objectified in our world perception our mental act of attention and by it has furnished art with a means which far transcends the power of any theater stage" (p. 38). And, in relation to memory, we have the unique "cut-back" (i.e., flashback) "as if reality has lost its own continuous connection and become shared by the demands of our soul" (p. 41). His main psychological and aesthetic principle holds that "the photoplay tells us the human story by overcoming the forms of the outer world, namely, space, time, and causality, and by adjusting the events to the forms of the inner world, namely attention, memory, imagination, and emotion" (p. 74). Photoplay enables "the free play of our mental experiences [to] reach complete isolation from the practical world through the perfect unity of plot and pictorial appearance" (p. 82).

By way of contrast, Swiss film scholar Hugo Mauerhofer (1949/1966) described the "cinematic situation" as a "modern *necessity*" with a "psychotherapeutical function" because it "makes life bearable for millions of people" (p. 234). In the post-World War II period, people were faced with harsh realities, and the cinematic experience enabled them to vicariously satisfy their longings and daydreams. Manohla Dargis (2011), writing in a *New York Times* article titled "Out There in the Dark, All Alone," noted that, in 1948, 90 million Americans went to the movies each week, and many more than that, one assumes, in Europe. Although Americans were not recovering from the material destructions of war, the threats still were fresh in their collective memories. I recall as a child in the 1950s attending popular war movies in the small French Canadian town where I lived. The genre remained with us for some time.

The cinematic situation offers "the most complete possible isolation from the outside world" (Mauerhofer, 1949/1966, p. 230) in which "no sources of light…except the screen itself" (p. 230) distract the viewer. In this "visual seclusion" (p. 230), the viewer's sense or experience of time and space is transformed. In the disjunction between cinematic time and mundane time, "the subjective impression is that time is passing more slowly," and this challenges the viewer with the potential experience of boredom and "creates a desire for *intensified action*" (p. 231) as embodied in "a concentrated form of film narrative" (p. 231). In a similar manner, the darkened room "causes objects to lose something of their distinct shape, thereby giving greater scope to imagination in interpreting the world around us" (p. 231), and this "partly removes the barrier between consciousness and the unconscious" (p. 231).

Mauerhofer (1949/1966), goes on to describe the "complete passivity and receptiveness" of the spectator such that there is a "psychological affinity between the *Cinematic Situation* and the state of sleep" (p. 232); films present us with "ready-made" dreams. The circumstance of "imminent boredom, intensified power of imagination and voluntary passivity, causes the unconscious to begin to communicate with the consciousness" so that the "whole arsenal of our repressions is sent in motion" (p. 232), including "our unfulfilled wishes and desires, our feelings of incomplete resignation, the daydreams which we do not or cannot realize" (p. 232). Thus, cinema provides "an unreal reality, half-way between everyday reality and the purely personal dream" (p. 232), one that changes "the entire state of mind of the cinema-goer," including "attitude, gait and gestures...for quite a while after leaving a cinema" (p. 233).

The shift from analog to digital consciousness and its embodiment in film implies a radical change in the "cinematic situation" and relations between viewer and film. Walsh (2008) underscores the fact that, in digital cinema, "the invisible intervals or cuts between images...are even less visible than they used to be" and this "forecloses on spaces of reflection emerging with moving image-repertoires" (p. 43). The "ever-increasing ability to consume and process images in an accelerated manner, in digital media the production of a continuous field of cuts has overridden the shock/critical reflection aspect of montage" (p. 43). Walsh cites Lev Manovich's (2001) notion of a "spatial montage narrative" in which the viewer becomes an editor "bringing to the forefront, one by one, numerous layers of looped actions that seem to be taking place all at once, a multitude of separate but co-existing realities" (Manovich, 2001, p. 320). Under these circumstances, simultaneity replaces succession, and the traditional notion of montage verges on becoming an anachronism. According to Walsh, time in the contemporary (i.e., digital age of electronic transmission) "no longer follows a linear order of successive moments, but has been taken over by technological metaphors" (p. 45). In contrast to Mauerhofer's romantic treatment of time, "In the contemporary mediascape, waiting and boredom are eradicated from dominant forms of the instant" (p. 49). Boredom plays a potentially important role in aesthetic experience; lying between past and future, it provides a locus for the viewer to "cultivate existence" (p. 49) and reflect on life.

Life in the digital age goes well beyond anarchic juxtapositions, random encounters, multiple sensations, and uncontrollable meanings. It also enters the world of hyper-*photogenie* in that fragments shaping experience lose reference to the mundane or material. The collage of fragments no longer appears to have boundaries. Theorizing about the nature of digital cinema addresses the very foundations of reference in language, touching in a romantic way on Martin Heidegger's treatment of the aesthetic. For Vivian Sobchack (2000), the digital morph effect defies perceived coherence and is paradoxically a "metaphysical object" in and of itself. Patrick Crogan (2000) cites the analysis by Samuel Weber (2000) of an "effect...that requires an audience to constitute it as an effect through their being affected by it" (p. 2). Crogan also cites Jim Collins's (1955) term "hypergeneric" film, which reflexively incorporates elements from various genres as part of its textual strategy to appeal to spectators.

The critical point here is that digital film abandons the traditional notion of reference that is present in analog film. The arbitrary relations to "things" that are represented requires that we rethink the very foundations of the "cinematic situation" in the new age of visual media. Although visual effects are the product of team efforts in the age of electronic transmission, the skilled viewer can recapitulate these efforts in the construction of image sequences that are meaningful to them. Ferri (2007) argues that we have entered a "*cyber* village" in which "The synergy between 'real' and 'virtual' space augments the presence of the film experience. The shadows of the film imagination are becoming deeper, clearer, and more colorful" (p. 67). The potential of the multisensory world of media to challenge the imagination lies at the heart of culture's aesthetic future.

Alain Cohen (2001) has proposed the concept of the "hyperspectator" since "the rise of new ways of viewing Hollywood films suggests the need for new mind models wherein the spectatorial subject actively helps to create the simulacra of 'virtual' Hollywood, as well as being created by it" (p. 152). The hyperspectator has access to all the materials that are stored and made available through the digitized hyperspace of bandwidth. These include "the must-films from the history of cinema, the sleepers, the epiphanic films unseen for lack of distributors, the cult films….the unavoidable mega-millions productions" (p. 159). Hyperspectators surf hyperfilms, "moving cross-referentially from film to film, from one director to another or from genre to genre, and into trans-national cinemas" (p. 161) as if they were hypertexts. This expresses the new freedom to create a lattice-work of film experiences in the comfort of home at a time of one's own choosing.

In essence, we see here a shift from the highly absorbed viewer in Mauerhofer's account of the 1940s "cinematic situation," to the more detached manipulator of hypertexts and hyperimages that rush by with ever increasing acceleration. In this new context, we find a dynamic equilibrium between Coleridge's "willing suspension of disbelief," which lies at the heart of aesthetic imagination, and the application of logical comparison that is central to everyday pragmatic cognition. The enhanced personal agency of viewers in the digital age enables them to construct hybridized images that are personally appealing. But we have to ask whether the abilities and heuristics of enhanced executive functioning produce only feelings of pleasure and excitement. The experience of deeper emotions requires an engagement with personal history and sensitivity to social context. This reconciliation of imagination and logic, of emotion and cognition, entails an ability to slow the digitization of mind in order to grasp the foundations of one's being.

When it comes to the "aesthetic situation," broadly defined, how is engagement with film different from viewing paintings or watching plays? First, it goes without saying that in all aesthetic media we find a dynamic balance between formal and expressive stylistic qualities. In paintings, there is the contrast in the Italian tradition between Florentine *desegno*, with its emphasis on highly structured composition, and Venetian *colore,* which implies the expressive use of color and texture. In theater, we find the contrast between an Enlightenment or Neoclassical emphasis on the choice of scenes, characters, and actions to manipulate the feelings of the audience and a Romanticist disposition to depict meaningful scenes from life in a concentrated manner (see Cupchik, 2002). In film, the linear and continuous unfolding of plot in accordance with a Hollywood model is contrasted with the use of montage for the purpose of shocking or surprising viewers into adopting fresh perspectives on life.

The theme of continuity relates to paintings, which can be understood as contrived out-takes from unfolding life episodes, either real or imagined. The interpretation of paintings is predicated on memory, in particular the recognition or recall of symbols, characters, and events; it is backward looking when it comes to time. To the extent that style is salient, these qualities of paintings can shape experiences in the moment. Thus, Impressionist or Pointillist brushstrokes make the viewer very aware of the surface of the artwork as an object in the here and now. When it is merged with the subject matter, atmosphere is created and an experience is molded. Theatrical plays take the problem of continuity one step further; they are very much in the present but imply the future, to the extent that scenes and acts unfold over time. The presence of actors in front of an audience cues realism because set and setting are treated in a symbolic and perfunctory manner.

Photoplays or films embody *photogenie* to the extent that they combine critical features of plays and artworks. On the one hand, they can present the unfolding narrative just as in a play, but with the luxury of flashbacks, parallel developments, and so forth. On the other hand, films have visual and acoustic salience, to the extent that they are presented on a large screen in a darkened room with surround sound. This sensory salience "transports" or absorbs the viewer into a virtual world wherein logic can be defied by the tricks of montage. In this sense, film, more than art or theater, affords the kinds of displacements and condensations characteristic of Freudian accounts of dreams. Films also imply a contrived simulation of everyday experience by drawing the viewer in with close-ups or affording aesthetic distance with panorama shots. In essence, we are invited to adopt the director's viewpoint as if we were present in the scene. All this is done *sotto voce* because we don't say to ourselves, "I am being drawn along by the director." Rather, we willingly suspend disbelief, as Coleridge would expect us to do. It is in this context that the needs and desires of audience members begin to match up with the qualities of the film and the intentions of the director.

The question then becomes: How do different aspects of the self interact or interface with different qualities of the film? To what depth of emotional processing does the viewer engage with the film? The contrast between feelings of excitement and pleasure, as opposed to emotions such as happiness, sadness, or fear, is central to our analysis. According to the *principle of affective covariation*, viewers will ride the surface of films that offer adventure and mere distraction in order to alleviate states of boredom or provide transient feelings of pleasure (see Cupchik, 2011a). The *principle of emotional absorption* holds that viewers will enter more profoundly into films that address unresolved and personally relevant emotional issues.

An Empirical Exploration of Film Reception

In this section, we introduce the relevant highlights of a study that examined relations between the self and experiences in the "cinematic situation." The changing nature of the self in the internet era was the topic of a recent lecture (Cupchik, 2010) and related publication (Cupchik, 2011b) that considered changes from an *analog self* during the Age of Mechanical Reproduction (Benjamin, 1969/1936) to the *digital self* during the Age of Electronic Transmission, in which viewers or audiences have much greater control over their media experiences. The analog self is seen as holistic, continuous, and deeply stratified, incorporating the meanings appropriate to particular stages of life. In relation to media experiences, the analog self is concerned with symbolic meaning and narrative coherence. By contrast, the digitized self is concrete, mechanistic, and compartmentalized, acting very much in the present to address transient needs. It is not constrained by personal history and can go anywhere in hyperspace, unencumbered by traditional values or meanings.

At least four dimensions of the self span the analog and digital ages: current (or actual) versus ideal, public versus private, implicit versus explicit, and engaged versus detached. The *current versus ideal self* contrast (Higgins, 1987) concerns how people perceive their current collections of skills or traits in comparison either with their own idealized state or preferred state favored by others. The *public versus private self* contrasts the "front room" in which people engage in self-presentation and impression management and the "back room" to which people can retreat, where they can relate quietly to themselves (Goffman, 1959). The contrast between an *engaged* versus a *detached* presence in social episodes relates to Bullough's (1912) treatment of "psychical" or aesthetic "distance" and his comparison between *under-* and *overdistancing*. Although people need to shift between being deeply absorbed in social situations or assessing them from an objective perspective, some might favor one over the other mode of engagement. The *implicit versus explicit* distinction contrasts qualities of the self that are nascent, personally relevant, and still in the process of being developed with qualities about which we are consciously aware.

A twenty-four item self-report survey was developed in an earlier study relating qualities of the self to internet usage that provided support for these four underlying dimensions (Amos, Cupchik, & Hilscher, 2012). The four primary factors are reviewed here. For Factor 1, *strong sense of self*, participants reported being everything they want to be; having a strong sense of self; saying exactly what they are thinking; and having confidence in their morals, identity, values, and capabilities. Factor 2, *uncertain sense of self*, involved individuals always trying to figure the self out, constantly thinking about their reasons for doing things, and questioning some aspects of the self. Factor 3, *actual self is not ideal*, represented a response in which participants said they often procrastinate but would like to learn how to use their time effectively, wanted to improve marks despite not yet having adjusted study skills, and felt they were careless with money but hope one day to live within their means. Factor 4, *private sense of self*, consists of three items: some aspects of the self are not shared with others, there is a preference for personal space when interacting, and the individual displays at times a highly self-critical attitude.

A survey with thirty-four items was developed to examine how participants responded to the "cinematic experience." Factor analysis disclosed thirteen factors that reveal the multidimensional nature of the "cinematic experience"; the ten main factors are reviewed here. Factor 1, *specialty downloader*, represented a combination of behaviors: Watching foreign films or films with subtitles, listening to the soundtracks from movies, and downloading movies. This resonates with the notion of the hyperspectator. Factor 2, *loses plot line*, contained: Often have difficulty following the movie's plot, tend to be detached when watching movies, and do not enjoy escapist or adventure movies. Factor 3, *social media commentator*, involved often commenting on movies using social media and believing it is very important to see movies when they are first released. This, too, is typical of audiences in the digital age of electronic transmission.

Revisiting narrative, the fourth factor, consisted of: Often watching movies on a personal laptop or handheld device, preferring movies with original plots over documentaries, and often rewatching movies. Factor 5, *personal reflection*, comprised: Enjoyment of films that promote personal reflection about one's life and a high level of agreement with the assertion that sometimes movies can put the viewer in touch with their unconscious. Factor 6, *style and dialogue*, involved a high degree of awareness of the cinematography in films and the view that the characters and dialogue (e.g., character's lines and narration) are important components of a film. Factor 7, *evaluating film versus advertisements*, involved deciding if one likes a film after it is over and strongly disliking ads at the beginning of a film. Factor 8, *realistic stars*, indicated a preference for realistic films featuring well-known actors. Factor 9, *controlling viewer*, characterized participants who often give up on a movie and want to control the movie-watching context; for instance, being able to pause the film and take a break when watching a film at home. Factor 10, *mood immersion* involved the view that a movie should match one's mood and be viewed in a darkened room, a view that extends Mauerhofer's ideas into the twenty-first century.

Correlations Among the Self and Film Factors

Three of the factors from the Self Survey were significantly correlated with factors derived from the Film Survey. Self Factor 1, *confident self*, correlated with Film Factor 3, *social media commentator* ($r = +.22$) and Film Factor 6, *style and dialogue* ($r = +.22$). Thus, students with a strong sense of self were prepared to comment on "just released" films and were tuned to the cinematography and dialogue.

Self Factor 3, *frustrated sense of self*, was negatively correlated with Film Factor 5, *personal reflection* ($r = -.36$) and positively correlated with Film Factor 10, *mood immersion* ($r = +.28$). Students experiencing frustration regarding control over their own lives prefer to avoid films that prompt reflection and deny that films can affect their unconscious (Film Factor 5). Instead, like Mauerhaufer's audiences, they want to sit in a darkened room and project their moods onto the cinematic situation (Film Factor 10).

Self Factor 4, *private self*, was positively correlated with Film Factor 7, *evaluating film versus advertisements* ($r = +.20$). Accordingly, participants who insist on maintaining personal space when interacting with others and keeping aspects of themselves private while sometimes being self critical take a longer time to decide whether they like a film, and they expressed a dislike for advertisements that precede films.

In summary, participants who displayed a *confident sense of self* and a *private sense of self* appeared to be quite "Enlightened" in their responses to films. They could become absorbed in films, appreciate their stylistic structure, and either express opinions readily or take time to formulate them. Participants who were *frustrated about aspects of their lives* expressed a more emotional and "Romantic" approach to film, feeling the tempo of films that matched their moods, which they preferred to watch in darkened spaces.

The Self in the Cinematic Situation

In this closing section, we integrate the theoretical ideas and empirical data relating aspects of the self to engagement in the "cinematic situation." The unifying idea is that common structural principles underlie changes in society, self, and the media. In the movement toward "modernism," technological and social changes accelerated over the past 200 years. With reference to the individual, we find the complementary development of personal agency to make choices, at least among Western European and North American people of means, occurring along with the potential fragmentation and related neuroses that result from finding oneself in a rapidly changing "everywhere now" world of communication (Zhao, 2005; 2006). At a cultural level, the shift from analog to digital technology expresses a shift from engagement in a world of continuous simulation (in representational art or narrative-based film) to the potential for syncretic combinations of media and meanings. As in the case of the Chinese logogram for "crisis," there is the complementary presence of both "opportunity" and "danger." However, in the midst of our rapidly changing world, we preserve the complementary relations between rationality and emotion that remain present in discourse since the Enlightenment and Romanticism of the eighteenth century. These two facets of our being, existential and organic, are central to our humanity and are perpetually in a dynamic flux. One question that we are struggling with concerns whether the change from an analog to a digital world is accompanied by a shift favoring rationality over emotion. By way of summary, examine the two columns in Table 6.1, which are not without paradoxes.

The first column displays critical concepts that might be related to the Enlightenment's rational approach to the world, whereas the second column incorporates concepts related to Romanticism's emotional and expressive approach to the world. The Enlightenment's pragmatic approach is oriented to accomplishing goals in a realistic manner, and this entails a logical comparison among choices. Feelings on the dimensions of pleasure-pain or arousal provide feedback about whether the choices helped to realize goals or led to frustration and failure. The Hollywood film offers an analog to this kind of life experience by providing a sense of continuity that enables a person to follow this simulation of life events. The goal of viewers is to get a sense for the unfolding narrative, in which events embody the world of action. In the process, they can identify with characters whose life experiences either approximate their own or fulfill their fantasies and desires. This kind of engaged experience is tied to the immediate and proximal world, which they accept as present before their eyes.

Romanticism offers a different treatment of the world, one in which imagination can accommodate seemingly contradictory or syncretic events and

Table 6.1 A Comparison of Critical Concepts

Enlightenment	Romanticism
Realism	Imagination
Logical	Syncretic
Comparison	Suspension of disbelief
Feelings	Emotions
Hollywood film	Avant garde cinema
Continuity	Discontinuous
Analog	Digital
Whole	Fragmented
See as	See That
World of action	World of Meaning
Identification	Transcendent—reflection
Proximal	Distal
Engaged	Detached
Localized	Everywhere at once

characters. This requires the temporary "suspension of disbelief," à la Coleridge, in order to accept represented events "as if" they were real. Avant garde cinema challenges the viewer by presenting discontinuities that do not fit with conventional "reality," and the digitizing process makes it possible to go beyond content to hybridized media, for example, by integrating film and cartoon, to create a new world. This prompts viewers to engage in an "effort after meaning" (Bartlett, 1932), which encourages reflection and a transcendent viewpoint. In this detached manner, they can adopt a distal perspective on the world and "see that" events occur for particular reasons in particular contexts. What began as an emotional encounter with the world transforms into an experience that encourages the person to find new meaning in life and the world or face existential fragmentation.

The findings relating the Self and Film Surveys fit quite nicely into the Enlightenment versus Romanticism or rational versus emotional framework. Participants who embodied a *confident* and *private sense* of *self* could become absorbed in films, appreciate their plot and stylistic structure, and either express opinions readily or take time to formulate them if they are more cautious. Participants who were more emotional and *frustrated about aspects of their lives* were sensitive to the tempo of films that matched their moods and preferred to watch films in darkened spaces. Thus, different aspects of the multidimensional self related to the "cinematic situation" in accordance with individual needs and dispositions.

This chapter explored diverse aspects of the self in relation to film. The continuities and discontinuities that reached across the individual frames of early films were consistent with a rapidly changing society and the challenge of fragmentation that individuals have faced since the late nineteenth century. The film as a medium offers Hollywood-style distraction, excitement, and pleasure for those in need of affect modulation. But it can also engage audiences in a search for meaning that addresses fundamental life issues and provides an opportunity to experience deep emotions and refresh one's soul with insight. As a situated experience, film can provide, in a darkened room, a sense of collective insulation from the challenges of life. The shift from analog to digital film reflects the enhanced personal agency that technology has afforded viewers in the late twentieth and early twenty-first centuries. There is a clear interplay between continuing efforts to enhance perceptual engagement by incorporating color, surround sound, three-dimensional experience, and so forth, and the detachment and metacognition that is afforded by handing control over to individuals sitting in front of computer screens in their homes.

References

Amos, J., Cupchik, G. C., & Hilscher, M. C. (2012). *The self and internet engagement.* (Unpublished manuscript). University of Toronto.

Arnheim R. (1957). *Film as Art.* Berkeley, CA: University of California Press.

Bartlett, F. C. (1932). *Remembering.* London: Cambridge University Press.

Beaudelaire, C. (1964). *The painter of modern life and other essays.* J. Mayne (Ed. and Trans.). London: Phaidon.

Benjamin, W. (1969). The work of art in the age of mechanical reproduction. H. Zohn (Trans.). In H. Arendt (Ed.), *Illuminations* (pp. 217–252). New York: Schocken Books. (Original work published 1936)

Bordwell, D. (2006). *The way Hollywood tells it.* Berkeley: University of California Press.

Bullough, E. (1912). 'Psychical distance' as a factor in art and as an aesthetic principle. *British Journal of Psychology,* 5, 87–98.

Charney, L. (1995). In a moment: Film and the philosophy of modernity. In L. Charney & V. R. Schwartz (Eds.), *Cinema and the invention of modern life* (pp. 279–294). Berkeley: University of California Press.

Cohen, A. J. J. (2001) Virtual Hollywood and the genealogy of its hyper-spectator. In M. Stokes & R. Maltby (Eds.), *Hollywood spectatorship. Changing perceptions of cinema audiences* (pp. 152–164). London: British Film Institute Publications.

Collins, J. (1995). *Architectures of excess: Cultural life in the information age.* New York: Routledge.

Crogan, P. (March, 2000). Things analog and digital. Special effects/Special affects: Technologies of the Screen Conference, University of Melbourne.

Cupchik, G. C. (2002). The evolution of psychical distance as an aesthetic concept. *Culture and Psychology, 8*(2), 155–188.

Cupchik, G. C. (August, 2010). *The digitized self in the age of the internet: What would Arnheim and McLuhan have to say about this?* Arnheim Award Address, American Psychological Association, San Diego, CA.

Cupchik, G. C. (2011a). Framing emotional responses to mass media. In K. Döveling, C. von Scheve, & E. Konijn (Eds.), *Handbook of emotion and mass media* (pp. 332–346). London: Routledge.

Cupchik, G. C. (2011b). The digitized self in the internet age. *Psychology of aesthetics, creativity, and the arts, 5*(4), 318–328.

Cutting, J. E., DeLong, J. E., & Nothelfer, C. E. (2010). Attention and the evolution of Hollywood film. *Psychological Science, 21*(3), 432–439.

Dargis, M. (2011). *Out there in the dark, all alone.* Retrieved from www.nytimes.com/2011/.../the-24-hour-movie-and-digital-technology.html

Erikson, E. H. (1950). *Childhood and society.* New York: Norton.

Ferri, A. J. (2007). *Willing suspension of disbelief: Poetic faith in film.* New York: Bowman and Littlefield.

Goffman, E. (1959). *The presentation of self in everyday life.* Garden City, NJ: Doubleday.

Higgins, E. T. (1987). Self-discrepancy: A theory relating self and affect. *Psychological Review, 94,* 319–340.

Hochberg, J., & Brooks, V. (1996). The perception of motion pictures. In E. C. Carterette & M. P. Friedman (Eds.), *Handbook of perception & cognition, Vol. 10: Cognitive ecology* (pp. 205–292). San Diego: Academic Press.

Iser, W. (1978). *The act of reading: A theory of aesthetic response.* Baltimore: John Hopkins University Press.

Jameson, F. (1972). *The prison-house of language.* Princeton, NJ: Princeton University Press.

Locke, J. (1997). *An essay concerning human understanding.* R. Woolhouse (Ed.). New York: Penguin Books. (Original work published 1690)

Manovich, L. (2001). *The language of new media.* Cambridge, MA: The MIT Press.

Mauerhofer, H. (1949/1966). Psychology of film experience. In R. D. MacCann (Ed.), *A montage of theories* (pp. 229–235). New York: Dutton.

Mitry, J. (1997). *The aesthetics and psychology of the cinema.* C. King (Trans.). Bloomington: University of Indiana Press. (Original work published in 1963)

Münsterberg, H. (1970). *The photoplay: A psychological study.* New York: Dover. (Original work published 1916)

Pudovkin, V. I. (1958). *Film technique and film acting.* London: Vision Press.

Shklovsky, V. (1988). Art as technique. In D. Lodge (Ed.), *Modern criticism and theory* (pp. 16–30). New York: Longman. (Original work published in 1917)

Simmel, G. (1950). The metropolis and mental life. H. H. Gerth (Trans.). In K. H. Wolff (Ed.), *The sociology of Georg Simmel* (pp. 409–424). New York: Free Press. (Original work published in 1903)

Sobchack, V. (2000). *Meta-Morphing: Visual transformation and the culture of quick change*. Minneapolis: University of Minnesota Press.

Walsh, M. (2008). The registration of the cinematic instant in film installation. *Spectator, 28*(2), 42–50.

Weber, S. (2000). *Special effects and theatricality*. Fourth Presidential Symposium of "Special Effects", Stanford University, February.

Zhao, S. (2005). The digital self: Through the looking glass of telecopresent others. *Symbolic interaction, 28*(3), 387–405.

Zhao, S. (2006). The internet and the transformation of the reality of everyday life: Toward a new analytic stance in sociology. *Sociological Inquiry, 76*(4), 458–474.

III THE PRODUCTION

7 THE PRODUCER–DIRECTOR DYAD

MANAGING THE FAULTLINE BETWEEN ART AND COMMERCE

Joris J. Ebbers, Nachoem M. Wijnberg, and Pawan V. Bhansing

The tension between art and commerce is a general feature of production in the cultural industries in general (Caves, 2000; Voss, Cable, & Voss, 2000) and of the film industry in particular (Delmestri, Montanari, & Usai, 2005; Holbrook & Addis, 2008). This is one reason why film production is of great interest from the perspective of social science and management theory. Another reason is the dominance of temporary organizational structures. Films—especially in the Netherlands—are predominantly produced by project-based organizations (PBOs), which can be defined as temporary organizations that dissolve as soon as the project is completed for which they were specifically set up (DeFillippi & Arthur, 1998; Starkey, Barnatt, & Tempest, 2000). These two features taken together have determined the basic shape of film production in the Netherlands.

Dealing with the tension between art and commerce is often handled by dividing primary responsibility for these two dimensions of performance among different individuals with different roles in each temporary PBO. Although the director is predominantly responsible for the artistic aspects of a film, the producer is predominantly responsible for the commercial aspects of a film. However, the division of authority between these key individuals is not always explicit or clear. Does the producer have a veto on decisions that will affect the budget during the production? Does the director have primary responsibility for recruiting and selecting other team members occupying artistic roles, such as the screenwriter or director of photography (DOP)?

Looking at these relations in a broader sense also means that one has to consider not just the single PBO, but also the group of people who regularly work together in a series of such PBOs. A *latent organization* is a form of organization that binds together "configurations of key actors in ongoing relationships that become active/manifest as and when projects demand" (Starkey et al., 2000, p. 299). Ebbers and Wijnberg (2009) presented evidence that precisely in the film industry these latent organizations, even though they only exist informally and on the basis of implicit and relational contracts, can be considered more "real" organizations from a management perspective than the temporary PBOs that do have a formal existence. Taking these longer term relations into account raises questions about the effects of stable and strong links among individuals, especially with respect to the core producer–director dyad. Does repeated collaboration between individuals occupying these two roles result in advantages or disadvantages with regard to the selection of team members or the efficient management of actual production?

Faultline theory (Bezrukova, Jehn, Zanutto, & Thatcher, 2009; Gibson & Vermeulen, 2003; Li & Hambrick, 2005) suggests that the most obvious and significant dichotomies among the members of groups or organizations can have a strong impact on the functioning of the group or organization as a whole. If the art versus commerce faultline is the most significant dichotomy in the organization of film production, then it makes sense to look closely at the specific roles that bridge this faultline: the producer–director dyad. This is especially relevant when this particular dyad can also be considered the dual executive team (Reid & Karambayya, 2009) of the project organization and of the latent organization. In general, the strongest ties are expected to arise between individuals who are most similar (McPherson, Smith-Lovin, & Cook, 2001), but in an organization, such as the latent organization that depends on relational contracts, the most essential ties might well be those that are most unlikely to arise and become strong. It is precisely these ties between dissimilar actors that constitute dyads that bridge the most important art versus commerce faultline in the organization.

For these reasons, this chapter focuses on the core dyad of director and producer. We show how and to what extent this dyad actually bridges the faultline between art and commerce. In addition, we focus on how the particular relationships between the members of this core dyad determine the performance of the PBO, as well as of the latent organization. We first briefly discuss PBOs, latent organizations, and faultline theory. Then, we consider how these theoretical approaches helps one to understand the practice of film production in temporary organizations. Next, we present data we collected in a series of interviews among Dutch directors and producers. Finally, we offer a brief conclusion.

Theory

Organizations, Project-Based Organizations, and Latent Organizations

The core insight of *transaction cost theory* is that firms exist because making use of markets to achieve specific results can be costly (Coase, 1937). The higher the costs of the market as a coordination mechanism, the more reason to incorporate transactions within the boundaries of the firm (Williamson, 1975). Large firms, however, also have important drawbacks, such as the principal–agent problem, which is related to internal coordination and monitoring of opportunistic behavior by employees (Alchian & Demsetz, 1972) and slow managerial decision-making processes that may hamper innovation (Thompson, 1965).

Partly to offset these two negative consequences of large bureaucratic organizations, flexible employment relations, the "boundary-less career," and looser contractual relationships between employers and employees have been on the rise (Arthur & Rousseau, 1996). Organizations want more flexible labor contracts so that they can react more quickly to uncertain market conditions and stay competitive and innovative. Short-term contractual labor relations are thought to be an important means to this end.

Arguably, the quintessential form of flexible organization is the PBO. A PBO can be defined as a temporary organization that ceases to exist as soon as the project, for which it was specifically set up, is completed (DeFillippi & Arthur, 1998; Jones, 1996; Starkey et al., 2000). The discontinuities inherent to PBOs, however, also bring high transaction costs (Williamson, 1981) that are involved in setting up this type of organization. For each project, one needs to search for members, negotiate contracts, and coordinate individual and collective actions. Short-lived and temporary organizations such as PBOs are less likely to develop more elaborate organizational structures to deal with multiple organizational objectives.

A way of dealing with these transaction costs in short-term PBOs is to form an informal organization by serially collaborating in a string of PBOs. Fundamental to these so-called latent organizations are long-term informal relationships between key professionals that become formal in temporary contracts for particular projects. By definition, latent organizations also lack formalized structures, just as they lack explicit and formal contracts. Instead, they can be considered to be governed by implicit and relational contracts (MacNeil, 1985;

Rousseau, 1990). These relational contracts are indissolubly linked to particular relationships, and the obligations and expectations that result from them are sustained by the value of the continuation of these relationships. Relational contracts allow for flexibility in dealing with unforeseen events, solidarity in problem solving, and openness in information sharing (Bull, 1987; Poppo & Zenger, 2002). The latent organization brings advantages that can remedy some of the problems of the PBO (Starkey et al., 2000). It provides the organizational continuity in which relational contracts and flexible rewarding can flourish.

Short-term PBOs are an especially common phenomenon in the cultural industries, such as the television (Starkey et al., 2000) and film industry (DeFillippi & Arthur, 1998; Jones, 1996; Starkey et al., 2000). In turn, the long-term latent organizations can be a way to solve contractual and behavioral difficulties in both the television (Starkey et al., 2000) and film industries. Ebbers and Wijnberg (2009) presented evidence that, especially in the film industry, these latent organizations, which only exist informally and on the basis of implicit and relational contracts, can be considered to be more real organizations than PBOs that have a formal existence.

Organizational Structure and Faultlines

Organizations are rarely, if ever, simple and homogenous. They often pursue many different activities and usually have many members who differ from one another along many dimensions. Moreover, there usually are many organizational objectives and ways to measure performance for each of them. At the same time, there are various means that can help organizations in dealing with all these multiplicities, such as the division of labor and designing a suitable organizational structure.

At a very basic level, it makes sense to distribute tasks among organizational members who are best suited to perform them. In larger organizations, this can lead to the establishment of functionally specialized departments, such as a research and development (R & D) department and a marketing department in an electronics manufacturer. Each of these departments then focuses on a particular range of activities, necessitating particular skills and capabilities and attracting employees with particular qualifications and orientations. In turn, this kind of departmental specialization can create new problems, precisely because this specialization can decrease the effectiveness of communication and decision making across departmental boundaries. This problem is often referred to as an *interface problem*. An example of an interface that has received much attention in the literature is the R & D versus marketing interface (Gupta, Raj, & Wilemon, 1986; Leenders & Wierenga, 2008).

Although grouping engineers in the R & D department and marketers in the marketing department can create interface problems, within each organizational unit there may also be differences between individuals. The tensions between different sets of objectives, orientations, or other personal characteristics can result in faultlines that have the potential to split the organization. Wherever there are groups, subgroups can be distinguished based on the presence or absence of particular characteristics within these groups. Even in the management team at the top of a large company, tension can exist between engineers on one side and people with a business science background on the other. These groups do not necessarily have to be formal groups, nor do they even need to be recognized as such by the involved actors. Lau and Murnighan (1998) introduced the term "faultlines" to describe the boundaries between two or more such subgroups. From an organizational perspective, these faultlines need to be monitored because the performance of the organization as a whole depends on how they are bridged and managed.

Much research has been done to study the effects of the existence of particular faultlines in groups or teams on collective performance (Bezrukova et al., 2009; Gibson & Vermeulen, 2003; Li & Hambrick, 2005). This stream of research has mostly focused on demographic attributes (Jehn, Chadwick, & Thatcher, 1997; Jehn, Northcraft, & Neale, 1999), but values (Bezrukova et al., 2009; Jehn, 1994; Probst, Carnevale, & Triandis, 1999) also have received attention as characteristics that can define faultlines. These group values denote the essential beliefs or orientations of individuals that are held in common in particular (sub-)groups and that determine the behavioral choices of these individuals. The more these group values differ between individuals on the two sides of the faultline, the more one can expect different decisions to be preferred by these individuals and the greater the potential for disunity and conflict at the intergroup or organizational level. Again, as briefly discussed earlier, a possible way to manage such faultlines is to create various departments in which particular group values are shared. The managerial problem then is transferred out of the groups or teams and toward the management of the organization as a whole.

In this chapter, we focus on one particular type of faultline, the artistic–commercial faultline, which is the one most readily apparent in the cultural industries in general and the film industry in particular. Given the importance of the tension between artistic and nonartistic or commercial objectives in the cultural industries, at first sight, it seems to make sense to have departmental specialization along those lines, with, on one side, those organizational members devoted to achieving artistic ends and, on the other, those members who have to ensure the economic success of the organization. Such organizations do exist, sometimes with the division going through all levels of the organization up to the artistic director and the commercial director, who jointly form the dual executive leadership (Reid & Karambayya, 2009).

Faultlines in Film Production and the Core Dyad

In cultural industries, one solution for dealing with the tension between artistic and nonartistic objectives is to have an artistic director and a business director leading the organization together. In fact, many authors (e.g., Caves, 2000; Holbrook & Addis, 2008) have pointed out that the dichotomy between artistic and nonartistic objectives is a major determinant of how organizations in the cultural industries behave. This suggests that, in the cultural industries, there may be a major faultline between artistic and nonartistic or commercial roles and objectives. In addition, this may imply that how this faultline runs through the organization and its parts, and how it is bridged and managed, could be a major factor in explaining organizational performance. In the film industry, this dichotomy is clearly identifiable. The director usually has the main responsibility for artistic matters, whereas the producer is responsible for the business side of filmmaking. These two roles can also be seen to reflect the dual leadership of film projects.

Although Hollywood in the first half of the twentieth century was characterized by the dominance of large, centralized, and vertically integrated organizations, the film industry in the past decades has become an example of a strongly decentralized industry. Films are most often produced by a group of independent firms and freelancers that are contracted to supply the resources needed in a project organization that is disbanded immediately after the film is completed. Currently, a career in the film industry—and in neighboring ones, such as television—is therefore a succession of temporary projects that result in a collection of film credits. It differs from a long career at one or a couple of firms, in which one is aiming for a progression through the ranks by internal promotions (Faulkner & Anderson, 1987).

The benefits of hierarchy in the old Hollywood studio system was that both producers and directors were tied to the studio with long-term contracts, and disagreements could be settled at a higher hierarchical level. An important side effect of the replacement of the old studios by a succession of PBOs is the increased difficulty in managing the dichotomy between art and commerce and the different objectives of producers and directors because projects are temporary and organizations are disbanded after completion of the film. Moreover, the artistic versus commercial success of films may have a different impact on the careers of producers and directors. On the one hand, the evaluation criteria for a producer's career are mainly related to the commercial success or potential of the films in which they participated. On the other hand, directors' careers may be more driven by their artistic performance, especially in terms of the awards that they have won.

Homophily denotes the phenomenon that contacts between similar people occur at a higher rate than do contacts among people who are dissimilar (McPherson et al., 2001). In general, it is assumed that being close in this sense will make it easier for ties to be established (Lazarsfeld & Merton, 1978). Just as network ties arise most easily between similar actors, it can be expected that relational contracts will come more easily into existence and are more likely to effectively govern relations between individuals when they are more similar to each other. At the same time, this argument suggests that precisely in such an informal organization—in which ties between similar individuals arise relatively easily—the most essential ingredients to organizational longevity and performance are the relationships between individuals who are *not* similar. This provides an argument for focusing on those relationships that seem to bridge the most important faultline.

The members of latent organizations include a wide variety of professionals involved in film projects, and links and relationships can exist between subgroups of any size. It has been suggested, however, that special attention be paid to dyadic relationships. Baker and Faulkner (1991) focused on dyads or collaborative pairs occurring among three roles: producer, director, and scriptwriter. They showed that, in the past, it was not unlikely that the roles of producer and director were combined in a single person. Thus, the faultline between art and commerce was bridged by pooling these diverging interests and responsibilities in a single individual. However, over time, there has been a trend toward specialization in the producer role and a clear division between commercial and artistic domains, with the former being occupied by the producer and the latter by the director or scriptwriter (Baker & Faulkner, 1991).

Other studies on network relations, such as that by Sorenson and Waguespack (2006), included vertical relations between the producer and distributor. Since both are mainly concerned with the business aspects of film projects, this can be classified as the core commercial dyad in film production. An important part of the study by Ferriani et al. (2005) focused on dyadic relations between the director and each of the other members of what Goldman (1983) regards as the core team of director, DOP, editor, production designer, and composer. All these dyads can be classified as artistic dyads in the film production process. Thus, none of these dyads crosses the faultline between art and commerce.

In this study, we focus on the producer–director dyad. As we indicated already, producers and directors are considered to represent the artistic and commercial poles in the project. From script development and preparations in preproduction, the actual shoot in the production phase, to postproduction activities such as editing, producers and directors are also often involved in the project for a longer time than any of the other actors. Of the mixed dyads of commercial and artistic roles, we would therefore expect the greatest benefits to result from these producer–director dyads because the artistic goal of the director wanting to build a reputation based on artistic performance can potentially be hindered by the producer's goal of keeping within budget and making a profit (Alvarez & Svejenova, 2002).

Directors may enhance their reputation by receiving awards (or nominations) for their contributions to films that lose money (DeFillippi & Arthur, 1998), whereas such results could at the same time be detrimental to the producer's reputation and scare off investors in future projects. A strong and stable producer–director dyad will help to even out these diverging artistic versus nonartistic goals and is therefore more likely to form the core of a stable latent organization. Moreover, to the extent that there are "managerial" relations within PBOs, it is the roles of producer and director that provide management, and, if they are perceived to form a stable dyad, other individuals will more readily accept instructions from either one of them. Finally, as we already suggested, the producer–director dyad constitutes the relationship that is least likely to be brought about and strengthened by the forces of homophily. Strong ties are less likely to form in this faultline-bridging dyad and, precisely because of this, the strength of this tie is potentially essential to a latent organization that depends on relational contracts.

In the next section, we present data about film production in the Netherlands, based on interviews with producers and directors. The case study will be structured along four main themes: (1) the division of roles and responsibilities among producers and directors, (2) the functioning of the producer–director dyad in selecting other members of the PBO, (3) the benefits of a stable producer–director dyad, and (4) the liabilities of a stable producer–director dyad.

Case Study

The following case study is built around quotes from semistructured face-to-face interviews that were conducted with producers and directors in 2007 and 2008. We interviewed a total of twenty-four producers and fourteen directors who were selected from the population of producers and directors involved in the production of feature films released in the previous 10 years. All producers were either (co-)owner or chief executive officer of production companies. Most of these production companies were also involved in the production of television drama, in some cases commercials, and, in rare cases, theater plays. We performed roughly 90-minute interviews that were tape-recorded and subsequently typed out verbatim. Finally, all informants were granted anonymity in the reporting of results.

Roles and Responsibilities

Roles and Responsibilities of Directors and Producers

Whereas the producer's predominant role and responsibility is concerned with finding adequate financial capital, managing contracts, guarding the budget, and scheduling and organizing the production process, the director's predominant role and responsibility is concerned with the ultimate look and feel of the film. Although some directors see a clear division of responsibilities, for example "producers provide the entire logistics and, as a director, you have a vision of what you want to achieve" (Director H), others have a broader view of the producer's role: "There are people that view a producer as a completely different person that is only concerned with financial matters. That financial part might be her specialty, but the substantive choices about what the film should be about and what it should look like, these are things we do together.... At the moment we are casting for my new film. At those moments, we talk simultaneously about whether an actress is bankable or capable of attracting a large audience. To me, that is just as crucial as that actress being a very interesting person who makes the film very different from a content perspective" (Director L).

Roles and Responsibility for Artistic Success

Because of their different roles and responsibilities and their different opinions as to the exact division and/or overlap between them, directors and producers may also be expected to have different opinions as to whom they eventually hold responsible for either artistic or commercial success. A first important indicator of tension across the faultline between art and commerce could therefore be disagreement between directors and producers about who is responsible for artistic or commercial success. In our interviews, we asked producers and directors in which order they hold their fellow project members responsible for either the artistic or commercial success of a film. In addition to the role of producer and director, we used a list of key team members, including the roles of scriptwriter, cast members, cameraman or DOP, editor, composer, and distributor. Tables 7.1 and 7.2 describe the extent to which producers and directors disagree with respect to responsibilities for artistic and commercial success.

Both producers and directors agree that the director has the key responsibility for the eventual artistic success of a film project. The view of producers

Table 7.1 Order of Responsibility for Artistic Success
According to Producers and Directors

Roles	Producer	Director	P—D
Director	1	1	=
Producer	2	5	−3
Scriptwriter	3	2	+1
Cast	4	4	=
Camera (DOP)	5	3	+2
Editor	6	6	=
Composer	7	7	=
Distributor	8	8	=

is summarized very well in this quote from a producer: "The director is ultimately most responsible for the artistic achievements of films. All the others on the [film] set of course also have a responsibility, but the director has the final responsibility" (Producer U). This view is confirmed by directors. "The director has ultimate creative responsibility for the film. For everything the DOP or composer does, I am ultimately responsible" (Director B). After the film has been completed, the role of the producer is to vie for broader artistic recognition at film festivals: "Later on the producer is the one who brings the film to the attention of [film] festivals and the like…A producer plays a very large role in this" (Director H).

In the first column of Table 7.1 we see listed the roles of the core members of a film project. The second column shows the order of responsibility as an average in the opinion of producers. The third column shows the same for directors. The

Table 7.2 Order of Responsibility for Commercial
Success According to Producers and Directors

Roles	Producer	Director	P—D
Producer	1	2	−1
Director	2	4	−2
Distributor	3	1	·+2
Scriptwriter	4	5	−1
Cast	5	3	+2
Editor	6	7	−1
Composer	7	8	−1
Camera (DOP)	8	6	+2

final column shows the difference in opinion between producers and directors as to the order of responsibility for the artistic success of a film. With respect to the coding, we should note that if a respondent gave the same score for two or more roles, each was coded as the average of these scores. For example, if a producer held the director and producer equally responsible, both would score a 1.5 (average of 1 and 2). Roles to which respondents did not assign a responsibility score were coded as the average of the remaining scores for each of them. For example, if a director held the editor, composer, and distributor equally least responsible, each was coded as a 7 (average of 6, 7, and 8).

Table 7.1 shows that producers and directors have a shared understanding about the artistic responsibility of the director, cast, editor, composer, and distributor. There is some disagreement (–3) however, with respect to the responsibility of the producer. Whereas producers see themselves as the second most responsible: "In my opinion the producer is actually just as important for artistic success as the director" (Producer V), directors place them at number 5. Part of this might be explained by the fact that even though a producer's direct influence on the artistic merits of a film could be limited, in the end, they are responsible for having green-lighted the film project in the first place. This is very well reflected in the following quote: "Being a producer, it [artistic failure] is always your fault. In that case, you just shouldn't have hired those people" (Producer H). There is a slight disagreement with respect to the scriptwriter (+1), but this might be related to the previous point. Finally, it should be noted that directors value the artistic input of the DOP/cameraman much more than the producer does (+2).

Roles and Responsibility for Commercial Success

Commercial success in the film industry is very difficult to predict. This could also explain why there is considerable disagreement between producers and directors about who is most responsible for commercial success (Table 7.2). To a certain extent, this is also a matter of choice because films channeled into art house releases, with lower anticipated revenues, can cross over to become big commercial successes, as a result of artistic acclaim at prestigious film festivals, for example. "It is generally very difficult to determine who is responsible for commercial success. It also depends on whether it was supposed to be a commercial success from the start or not. It is possible that originally a film was not intended to be a commercial film, but afterward became one, and vice versa" (Director F).

Producers and directors nearly agree that the producer has the prime responsibility for the commercial success of a film (–1). To put it simply: "The buck stops here" (Producer C). Producers, however, hold directors much more responsible for commercial success than the directors do themselves. There is a fair gap between the two (−2). This also depends on who takes the initiative in setting up a new film project in the first place. "When you, as a producer, ask a writer to write a script and, subsequently, you hire a director, then of course you as a producer are responsible. But here in the Netherlands, it is not unusual for directors or writers to approach you with a script" (Producer N). In addition, although producers do not hold a scriptwriter responsible for commercial success (because it is a producer's decision to greenlight the script), they do hold directors responsible for how the script is turned into a film: "It may be that a writer delivers a brilliant script. But it can be completely ruined by the director" (Producer I).

Although—according to directors and producers—distributors do not play a role in a film's artistic success, they do play quite an important role in the commercial success of a film. The distributor's role and responsibility is marketing the film, determining the size of the release in terms of number of prints that will be distributed to film theaters, and making deals with these film theater owners about sharing the revenues. "The producer and I come with a film and then the distributor must cash it in. We put the ball on the spot, and he should score" (Director B). But at the same time a distributor "cannot turn a [bad] film into a success…and alternatively, they can screw up by targeting the wrong audience, bad publicity, lack of marketing, and giving a small film a big release and vice versa" (Producer C).

Interestingly enough, there is considerable disagreement between producers and directors as to the degree to which they hold distributors responsible. Directors hold distributors more responsible for commercial success than do producers (+2). "The distributor should be at the top, because if he determines that the film is released in 100 copies, then at least 50,000 people will go and see the film. Rather, if a film is released with only six copies, no one will see that film" (Director A). However, it is very difficult to determine who is responsible for commercial success because it all adds up. "I think that if the same film was made by a director who made it a lesser film—to put it bluntly—that because of the casting and the way it is promoted by the producer and distributor, the first blow would have been the same. The first 300,000 visitors would come just the same. This would be the result of [good] promotion, casting, genre, and marketing. But, after that, the film should be on its own legs. If the film is not good, it will stop after 300,000 visitors.… So, in some cases, I think the most important factor for the commercial success of the film is the director. But, on the other hand, if the same film would not have been marketed that well, there wouldn't have been a lot of visitors to start with" (Director M).

The previous quote already hints at the importance of cast members (in terms of the lead actor and/or actress) for commercial success. As you can see, there is considerable disagreement as to the bankability or value of cast members in attracting a large audience. Some producers believe that cast members have star power that can aid in turning a film into a commercial success. "We are now making a film with [actor]. This film you have to market completely around [actor]. You have to offer something in return because his name is worth money" (Producer A). Part of the contract states that cast members are also required to promote the film in the press to build publicity. "Actors and directors, since it is written in their contracts, know that they must cooperate with regard to press, promotion, and publicity" (Producer I). Some producers also believe that, in addition to the cast, certain well-known directors can also draw an audience: "It is about the director who is known from this or that film and the bankability of the cast" (Producer D). Nevertheless, in general, producers seem to agree that, in the Netherlands, cast members are not bankable. "In the Netherlands, people do not go to the films because it features a certain actor" (Producer G).

The Producer–Director Dyad and Project Team Selection

Producers and Directors in the Team Selection Process

The previous section makes clear that there can be disagreement between directors and producers as to which other team members they hold responsible for artistic and commercial success. With respect to both artistic and commercial success, directors rate the input of the DOP much higher than producers do. In addition, directors also hold distributors and cast members much more responsible than producers do. Although eventual—commercial even more than artistic—success is difficult to predict and therefore difficult to attribute to individuals, one might expect that this disagreement between producers and directors could manifest itself in the selection process of other individual team members for each film project.

The division between artistic and commercial roles and responsibilities and the possible faultline between the two is neatly summarized by the following quote: "In my opinion, the director, editor, and composer are stacked together and the producer, distributor, and cast are stacked together" (Producer I). As we saw earlier, the director is mainly responsible for the artistic look and feel of a film and is also ultimately responsible for the work of the other artistic team members, such as the editor, DOP, and composer. One would therefore expect that the director has the strongest voice in the selection of these team members. Conversely, the producer is predominantly responsible for the business aspects of the film. Since distributors and, to some extent, cast members can play an important role in attaining commercial success, one would expect that the producer has a strong voice in the selection of these team members.

However, who precisely has the strongest voice, the director or producer, also depends on who had the original idea or initiated a particular film project. As we already briefly mentioned, it is not uncommon for directors to approach a producer either with an idea or a script that they may even have written themselves. "It really depends. Sometimes it is the director, sometimes the writer, and sometimes the producer. Sometimes the director is also the writer. Sometimes I come up with a plan and I hire a writer to work on it" (Producer B). Naturally, the one who owns the intellectual property overall has a stronger voice in team selection. "If the producer is the initiator, then he will have a greater say in the selection of the cast and crew. If I myself, or together with a scriptwriter, initiate a project and subsequently approach a producer, I will be in a much stronger position" (Director J).

In general, however, there are no specific contractual agreements between producers and directors in which they demand specific individuals to be part of the team. "I don't have anything written down about which specific individuals I want to work with, but that I do have a voice in it. The producer cannot force me to work with someone I do not want to work with. There are no specific names in it [the contract], but it does state that we should agree" (Director E). This is confirmed by producers. "That's often what you and the director determine together. You both need to be able to work with that person. When either of the two really does not see it work, you should not do it. Then you get a forced collaboration and that never works" (Producer A). Although there are no upfront contractual obligations that determine team selection, and directors and producers both need to agree on who is to join, in practice, either the producer or the director has a dominant voice in relations to specific roles.

Dominance of Directors Versus Producers in the Team Selection Process

Apart from the roles of producer and director, the roles of other professionals involved in a film project also come with specific tasks and responsibilities that, in turn, shape the particular relations between each of them and the members of the core dyad. In what follows, we focus on the same roles discussed in the previous sections (Tables 7.1 and 7.2. Since each film is a unique project that may require very specific skills and resources, the selection process for team members is also partly determined by the nature of the project at hand. The film's specific genre, for example, may influence the selection of team members: "Sometimes you have a specific editor for each project. A certain editor is better in drama than in comedy or suspense" (Director H). In addition, the choice of whether the film is intended to be an art house film or a mainstream film will also influence the selection of team members. "The composer has a great deal of influence on the feel of a film. Just by listening to the music, you can already hear whether something is art house or mainstream and... [being a DOP] you need to know what kind of film you're shooting. For example, if you are shooting a commercial film, then the film needs to get the look that it deserves" (Director F).

Although the specific choice may depend on the nature of the film project, directors have the dominant voice in selecting the film crew for the main creative roles. After asking directors which are the most important artistic roles in addition to those of director and scriptwriter, directors confirm that "you can see some roles as purely creative: the DOP, composer, and editor" (Director M). When asking directors, with respect to the selection process, in which roles their voice is dominant, it is clear that this is especially the case with respect to precisely these three key creative roles. This is highlighted by the following quotes: "I am very loyal. For example, I nearly almost work with the same DOP and composer.... I always try to work with the same editor, but that is not always possible" (Director N). "I have two [DOPs] that I like to work with, it will be difficult for me to collaborate with a third. It should preferably be someone I know and previously worked with. There are a few options. The choice of one of these two depends on the style of the film" (Director F). "The editor is almost always my choice. I make a choice and they say 'OK.' That is also a good thing because it's my regular editor" (Director M).

Both the key creative roles and the dominant influence of the director in their selection—except to some extent for the composer—are largely acknowledged by producers in the following quotes. "A cameraman, editor, and composer are very crucial in determining the style and form. I select them for each specific project depending on its style. I will first see which persons I know myself, but the director has his preferences as well" (Producer J). Another producer confirms this: "You do have preferences, but it all depends on what type of film it is, who the director is.... It may be that it is all tied to the director" (Producer A). "In the case of DOPs... we usually follow the preferences of the director. This also applies to the editor. The composers we search together with the director" (Producer G). "It often depends on the director. I know that if I work with this particular director, I get this editor.... People know that they often work together" (Producer A).

The producer is especially dominant in the selection of the film distributor. This is perfectly illustrated by the following quote from a producer: "Before we start with the actual film shoot, we already have close contact with the distributor. We do this because we think that it is important that the relationship between the producer and distributor is properly coordinated. In this respect, we are unlike many other producers. Many producers make a film and pass the baton to the distributor when the film is finished. The distributor generally runs a great risk with a film and, in order to reduce the risks, the distributor may give a film a small release. That means limited marketing and few copies. So this becomes a kind of self-fulfilling prophesy. For us, it is important that, in an early stage and in consultation with the distributor, we determine the target audience, how that audience will be reached, and what the marketing strategy will look like. If, as a producer and distributor, you determine the marketing strategy at an early stage, the risk to the distributor will be a lot smaller. We also often collaborate with the same distributor, as a result of which you are better able to coordinate the collaboration" (Producer U).

This quote shows that whereas the dominance of the director in the selection process is based on strong ties with artistic members of the film project, the dominance of the producer is in many cases the result of strong ties with the other main commercial party involved in the film project: the film distributor. The director is hardly ever involved with the distributor. "I do not interfere with the selection of a distributor, that's a producer issue" (Director E). Even if they wanted to, it is very difficult for directors to influence the relation between the producer and distributor. "In a possible future project [with the same producer], I would prefer a different distributor, but there's a special bond between this producer and distributor, so I do not think that I will be able to make that happen. That is something where the producer's voice is more important than mine" (Director F).

Conflicts Between Producers and Directors in the Selection Process

The influence of the producer in the selection process becomes more important, however, when the director's choice of team members interferes with the producer's commercial interests. "The vote of the producer is especially decisive where important financial interests are at stake. As long as this is not the case, there will not be any tampering with the artistic integrity of the director" (Director D). However: "Sometimes they [selection criteria] indeed diverge. This obviously has to do with money or preference or antipathies of a producer" (Director E). Producers need to strike a balance between the skills of prospective team members and the price they have to pay for them. "In most cases, it is the average between the person capabilities, isn't he too expensive, and doesn't he demand too much" (Director A).

An important conflict between producers and directors revolves around the selection process of cast members or lead actors and actresses. "Producers will always meddle with the [selection of] cast members. Commercial considerations of the producer in the choice of key cast members can cause friction" (Director F). Although a number of directors and producers doubt the existence of star power in the Netherlands, an important reason why producers may have a strong preference for certain cast members is that their bankability—or capability to draw an audience to the cinemas—will help them to persuade investors or distributors to invest in their project. "Sometimes it is easier to convince a distributor when you say that you have certain actors or actresses in the film" (Producer J). Especially in mainstream (as opposed to art house) film projects, it is not unlikely that the selection decision may switch to the commercial side of the art–commerce faultline because it is, to a considerable degree, determined by the commercial producer–distributor dyad. "It may be that the distributor says 'take this or that lead actor, because it makes it easier for me to design a [marketing] campaign.' So he does sort of have an influence on the choice of actors" (Producer N). Although directors can refuse to work with certain cast members, they do discuss the selection with the producer at length. "If a film is to be a commercial success, this is a matter for the producer and me together. You talk about it constantly; the kind of actors that you cast. It is important that you monitor the genre or type of film" (Director E).

The Influence of Loyalty and Past Collaborations on the Selection Process

In addition to differences in taste between the producer and director and the cost of contracting certain team members, relations based on past collaboration also play an important role in team selection processes. "As a producer, you can't tie people [to your organization] with a permanent contract. You don't have the money for that. Moreover, the director also has his own friends that he is trying to smuggle in" (Producer K).

On the one hand, these preferences for professionals one has worked with in the past may simply be a matter of familiarity or trust. "Naturally, in certain cases it is more pleasant to work with people that you know. You know what you have both in terms of personality and quality" (Producer B). As we saw earlier, producers and directors tend to be quite loyal and have built their own networks of professionals they like to work with. Naturally, they will try to get these individuals on their team. "You have your own network with many people in [different] departments you regularly work with that you want to try to advise to your director" (Producer B). Both producers and directors, however, see the risk involved when the team members of a film project are too loyal to the other party. "Producers generally find it scary when the crew originates too much from the personal sphere of the director because it means that they [the producers] have less control" (Director B).

On the other hand, however, past collaboration can lead to varying degrees of obligations and expectations toward particular professionals that may influence the selection process. In the (Dutch) film industry, there is often a lack of money and when financial resources are tight loyalty can become important. "it [loyalty] is also financial. I have made many small films where there was not much money. Much of the people who participated in these [small productions] also did very big things [productions]" (Director F). Producers also engage in this form of informal cross-subsidization between projects. "When I ask someone to work for less, I can't do it again the next time. I feel that I have an obligation to ensure that person must be compensated with a next project. It happens very often that you ask people to work for less than normal, but as a producer this creates obligations for the next project" (Producer J).

Effects of the Stability of the Producer–Director Dyad

Long-Term Relations and Producer–Director Dyads

As discussed earlier, we are especially interested in the producer–director dyad since this is the most important dyad from a management perspective. The stability of this dyad or the degree of loyalty between producer and director varies quite a lot. "Some directors are loyal, but others are not. The last group wanders from producer to producer" (Producer O). Some directors are highly skeptical about loyalty and distrust the intentions of producers. "It's a business relation. There is no other relation. It has been a long time ago since I last fell for pleas for so-called loyalty: 'Do something for us now for the good cause' and things like that. I always demand money. There is no loyalty" (Director G). Alternatively, there are also producers who question the loyalty and commitment of directors and other crew members: "We are not tied to anything because people have things running with six other producers. They have many irons in the fire.... There is a lot of shopping around among screenwriters and directors" (Producer D).

On the basis of our interviews with producers, we found that 21 percent of the production companies had both producers and directors as shareholders. From the interviews with directors, we know that 14 percent of them indicated that they were joint shareholder in a production company. In general, however, there are no formal long-term contractual relations between producers and key creative individuals, such as directors or scriptwriters. Often, this is not simply the result of opportunism, but due to the high uncertainty that characterizes the film industry. Since it is very difficult to predict the success of films, it is also very difficult to finance (especially independent) film productions. In addition, and possibly as a result, most film production companies are very small and have little stability or continuity that would allow them to be able to offer long-term employment contracts to key creative individuals. The average Dutch film production company has only 4.25 full time employees (FTEs), of which 1.5 are its owners.

Although many producers would like to offer long-term contracts to key creative individuals, such as directors and scriptwriters, they say they cannot afford to because of the high risks involved. "You try to build a long-term relationship with people you're satisfied with. But because being a producer you have so little financial elbow room, you can't offer anyone anything. I can't say: come and work for us for 2 years" (Producer G). Although highly uncommon, the same producer gives an example of a long-term contract that he made with a specific director. "I did once offer [Director E] a salary for a certain period of time, whether we had work for him or not, because we really wanted to do a project with him, and did not want him to go to another producer" (Producer G). It is more common for producers to tie in a specific director by offering a series of projects on an individual contract basis. "In the meantime, they kept me occupied and on standby in case [film] would get greenlighted. I did not have a contract, but they always tried to let me do a number of [television] series in order to keep me tied to their firm" (Director E).

Although formal long-term employment contracts are uncommon, the majority of producers prefer stable long-term relations with freelancers. "We have no permanent employees. You naturally reestablish contact when the previous collaboration was successful.... This is not something that is written down in contracts" (Producer N). Since success is difficult to predict in the film industry, some producers even continue a relation when the previous project was not successful. "You also build significant joint experience. That's important, even if things go wrong. I prefer a company where it goes wrong once and where it goes well the next time instead of having to work with an uncertain factor every time" (Producer R). Producers are especially keen on building relationships with directors and scriptwriters who—in their view—are the key individuals in film production. Producers consider them the heart of their firms, even though they are freelancers. "The important thing as a [production] company is to tie directors and screenwriters to your company. This allows you to get a certain profile as to the type of films that you make, and it also determines your image as a producer. Those people should be the heart of your business. You try to build some form of relationship with them in order to keep them tied" (Producer J).

Directors generally also prefer to collaborate with a small number of producers. In addition to those directors who are joint shareholders in a production company, there is also the director who works exclusively for a single producer without any contractual obligations to do so. "I'm not even sure whether this is written down in a contract, but in principle I am not setting up relationships with other producers. This is an important thing because almost nobody else does this.... After my graduation, I was immediately picked up by the producer with whom I still work. I therefore tied myself to this producer, but it is completely informal. Any day, we can say: 'we go and work with someone else,' but it is a very strong partnership.... We have very often thought about starting a firm together, but then you really need to have the same goals. My goal is to make my own films and not those of others, so I don't want to spend too much time developing other people's projects" (Director L).

The majority of directors prefer to collaborate with a limited number of producers. "I have a preference for a close cooperation with one or a few producers" (Director M). This is especially the case when the director is also the writer of his or her own script (so-called hyphenates). They often develop these ideas for scripts in close collaboration with a producer. "I've always been independent, but since 2 years I have a verbal agreement with [producer A]. This means that I offer all my new plans for films to them first. If they are not interested, I will go to another producer" (Director A). The following director is known in the industry for shopping around for the best deals with any production company, but he also indicates a preference for a stable relation. "At the moment, I am not tied to any [production] company, but that is likely to change in the future.... I want to do this because I have the idea that there are very interesting things happening in the world when, at some point, a director and producer become a tandem" (Director F).

Benefits of Stable Producer–Director Dyad During Selection

Producers and directors who have strong ties are more likely to trust each other in the selection process of the other project team members. This is confirmed by the following two directors. "If you have already worked with someone before, there will be more trust and everything [in the selection process] will be easier. You have to get to know each other" (Director E). Producers may also be more inclined to hire a project team member for which a director has a strong preference, even though this person may be more expensive than the producer was initially willing to spend: "You have to be able to trust that someone [a producer] can really take into consideration both the costs and the benefits. That you spend your money on people who might be a bit expensive, but at the same time, do deliver excellent work, and that, on other fronts, you can cut some costs" (Director H).

A stable relation between producers and directors makes contract negotiations easier. This is especially important for producers since they are the ones who have to guard the budget. "These people grow with our company. It also means that you can reward flexibility. They work for us for the amount that is available in the budget. Depending on the size of the budget, this amount is sometimes higher and sometimes lower. This means that we do not need to have complex negotiations because they trust us to reward them within the possibilities of the budget. It also offers us the possibility to even out payments over successive projects" (Producer U). Moreover, a director may also act as a go-between between the producer and other potential team members during contract negotiations. "I have the role of good cop, in the sense that I can explain to one department that another department gets even less. Ultimately, in the phase that the money is being distributed, everyone doesn't just want money for himself in terms of salary, but also for his department to do things with. They want the best for the film, but this is not always possible. In these matters, I have a soothing effect. I provide each of them with information. This is really a kind of good cop bad cop idea" (Director L). The following director phrases it slightly differently: "If I already know in advance from the producer how much money is available, then I could potentially approach these people using my charm and say: Would you rather not do it? Can't you do it for a bit less? It would be so nice to work together again" (Director K).

In addition, the flexibility of a producer in the selection process is constrained by the director's network of past collaborations and vice-versa. Directors as well as producers often have a few individuals for each role that they prefer to work with. One of the producers states that: "if there are twenty roles on a [film] set, we always have a preference for three or four [people]. That means we have a pool of eighty, a solid club of eighty, from which we choose. This is the pool that we like to work with" (Producer C). However, the selection of the project team to a large extent depends on the director. "You build [a team] around the directors you choose" (Producer S). In addition to the fact that a stable producer–director dyad leads to more trust, it also makes the selection process considerably easier because their networks of past collaborations overlap. "Because of trust and past experience, it becomes easier to build a crew since you are already very much [fishing] in the same pond. They [producers] often work with the same people with whom I work" (Director M).

Finally, these overlapping networks are valuable to producers since directors are more inclined to work with people from their own network, and it allows them to offer crew members deals for a package of projects at a discount. "You can provide someone with work for a long period at a discount" (Producer E). For example, with respect to DOPs: "If you know that a DOP will be doing two projects in a row with you, you can bundle the negotiations for the two projects. A deal of 40 days for us is cheaper than two separate deals of 20 days" (Producer K). The following director acknowledges this: "Especially when you have a long-term relation, the producer will try to push his own people. He wants you to build a long-term collaboration with them" (Director B). Although the benefits of a stable producer–director dyad are valuable in the selection of team members, they are arguably even more important during the actual shooting of the film.

Benefits of Stable Producer–Director Dyad During Production

For producers, it is crucial to be able to exert a certain degree of control over the team shooting the film. "The team that is shooting the film is very important. You have to monitor this well, otherwise things can easily get out of hand.... If you do not have much control over a film, also from an artistic view it does not make much sense for me to make a film" (Producer Q). Directors, however, run the risk of having to compromise their artistic vision because producers cut the supply of money during the shoot. "In [film] for example, we produced under conditions that I did not want. At one point, we agreed among all heads of department: we will keep it fun, but clearly this it is not the project that we had in mind anymore. [The budget] was increasingly being cut and scraped in ways we had not anticipated. At that point, you have the choice to either quit or to continue. It the latter case, you have to accept that it [the film] will become somewhat less good" (Director E). In situations like this, there is a risk to the producer that the director will rally the crew against him or her. However, when there is a long-term relationship with a producer, directors "won't stir up the crew against the producer" (Director H) and "will be more inclined to give the producer the benefit of the doubt" (Director J).

Especially during the actual shooting, it is important to have a mutual understanding of the need to balance the commercial objectives of the production department and the artistic objectives of those on the film set. It is important "that there is not a relationship of us against the production [department], or us and the people who always say: 'we don't have money for that.' I always want a quadrangle between the executive producer, director, DOP, and the first assistant director. These four people must feel that they are a team and agree with respect to all three aspects: what is financially possible, what is practically feasible, and what are our wishes with respect to the content—all four of them have to believe that these three things are equally important, rather than 'I just want this and you just find out how you manage this financially.' These people are not welcome. It also shows respect for each role, and respect that you believe that everyone only wants one thing and that is to make a beautiful film, and not pocketing a lot of money, exploiting people, or not feeling like exploring alternatives, but just saying that 'something cannot be done,' or only dreaming of the most beautiful shots. But, just as well, I do not want to judge a director in terms of: 'But you always think the sky is the limit'" (Producer X).

In cases in which there is a stable producer–director dyad, it is easier to deal with these inherent conflicts between producers and directors, which can easily be exacerbated by the many contingencies that characterize film shoots. "A director who has the long-term relationship with a producer in mind will have more eye for the balance between artistic feasibility, financial feasibility, and practical feasibility from a production perspective. You're no good to me when you as a director think that nothing has anything to do with you, except the content of the film" (Producer X). This is confirmed by the following director: "Discussions are more to the point: What are we going to do and how are we going to do it within the boundaries of time and the financial resources that are available? What choices do we make? Which scenes are important? It is more about brainstorming and discussion rather than conflict" (Director N). Another director adds that "the more you talk about things, the more they [producers] tell you what they are doing, the more I can influence that, and the more it is just an open, transparent, and organic whole rather than you being suddenly confronted with all kinds of issues" (Director F). It also means that producers can more safely challenge directors, and it works the other way around: "If a producer knows that you have a long-term relation with one another, he will take more risks in being critical without running the risk that the director will go to a different producer. The more stable the collaboration, the more critical he can be towards me" (Director B).

Stable producer–director dyads can either be formal and based on long-term contractual relations that exceed the individual project, or they can be informal, based on serial collaboration in successive projects.

First, when producers and directors are joint shareholders in a film production company, conflicts between commerce and art can be settled at the firm level. "The advantage in our company is that we all have experience in directing and producing. This is an advantage because we can settle the conflicting interests of the director and producer internally. As a director, you have certain demands and wishes, but at the same time, you know that as a producer you need to keep an eye on proportionality. So as a director, I correct myself as it were.... You avoid all sorts of problems because you know the implications in advance" (Producer/director U).

Second, however, stable producer–director dyads are, in most cases, informal relations based on serial collaboration in successive project organizations. The same producer/director continues: "You often see that certain directors often work with certain producers. Then it is very similar to what happens within our company. In that case, all those forces have been given a place. You are doing the same thing and you feel at ease with one another. The challenge is to avoid a split in the team" (Producer/director U). Or, in the words of a director: "you become a bit of a co-producer, and the producer becomes a bit of a co-director. So you operate as a team" (Director K).

Liabilities of a Stable Producer–Director Dyad

In the previous section, we focused on the benefits of stable relations between producers and directors. In this last section, we briefly discuss some of the liabilities of stable producer–director dyads.

Most of these liabilities are related to producers or directors becoming overly dependent on each other. Usually, this is a more serious problem for directors because they are generally involved in fewer projects than are producers. "A disadvantage [of a stable relation] is that they [producers] lose confidence in our collaboration and suddenly see much more opportunities for collaboration with others than I do. The difference between a producer and director, among other things, is that most producers are involved in several projects in a year while I can technically do not much more than one project per year" (Director M). Another director shares that: "I want to spread my collaborations with producers. I do not want all my projects to be with one producer, I find this too risky. At any moment, in the heat of the battle, your work relationship can come under pressure. You'll get the most stupid problems, like having to buy back your own projects from producers who want to see money for them" (Director D).

In addition to becoming too dependent on a single producer, directors also simply miss out on other valuable opportunities with other producers. Loyalty may become problematic when "you are acting so loyal that you do not seize particular opportunities with other producers. Of course, it is true that expectations will grow: 'why are you suddenly [working] with someone else?'" (Director C). According to the following producer, it is especially inexperienced directors who run the risk of being loyal to only a single producer. "Directors are naïve when they are young…they are willing to commit to a single producer without any contract…. Most directors discover after 2 or 3 years that they must spread their attention" (Producer K).

Some producers also encourage directors to spread their risks because of the uncertain nature of the industry; they cannot offer them a stable supply of work. "I always tell directors that they need to have several irons in the fire, and therefore also need to do projects with other producers. They know that I would offer them a permanent contract if I could afford to. I encourage them to also get involved in other projects. I have had so many people crying here at this table who had freed up their agenda and turned down a number of projects and don't know what to do anymore. I can't guarantee anyone that there will be a new film coming up" (Producer X).

In addition to overreliance on a single source of work, it is also difficult for directors to negotiate a higher remuneration when they have a stable relation with a producer. First, producers know what they earned in past projects and use that as a benchmark. "When you work with the same producer, it is also problematic to suddenly ask for substantially more money. I can do this more easily when I start working with another producer. With respect to remuneration and negotiation about the terms of your contract, it is easier and better to work with several producers. The competition among producers works in my favor, which means that I can demand more on all fronts" (Director E). Second, directors may more easily take salary cuts because of budgetary issues. "It's tricky because I am also sort of part of the company, and therefore tend to think too much in line with the producer, while my agent says: 'you have to go for your full pay because the money has been made available because of you,' then I tend to say 'yes, but I know because of information that, if I do that, it will be difficult to make the film.' In those situations, I am inclined not to do it, not to demand the maximum because this could mean that I run the risk of the project not going through" (Director B).

Finally, the film industry is a creative one and therefore depends on a fresh flow of new ideas that can often result from new encounters with other film professionals. This is something that both directors and producers mention on several occasions. "It is always good to work with several teams. Otherwise, you will get stuck in routines and it's always good to see how other people do certain things. It also keeps you fresh. It provides you with new ideas" (Producer G). "It [the relation] can become worn and therefore it is good to renew. You're too easy on one another.... A new person can also excite you and give you a whole new view. They can also involve you in things that the other person kept you out of and you knew nothing about" (Director J).

Conclusion

There is broad evidence of continuity or repeat collaboration in the film industry (Delmestri et al., 2005; Ferriani, et al., 2005), and it has been proposed to look at these groups of serially collaborating individuals as members of so-called latent organizations (Starkey et al., 2000). In the case presented here, we specifically focused on how the core dyad of producer and director functions to manage the tensions generated by the artistic–commercial faultline. Whereas the producer's predominant role and responsibility is concerned with finding adequate financial capital, managing contracts, guarding the budget, and scheduling and organizing the production process, the director's predominant role and responsibility is concerned with the ultimate look and feel of the film. Precisely because the individuals fulfilling these two roles are at different sides of the faultline, the link between them bridges it.

We took a closer look at the actual division of roles and responsibilities among producers and directors, and we particularly focused on how the dyad operated in selecting other members of the team. Next, we looked at the advantages and disadvantages of a stable producer–director dyad as perceived by producers and directors. The responses of producers and directors show that they do see their roles as being mainly on one or the other side of the faultline. At the same time, they may have different estimates of the other team members' importance for artistic or commercial results. This can lead to further differences of opinion with regard to the selection of other team members. The producers and directors recognized the importance of a stable and strong link between them. Although some potential disadvantages were clearly noted—staleness, lack of flexibility— longer term close collaboration has great importance in managing the dual objectives of film production, to the benefit of the performance of the PBO, as well as of the latent organization.

Acknowledgments

This research has been made possible with the help of the Netherlands Organisation for Scientific Research—Nederlandse Organisatie voor Wetenschappelijke Onderzoek (NWO)—under grant number 400-07-160.

References

Alchian, A., & Demsetz, H. (1972). Production, information costs, and economic organization. *American Economic Review, 62*(5), 777–795.

Alvarez, J. L., & Svejenova, S. (2002). Symbiotic careers in movie making: Pedro and Agustm Almodovar. In M. Peiperl, M. Arthur, R. Goffee, & N. Anand (Eds.), *Career creativity: explorations in the remaking of work* (pp. 183–208). Oxford: Oxford University Press.

Arthur, M. B., & Rousseau, D. M. (1996). *The boundaryless career: A new employment principle for a new organizational era.* Oxford: Oxford University Press.

Baker, W. E., & Faulkner, R. R. (1991). Role as a resource in the Hollywood film industry. *American Journal of Sociology, 97*(2), 279–309.

Bezrukova, K., Jehn, K. A., Zanutto, E. L., & Thatcher, S. M. B. (2009). Do workgroup faultlines help or hurt? A moderated model of faultlines, team identification, and group performance. *Organization Science, 20*(1), 35–50.

Bull, C. (1987). The existence of self-enforcing implicit contracts. *Quarterly Journal of Economics, 102,* 147–159.

Caves, R. E. (2000). *Creative industries contracts between art and commerce.* Cambridge, MA: Harvard University Press.

Coase, R. H. (1937). The nature of the firm. *Economica, 4*(16), 386–405.

DeFillippi, R. J., & Arthur, M. B. (1998). Paradox in project-based enterprise: The case of film making. *California Management Review, 40*(2), 1–15.

Delmestri, G., Montanari, F., & Usai, A. (2005). Reputation and strength of ties in predicting commercial success and artistic merit of independents in the Italian feature film industry. *Journal of Management Studies, 42*(5), 975–1002.

Ebbers, J. J., & Wijnberg, N. M. (2009). Latent organizations in the film industry: Contracts, rewards and resources. *Human Relations, 62*(7), 987–1009.

Faulkner, R. R., & Anderson, A. B. (1987). Short-term projects and emergent careers: Evidence from Hollywood. *American Journal of Sociology, 92*(4), 879–909.

Ferriani, S., Corrado, R., & Boschetti, C. (2005). Organizational learning under organizational impermanence: Collaborative ties in film project firms. *Journal of Management and Governance, 9*(3-4), 257–285.

Gibson, C., & Vermeulen, F. (2003). A healthy divide: Subgroups as a stimulus for team learning behavior. *Administrative Science Quarterly, 48*, 202–239.

Goldman, W. (1983). *Adventures in the screen trade.* New York: Scribner.

Gupta, A. K., Raj, S. P., & Wilemon, D. (1986). A model for studying R&D. Marketing interface in the product innovation process. *Journal of Marketing, 50*(2), 7–17.

Holbrook, M. B., & Addis, M. (2008). Art versus commerce in the movie industry: A two-path model of motion-picture success. *Journal of Cultural Economics, 32*(2), 87–107.

Jehn, K. A. (1994). Enhancing effectiveness: An investigation of advantages and disadvantages of value-based intragroup conflict. *International Journal of Conflict Management, 5*(3), 223–238.

Jehn, K. A., Chadwick, C., & Thatcher, S. M. B. (1997). To agree or not to agree: The effects of value congruence, individual demographic dissimilarity, and conflict on workgroup outcomes. *International Journal of Conflict Management, 8*(4), 287–305.

Jehn, K. A., Northcraft, G. B., & Neale, M. A. (1999). Why differences make a difference: A field study of diversity, conflict, and performance in workgroups. *Administrative Science Quarterly, 44*(4), 741–763.

Jones, C. (1996). Careers in project networks: The case of the film industry. In M. B. Arthur & D. M. Rousseau (Eds.), *The boundaryless career: A new employment principle for a new organizational era* (pp. 58–75). New York: Oxford University Press.

Lau, D. C., & Murnighan, K. (1998). Demographic diversity and faultlines: The compositional dynamics of organizational groups. *Academy of Management Review, 23*(2), 325–340.

Lazarsfeld, P. F., & Merton, R. K. (1978). Friendship as a social process: A substantive and methodological analysis. In M. Berger, T. Abel, & C. H. Page (Eds.), *Freedom and control in modern society* (pp. 18–66). New York: Octagon Books.

Leenders, M. A. A. M., & Wierenga, B. (2008). The effect of the marketing–R&D interface on new product performance: The critical role of resources and scope. *International Journal of Research in Marketing, 25*(1), 56–68.

Li, J., & Hambrick, D. C. (2005). Factional groups: A new vantage on demographic faultlines, conflict, and disintegration in work teams. *Academy of Management Journal, 48*(5), 794–813.

MacNeil, I. R. (1985). Relational contract: What we do and do not know. *Wisconsin Law Review,3,* 483–525.

McPherson, M., Smith-Lovin, L., & Cook, J. M. (2001). Birds of a feather: Homophily in social networks. *Annual Review of Sociology, 27,* 415–444.

Poppo, L., & Zenger, T. (2002). Do formal contracts and relational governance function as substitutes or complements? *Strategic Management Journal,23*(8), 707–725.

Probst, T. M., Carnevale, P. J., & Triandis, H. C. (1999). Cultural values in intergroup and single-group social dilemmas. *Organizational Behavior and Human Decision Processes, 77*(3), 171–191.

Reid, W., & Karambayya, R. (2009). Impact of dual executive leadership dynamics in creative organizations. *Human Relations, 62*(7), 1073–1112.

Rousseau, D. M. (1990). New hire perceptions of their own and their employer's obligations: A study of psychological contracts. *Journal of Organizational Behavior, 11*(5), 389–400.

Sorenson, O., & Waguespack, D. (2006). Social structure and exchange: Self-confirming dynamics in Hollywood. *Administrative Science Quarterly, 51*(4), 560–589.

Starkey, K., Barnatt, C., & Tempest, S. (2000). Beyond networks and hierarchies: Latent organizations in the UK television industry. *Organization Science, 11*(3), 299–305.

Thompson, V. A. (1965). Bureaucracy and innovation. *Administrative Science Quarterly, 10*(1), 1–20.

Voss, G. B., Cable, D. M., & Voss, Z. G. (2000). Linking organizational values to relationships with external constituents: A study of nonprofit professional theatres. *Organization Science, 11*(3), 330–347.

Williamson, O. E. (1975). *Market and hierarchies: Antitrust implications.* New York: Free Press.

Williamson, O. E. (1981). The economics of organization: The transaction cost approach. *American Journal of Sociology, 87*(3), 548–577.

8

NETWORKS AND REWARDS AMONG HOLLYWOOD ARTISTS

EVIDENCE FOR A SOCIAL STRUCTURAL ORDERING OF CREATIVITY

Gino Cattani and Simone Ferriani

Organizational research on individual creativity has expanded rapidly in the past decade. Initially focused on the individual traits presumed to affect creativity (Sternberg, 1985; Tardif & Sternberg, 1988), over the years, this research has concentrated more squarely on the role of social interactions and social facets of the environment (Amabile, 1988; Glynn, 1996; Woodman, Sawyer, & Griffin, 1993). Building on social psychologists' key idea "that the creative individual be placed within a network of interpersonal relationships" (Simonton, 1984, p. 1273), organizational scholars interested in the social side of creativity recently have begun to incorporate social network concepts into their models and explanations of the determinants of individual creativity to gain deeper understanding of how creative work is generated (Burt, 2004; Perry-Smith & Shalley, 2003; Uzzi & Spiro, 2005).

These studies have shown how the adoption of a social network perspective is fruitful in informing creativity literature and thus enhancing our understanding of creativity at work. Yet, by focusing mainly on structural explanations of creativity, this research has left largely underexplored another key dimension of creativity: the need for field legitimation; that is, the process by which the new and unaccepted is rendered valid and accepted through field consensus (Johnson, Dowd, & Ridgeway, 2006; Zelditch, 2001). We seek to fill this gap by integrating established sociological perspectives on creativity that emphasize how creativity is embedded in networks of social relationships and support (Csikszentmihályi, 1994; 1996; Uzzi & Spiro, 2005) with recent research on legitimacy that uses an audience–candidate interface framework (Cattani, Ferriani, Negro, & Perretti, 2008; Zuckerman, 1999; Zuckerman, Kim, Ukanwa, & von Rittman, 2003). The framework that we advance explains audiences' (henceforth *evaluators*) rewarding of candidates' (henceforth *agents*) creative work as a function of candidates' positioning within the social structure of their field, as well as of the type of audience under consideration. In particular, we suggest that evaluators who are industry peers—that is, members who occupy the same social position within the field as the agents they evaluate and therefore may compete for the same material and symbolic resources—tend to reproduce dominant social beliefs and norms. As a result, they are more likely to grant recognition to agents who are "core" rather than "peripheral" members of the network. This sociostructural ordering of creativity, whereby disproportionate benefits accrue to highly embedded agents, makes it especially hard for peripheral agents to gain peer evaluators' attention, thus reducing the chance that their creative work will be legitimated. By accentuating inequalities in status, resources, and opportunities between core and peripheral agents, a sociostructural ordering of creativity resonates with the so-called "Matthew effect" in science, which shows how recognition for scientific work tends to be skewed in favor of established scientists (Merton, 1968).

We explore these ideas within the context of the Hollywood motion picture industry, which we traced over the period 1992–2004. This industry provides an ideal context for testing the implications from our theoretical framework. First, the industry has long embraced arrangements featuring flexible and short-term relationships that rely on enduring networks, in which mutual trust and reputations have been cemented over time (Faulkner & Anderson, 1987). Second, the industry grants systematic recognition to its members for their creative achievements through a large number of organizations that bestow awards on those seen as having made significant contributions to the field (Gemser, Leenders, & Wijnberg, 2008; Simonton, 2004a). In particular, in this study, we consider industry "peers" as the focal audience of evaluators. Third, creativity is central to the film production process since each movie is a unique product whose completion requires the sustained collaboration of several individuals (Simonton, 2004b).

Social Structure and Rewards

The relationship between institutional norms and standards and how creativity becomes manifest is central to our explanation of why and how we should expect evaluators' attributions of creativity to map onto the social networks of the field.

In this chapter, we refer in particular to the degree of sociostructural embeddedness because agents who are deeply embedded in their social system are more likely to conform to those norms that characterize their area of expertise and thus reproduce ideas or styles currently deemed acceptable. As Jones and colleagues (1997, p. 929) pointed out: "The more structurally embedded (e.g., the more connected and frequently interacting) the industry participants, the more deeply they share their values, assumptions and role understandings." Strong structural embeddedness also makes deviance from existing norms and standards harder to hide and, therefore, more likely to be punished (Granovetter, 1985). In contrast, agents who are less deeply embedded and not subject to such strong assimilative pressures are freer to pursue divergent ideas (White, 1993).

The core–periphery imagery provides an intuitive and evocative illustration of this sociostructural trade-off between demands for conformity and freedom to diverge (Cattani & Ferriani, 2008). Insofar as individual agents remain peripheral to their social field, they can more easily attend to fresh new ideas, knowledge, and perspectives without the anxiety of clashing with the field's accepted rules (Perry-Smith & Shalley, 2003)—which in turn results in radically new solutions (i.e., technologies, theories, practices, etc.) often being pioneered at the fringe or periphery of a given social field (Leblebici, Salancik, Copay, & King, 1991). For instance, the famous abstract Italian painter Giorgio Morandi once said: "When most Italian artists of my generation were afraid to be too 'modern' or 'international' and not 'national' or 'imperial' enough, I was left in peace, perhaps because I demanded so little recognition. In the eyes of the Grand Inquisitors of Italian art, I remained but a provincial professor of etching at the Fine Arts Academy of Bologna" (quoted in Kramer, 1981). However, insulation from conformity pressures also means that peripheral agents are likely to suffer a legitimacy denial due to their departure from evaluators' normative expectations and standards. In addition, peripheral agents usually have only limited ability to mobilize attention from within their own field. As Collins (2004, p. 436) noted, "a peripheral position condemns one to coming too late into the sophisticated centre of the action." As individual agents progress toward the core and thereby become more embedded within the field's social structure, deviant ideas are foreclosed and adherence to the field's institutionalized norms and standards is increasingly stimulated and even rewarded. But proximity to the core also implies greater leverage to elicit attention from relevant evaluators. Thus, not only are core agents more likely to produce work that adheres to norms and standards that reflect evaluators' beliefs and preferences, but they also have superior access to the material and symbolic resources they need to further their work.

Following these arguments, it is plausible to expect evaluators to exhibit a systematic tendency to favor core players relative to peripheral ones when relinquishing symbolic and material resources. This prediction appears especially warranted insofar as evaluators have strong, uniform incentives to enforce established norms and standards of evaluation and thereby preserve the institutional logics of their field. For example, this is likely the case when evaluators are peers from the same community.[1] In fact, peer evaluators are likely not only to have vested interests in preserving the status quo but also to use their influence to protect it. Sociologists of art and science have provided extensive evidence about peer resistance (Merton, 1968; White & White, 1965). As an example of this dynamic, consider the French Academy of Fine Arts (Académie des Beaux Arts) in the nineteenth century. The French Academy assessed artwork and rewarded artists based on the evaluation of gatekeepers who were members of the Academy. Success in the system depended on receiving recognition from the Academy. In theory, the artist's work was evaluated objectively; in practice, the gatekeepers increasingly attempted to maintain their own power and that of their followers. As a result, artists associated with Academy members were more likely to win awards. Over the years, the members of the Academy took turns obtaining symbolic rewards for their own students, thus effectively assuring the continuity of the Academy's orthodoxy (White & White, 1965).

In science, medical specialists have a long history of resisting inventions from what they define as "the outside": Pasteur, for instance, faced violent resistance from contemporary medical specialists when he advanced his germ theory. He regretted that he was not a medical specialist, whom he felt regarded himself as a "mere" chemist poaching on their scientific preserves and thus not worthy of their attention (Olmsted & Fulton, 2008). In addition, when evaluators are peers, agents who are positioned at the core of a given field's social structure are more likely to share particular cognitive and social networks with them, resulting in a strong bias toward work emanating from the core. This effect has been documented in academic evaluation systems, in which evaluators are typically established scholars who inevitably "have students, colleagues, and friends with whom they share what is often a fairly small cognitive universe and they are frequently asked to adjudicate the work of individuals with whom they have only a few degrees of separation.... Evaluators [therefore] often favour their own type of research while being firmly committed to rewarding the strongest proposal" (Lamont, 2009, p. 8).

The previous arguments suggest the existence of a socially structured ordering of creativity whereby a disproportionate amount of symbolic and material resources accrue to those at the core of the social field. They point, in other words, to a misallocation of recognition as predicated by the notion of cumulative advantage and disadvantage, known in science as "the Matthew effect" —the tendency for eminent scientists to receive disproportionate credit for their work compared to comparable scientific contributions by relatively unknown scientists

(Merton, 1968). This perspective echoes Collins's (1998, p. 61) concern: "Are we dealing only with fame, not with creativity itself?" Collins effectively questions why many creative individuals were "buried in obscurity" because they never received credit for their works: "This is a powerful image because it sustains most of us intellectuals, who rarely get the credit we think we deserve" (1998, p. 61).

Although the Matthew effect implies the existence of a social stratification in science that translates into a de facto hierarchical structure based on reputation (whereby eminent scientists stay at the top of the "pyramid" and unknown ones at its bottom), the distinction between core and peripheral agents instead depends on their degree of embeddedness within the social field and hence the extent to which they tend to conform, as well as their ability to leverage social network resources to enhance visibility. In light of the previous considerations, we thus argue that evaluators who are industry peers tend to reproduce dominant social beliefs and norms and hence are more likely to grant recognition to core as opposed to peripheral members of a given field's the social network.

Setting and Data

Our analysis is situated within the context of the Hollywood film industry. This is a very promising setting in which to study the relationship among social structure, peers' evaluation, and rewards for creativity. First, as we noted before, creativity is central to the film production process since each movie is a unique product that requires the collaborative work of cast and crew members. These diverse contributions are both so individualized in terms of their specialization, and so essential to a movie's success, that special honors (e.g., the Academy Awards) have been established to recognize those contributors whose work is judged to be noteworthy in each specialty (Simonton, 2004b). Thus, this is an industry that allows us to study simultaneously the peers who evaluate and the individual agents who compete with one another for their approval. In this industry context, the results of these evaluations are made (very) public every year through the conferring of prestigious awards that celebrate outstanding cinematic achievements, which establish a level of social validation in the field unachievable by other means (Cattani & Ferriani, 2008; Simonton, 2004a; 2004b).

Our data consist of the population of crew and cast members (hereafter "professionals") who worked on at least one of the 2,297 movies distributed in the United States by the eight major studios—that is, the seven historical majors plus the more recently founded (1994) Dreamworks—and their various subsidiaries over the 12-year period from 1992 to 2004. We collected information on the composition of the production team of each movie in the sample, as well as the level of recognition their creative work on each movie had gained by recording the awards and nominations each profession-al's work had received from several award-granting organizations. Although movie making is essentially a collaborative venture—the list of "credits" at the close of any movie shows the wealth of individuals who contribute their creative input, unique talents, and technical expertise to each project—only a very restricted group of people is normally credited (in terms of awards) with the critical creative work. Our analysis focused on the following set of profes-sionals: producer, director, writer, leading actor/actress, editor, cinematogra-pher, production designer, and composer. Using the Internet Movie Database (IMDB), we then identified 12,679 of these "critical creators" as distributed across these eight roles in the movies in our dataset.

Finally, to unveil the sociorelational fabric of the industry, we analyzed the bipartite affiliation network between professionals and movies. An *affiliation net-work* is a network of vertices connected by common group memberships as in proj-ects, teams, or organizations. We thus constructed networks of film professionals in which a link between any two professionals indicates collaboration on the making of a movie. In the global network, professionals are directly connected to each other when they worked on the same movie project and indirectly connected when they are linked through at least one professional who worked on two or more movies. The affiliation network was therefore created starting from an individual-by-movie matrix X where $x_{ij} = 1$ if the ith individual participated in making the jth movie, and $x_{ij} = 0$ otherwise. We then multiplied matrix X and its transpose X', whose ijth cell indicates the number of movies to which both professional i and professional j contributed. This value can be interpreted as an index of the strength of social proximity between the two individuals (Borgatti & Everett, 1997).

We used a 3-year moving window to control for the duration of each tie, hence making the adjacency matrixes time varying (but the results are qualita-tively similar when different time windows—e.g., a 2- or 4-year window—are used in the analysis). We started with the core crewmembers who worked in 1995 and used the earlier 3-year data to construct the accumulative relational profiles. We then used the resulting ten time-varying matrices to compute all individual level network measures.

Variables

Dependent Variable

We used a discrete-choice approach to model the industry's peer–agent evalu-ation process, in which peer evaluators select agents' work by bestowing an award or nomination. In this context, the evaluators are the following peer-based awarding organizations: the Academy of Motion Picture Arts and Sciences, the

Producers Guild of America, the Directors Guild of America, the Writers Guild of America, the Screen Actors Guild, the Art Directors Guild, the American Society of Cinematographers, the American Cinema Editors, and the Film Independent (originally Independent Feature Project/West). We collected data on the accolades awarded by them in each year.[2] The primary data sources were Tom O'Neil's (2003) Movie Awards and the organization's official web sites. The dependent variable thus takes the value 1 when, in a given year, a professional receives one award/nomination from one of the previous awarding organizations, and 0 otherwise.

Independent Variable

To detect the core–periphery structure in our data, we followed the procedure implemented in UCINET (Borgatti, Everett, & Freeman, 2002) using a genetic algorithm. The definition of the core here is a group of nodes that are connected to all other nodes of the core and the periphery. The periphery is defined as a group of nodes that are not connected to each other but only to the nodes in the core. The algorithm is designed to maximize the density within the core (between the regions belonging to the core) and to minimize the density within the periphery (in an ideal core–periphery structure, there are zero relations between the peripheral nodes). Since the density of the core–periphery interaction has no ideal value, these observations are treated as missing (see Appendix for the formalized version of this algorithm). Using this procedure, we created the binary variable *Individual Core–Periphery*—which takes on the value 1 when individuals are partitioned into the core and 0 for those who are partitioned into the periphery of the Hollywood network. We created this variable adopting a 3-year moving window; that is, for the 3 years (t-3, t-2, and t-1) prior to the focal year t (the results do not vary much using a different time window). The measure was computed using UCINET VI (Borgatti et al., 2002). It is worth noting that although all agents in the core are highly central, as calculated by virtually any measure, not every set of central agents forms a core. Indeed, they "may have high centrality by being strongly connected to different cohesive regions of the graph and need not have any ties to each other" (Borgatti & Everett, 1999, p. 393).

Control Variables

To rule out possible alternative explanations for the hypothesized relationships, we included several control variables in the final model specification:

- *Team Reputation.* An individual's status stems from both his or her past achievements and the status of his or her partners, and the individual can receive greater recognition by collaborating with higher status colleagues. This implies that "higher status affiliations help to increase returns to a given quality of output" (Benjamin & Podolny, 1999, p. 565). We accounted for these possibilities by measuring the quality of the team as the average number of accolades team members other than the focal individual had received in the 3 years (i.e., t-1, t-2, and t-3) prior to the focal year t.

- *Individual Role.* As noted earlier, our analysis is focused on a restricted group of professional roles and because each one embodies different artistic and technical dimensions and draws on diverse cognitive and practical abilities, the assumption that the same relational mechanisms are equally important across different roles might be inappropriate. Controlling for role is also important because different organizations bestow awards in different role categories, and the number of these has changed over time in some cases. Whereas the Academy of Motion Picture Arts and Sciences and Film Independent tend to assign awards to all (or most) categories (thus covering all roles in the analysis), the various guilds only award their members. As a result, individuals performing roles with more award categories have greater chances of receiving accolades for their creative work. We accounted for this possibility and professionals' particular roles by including a fixed effect for the role each professional performed in a given movie. This was achieved in SAS using the STRATA statement, which considers each role as a separate stratum—that is, grouping all observations for each role in the process of constructing the likelihood function. When the same professional covered multiple roles in the same movie or across different movies, the attribution was based on the role he or she undertook most often during the study period.

- *Individual Degree of Control.* Prior research has shown how intrinsic motivation is more conducive to creativity than is extrinsic motivation (Amabile, 1996). When the primary motivations are interest in and enjoyment of an activity, outputs tend to be more creative than when the motivation is achieving goals set by others. It is thus quite possible that individuals performing multiple roles also have more freedom in the pursuit of their goals and are in a better position to express their skills and talents. As a result of being more intrinsically motivated, they are more likely to generate creative work and even increase their visibility in the field. We therefore created the variable *Individual Degree of Control* to capture the extent to which professionals enjoy enough latitude to express their creativity; we did so by measuring the average number of different roles each performed in his or her movies in a given year. Although in most cases there was only one specialist per role, a professional sometimes performed multiple roles in a single movie (e.g., Clint Eastwood was director, actor, and producer for *Unforgiven* in 1992) or the same role was collectively performed by multiple individuals (e.g., Joel and Ethan Cohen co-directed *Fargo* in 1996).

- *Individual Artistic Reputation.* Peers' judgments are influenced by agents' past achievements (Podolny, 1993): A high number of accolades in an individual's career would probably indicate an exceptional talent and skills. Past research in the film industry also suggests that the most successful professionals often enjoy preferential access to better resources and information (Faulkner & Anderson, 1987). Since recognition through accolades is highly valued by industry members, recipients enjoy greater media attention than do their lower status counterparts (Hsu, 2005). Accordingly, we controlled for an individual professional's talent and skills by creating the variable *Individual Artistic Reputation*; that is, the number of awards won and nominations gained by each professional in the 3 years (i.e., t-3, t-2, and t-1) prior to the focal year t (again, the results did not change with a different time window).

- *Individual Commercial Reputation.* Following previous research (e.g., Elberse, 2007), we looked at a professional's *commercial* reputation based on how well or poorly his or her movies had fared commercially. Specifically, we computed the cumulative number of "top ten box office" movies in each year in which each professional worked until the year prior to the focal one using data on top-grossing movies from the IMDB online database. We chose the number of "top ten box office" movies in a given year to have a conservative measure of each professional's commercial reputation. But the results are qualitatively similar when the top twenty or top thirty box office movies are used.

- *Movie Sequel.* The extent to which movies reflect a genuine search for artistic novelty or focus instead on more formulaic content (which one could say was the case with sequels) might affect the likelihood of a professional receiving an accolade. This variable was thus computed as a dummy, taking the value 1 when a movie was a sequel and 0 otherwise.

- *Movie Rating.* Another important factor in measuring the level of creativity inherent in a particular movie is the rating assigned to it by the Motion Picture Association of America (MPAA). Ratings signal the degree of sexually graphic sequences, violence, and strong language in a movie. Prior research suggests that features produced for mature audiences (R and NC-17) perform less well at the box office (Ravid, 1999). Movies rated G, PG, and PG-13 have greater audience potential, and, indeed, movie theater's landlords may sometimes contractually prohibit theaters from showing NC-17 films. As a result, studios quite often exert some pressure on producers and directors to ensure films receive a rating aligned with their market aspirations. This practice can obviously constrain creativity. We accounted for this by including a categorical variable with six categories: G, PG, PG-13, R, NC-17, and no available rating.

- *Movie Genre*. The likelihood of an accolade being bestowed could also depend on movie genre, on the premise that a movie's artistic content might vary across genres: one could argue that a professional working on an action movie is less likely to gain such recognition because action movies typically reflect more formulaic conventions. We created a categorical variable (with eighteen categories) to control for each movie's genre using data from the American Film Institute (AFI).
- *Number of Movies*. The chance of receiving an award or nomination is also likely to depend on the number of movies each professional makes in a given year. Also, as they make more movies, the very same professionals can expand the number of ties to other professionals in the industry, which in turn can affect the chance of receiving an award or a nomination. Accordingly, we controlled for the number of movie a professional was involved in during the focal year.
- *Awarding Organizations*. We accounted for the impact of stable unobserved differences between the selected groups of peer evaluators by stratifying by awarding organizations, which is tantamount to estimating a fixed effects model for awarding organizations.
- *Year*. Since we had no a priori expectations about the existence of time trend(s) over the study period, we controlled for the effect of all unobserved factors (e.g., macroeconomic trends, changes in taste or fashion, and other factors that might affect the movie industry) that might affect peers' evaluation by also stratifying by year.

Model

For any given role, we modeled the impact of a professional's characteristics on the probability of a peer-based awarding organization bestowing an accolade on that professional rather than any other. This can be framed as a series of discrete choice problems, with one professional selected in each category (role) each year from a discrete set of professionals. Let y_{ij} be equal to 1 if awarding organization i (with $i = 1, \ldots, n$) chooses option j (with $j = 1, \ldots, J_i$), 0 otherwise; and x_{ij} be a vector of explanatory variables describing option j for awarding organization i. The number of possible choices is J_i to indicate that different peer-based awarding organizations may have different sets of options to choose from. The conditional logit model introduced by McFadden assumes the following general form:

$$\Pr\left(y_{ij} = 1\right) \frac{e^{\beta x_{ij}}}{e^{\beta x_{i1}} + e^{\beta x_{i2}} + \cdots + e^{\beta x_{iJi}}} \tag{1}$$

This equation implies that the odds awarding organization i will choose professional j over professional k is given by the difference in the vector of explanatory variables describing each option as

$$\exp\{\beta(x_{ij}-x_{ik})\} \tag{2}$$

If the values of any explanatory variable are the same, then this variable has no effect on the choice between professional j and professional k. Suppose that awarding organization i has a stable preference for each option j, denoted μ_{ij}, and that the actual utility U_{ij} for a particular option varies randomly around μ_{ij} so that

$$U_{ij} = \mu_{ij} + \varepsilon_{ij} \tag{3}$$

where ε_{ij} is a random variable having a standard extreme value distribution and the ε_{ij}'s are independent across the different options. If an awarding organization chooses the option with the highest utility U_{ij}, and if the logarithm of μ_{ij} is a linear function of the explanatory variables, then the probability that awarding organization i chooses option j is given by equation (1).[3]

Results

Tables 8.1 and 8.2 present the descriptive statistics and the correlation values, which are relatively low. We also checked for the existence of multicollinearity by computing the variance inflation factors (VIFs) using PROC REG in SAS and found it was not a problem. As mentioned before, we estimated these models by stratifying by organization, role, and year.

Table 8.3 presents the coefficient estimates for the discrete choice models predicting the likelihood that peer organizations will choose to give an accolade. Model 1 is the baseline model, with all controls. Although the coefficient estimates are not reported, the overall impact of the dummies for *movie genre* and *movie rating* are significant. The coefficient estimate of the variable *Movie Sequel* is significant, and the sign of the coefficient is in the expected direction, showing that professionals working in movies that are more formulaic are less

Table 8.1 Descriptive Statistics

Variable	Mean	Std Dev	Min	Max
Audience (stratifying variable)			1	8
Role (stratifying variable)			1	8
Year (stratifying variable)			1992	2004
Movie Genre (categorical)			1	18
Movie Rating (categorical)			0	5
Movie Sequel	0.098	0.298	0	1
Team Reputation	0.548	1.048	0	16.417
Individual Degree of Control	1.202	0.562	1	7
Individual Commercial Reputation	0.351	0.896	0	12
Individual Artistic Reputation	0.095	0.358	0	9
Individual Number of Movies	1.580	1.026	1	15
Individual Core-periphery	0.004	0.065	0	1

likely to receive an accolade. Professionals working in a team whose members received accolades in previous years (*Team Reputation*) are more likely to receive themselves an accolade, a result consistent with findings from Rossman et al. (2010). At the individual level, the quality of each professional's human capital

Table 8.2 Pearson Correlation Coefficients

Variable	1	2	3	4	5	6	7
1. Movie Sequel	1						
2. Team Reputation	0.023	1					
3. Individual Degree of Control	−0.018	0.094	1				
4. Individual Commercial Reputation	−0.038	0.199	0.022	1			
5. Individual Artistic Reputation	0.020	0.238	0.091	0.158	1		
6. Individual Number of Movies	(0.000)	0.085	0.518	0.261	0.085	1	
7. Individual Core–Periphery	−0.055	0.041	0.171	0.081	0.027	0.260	1

All correlations significant at the <.001 level, with the only exception of the correlation reported in parenthesis (not significant).

Table 8.3 Results for Discrete Choice Model Predicting Peers' Choice

Variables	Model 1		Model 2	
	Coeff.	Std. Err.	Coeff.	Std. Err.
Movie Genre (dummies)	Included	—	Included	—
Movie Rating (dummies)	Included	—	Included	—
Movie Sequel (dummy)	−0.721**	0.144	−0.768**	0.146
Team Reputation	0.196**	0.015	0.195**	0.015
Individual Degree of Control	0.386**	0.050	0.396**	0.050
Individual Commercial Reputation	0.171**	0.022	0.169**	0.022
Individual Artistic Reputation	0.387**	0.039	0.383**	0.040
Individual Number of Movies	−0.135**	0.032	−0.156**	0.032
Individual Core–Periphery			0.793**	0.251
Fixed Effects:				
Awarding Organization	Included		Included	
Year	Included		Included	
Individual Role	Included		Included	
ChiSq vs. Null	1982.23**		1990.98**	
ChiSq vs. Model 1			18.18**	
Number of Strata	266		266	
Number of Observations	82594		82594	

* p < 0.05, ** p < 0.01—Two-tailed tests for all variables.

(*Individual Artistic Reputation*) and the number of roles each professional performed in the same movie (*Individual Degree of Control*) turned out to be significant and in the postulated direction. Similarly, professionals whose status stems from having worked in the past in commercially successful movies (*Individual Commercial Reputation*) was significant, suggesting that they enjoy greater visibility and therefore are more likely to receive an accolade. By contrast, when professionals work on more than one movie per year (*Individual Number of Movies*), the likelihood that they will receive an accolade declines, possibly because the quality of their performance deteriorates as they get involved in too many projects. The global test of the null hypothesis that all the coefficients are equal to 0 is highly statistically significant (the likelihood ratio test is 1982.23 with 27 df and Pr > ChiSq = 0.0001).

Model 2 shows the results after we entered our variable of central theoretical interest, *Individual Core–Periphery*. The coefficient (0.793) is in the hypothesized direction and is statistically significant ($p < 0.001$), either by a Wald test or a likelihood ratio test. The odds ratio of $\exp(0.793) = 2.21$ indicates that core professionals have an odds of receiving an accolade that is more than double the odds of those in the periphery. Also, all the control variables are significant, and the signs of their coefficients remain unchanged relative to the baseline.

A potential problem in the analysis is that the likelihood of being rewarded by peers might affect a professional's position in the core or the periphery of the field. At a general level, we believe that the way we constructed the core–periphery measure makes it unlikely that our results are driven simply by reverse causation. For a professional in a given year, the core–periphery measure is constructed from affiliation data for the 3 preceding years. Creative performance is then taken as the award bestowed in the focal year. Thus, we relate individuals' likelihood of being consecrated to their past network position.

Discussion and Conclusions

Over the past 20 years, increasing sociological evidence has accumulated suggesting that creativity is very often embedded within broader social structures that shape access to both novel ideas and social support. Creative achievements in fields as diverse as science, art, and business all exhibit a very similar pattern, in that "creators" are embedded in a network of actors who share ideas and act as both critics and supporters of each other's work (Collins, 1998; Simonton, 1999; Uzzi & Spiro, 2005). These accounts do not deny the role of individual talents and/or dispositions, but they suggest that these qualities are mobilized and channeled into a context of intersecting relationships through which conventions are learned and ideas recombined. The present study has expanded on this line of work by establishing a framework for understanding creativity as a joint result of sociostructural conditions at the individual level and social systems making judgments about individuals' efforts.

Building on socioinstitutional perspectives on creativity (Csikszentmihályi, 1996; Ford, 1996) and combining structural explanations of creativity with recent organizational insights on the social structure of consensus (Cattani, Ferriani, Negro, & Perretti, 2008), we framed the relationship between novelty and its recognition as an ongoing tension between the core and periphery of the social field. We also noted that whether these creative efforts are socially validated, and therefore rewarded, depends on the norms and standards of judgment used by relevant evaluators, which in turn reflect evaluators' incentives to preserve the institutional logics of the field. We reasoned that individuals positioned closer to the core of their field are more likely to appeal to peer evaluators because closeness to the core induces adherence to the prevailing field's norms and standards.

Our results suggest that rewards for creativity are socially structured: where individuals stand within the field's social structure may affect the recognition of their work and thus shape their reputation for creativity. This is an important finding that complements the vast research that has treated individual abilities as the main explanation for the production of creative work (Gardner, 1993; Sternberg, 1985). As a result, little attention has been devoted to how creativity is shaped by a wider set of constraints that operate via social validation and are enforced by external evaluators. This chapter shows how creativity is embedded in patterns of relationships and judged by evaluators (gatekeepers) who participate in the social stratification of the field by granting or denying recognition to individuals' creative work. Also, by focusing on peer evaluators and sociostructural conditions affecting the process of validation, our study extends research on the determinants of social stratification that tends to focus on agents (e.g., individuals, organizations) vying for recognition rather than on the gatekeepers responsible for conferring it. Research on the social structure of markets, for instance, has predominantly looked at attributes such as the position in the status ordering of market actors and its effect on the opportunities available to them (Benjamin & Podolny, 1999; Podolny, 1994). Conversely, drawing from the audience–candidate framework (Zuckerman, 1999), organizational ecologists have only recently started to explicitly incorporate audience (evaluator)-level features and variables in their models of organizational survival (Hannan, Pólos, & Carroll, 2007; Hsu & Hannan, 2005).

Our research contributes to this line of inquiry by establishing a theoretical and empirical framework for better appreciating the influence that peer evaluators may have on the distribution of rewards to individual agents, independent of agents' specific attributes. Our findings thus enhance current understanding of competitive dynamics in markets by highlighting the influence of agents' position in the social structure on their ability to establish themselves as legitimate players in the market. The finding that there is a significant relationship between individuals' position in the social structure and their likelihood of appealing to relevant peers provides considerable empirical substance to Merton's (1968) central claim that to investigate the processes shaping the advancement of knowledge in a given field, it is important to consider the social mechanisms that curb or facilitate the incorporation of possible contributions into the domain.

Based on our theoretical framework, individuals who are routinely peripheral to the field and therefore not deeply (if at all) assimilated into existing norms and standards will struggle to achieve symbolic and material resources for their creative efforts. This is typically the case, for instance, of mavericks in the art world. Unlike core individuals who are tied to the field's center of influence and are therefore likely to follow more conventional perspectives in their work, mavericks retain some loose connection with their field "but no longer partici-pate in its activities.... They propose innovations the art world refuses to accept as within the limits of what it ordinarily produces" (Becker, 1982, p. 233). As an illustration, consider iconic film director Stanley Kubrick's decision to reject the production logics of the Hollywood establishment (which he referred to as "film by fiat, film by frenzy") and move to a secluded town in England in 1962, despite the success of his last Hollywood production *Spartacus* (Ciment, 2003). Frustrated by the lack of creative freedom in Hollywood, he established his own independent production company in the United Kingdom. Film histo-rians and critics now concur that Kubrick's cinematic creativity benefited from his radical decision because he started to explore themes and ideas that were far removed from Hollywood's prevailing canons, yet he also suffered a significant legitimacy discount for standing outside the establishment, which never granted him an Academy Award for best picture or director. These ideas are also con-sistent with Kuhn's (1970) argument that exponents of a dominant paradigm often will counter fundamental novelties, which typically originate from the periphery of the field, because they are subversive and pose a challenge to the existing paradigm. Clearly, these processes of social selection that regulate the allocation of rewards can counter efforts to introduce new ideas and practices that do not conform to the dominant conventions. They also raise the broader question of how change is triggered in an established institutional field when new ideas and practices, once introduced, challenge the position of established participants (Leblebici et al., 1991). This is a fundamental question that merits further investigation.

The study suffers from obvious limitations that nevertheless represent oppor-tunities for future research. First, we studied an art field rather than a scientific one in which knowledge can be more easily codified and evaluation of changes is likely to be premised more on technical criteria than on the fit with normative criteria (Becker, 1982). As a consequence, the results should be generalized with caution to other settings where external evaluations might be related more closely to technical prowess and mastery. Also, it is important to stress how, from our data, we can only observe evaluators' choice—the awarding of an accolade—but not the process leading to the final choice. The complex process by which evalu-ators screen and select falls outside the scope of this study. A different research design and analytical approach (e.g., an ethnographic study or a survey) would be better suited to address this question explicitly. Finally, we looked only at peer evaluators who are likely to have a vested interest in preserving existing institutional field arrangements and therefore oppose attempts to challenge or depart from them. Focusing on critics might, however, offer a completely different picture. Critics and peers have, in fact, different incentives, in that critics' reputation within the field depends significantly on their ability to discover new talents. The role of critics and, more generally, of different kinds of evaluators in creating countervailing mechanisms that may curb the sociostructural ordering of creativity is an important area of research that deserves future attention. For instance, contexts such as the Cannes Film Festival and the Venice Film Festival, where the composition of juries in terms of peers and critics has varied dramatically over their long history, provide exciting empirical settings for further exploring and extending the ideas developed here.

Notes

1. The assertion that peer evaluators conservatively allocate resources and recognition is recurrent but not absolute. Because these individuals are often high-status members of their professional community, they may have a significant degree of latitude in endorsing deviant ideas without worrying too much about being penalized for their unconventional choices. Evidence consistent with this idea can be found in Phillips and Zuckerman (2001). It should be noted, however, that the question of whether high status favors or hinders departure from established norms and standards is still open, and competing perspectives have been offered on this matter (for a recent discussion, see in particular Phillips, Turco, & Zuckerman [2010]).

2. We focused on these organizations for various reasons. All have been in existence for several years and are widely regarded as reliable and competent organizations. As Gemser et al. (2008, p. 31) noticed, "the announcements of the winners of all these awards receive national coverage in the printed press and/or on national television, and the jury process is transparent for the outside world." Together, the selected awards reflect the judgments of hundreds of interested expert peers from the worlds of film practiced in identifying and rewarding exceptional filmmaking achievement. The range of awards used in the analysis allow us to minimize the risk of including only awards—e.g., Oscars—whose assignment is sometimes driven by commercial considerations (Holbrook, 1999).

3. If these conditions are satisfied, the conditional logit model is reasonable because the assumption of the independence of irrelevant alternatives (IIA), a key assumption of the discrete choice model, is not violated (Allison, 1999). This means that the odds of choosing option j rather than option k are not affected by the other available options. The IIA assumption can only be tested when awarding organizations are presented with different choices. In our context, it is reasonable to assume IIA because

"nominees are unlikely to be considered close substitutes for one another" (Pardoe & Simonton, 2007, p. 381). A possible exception to IIA might be the relatively rare occasion when a professional receives multiple nominations in the same category in the same year. In the case of Oscars, for example, this has happened only very rarely— for example, for best director (Clarence Brown in 1930, Michael Curtiz in 1938, and Steven Soderbergh in 2000)—because "the Oscar rules prevent this from happening in the lead acting categories" (Pardoe & Simonton, 2007, pp. 381–392). Similar considerations hold for other awards as well. In the analysis, we stratified by awarding organization, professional's role, and year. We estimated the conditional logit model by maximum likelihood using PROC LOGISTIC in SAS (version 9.1).

References

Allison, P. D. (1999). *Logistic regression using the SAS system: Theory and application.* Cary, NC: SAS Institute.

Amabile, T. M. (1988). A model of creativity and innovation in organizations. In B. M. Staw & L. L. Cummings (Eds.), *Research in organizational behavior* (pp.123–167). Greenwich, CT: JAI Press.

Amabile, T. M. (1996). *Creativity in context.* Boulder, CO: Westview Press.

Becker, H. S. (1982). *Art worlds.* Berkeley: University of California Press.

Benjamin, B. A., & Podolny, J. M. (1999). Status, quality, and social order in the California wine industry. *Administrative Science Quarterly, 44*(3), 563–589.

Borgatti, S. P., & Everett, M. G. (1997). Network analysis of 2-mode data. *Social Networks, 19,* 243–269.

Borgatti, S. P., & Everett, M. G. (1999). Models of core/periphery structures. *Social Networks, 21,* 375–395.

Borgatti, S. P., Everett, M. G., & Freeman, L. C. (2002). *Ucinet 6 for Windows: Software for Social Network Analysis.* Harvard, MA: Analytic Technologies.

Burt, R. (2004). Structural holes and good ideas. *American Journal of Sociology, 110,* 349–99.

Cattani, G., & Ferriani, S. (2008). A core/periphery perspective on individual creative Performance: Social networks and cinematic achievements in the Hollywood film industry. *Organization Science, 19*(6), 824–844.

Cattani, G., Ferriani, S., Negro, G., & Perretti, F. (2008). The structure of consensus: Network ties, legitimation and exit rates of U.S. feature film producer organizations. *Administrative Science Quarterly, 53*(1), 145–182.

Ciment, M. (2003). *Kubrick: The definitive edition.* New York: Faber and Faber.

Collins, R. (1998). *The sociology of philosophies: A global theory of intellectual change.* Cambridge: Harvard University Press.

Collins, R. (2004). Collaborative circles: Friendship dynamics and creative work. *Social Forces, 83*(1), 433–435.

Csikszentmihályi, M. (1994). The domain of creativity. In D. H. Feldman, M. Csikszentmihályi, & H. Gardner (Eds.), *Changing the world: A framework for the study of creativity* (pp. 135–158). London: Praeger.

Csikszentmihályi, M. (1996). *Creativity, flow and the psychology of discovery and invention*. New York: Harper Collins.

Elberse, A. (2007). The power of stars: Do star actors drive the success of movies? *Journal of Marketing, 71*(4), 102–120.

Faulkner, R. R., & Anderson, A. B. (1987). Short-term projects and emergent careers: Evidence from Hollywood. *American Journal of Sociology, 92*, 879–909.

Ford, C. (1996). A theory of individual creative action in multiple social domains. *Academy Management Review, 21*, 1112–1142.

Gardner, H. (1993). *Creative minds*. New York: Basic Books.

Gemser, G., Leenders, M. A. A. M., & Wijnberg, N. M. (2008). Why some awards are more effective signals of quality than others: A study of movie awards. *Journal of Management, 34*(1), 25–54.

Glynn, M. A. (1996). Innovative genius: A framework for relating individual and organizational intelligences to innovation. *Academy of Management Review, 21*,1081–1111.

Granovetter, M. (1985). Economic action and social structure: The problem of embeddedness. *American Journal of Sociology, 49*, 323–334.

Hannan, M. T., Pólos, L., & Carroll, G. R. (2007). *Logics of organization theory: Audiences, codes, and ecologies*. Princeton, NJ: Princeton University Press.

Holbrook, M. B. (1999). Popular appeal versus expert judgments of motion pictures. *Journal of Consumer Research, 26*, 144–155.

Hsu, G. (2005). Evaluative schemas and the attention of critics in the US film industry. *Industrial and Corporate Change, 15*(3), 467–496.

Hsu, G., & Hannan M. T. (2005). Identities, genres, and organizational forms. *Organization Science, 16*, 474–490.

Johnson, C., Dowd, T. J., & Ridgeway C. L. (2006). Legitimacy as social process. *Annual Review of Sociology, 32*, 53–78.

Jones, C., Hesterly, W., & Borgatti S. P. (1997). A general theory of network governance: Exchange conditions and social mechanisms. *Academy of Management Review, 22*, 911–945.

Kramer, H. (1981). Art view: Giorgio Morandi: A quality of private mediation. *New York Times*, December 6 available online at http://www.nytimes.com/1981/12/06/arts/art-view-giorgio-morandi-a-quality-of-prvate-mediation.html

Kuhn, T. (1970). *The structure of scientific revolutions* (2nd ed.). Chicago: Chicago University Press.

Lamont, M. (2009). *How professors think*. Cambridge, MA: Harvard University Press.

Leblebici, H., Salancik, G. R., Copay, A., & King T. (1991). Institutional change and the transformation of inter-organizational fields: An organizational history of the U.S. radio broadcasting industry. *Administrative Science Quarterly, 36*(2), 333–363.

Merton, R. K. (1968). The Matthew effect in science. *Science, 159*(3810), 56–63.

Olmsted, J. M. D., & Fulton J. F. (2008). *Francois Magendie: Pioneer in experimental physiology and scientific medicine in nineteenth century France.* Whitefish, MT: Kessinger Publishing.

O'Neil, T. (2003). *Movie awards* (Rev. ed.). New York: Perigee Trade.

Pardoe, I., & Simonton D. K. (2007). Applying discrete choice models to predict academy award winners. *Journal of the Royal Statistical Society: Series A (Statistics in Society), 171*(2), 375–394.

Perry-Smith, J. E., & Shalley C. E. (2003). The social side of creativity: A static and dynamic social network perspective. *Academy of Management Review, 28*(1), 89–106.

Phillips, D. J., & Zuckerman, E. W. (2001). Middle-status conformity: Theoretical restatement and empirical demonstration in two markets. *American Journal of Sociology, 107*(2), 379–429.

Phillips, D. J., Turco, C. J., & Zuckerman E. W. (2010). High-status conformity and deviance: Pressures for purity among U.S. corporate law firms (Working Paper). Massachusetts Institute of Technology.

Podolny, J. M. (1993). A status-based model of market competition. *American Journal of Sociology, 98*, 829–872.

Podolny, J. M. (1994). Market uncertainty and the social character of economic exchange. *Administrative Science Quarterly, 39*(3), 458–483.

Ravid, S. A. (1999). Information, blockbusters, and stars: A study of the film industry. *Journal of Business, 72*, 463–492.

Rossman, G., Esparza, N., & Bonacich P. 2010. I'd Like to Thank the Academy, Team Spillovers, and Network Centrality. *American Sociological Review, 75*(1), 31–51.

Simonton, D. K. (1984). Artistic creativity and interpersonal relationships across and within generations. *Journal of Personality and Social Psychology, 46*, 1273–1286.

Simonton, D. K. (1999). *Origins of genius: Darwinian perspectives on creativity.* Oxford: Oxford University Press.

Simonton, D. K. (2004a). Film awards as indicators of cinematic creativity and achievement: A quantitative comparison of the Oscars and six alternatives. *Creativity Research Journal, 16*, 163–172.

Simonton, D. K. (2004b). Group artistic creativity: Creative clusters and cinematic success in 1,327 feature films. *Journal of Applied Social Psychology, 34*(7), 1494–1520.

Sternberg, R. J. (1985). *Beyond IQ: A triarchic theory of human intelligence.* New York: Cambridge University Press

Tardif, T. Z., & Sternberg R. J. (1988). What do we know about creativity? In R. J. Sternberg (Ed.), *The nature of creativity: Contemporary psychological perspectives* (pp. 429–440). Cambridge: Cambridge University Press.

Uzzi, B., & Spiro, J. (2005). Collaboration and creativity: The small world problem. *American Journal of Sociology, 111*, 447–504.

White, H. C. (1993). *Careers and creativity: Social forces in the arts.* Boulder, CO: Westview Press.

White, H. C., & White, C. A. (1993). *Canvases and careers. Institutional change in the French painting world.* New York: Wiley. (Original work published 1965)

Woodman, R. W., Sawyer, J. E., & Griffin, R. W. (1993). Toward a theory of organizational creativity. *Academy of Management Review, 18*(2), 293–321.

Zelditch, M. (2001). Processes of legitimation: Recent developments and new directions. *Social Psychology Quarterly, 64,* 4–17.

Zuckerman, E. W. (1999). The categorical imperative: Securities analysts and the legitimacy discount. *American Journal of Sociology, 104,* 1398–1438.

Zuckerman, E. W., Kim, T-Y., Ukanwa, K., & von Rittman J. (2003). Robust identities or non-entities? Typecasting in the feature film labor market. *American Journal of Sociology, 108,* 1018–1074.

Appendix: The Core–Periphery Algorithm

The discrete version of the core–periphery algorithm is formalized by Borgatti and Everett (1999) as

$$\rho = \sum_{ij} \alpha_{ij} \delta_{ij} \tag{1}$$

$$\delta_{ij} = \begin{cases} 1 & \text{if } c_i = CORE \text{ and } c_j = CORE \\ 0 & \text{if } c_i = PERIPHERY \text{ and } c_j = PERIPHERY \\ . & \text{otherwise} \end{cases} \tag{2}$$

where ρ is a measure for the correlation between the real network structure and the theoretical structure, which is maximized if A (the matrix of a_{ij}) and Δ (the matrix of δ_{ij}) are the same. In the equations, a_{ij} indicates the presence or absence of a relation between actor i and j, c_i refers to the group (core or periphery) actor i belongs to and $\delta_{i,ij}$ indicates the presence or absence of a relation between actor i and j in the ideal image. In the equations, $a_{\cdot ij}$ indicates the presence or absence of a relation between actor i and j in the observed data, c_i refers to the group (core or periphery) actor i belongs and δ_{ij} indicates the presence or absence of a relation between actor i and j in the ideal core–periphery image. Where ρ is a measure for the correspondence between the real network structure and the theoretical structure, which is maximized if A (the matrix of α_{ij}) and Δ (the matrix of $\delta_{\cdot ij}$) are the same. Note that "." indicates a missing value. The reason is that off-diagonal regions (core-to-periphery ties and periphery-to-core) of the ideal core–periphery matrix are treated as missing data: the genetic algorithm thus seeks only to maximize density in the core and minimize density in the periphery, without regard to the density of ties between those off-diagonal regions. The genetic algorithm is designed to find the core–periphery partition that maximizes the fit statistic (ρ). The partition obtained by applying model (2) to our data then places the various actors either in the core or the periphery.

9

STRATEGIC ASSETS AND PERFORMANCE ACROSS INSTITUTIONAL ENVIRONMENTS

Allègre L. Hadida

Do institutions in different geographic locations affect motion picture performance, and do the strategic assets deployed by cinema studios operating from different countries similarly contribute to the commercial success and creative merit of the motion pictures they produce? Conceptual responses to these questions generally fall into two camps.

According to new institutional economics (NIE), external institutional factors act to shape organizations' long-term economic performance (North, 1990). They enable or restrict the strategic options offered to film studios and therefore confine differences among studios across countries. According to the resource-based view (RBV), organizations, including film studios, create sustainable competitive advantages through the effective exploitation and unique combinations of valuable, rare, difficult to imitate, and hard to substitute strategic assets (Amit & Schoemaker, 1993; Barney, 2003).[1]

So far, NIE research has explored how institutional environments influence individual firms' choices of arms-length relationships, fully integrated hierarchies, or strategic alliances to rule their transactions (Williamson, 1999). It has also investigated how organizations develop dedicated "nonmarket" strategies, including lobbying, to better deal with institutional incentives (Baron, 2000). However, it has rarely looked into the nature of the strategic assets that enable these choices. Liebeskind (1996) noted that firms develop capabilities aimed at protecting valuable knowledge from expropriation and imitation. Such institutional capabilities are highly dependent on the regulatory context in which firms operate because courts act to enforce laws on proprietary resources. Oliver (1997) also acknowledged the role of the institutional context, including regulatory pressures, in shaping the resource selection decisions of individual firms. Her study, however, focused on issues of social isomorphism, conformity, and stability within the organization (as per DiMaggio & Powell, 1983), rather than on the economic interactions between institutions and strategic assets. Last, Ghertman and Hadida (2005) modeled the shift in competitive advantage from early French cinema entrepreneurs over to their US counterparts as the consequence of the interplay of diverging institutions, firm structures, and strategic assets in the two countries. This research illustrated, in particular, the damaging economic impact on the French cinema industry of several institutional decisions taken by French governments before World War I.

Likewise, RBV research did not expand on the influence of national institutions (Henderson & Mitchell, 1997; Teece, Pisano, & Shuen, 1997) on strategic asset development and performance. Miller and Shamsie (1996) investigated the types of resources developed and used by Hollywood studios during and after their Golden Age. In spite of choosing a distinctively institutional event to delineate time periods (namely, the 1948 anti-trust Paramount Decrees, which caused the vertically integrated production and distribution studios to divest from exhibition), they exclusively modeled their study along competitive (rather than institutional) dimensions. Similarly, Weinstein (1998) attributed the demise of the studio system to the reduced demand for motion pictures initiated in the 1930s, and saw the implementation of the Paramount Decrees as a logical economic response to this decline. From 1938 onward, decreases in the number of films released and in box office revenue paralleled the drop in relative consumer spending on cinema (Robins, 1993). Faced with lower demand and excess supply, studios started to sell land for urban development and stopped employing actors on salary (Weinstein, 1998).

This chapter extends this existing body of research by conceptually linking the NIE and RBV to investigate the influence of the institutional environment of cinema on asset development and motion picture performance. In the wake of Mezias and Boyle (2005), it studies the influence of the legal environment on film studios' resource portfolios. It does so in two distinct institutional settings, the United States and France, over a decade of relative institutional stability in both countries. Following a suggestion made by Eliashberg, Elberse, and Leenders (2006), this chapter also looks into the trade-offs made by the studios between commercial and creative objectives in their product development process.

Conceptual Foundations

New institutional economics posits that human beings create institutions aimed at supporting property rights and contracts to decrease the uncertainties of transactions among economic agents (Coase, 1937). Institutions bring order to human interactions by guiding and framing them (Denzau & North, 1993). They may be defined as informal constraints (e.g., codes of conduct, norms of behavior, conventions and social practices), formal rules (e.g., political and judicial rules, economic rules and contracts), and the effectiveness of their enforcement, most notably by courts, public organizations, and governments through regulation (North, 1990). Institutional incentives reflect informal constraints and directly stem from formal rules and the effectiveness of their enforcement. Entrepreneurs and managers play the game under existing rules or lobby to change them. Although institutions explain differences in economic development and performance across countries, no single institutional setting is universally optimal, and the impact of institutions on economic performance varies widely from one country to the next (Engerman & Sokoloff, 1997). National borders consequently constitute relevant boundaries of the relationships among institutional incentives, strategic assets, and performance.

The resource-based view posits that the value of a strategic asset reflects its ability to exploit opportunities and/or neutralize threats in a firm's competitive environment (Arora & Gambardella, 1997). Accordingly, the latter both shapes and is shaped by a firm's strategies (Henderson & Mitchell, 1997; Lecocq & Demil, 2006). As information travels faster, key resources and industry best practices spread more widely (Porter, 1996) and learning ecologies of shared practices and routines develop (Lampel & Shamsie, 2003). Within a given industry, the strategic assets needed for production may therefore be increasingly similar across firms and countries.

Accordingly, most film studios developed unique "house-styles" (Sedgwick, 2002) and quasi-exclusive relationships with specific artists and technicians during the "golden age" of Hollywood (1930–1949). Specific "star–genre combinations" (Schatz, 1997)—for instance, Bing Crosby in Paramount musicals or James Cagney in Warner Brothers' crime dramas (Gomery, 1986)—cemented these studios' distinctive identities (Rosten, 1941). The vertical disintegration era that followed and an open market for resources, including actors, led to a uniformization of the studios' assets and output and to the dilution of their distinctive identities. Increases in international co-productions have also led producers from different countries to resort to the same pool of bankable and geographically mobile actors and directors and international audiences to develop similar tastes.

Even so, differences in institutional environments may cause variations in the way organizations assemble the assets needed for production. In the NIE framework, firms are expected to develop strategies in response to their incentive structure, which changes as institutions evolve (North, 1990). In the RBV, such strategies would result in the creation and development over time of distinctive strategic assets. Hence, stretching the RBV and NIE perspectives posits that firms are expected to develop specific assets to shape and respond to their institutional environment. Whereas the previous assertion is straightforward in NIE (Liebeskind, 1996), it is less so in the RBV, which is less mindful of firms' institutional environments.

Model

By definition, the relative inimitability of strategic assets relies on their imperfect mobility (Barney, 1991), and the exploitation of perfectly mobile resources with no firm-specific ties cannot lead to a sustainable competitive advantage (Peteraf, 1993). And yet, organizations, including film studios, increasingly rely on perfectly mobile free agents (Jones & DeFillippi, 1996) and expect to create and sustain value from their temporary combinations. The imperfect mobility of assets has consequently become, at best, contingent on the nature of the organization that controls them (Anand & Singh, 1997) as sources of rents elude any organization's direct individual control to reside in its network of partners (Dyer & Singh, 1998). In such circumstances, a focus on individual projects allows for a relatively straightforward identification of the strategic assets used in film production and that are most likely to determine performance. It may also unveil better insights into strategic assets and their combinations in specific activities (DeFillippi & Arthur, 1998).

Uncertainties in the evolution of individual careers also justify investors' and customers' interest in the track record of project participants (Faulkner & Anderson, 1987). Following Hadida (2010), and building on existing research on the economics of superstars (Rosen, 1981), typecasting (Zuckerman, Kim, Ukanwa, & Von Rittmann, 2003), and reputation (Hall, 1993; Rao, 1994; Weigelt & Camerer, 1988), *track record* is hereby defined as the tangible manifestation of the accumulative capability of project participants to induce customer trial (commercial track record) and/or peer recognition (creative track record). The continually reproduced system of inequality that this definition entails also rests on the assumption of a "Matthew effect," defined as the incremental buildup of recognition for individuals or teams of significant repute and the denial of such appreciation to those who have not yet made their mark (Merton, 1968).

In cinema, three categories of project participants beg particular attention. First, film producers take the initiative and responsibility for a film's development and completion. They set up its budget and supervise all its financial and administrative aspects. Second, directors are responsible for a film's creative form. They collaborate with producers on staffing and casting and supervise the creative elements of the film production and postproduction phases. Third, lead actors play a significant part in the making and promotion of a movie, mainly thanks to their high visibility with audiences. Figure 9.1 introduces a conceptual model of the link between the track record of these key participants (hereby defined as strategic assets) and above-average film performance across institutional contexts. All relationships (represented as arrows) between latent variables (oval shapes) are positive. The model also illustrates film performance both in commercial and creative terms, reflecting thus the complex nature of cinema projects.

Creative track record is hereby defined as the tangible manifestation of the accumulative capability of project participants to be praised for their creative achievements. Being nominated for or winning a prestigious film award grants membership to an exclusive network. The creative merit of a movie also rests more on the combination of individual talents than on the latter considered in isolation. The creativity of a director is nothing without actors, cinematographers, technicians, and other specialized contributors to channel it. Likewise, these film professionals cannot feature in a movie without a director and a producer to overview its creative and economic components, respectively. Creative track record is therefore defined for a film project as a whole rather than for its individual participants. The stronger the creative track record associated with a movie, the higher its creative merit (Hadida, 2010). For instance, *Forrest Gump* (Robert Zemeckis, 1994), featuring Academy Award winners Tom Hanks (best actor,

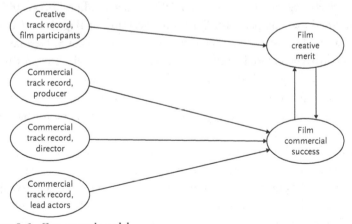

FIGURE 9.1 Conceptual model.

Philadelphia, 1993), Sally Field (best actress, *Norma Rae*, 1979, and *Places in the Heart*, 1984), Ken Ralston (best visual effects, *Death Becomes Her*, 1992), Arthur Schmidt (best film editing, *Who Framed Roger Rabbit* (1988), and Nancy Haigh (best set decoration, *Bugsy*, 1991), went on to win six Academy Awards in 1995, including for Hanks, Ralston, and Schmidt.[2]

The definition of commercial track record mirrors that of creative track record, albeit in a disaggregated form. Producers' commercial track record initially rests on their ability to detect those film projects with most box office potential. It subsequently relies on their expertise to guarantee their timely completion. In time, the accumulation of these two capabilities allows producers to become increasingly proficient and potentially enhances their film' commercial success. Similarly, directors may establish over the years a style and know-how that secure them a loyal audience.[3] Last, lead actors, through their acting abilities and choices of films and roles, are also likely to develop fan following and a proven commercial track record.

Yet, existing research yields contradictory evidence. The relationship between a producer's commercial track record and a film's commercial success is generally positive (e.g., De Vany & Walls, 2002; Sorenson & Waguespack, 2006). However, results range from strong (e.g., Bagella & Becchetti, 1999; Delmestri, Montanari, & Usai, 2005; Hadida, 2010) to limited or no evidence (e.g., Jansen, 2005; Liu, 2006; Sochay, 1994) of a positive relationship between a director's commercial track record and film commercial success. Similarly, they range from strong (Elberse & Eliashberg, 2003; Faulkner & Anderson, 1987; Sochay, 1994) to limited or no (e.g., Litman, 1983; Smith & Smith, 1986) and even negative evidence (Chang & Ki, 2005; Ravid, 1999) of a positive relationship between lead actors' commercial track record and film commercial success.

Furthermore, none of the empirical studies investigating these relationships, bar two (Neelamegham & Chintagunta, 1999; Elberse & Eliashberg, 2003), provides international comparisons. With the exception of Bagella and Becchetti (1999, Italy), Delmestri et al. (2005, Italy), and Jansen (2005, Germany), they are also exclusively centered on the United States and Canada. The present analysis purports to introduce institutional explanations based on contrasted national intellectual property regimes and social practices to hypothesized differences in the relative contribution of strategic assets to motion picture performance in the United States and in France.

Indeed, the legal environment and industrial structure of cinema in the United States and in France stand out as archetypes of contrasting intellectual property regimes and social practices in common law–based and in civil law–based countries. Intellectual property regimes are key institutions (Liebeskind, 1996; North, 1990). They capture patterns of investment and growth (Acemoglu, Johnson, &

Robinson, 2001) and shape local firms' strategies and assets portfolios in a given country to make those strategic assets most valued by organizations in that country potentially unsuitable in another. Intellectual property regimes rest respectively on copyright laws in common-law countries, including the United States, and on authors' rights in civil-law countries, including France.[4]

The 1976 US Copyright Act guarantees the rights of investors in cultural products, including films, and considers producers as the main authors of cinema projects. Directors are seen as short-term contractors: they do not retain moral rights on their work, and they often relinquish their copyrights to producers. By contrast, the French Authors' Rights are extremely protective of writers and directors. They acknowledge their moral rights in respect of their name, their authorship, and the integrity of their creations. Bestowing moral rights on directors undercuts the power of producers and gives way to new interactions and informal institutions, in the form of deeply embedded social and professional practices.

Consider first the film production process. Producers decide on a film's final editing cut in the United States, whereas directors do in France. By law, US producers must raise the full production budgets of their films, whereas French producers are only required to invest 30 percent and may call on state subsidies, television channels, and private investors for the remaining 70 percent. They are less at professional risk than their US colleagues, whose budgets are also likely to be ten times higher.[5] Although the US cinema industry is a blockbuster economy, in which producers invest massively on prospective "home-runs" (Baker & Faulkner 1991), French producers tend to hedge their bets across smaller films in the hope that one of them will prove. US producers take more financial risks and also benefit from higher prestige and visibility than their French counterparts: after a film has been released, the US Academy Award (Oscar) for best picture is handed to producers, whereas its French equivalent (César) goes to directors. It is therefore likely that, all things being equal, strategic assets linked to producers would contribute more to commercial performance in the United States (a common-law country) than in France (a civil-law country).

This hypothesized relationship points to the fact that because strategic assets are developed at least partially to respond to external industry and institutional factors, film projects become grounded in the microeconomic, strategic, and institutional environment surrounding their participants—with significant consequences on performance. Accordingly, the institutional environment strongly influences the social practices and choices of film professionals, even as the actions of specific film producers and movie studios endogenously shape the nature of national institutions over time (Furman & MacGarvie, 2007; Ghertman & Hadida, 2005).

Differentiating next between the commercial and creative dimensions of performance allows us to partially account for the complexity of this concept (Coff, 1999). Because the dual foundation of cinema as business and art makes it difficult to determine *ex ante* whether commercial success breeds creative merit or vice-versa, the empirical test reported here investigates the relationship between commercial success and creative merit both ways (also in Hadida, 2010). Regardless of institutional environments, I hypothesize that the commercial success of a movie may positively impact its creative merit and that, alternatively, the creative merit of a movie may positively impact its commercial success.

Investigating this relationship both ways addresses the often neglected issue of the relative importance of creative and commercial priorities in creative projects (Hadida, 2010; Hirsch, 2000). Even so, such a research strategy may appear counterintuitive, as several authors have documented frictions between art and business (Caves, 2000; Holbrook, 1999). Negative correlations between awards and moviegoers' film selection criteria (Holbrook, 2005) confirm that the commercial and creative dimensions of film performance are distinct. However, alternative demonstrations of positive correlations between them (Delmestri et al., 2005; Ginsburgh, 2003) illustrate that these two dimensions cannot be considered antagonistic.

Methods

Data

The data collected to test these hypothesized relationships are presented in their entirety in a related paper (Hadida, 2013) and only briefly summarized herein. They consist of two representative samples of movies produced and released from 1988 to 1997 in the United States and in France, respectively. This relatively stable period of study was chosen to guarantee that films in the US and French datasets were homogenous with respect to their sources of funding.

The statistical test, as detailed in Hadida (2013), follows the standard four steps of structural equation modeling under a maximum likelihood procedure. To increase result accuracy, tests were also performed exclusively on fully informed data. The final sample consists of two groups of 1,784 US films (Group 1: United States) and 1,158 French films (Group 2: France). They represent 48 percent and 81 percent, respectively, of all films produced and released in these countries from 1988 to 1997 inclusive (www.mpaa.org; www.cnc.fr). The final sample selection criteria mirror those used in previous studies (Cerridwen & Simonton, 2009). Likewise, although it does not include the full population of movies released in both countries over the 1988–1997 decade, the sample of 1,784 and 1,158 films is reasonably large; it is representative of movies distributed in mainstream movie theaters in both countries; and it exhibits noteworthy variations on all the variables taken into consideration in the study.

The films are evenly distributed along the 1988–1997 decade in both countries. All financial data were collected from the investment banking services firm Houlihan, Lokey, Howard, and Zukin (HLHZ) in the United States and from the National Cinema Centre (CNC) in France. Qualitative data sources include trade publications *Variety, Studio Magazine,* and *Le Film Français*; yearly reference publications *Quigley Entertainment Almanac* and *L'Année Cinématographique* (1985–1997); and the websites oscars.org, lescesarsducinema.com, and imdb. com. Correspondence between the qualitative data (e.g., name of directors, lead actors, and producers) collected from different sources was carefully checked through a random draw of two subsamples of 20 percent (one per country) of all films in the sample. This step guaranteed the internal validity of the final database.

In line with earlier longitudinal studies of the film industry (Miller & Shamsie, 2001; Nelson, Donihue, Waldman, & Wheaton, 2001; Robins, 1993), all financial data were converted to constant 1988 monetary units to compensate for inflation. All variables associated with the two lead actors were also aggregated, and all manifest variables were standardized to facilitate their comparison and the interpretation of structural equation results (McDonald & Ho, 2002, p. 69).

Performance Criteria

Peer recognition is the dominant selection system in cinema (Holbrook, 1999) and was therefore chosen to illustrate *film creative merit*. Following Anand and Watson (2004), the two variables chosen to illustrate the creative dimension of performance relate to the institutional recognition of the film by peers in the emblematic Oscar (US) and César (France) annual ceremonies: "scholarly opinion tends to regard the Oscars as 'an *institutionalized* measure of film quality' or a 'legitimate yardstick of film excellence'" (Holbrook, 1999, p. 149). The Césars play an equivalent social structuration role in France. In both countries, each profession votes for its own, except for the best foreign-language, documentary, and feature film, which all voters designate. *Total Nominations* is the total number of Oscar (US) or César (France) nominations received by a film. To avoid artificially inflating its correlation to *Total Nominations, Share of Awards* is the percentage ratio of nominations that were followed by awards. Previous studies used similar indicators (e.g., Holbrook, 1999; Nelson et al., 2001; Sochay, 1994) as dimensions of independent variables.

Opening box office results (BO) give a relatively independent account of a film's initial appeal. As in Eliashberg and Shugan (1997) and Elberse and

Eliashberg (2003), the first manifest indicator of latent variable *film commercial success*, *BO Initial*, is defined as a film's total domestic BO upon release.[6] Following Sochay (1994), Ravid (1999), and Liu (2006), *BO Total*, the second manifest indicator of *film commercial success*, reflects a film's domestic BO throughout its theatrical run. By definition, *BO Initial* is a subsample of *BO Total*. Yet no linear mathematical relationship links the two variables. Using both instead of a single manifest construct allows accounting for the short- and long-term components of commercial performance. Using two manifest variables to illustrate a single latent construct also conforms to the measurement norms of structural equation modeling (McDonald & Ho, 2002, p. 67).

Cinematic Predictors

Film participants' creative track record closely mirrors creative merit. Likewise, *Past Nominations* estimates the total number of Oscar (US) or César (France) nominations of the film's producer, director, and two lead actors; *Past Share of Awards* is the transformation ratio (in percentage) of nominations that led to awards in the three years before a film's release.

Four distinct components illustrate commercial track record: brand awareness, experience, specialization, and quasi-vertical integration in distribution. Differences in the final combinations of these four manifest indicators reflect the varied roles undertaken by producers, directors, and lead actors on film projects and the distinct performance indicators they are assessed against.

Brand awareness is defined as the commercial potential that may be derived from the past commercial successes of key participants in a film project (Kapferer, 2001). *Director's Accrued BO* and *Actors' Accrued BO* assess cumulative brand awareness as the accumulated gross BO of all the films of the director and two lead actors, respectively, released in the three years before the film's release. The choice of a three-year time span mirrors similar studies (e.g., Lampel & Shamsie 2003; Mintzberg & McHugh, 1985; Sorenson & Waguespack, 2006). It is also coherent with an average time-to-market of eighteen months, to which the duration of theatrical exhibition, which ranges from a few days to over a year, is then added. *Director's Latest BO* and *Actors' Latest BO* were created to reflect differences in career cycles of directors and performers[7] and the shared industry belief that "one is only as good as one's last credits" (Faulkner & Anderson, 1987; Swami, Eliashberg & Weinberg, 1999). They respectively represent the gross BO of the previous film of the director and two lead actors, regardless of its release date.

Past experience is the second component of commercial track record. In addition to signaling a growing command of film participants' skills, it also increases their exposure within the filmmaking community and to general audiences. The participants with most experience should increase a film's potential for commercial success while limiting economic and financial risks associated with its production. Thus, they should be contacted most for new projects. Empirical works based on the RBV similarly take into account the professional track record of top executives (Eisenhardt & Schoonhoven, 1996; Miller & Shamsie, 2001) and employees (Pennings, Lee, & Van Witteloostuijn, 1998), measured as the number of years spent in their position or industry. *Producer's Experience* hereby estimates the number of movie projects the producer managed in the three years before a film's release. Likewise, *Director's Experience* and *Actors' Experience* measure the number of films directed by the director and starred in by at least one of the two lead actors in the three years preceding a film's release.

Specialization is the third component of commercial track record. Well-known brand names reduce the commercial risks associated with new product launches. Increased brand specialization, by limiting opportunities for unrelated expansion, also prevents brand owners from tarnishing the reputation of the brand (Aaker, 1990). Similarly, actors who develop strong path dependencies in specific roles are generally more successful than their unfocused colleagues (Zuckerman et al., 2003). *Producer's Specialization* assesses the specialization of a producer through the percentage of film projects managed in the previous three years that were of the same genre as the indexed film.

The last component of commercial track record, *Producer-Distributor Projects*, measures the number of films in common, in the three years before a film's release, between its producer and main domestic distributor. It illustrates a distributor's willingness to invest in a movie on the basis of its participants. Because they are, to a great extent, assembled by producers, *Producer-Distributor Projects* qualifies as an indicator of producers' commercial track record.

Results

I performed a multiple group analysis in Amos 18 to compare the two distinct populations of US movies produced and released in the United States (Group 1) and French movies produced and released in France (Group 2) from 1988 to 1997. This analysis, detailed in Hadida (2013), confirmed that although the two groups are distinct, they may still be assessed with the same structural equation model (Bollen, 1989, p. 358). Table 9.1 displays the structural equation modeling results, together with critical ratios (z-tests) for differences between regression coefficients (parameters) in the US and French structural models.

The analysis of these results leads to two main observations. First, the critical ratio for differences in the relationship between the commercial track record of the producer and the commercial success of the movie in the United States and in

Table 9.1 Results of Structural Equation Modeling, United States and France

Measurement Model	United States (n = 1,784)	France (n = 1,158)
Regression Coefficient, Latent Variable—Manifest Variable[a]		
Film participants Creative track record—Past Nominations	1 (0.868)	1 (0.898)
Film participants Creative track record—Past Share of Awards	0.620*** (0.510)	0.453*** (0.464)
Producer Commercial track record—Producer-Distributor Projects	0.906*** (0.819)	0.599*** (0.653)
Producer Commercial track record—Producer's Specialization	0.740*** (0.689)	0.743*** (0.698)
Producer Commercial track record—Producer's Experience	1 (0.956)	1 (0.964)
Director Commercial track record—Director's Accrued BO	1 (1.000)	1 (1.000)
Director Commercial track record—Director's Latest BO	0.783*** (0.790)	0.778*** (0.711)
Director Commercial track record—Director's Experience	0.576*** (0.644)	0.561*** (0.552)
Lead actors Commercial track record—Actors' Accrued BO	1 (1.000)	1 (0.928)
Lead actors Commercial track record—Actors' Latest BO	0.722*** (0.728)	0.696*** (0.703)
Lead actors Commercial track record—Actors' Experience	0.678*** (0.732)	0.785*** (0.730)
Film creative merit—Total Nominations	1 (0.854)	1 (0.975)
Film creative merit—Share of Awards	0.711*** (0.544)	0.850*** (0.834)
Film commercial success—BO Total	1 (1.000)	1 (1.000)
Film commercial success—BO Initial	0.779*** (0.836)	0.563*** (0.785)
Covariances (correlations) between independent variables		
Producer Commercial track record—Director Commercial track record	0.113*** (0.098)	0.149*** (0.158)
Producer Commercial track record—Lead actors Commercial track record	0.082* (0.074)	0.174*** (0.172)
Producer Commercial track record—Film participants Creative track record	0.140*** (0.160)	0.587*** (0.497)

Director Commercial track record—Lead actors Commercial track record	0.478*** (0.379)	0.254*** (0.275)
Director Commercial track record—Film participants Creative track record	0.244*** (0.244)	0.330*** (0.305)
Lead actors Commercial track record—Film participants Creative track record	0.351*** (0.372)	0.717*** (0.615)
Error terms: e_{33} (Director's Experience) – e_{43} (Actors' Experience)	0.089*** (0.163)	0.084*** (0.145)

Structural Model[a]

Film participants Creative track record → Film creative merit	0.186*** (0.232)	0.222*** (0.216)
Producer Commercial track record → Film commercial success	0.080*** (0.072)	0.006[ns] (0.006)
Director Commercial track record → Film commercial success	0.254*** (0.261)	0.285*** (0.257)
Lead actors Commercial track record → Film commercial success	0.291*** (0.283)	0.306*** (0.298)
Film commercial success → Film creative merit	0.194*** (0.314)	0.482*** (0.411)
Film creative merit → Film commercial success	0.290*** (0.179)	0.223*** (0.261)

Square Multiple Correlations (R^2)

Film commercial success	0.366	0.474
Film creative merit	0.273	0.419
Stability index of nonrecursive model	0.056	0.107

Critical Ratios for Differences between Parameters

Film participants Creative track record → Film creative merit	0.751[ns]
Producer Commercial track record → Film commercial success	−2.283**
Director Commercial track record → Film commercial success	0.880[ns]
Lead actors Commercial track record → Film commercial success	0.405[ns]

(continued)

Table 9.1 (Continued)

Measurement Model	United States (n = 1,784)	France (n = 1,158)
Square Multiple Correlations (R²)		
Film commercial success → Film creative merit		3.845**
Film creative merit → Film commercial success		−0.713[ns]
Fit Indexes		
Chi-square		1282.443
Degrees of freedom and number of parameters		159 and 81
RMR and RMSEA		0.054 and 0.049
GFI and AGFI		0.946 and 0.919
CFI		0.949

[a] Items in parentheses are standardized values.

*** $p < 0.001$ (two-tailed); ** $p < 0.05$ (two-tailed); * $p < 0.01$ (two-tailed); [ns] nonsignificant.

AGFI, adjusted goodness-of-fit; CFI, comparative fit index; GFI, goodness-of-fit; RMSEA, root mean square error of approximation; RMR, root mean residual.

France is statistically significant ($-2.283, p < .05$), indicating a marked difference between the two countries. In the United States, the producer's commercial track record has a statistically significant impact, although weak, on film commercial success ($0.072, p < .001$).[8] In France, this impact is positive but nonsignificant. In contrast, the commercial track records of the director and lead actors significantly impact commercial performance in both countries, with no significant difference in these relationships between samples. In the United States and France, the commercial success of a movie rests more on the creative teams of artists assigned to a film project than on its producers' commercial track records. This confirms the producer's key role as a behind-the-scenes assembler and coordinator of other strategic assets and reflects the relative importance of this function in the two countries. As anticipated, US producers, who bear more financial risks and work in an institutional environment in which cinema is primarily perceived as an industry, hold a more central position than their French counterparts.

Second, the model hypothesized that the commercial success of a movie may positively impact its creative merit. At least in the short term, attendance is logically bound to precede (and potentially affect) the outcome of US and French awards, for which films are nominated after release. The impact of film commercial success on film creative merit is stronger, however, in France ($0.411, p < .001$) than in the United States ($0.314, p < .001$). In both countries, nominated and award-winning movies are also either maintained on screens or re-released to coincide with the local award ceremony. Hypothesizing that the creative merit of a movie may positively influence its commercial success directly accounts for the effectiveness of such strategies. The relationship between creative merit and commercial success is statistically significant both in the United States (0.179, $p < .001$) and in France ($0.261, p < .001$), again with a stronger effect in France. This finding partly contradicts Hadida's (2010) conclusion that US moviegoers do not typically opt for a film on the basis of its creative merit. Even so, the R^2 of 0.273 associated with *film creative merit* is weaker in the United States than that of *film commercial success* (0.366), whereas the R^2 of *film creative merit* (0.419) is almost as strong in France as that of *film commercial success* (0.474).

Associated with a statistically significant critical ratio for differences in the relationship between film commercial success and film creative merit in the two countries ($3.845, p < .005$), these results mirror US producers' and filmgoers' vision of cinema as primarily an industry. In contrast, their French counterparts seem to consider cinema as both (and almost equally) art and industry.

Supplementary analyses corroborate these findings. Five statistical controls were introduced separately in the model without substantially affecting its structure in either country. Using *year of release* as a control variable (as in Smith & Smith, 1986) illustrates the rise in average production costs in the decade under scrutiny, from US$18.1 to 53.4 million in the United States and from US$3.4 to 5.4 million in France.[9] In contrast, the influence of creative track record on film creative merit and of film commercial success on film creative merit declined in the two countries from 1988 to 1997, whereas the influence of creative merit on commercial success increased in France. These results may reflect a renewal of creative forces over time. The introduction of the film's *month of release* as a control (also in Krider & Weinberg, 1998) confirms the seasonality of the theatrical market. In the United States in particular, it illustrates the industry practice of selecting a film's release date according to its BO potential. Positive and significant correlations between a film's month of release and its creative merit also substantiate that the later the film is released in the year, the more likely it is to be nominated for and to win an Oscar—an effect that may be self-fulfilling, as studios tend to release their films with the highest award potential late in the year.

A third statistical control, *genre* (also used as an independent variable by Litman [1983] and Eliashberg and Shugan [1997]), did not have a substantial impact on performance in either country. Consistent with earlier studies of product reputation (Milgrom & Roberts, 1986), the more track record resources are associated with the film and the higher its *budget*, the more initial *screen coverage* (as in Neelamegham & Chintagunta, 1999) it gets, and the more BO (and also indirectly, creative merit) it generates.

Discussion and Conclusion

So far, existing research linking strategic assets to institutions has focused on explaining the emergence of institutional capabilities (Liebeskind, 1996) and of resource strategies (Baron, 2000; Oliver, 1997) aimed specifically at dealing with institutional pressures. The model developed in this chapter and its empirical demonstrate that institutions also condition the allocation and valuation of strategic assets with primary purposes other than relaxing institutional constraints. Thus, even though resources and capabilities necessary for production in the same industry are comparable in the United States and in France, their relative contribution to performance differs in these two countries.

Findings relative to the contribution of producer track record assets to commercial performance and to the relative importance of creative merit across countries echo the unique position of producers and directors in the United States and in France. Under the US Copyright Law, producers call the shots: writers and directors do not retain moral rights and are often only perceived as salaried technicians. In contrast, directors in France are "auteurs," a status both created and reinforced by the French law on Authors' Rights. Their prestige rests on talent, merit, and eccentricity, and places them at the core of the postrevolution cultural elite (Heinich, 2005).

Even so, creative merit and commercial success are complementary in both countries. Their dual use uncovers consistency in US and French film finance (mostly private vs. partly public), perception of cinema (primarily industry vs. art), and industry professionals' and moviegoers' social practices and consumption decisions. It therefore opens new perspectives on the institutional value system of US and French cinemas. More than a "cultural exception" (Farchy, 1999), existing institutional frameworks at country and industry levels induce strong coherence in film production systems and financial structures, spectators' viewing preferences, and creative achievement criteria in the United States and France. They result in a blockbuster industry and a strong defense of free-market cinema production and distribution in the United States and in a wide diversity of films produced and distributed and a complex system of subsidies in France.

The informal and formal institutional contexts of the US and French film industries are also deeply embedded in the broader historical and institutional contexts of both countries. The latter partially explains why the French film *Intouchables* (Eric Toledano and Olivier Nakache, 2011), 2011's "cultural event of the year"[10] and the third highest-grossing film of all time in France, may elicit much less enthusiasm and more racial sensibility in the United States. A few months before its May 25, 2012 US release, *Variety* critic Jay Weissberg accused the movie of displaying, in its treatment of actor Omar Sy's Senegalese character Driss, "the kind of Uncle Tom racism one hopes has permanently exited American screens." "Tellingly," Weissberg writes, the character "in real life is Arab, not black."[11] Although the movie does play on social and cultural clichés, this statement was received with bewilderment in France, where minorities of multiple ethnic origins get along and live together in the same housing estates.[12]

This example illustrates the idea that, just as institutions explain differences in economic performance across countries at the macroeconomic level (Acemoglu et al., 2001; Engerman & Sokoloff, 1997; North, 1990), they may also condition the predictors of performance at the project level of analysis. The present research shows that the effect of institutions on strategic assets and project performance varies across countries in the same industry.

Unlike previous studies, however, the present research does not aim at determining whether institutions and property rights in the Anglo-Saxon common-law tradition may be better suited to economic development and performance than those in the French civil-law tradition (La Porta, Lopez de Silanes, Syhleifer, & Vishny, 1999) or whether the negative effects of French institutions may have been overestimated (Acemoglu et al., 2001). To do so, thorough longitudinal comparisons carried out in the two film industries since their inception may be necessary. Inasmuch as film performance is measured in economic as well as creative terms, the conclusions of such studies may not be clear cut and may lead to interesting contributions to research on the importance of legal origins in economic and cultural development.

Empirical research comparing more than two populations (unless, as is the case here, they are particularly emblematic and epitomize two diverging dominant views of a same industry), several time periods, and other industries across institutional environments may further extend the findings presented here. The present focus on intellectual property regimes and social practices may also be broadened to other forms of institutions. This chapter will hopefully pave the way to many other studies aimed at further exploring and uncovering the fascinating relationship among institutions, strategic assets, and performance across countries.

Acknowledgments

I wish to thank Dean K. Simonton and James C. Kaufman for their invitation to contribute a chapter to *The Social Science of Cinema*, and for their editorial support and advice throughout its development. The data and methods used in the analyses presented here were introduced in more detail in Hadida, A. L. (2013): "Institutions, assets combinations and film performance: A US-French comparison." *Psychology of Aesthetics, Creativity and the Arts*, 7(2), 155–170. All errors and omissions remain mine.

Notes

1. Following Amit and Schoemaker (1993), *resources* are hereby defined as inputs into an organization's production process, *capabilities* as dynamic combinations of resources, and *strategic assets* as resources and capabilities at the source of above-average organizational performance.
2. This Matthew effect is even more marked when considering nominations alone and nominations as well as awards.
3. Even so, few productions reach blockbuster status, and most attempts to produce high-revenue properties fail (Faulkner & Anderson, 1987).
4. Over the years, the United States and France have introduced civil law- and common law-based innovations to their legal apparatus, respectively. Thus, copyright laws (for instance) also exist in France. The present chapter, however, focuses on the prevalent legal system and intellectual property regimes in the two countries and on their paramount influence on corporate and social practices.

5. In 1997, average movie production costs amounted to US$5.4 million in France versus US$53.4 million in the United States, and gross box office income in France totaled US$934 million versus US$6.36 billion in the United States (www.cnc.fr).

6. To reflect differences in release days and weekly consumption patterns, *BO Initial* encompasses BO revenues on Friday, Saturday, and Sunday in the United States and on Wednesday, Thursday, and Friday in France.

7. For instance, some actors and directors (e.g., Stanley Kubrik, Terrence Malick) allow more than three years to elapse between films.

8. All parameters mentioned here and in the rest of the chapter are standardized.

9. This tendency, which persisted in recent years, also echoes, after 1997, the sharp development of the DVD market. It further reinforces the cycle of specialization of lead actors in blockbusters, thus supporting Zuckerman's et al. (2003) conclusions on typecasting.

10. http://next.liberation.fr/cinema/01012379401-intouchables-evenement-culturel-de-l-annee-pour-les-francais

11. http://www.variety.com/review/VE1117946269?refcatid=31

12. http://articles.latimes.com/2012/jan/01/world/la-fg-france-untouchables-20120102

References

Aaker, D. A. (1990). Brand extensions: The good, the bad, and the ugly. *Sloan Management Review, Summer*, 47–56.

Acemoglu, D., Johnson, S., & Robinson, J. A. (2001). The colonial origins of comparative development: An empirical investigation. *American Economic Review, 91*(5), 1369–1401.

Amit, R., & Schoemaker, P. J. H. (1993). Strategic assets and organizational rent. *Strategic Management Journal, 14*(1), 33–46.

Anand, J., & Singh, H. (1997). Asset redeployment, acquisitions and corporate strategy in declining industries. *Strategic Management Journal, 18*, 99–118.

Anand, N., & Watson, M. R. (2004). Tournament rituals in the evolution of fields: The case of the Grammy Awards. *Academy of Management Journal, 47*(1), 59–80.

Arora. A., & Gambardella, A. (1997). Domestic markets and international competitiveness: generic and product-specific competencies in the engineering sector. *Strategic Management Journal, 18*, 53–74.

Bagella, M., & Becchetti, L. (1999). The determinants of motion picture box office performance: Evidence from movies produced in Italy. *Journal of Cultural Economics, 23*(4), 237–256.

Baker, W. E., & Faulkner, R. R. (1991). Role as resource in the Hollywood film industry. *American Journal of Sociology, 97*(2), 279–309.

Barney, J. B. (1991). Firm resources and sustained competitive advantage. *Journal of Management, 17*(1), 99–120.

Barney, J. B. (2003). *Gaining and sustaining competitive advantage* (2nd ed.). Englewood Cliffs, NJ: Prentice Hall.

Baron, D. P. (2000). *Business and its environment* (3rd ed.). New York: Prentice Hall.

Bollen, K. A. (1989). *Structural equations with latent variables.* New York: John Wiley and Sons.

Caves, R. E. (2000). *Creative industries: Contracts between art and commerce.* Cambridge, MA: Harvard University Press.

Cerridwen, A., & Simonton, D. K. (2009). Sex doesn't sell—Nor impress! Content, box office, critics, and awards in mainstream cinema. *Psychology of Aesthetics, Creativity, and the Arts, 3*(4), 200–210.

Chang, B.-H., & Ki, E.-J. (2005). Devising a practical model for predicting theatrical movie success: Focusing on the experience good property. *Journal of Media Economics, 18*(4), 247–269.

Coase, R. H. (1937). The nature of the firm. *Economica, 4*(16), 386–405.

Coff, R. W. (1999). When competitive advantage doesn't lead to performance: The resource-based view and stakeholder bargaining power. *Organization Science, 10*(2), 119–133.

De Vany, A., & Walls, W. D. (2002). Does Hollywood make too many R-rated movies? Risk, stochastic dominance, and the illusion of expectation. *Journal of Business, 75*(3), 425–451.

DeFillippi, R. J., & Arthur, M. B. (1998). Paradox in project-based enterprise: The case of film making. *California Management Review, 40*(2), 125–139.

Delmestri, G., Montanari, F., & Usai, A. (2005). Reputation and strength of ties in predicting commercial success and artistic merit of independents in the Italian feature film industry. *Journal of Management Studies, 42*(5), 975–1002.

Denzau, A. T., & North, D. C. (1993). *Shared mental models: Ideologies and institutions.* Working Paper, Center for Politics and Economics, Claremont Graduate School and Center for the Study of Political Economy, Washington University, St. Louis, MO.

DiMaggio, P. J., & Powell, W. W. (1983). The iron cage revisited: Institutional isomorphism and collective rationality in organizational fields. *American Sociological Review, 48*(2), 147–160.

Dyer, J. H., & Singh, H. (1998). The relational view: Cooperative strategy and sources of interorganizational competitive advantage. *Academy of Management Review, 23*(4), 660–679.

Eisenhardt, K. M., & Schoonhoven, C. B. (1996). Resource-based view of strategic alliance formation: Strategic and social effects in entrepreneurial firms. *Organization Science, 7*(2), 136–150.

Elberse, A., & Eliashberg, J. (2003). Demand and supply dynamics of sequentially released products in international markets: The case of motion pictures. *Marketing Science, 22*(3), 329–354.

Eliashberg, J., Elberse, A., & Leenders, M. A. (2006). The motion picture industry: Critical issues in practice, current research, and new research directions. *Marketing Science, 25*(6), 638–661.

Eliashberg, J., & Shugan, S. M. (1997). Film critics: Influencers or predictors? *Journal of Marketing, 61*(2), 68–78.

Engerman, S. L., & Sokoloff, K. L. (1997). Factor endowments, institutions, and differential paths of growth among new world economies. In S. Haber (Ed.), *How Latin America fell behind* (pp. 260–304). Stanford, CA: Stanford University Press.

Farchy, J. (1999). *La fin de l'exception culturelle?* Paris: CNRS Editions.

Faulkner, R. R., & Anderson, A. B. (1987). Short term projects and emergent careers: Evidence from Hollywood. *American Journal of Sociology, 92*, 879–909.

Furman, J. L., & MacGarvie, M. J. (2007). Academic science and the birth of industrial research laboratories in the U.S. pharmaceutical industry. *Journal of Economic Behavior & Organization, 63*(4), 756–776.

Ghertman, M., & Hadida, A. L. (2005). Institutional assets and competitive advantage of French over U.S. cinema: 1895-1914. *International Studies of Management and Organization, 35*(3), 52–83.

Ginsburgh, V. (2003). Awards, success and aesthetic quality in arts. *Journal of Economic Perspectives, 17*(2), 99–112.

Gomery, D. (1986). *The Hollywood studio system.* London: BFI-McMillan.

Hadida, A. L. (2010). Commercial success and artistic recognition of motion picture projects. *Journal of Cultural Economics, 34*(1), 45–80.

Hadida, A. L. (2013). Institutions, assets combinations and film performance: A U.S.-French comparison. *Psychology of Aesthetics, Creativity and the Arts, 7*(2), 155–170.

Hall, R. (1993). A framework linking intangible resources and capabilities to sustainable competitive advantage. *Strategic Management Journal, 14*, 607–618.

Heinich, N. (2005). *L'elite artiste: Excellence et singularité en régime démocratique.* Paris: Gallimard.

Henderson, R., & Mitchell, W. (1997). The interactions of organizational and competitive influences on strategy and performance. *Strategic Management Journal, 18*, 5–14.

Hirsch, P. M. (2000). Cultural industries revisited. *Organization Science, 11* (3), 356–361.

Holbrook, M. B. (1999). Popular appeal versus expert judgments of motion pictures. *Journal of Consumer Research, 26*, 144–155.

Holbrook, M. B. (2005). The role of ordinary evaluations in the market for popular culture: Do consumers have "good taste?" *Marketing Letters, 16* (2), 75–86.

Jansen, C. (2005). The performance of German motion pictures, profits and subsidies: Some empirical evidence. *Journal of Cultural Economics,29*, 191–212.

Jones, C., & DeFillippi, R. J. (1996). Back to the future in film: Combining industry and self-knowledge to meet the career challenges of the 21st century. *Academy of Management Executive, 10*(4), 89–103.

Kapferer, J.-N. (2001). *Re inventing the brand: Can top brands survive the new market realities?* London: Kogan Page.

Krider, R. E., & Weinberg, C. B. (1998). Competitive dynamics and the introduction of new products: The motion picture timing game. *Journal of Marketing Research, 35*(1), 1–15.

La Porta, R., Lopez de Silanes, F., Syhleifer, A., & Vishny, R. W. (1999). The quality of government. *Journal of Law, Economics and Organization, 15*(1), 222–279.

Lampel, J., & Shamsie, J. (2003). Capabilities in motion: New organizational forms and the reshaping of the Hollywood movie industry. *Journal of Management Studies, 40*(8), 2189–2210.

Lecocq, X., & Demil, B. (2006). Strategizing industry structure: The case of open systems in a low-tech industry. *Strategic Management Journal, 27*(9), 891–898.

Liebeskind, J. P. (1996). Knowledge, strategy, and the theory of the firm. *Strategic Management Journal, 17*, 93–107.

Litman, B. R. (1983). Predicting success of theatrical movies: An empirical study. *Journal of Popular Culture, 16*, 156–175.

Liu, Y. (2006). Word of mouth for movies: Its dynamics and impact on box office revenue. *Journal of Marketing, 70*, 74–89.

McDonald, R. P., & Ho, M.-H. R. (2002). Principles and practice in reporting structural equation analyses. *Psychological Methods, 7*(1), 64–82.

Merton, R. K. (1968). The Matthew Effect in science. *Science, 159* (3810), 56–63.

Mezias, S. J., & Boyle, E. (2005). Blind trust: Market control, legal environments, and the dynamics of competitive intensity in the early American film industry, 1893–1920. *Administrative Science Quarterly, 50*, 1–34.

Milgrom, P., & Roberts, J. (1986). Price and advertising signals of product quality. *Journal of Political Economy, 94*, 796–821.

Miller, D., & Shamsie, J. (1996). The resource-based view of the firm in two environments: The Hollywood film studios from 1936 to 1965. *Academy of Management Journal, 39*(3), 519–543.

Miller, D., & Shamsie, J. (2001). Learning across the life cycle: Experimentation and performance among the Hollywood studio heads. *Strategic Management Journal, 22*(8), 725–745.

Mintzberg, H., & McHugh, A. (1985). Strategy formation in an adhocracy. *Administrative Science Quarterly, 30*, 160–197.

Neelamegham, R., & Chintagunta, P. (1999). A Bayesian model to forecast new product performance in domestic and international markets. *Marketing Science, 18*(2), 115–136.

Nelson, R. A., Donihue, M. R., Waldman, D. M., & Wheaton, C. (2001). What's an Oscar worth? *Economic Inquiry, 39*(1), 1–16.

North, D. C. (1990). *Institutions, institutional change, and economic performance.* New York: Cambridge University Press.

Oliver, C. (1997). Sustainable competitive advantage: Combining institutional and resource-based views. *Strategic Management Journal, 18*(9), 697–713.

Pennings, J. M., Lee, K., & Van Witteloostuijn, A. (1998). Human capital, social capital, and firm dissolution. *Academy of Management Journal, 41*(4), 425–440.

Peteraf, M. A. (1993). The cornerstones of competitive advantage: A resource-based view. *Strategic Management Journal, 14*, 179–191.

Porter, M. E. (1996). What is strategy? *Harvard Business Review, November-December*, 61–78.

Rao, H. (1994). The social construction of reputation: Certification contests, legitimation, and the survival of organizations in the American automobile industry: 1895-1912. *Strategic Management Journal, 15*, 29–44.

Ravid, S. A. (1999). Information, blockbusters, and stars: A study of the film industry. *Journal of Business, 72*(4), 463–492.

Robins, J. A. (1993). Organization as strategy: Restructuring production in the film industry. *Strategic Management Journal, 14*, 103–118.

Rosen, S. (1981). The economics of superstars. *American Economic Review, 71*(5), 845–858.

Rosten, L. C. (1941). *Hollywood: The movie colony, the movie makers.* New York: Harcourt, Brace and Co. Inc.

Schatz, T. (1997). *Boom and bust: American cinema in the 1940s.* Berkeley: University of California Press.

Sedgwick, J. (2002). Product differentiation at the movies: Hollywood, 1946 to 1965. *Journal of Economic History, 62*(3), 676–705.

Smith, S. P., & Smith, V. K. (1986). Successful movies: A preliminary empirical analysis. *Applied Economics, 18*, 501–507.

Sochay, S. (1994). Predicting performance of motion pictures. *Journal of Media Economics, 7*(4), 1–20.

Sorenson, O., & Waguespack, D. (2006). Social structure and exchange: Self-confirming dynamics in Hollywood. *Administrative Science Quarterly, 51*, 560–589.

Swami, S., Eliashberg, J., & Weinberg, C. B. (1999). SilverScreener: A modeling approach to movie screens management. *Marketing Science, 18*(3), 352–372.

Teece, D. J., Pisano, G., & Shuen, A. (1997). Dynamic capabilities and strategic management. *Strategic Management Journal, 18*(7), 509–533.

Weigelt, K., & Camerer, C. (1988). Reputation and corporate strategy: A review of recent theory and applications. *Strategic Management Journal, 9*, 443–454.

Weinstein, M. (1998). Profit-sharing contracts in Hollywood: Evolution and analysis. *Journal of Legal Studies, 27*(1), 67–112.

Williamson, O. E. (1999). Strategy research: Governance and competence perspectives. *Strategic Management Journal, 20*(12), 1087–1108.

Zuckerman, E. W., Kim, T.-Y., Ukanwa, K., & Von Rittmann, J. (2003). Robust identities or nonentities? Typecasting in the feature-film labor market. *American Journal of Sociology, 108*(5), 1018–1074.

IV THE RECEPTION

10 ANALYZING THE ACADEMY AWARDS

FACTORS ASSOCIATED WITH WINNING AND WHEN SURPRISES OCCUR

Iain Pardoe and Dean Keith Simonton

Each year, hundreds of millions of people worldwide view the televised Academy Awards ceremony to see the Academy of Motion Picture Arts and Sciences (AMPAS) recognize outstanding achievement in film in the previous year. Since 1928, AMPAS members have voted for the nominees and final winners of Academy Awards, more popularly known as Oscars, in such categories as best picture, directing, acting, and writing. The Oscars are broadly viewed to be the foremost awards of their kind, given that the almost 6,000 members of AMPAS are among the most prominent figures in the film industry. Besides honoring cinematic accomplishments, Oscars have almost immediate practical repercussions (reviewed in Simonton, 2011). For example, winning a Lead Actor or Lead Actress Oscar increases the income that recipients can later command and enhances the quality of screenplays that are sent to their agents. In addition, Oscar nominations and awards can boost the box office performance of nominated and winning films by millions of dollars. However, although a film's production costs are positively correlated with gross earnings, there is little, if any, association between budget and the most important movie awards, such as the Oscars for directing, acting, and screenplay (Simonton, 2011).

Yet are these repercussions of Oscar recognition justified? Or, as many critics believe, are the Academy Awards contaminated by provincial Hollywood politics and tastes (see, e.g., Peary, 1993). If the latter, then the awards lose merit and thus may be somewhat unjust. This question has been addressed in two major ways.

First, investigators can simply determine whether Oscar nominations and awards are positively and strongly related to alternative ways of assessing cinematic achievements. For instance, Oscar recognition is strongly associated with other awards, such as the Golden Globes bestowed by the Hollywood Foreign Press Association, a group of Southern California-based international journalists, and with critical acclaim, such as gauged by the ratings that films receive in various movie guides (Simonton, 2004). On the basis of these and other statistical relationships, Simonton observed, "Those who take an Oscar home can have a strong likelihood of having exhibited superlative cinematic creativity or achievement" (p. 171). In fact, among all major awards, the Oscars appear to be the most significant indicators of merit (Ginsburgh, 2003; Simonton, 2004).

Second, investigators can pursue a more ambitious predictive modeling strategy. Rather than simply surveying correlations between pairs of variables, models for predicting Oscar outcomes can provide more detailed information about the magnitude of correspondence between the variables and the number and extent of prediction errors. Pardoe and Simonton (2008) developed this second strategy by building a model to predict the winners of the four major Academy Awards—best picture, directing, actor in a leading role, actress in a leading role—from those nominated in each year since 1938 (earlier years had yet to accumulate sufficient information to provide satisfactory predictions).

This chapter extends the latter work and includes additional results for the years 2007–2010. The outline of the chapter is as follows. The first section describes the data used—since the goal is to predict the eventual winner from a list of nominees, any information on the nominees that is available before the announcement of the winner is potentially useful, including other Oscar category nominations, previous nominations and wins, and other (earlier) movie awards. The second section motivates the discrete choice models used to provide annual predictions and discusses the modeling process. The modeling approach allows 1-year-ahead, out-of-sample prediction of the four major Oscars from 1938 to 2010. Presentation of the final results in the third section includes insights into how predictable the four major Oscars are, which factors play an important role in the predictions, and also how these have changed over time. It is also revealing to identify past winners with an exceptionally low estimated probability of winning and past nominees with a very high estimated probability of winning who did not actually win. The fourth and final section contains a discussion.

Data

All data have been obtained from the Internet Movie Database (IMDB; us.imdb. com; Simonton, 2011). Table 10.1 outlines the explanatory variables or factors used to predict the four major Oscar winners from 1938 to 2010 and also provides data ranges for the predicted years' awards (each variable was included only for the years in which it provided some predictive power). Additional details on the variables follow.

Oscars

Movies with nominees for best picture and directing often also have multiple nominees in other categories, and the chances of winning are generally thought to increase the higher the total number of nominations. For instance, the median number of nominations for winners of the best picture and directing

Table 10.1 Explanatory Variables Used to Predict the Four Major Oscar Winners from 1938 to 2010 and the Data Ranges

Variable	Best Picture	Directing	Lead Actor	Lead Actress
Total Oscar nominations	1938–2010	1939–2010	–	–
Directing Oscar nomination	1938–2010	–	–	–
Best Picture Oscar nomination	–	1944–2010	1939–2010	1939–2010
Golden Globe (drama)	1946–2010	–	1944–2010	1944–2010
Golden Globe (musical or comedy)	1956–2010	–	1965–2010	1952–2010[1]
Guild Award	1951–2010[2]	1951–2010[3]	1995–2010	1996–2010
Previous Oscar nominations[4]	–	1938–2010	1938–2010	–
Previous Oscar wins[4]	–	–	1939–2010	1938–2010
1st front-running movie	1938–2010	1938–2010	1938–2010	1938–2010
2nd front-running movie	1959–2010	1959–2010	1959–2010	1959–2010
3rd front-running movie	1959–2010	1959–2010	1959–2010	1959–2010

[1] Variable dropped between 1961 and 1972 because the standard error greatly exceeded the estimate.

[2] Directors Guild of America for 1951–1988, Producers Guild of America for 1989–2010.

[3] Separate indicators were not included for both the Golden Globe Best Director and Directors Guild of America awards from 1949 on because of collinearity between the two awards.

[4] Transformed to natural logarithms.

Oscars since their inception (1928–2010) is eight, whereas the median number of nominations for losing nominees is five.

Nominees tend to fare better if they are nominated for movies receiving best picture and/or directing Oscar nominations. We can note the following exceptions: (a) only three movies have won the best picture Oscar without also receiving a directing nomination (*Wings* in 1928, *Grand Hotel* in 1932, and *Driving Miss Daisy* in 1989; in 1928, the best unique and artistic picture winner, *Sunrise*, also did not receive a directing nomination); (b) only two directors have won a directing Oscar for a movie that did not receive a best picture nomination (Lewis Milestone for *Two Arabian Nights* in 1928 and Frank Lloyd for *The Divine Lady* in 1929); (c) only fourteen actors have won the lead actor Oscar for a movie that did not receive a best picture nomination (most recently, Jeff Bridges for *Crazy Heart* in 2009); and (d) only twenty-seven actresses have won the lead actress Oscar for a movie that did not receive a best picture nomination (most recently, Marion Cotillard for *La Vie en Rose* in 2007).

Golden Globes

The Hollywood Foreign Press Association has awarded its Golden Globes every year since 1944 to honor achievements in film during the previous calendar year. Since Oscars are presented some time after Golden Globes (up to 2 months later), winning a Golden Globe often precedes winning an Oscar. The following five facts should be noted: (a) of the sixty-eight best picture Oscar winners from 1943 to 2010, thirty-five had previously won the Golden Globe for best picture (drama); (b) the Golden Globe award for best picture was separated into two distinct categories in 1951, namely, drama and musical or comedy, and of the sixty best picture Oscar winners from 1951 to 2010, ten had previously won the Golden Globe for best picture (musical or comedy); (c) of the sixty-eight directing Oscar winners from 1943 to 2010, thirty-six had already won the Golden Globe for best director; (d) of the 137 lead acting Oscar winners from 1943 to 2010, forty-four males had previously won the Golden Globe for lead actor (drama) and thirty-five females had previously won the Golden Globe for lead actress (drama); and (e) of the 123 lead acting Oscar winners from 1950 to 2010, six males had previously won the Golden Globe for lead actor (musical or comedy) and thirteen females had previously won the Golden Globe for lead actress (musical or comedy).

Other Cinematic Honors

The Directors Guild of America has been awarding its honors for best motion picture director since 1949 (with all but two early awards made before the announcement of the directing Oscar). Since 1989, the Producers Guild of America has been awarding its honors to the year's most distinguished producing effort (with all but the first awarded before the announcement of the best picture Oscar). Since 1994, the Screen Actor's Guild has awarded five statuettes, known as "The Actor," for achievements in film (always before the Oscar ceremony), including male actor in a leading role and female actor in a leading role. We observe the following particulars: (a) of the forty best picture Oscar winners from 1949 to 1988, thirty-one had already won a Directors Guild of America award (and two would subsequently win one); (b) of the twenty-two best picture Oscar winners from 1989 to 2010, fourteen had already won a Producers Guild of America award (and one would subsequently win one); (c) of the sixty-two directing Oscar winners from 1949 to 2010, fifty-five had already won a Directors Guild of America award (and one would subsequently win one); and (d) of the thirty-four lead acting Oscar winners from 1994 to 2010, thirteen males had already won a Screen Actor's Guild award and thirteen females had already won one.

Nominees for directing and lead actor seem to have an *increased* chance of winning the more times they have been *nominated* in previous years, whereas nominees for lead actor and lead actress seem to have a *decreased* chance of winning the more times they have *won* in previous years. These variables have been log-transformed because they are highly skewed.

Finally, we note the following four facts: (a) 18 percent of directing Oscar nominees with no previous directing nominations have won the Oscar, whereas 23 percent of directing Oscar nominees with one or more previous directing nominations have won; (b) 19 percent of lead actor Oscar nominees with no previous lead actor nominations have won the Oscar, whereas 23 percent of lead actor Oscar nominees with one or more previous lead actor nominations have won; (c) 23 percent of lead actor Oscar nominees with no previous lead actor wins have won the Oscar, whereas 12 percent of lead actor Oscar nominees with one or more previous lead actor wins have won; and (d) 24 percent of lead actress Oscar nominees with no previous lead actress wins have won the Oscar, whereas 13 percent of lead actress Oscar nominees with one or more previous lead actress wins have won.

Other Predictor Variables

The indicator variable for the first "front-running movie" allows for the possibility that the chance of a nominee winning an Oscar could be linked to the fortunes of other nominees for the same movie. Each year, a handful of movies are often considered to be the Oscar front-runners—movies with multiple nominations in the more high-profile categories (including best picture, directing, and acting). To identify these front-runners, the Oscar categories were ranked each year based on previous best picture Oscar winners (for instance, the directing category usually ranks highly since best picture Oscar winners nearly always also have a directing nomination). Then, a "nomination score" was calculated for each movie nominated for one of the four major Oscars based on these rankings (e.g., movies with many nominations in the top-ranked categories have higher nomination scores than do movies with fewer nominations). The indicator variable then identifies the top front-runner as the movie with the highest nomination score and takes the value 1 for all nominees associated with this movie. Indicator variables for the second and third front-running movies were derived similarly.

Although a variable for previous directing Oscar nominations is included, adding a variable for the number of previous directing Oscar *wins* tended to worsen rather than improve predictions. Conversely, although a variable for previous lead actress Oscar wins is included, adding a variable for the number of previous lead actress Oscar *nominations* tended to worsen predictions. Also, although a variable for the total number of nominations improves predictions of the best picture and directing Oscar winners, such a variable worsens predictions of the lead acting Oscar winners.

It is well documented that female winners of acting Oscars tend to be younger than male winners (Simonton, 2011). However, the age differences within gender between Oscar winning and losing nominees are less dramatic. Lead actress nominee ages have increased over time, with winning nominees tending to be slightly younger than losing nominees. Lead actor nominee ages have also increased over time, with winning nominees tending to be slightly older than losing nominees initially, but tending to be slightly younger more recently. Age effects of this nature on the chance of winning a lead acting Oscar can be picked up by adding *age* and *age-squared* variables (i.e., quadratic terms) to the models for lead actor and lead actress. Nevertheless, incorporating quadratic terms for age into the models failed to improve predictions of winners.

Other variables that were investigated but that did not improve results include supporting actor Oscar nominations and wins, genre of the nominated movie (drama, comedy, etc.), Motion Picture Association of America rating (PG, R, etc.), running time (i.e., length of the movie), release date, movie critic ratings, and other pre-Oscar awards (e.g., New York Film Critics Circle, Los Angeles Film Critics Association, National Society of Film Critics, and National Board of Review). Some of these, although perhaps correlated to some extent with Oscar wins, failed to improve on variables already included—for example, of all the pre-Oscar awards, the Golden Globes and Guild awards are the most predictive of future Oscar wins. Other variables were excluded partly due to difficulties in obtaining reliable measurements over time. For instance, it is difficult to find a long time series of consistent movie critic ratings that would have been available before a particular year's Oscar results.

Estimation

The goal is to predict the four major Oscar winners for each year from 1938 to 2010 using any information on the nominees that is available before the announcement of the winner. This can be framed as a series of discrete choice problems, with one winner selected in each category each year from a discrete set of nominees (usually five, although up until 1936, the number of directing and acting nominees varied between three and eight, whereas up until 1944, the number of best picture nominees varied between five and ten, and, for the last 2 years, the number of best picture nominees has been ten).

In this particular discrete-choice application, the explanatory variables described in the previous section take different values for different response (nominee) alternatives. McFadden (1974) proposed a discrete-choice model for just such a case where explanatory variables are characteristics of the choice alternatives. This model also permits the choice set to vary across choice experiments, which in this case are each of the four categories (best picture, directing, lead actor, lead actress) in each of the years (1938–2010). The model produces estimates of the probability that a particular nominee will win in his or her respective category given the nominee's values for the explanatory variables—see Pardoe and Simonton (2008) for details.

McFadden originally referred to this model as a conditional logit model. In contrast to this model, in which the explanatory variables are characteristics of the choice alternatives, a similar model in which the explanatory variables are specific to the choice situation (and constant across alternatives) is the multinomial logit model. However, it can be shown that the two models are equivalent, and the distinction between them is somewhat artificial. Both types of explanatory variable can be handled together within the same framework with appropriate use of interactions (although the resulting model is sometimes called a *mixed logit (ML) model*, we reserve this terminology for the hierarchical model discussed later). Within such a framework, the model is often just called the multinomial logit (MNL) model, and we follow that lead here.

Multinomial Logit Model

The MNL model exhibits a property known as the *independence of irrelevant alternatives*, or IIA. For instance, in a choice set containing two alternatives, the addition of a third alternative can have no impact on the ratio of the probabilities of choosing each alternative. In other words, the new alternative gains share proportionately from the choice shares of the existing alternatives in the set. There exist contexts in which this property fails to describe observed behavior. For instance, suppose there are two soft drink beverages available in a choice set, one cola flavored and the other lemon flavored, say. The introduction of an alternative cola flavored soft drink (with a different name but otherwise indistinguishable from the existing cola) would most likely take most of its market share from the other cola rather than equally from both existing drinks. However, in the Oscars application, it seems reasonable to assume IIA, since nominees are unlikely to be considered close substitutes for one another. Exceptions to this might be nominated movies of the same genre that are closer substitutes than those from different genres or the relatively rare occasion when an individual receives multiple nominations in a category in the same year. To date, this latter phenomenon has happened only three times for directing (Clarence Brown in 1930, Michael Curtiz in 1938, and Steven Soderbergh in 2000); the Oscar rules prevent this from happening in the lead acting categories (that Jamie Foxx received nominations for both lead and supporting roles for 2004 films does not constitute an exception). Independence of irrelevant alternatives is also supported by the manner in which the winner is selected (using plurality voting) as the nominee who receives the most votes from all active and lifetime members of AMPAS. Pardoe and Simonton (2008) also evaluated the IIA assumption empirically and concluded that the IIA assumption seems reasonable for this application.

Mixed Logit Model

An extension of the MNL model that places a probability distribution on some or all of the explanatory variable parameters is the ML model, also known as random parameters or random coefficients or random effects logit, or, from a Bayesian perspective, hierarchical MNL. (We use the ML terminology here since it appears to be the most common in current discrete choice literature.) The ML model generalizes the earlier MNL model so that the explanatory variable parameters are specific to each choice experiment, and the (unconditional) probability of selecting a particular alternative averages over a mixing distribution.

Two important features of the ML model in this context are that it does not require the IIA assumption, and it can approximate any random utility choice model to any degree of accuracy through appropriate specification of the mixing distribution. Mixed logit models are often most successfully applied in situations in which the choice experiments are represented by individuals making the choices, and either demographic data are available on the individuals, or the individuals make repeated choices over a sequence of similar choice experiments (i.e., panel data), or both. These additional data facilitate estimation of the ML model since they provide additional information on the distribution of the individual explanatory variable parameters. In the application considered here, the "individuals making the choices" are the choice experiments (each category within each year), which have no repeated measurements (each Oscar competition is essentially unique) and which have no obvious associated data equivalent to demographics. Thus, for this particular application, it is not clear that a ML model will necessarily outperform the MNL model (which can be thought of as a special case of the ML model with a degenerate distribution for the mixing distribution). Furthermore, Pardoe and Simonton (2008) compared the performance of both models and results slightly favored the MNL model over the ML model.

Software Implementation

The MNL and ML models can be fit with a variety of statistical software packages. Pardoe and Simonton (2008) experimented with two estimation methods: classical maximum likelihood using NLOGIT and Bayesian estimation using WinBUGS. NLOGIT is one of the main software packages for MNL estimation using maximum likelihood, whereas WinBUGS uses Bayesian estimation techniques based on Markov Chain Monte Carlo (MCMC) simulation. Both packages are relatively user-friendly, although they do require some limited programming. WinBUGS code for the MNL and ML models considered in this paper is available at http://www.iainpardoe.com/refereed.htm.

All data available before the announcement of the 1938 Oscars are used to fit a model that can predict the winners for that year. Then, the actual outcome of the 1938 Oscars is appended to the previous dataset and used to fit a new model, which can predict the winners of the 1939 Oscars. The process repeats, adding new variables as they become available, up to the most recent Oscars, for 2010.

A potential difficulty of using Bayesian estimation here is specification of the prior distributions for the model parameters. For the MNL model, standard non-informative normal priors for the explanatory variable parameters (independent, centered at zero, with variance 10) produced stable results with reasonable predictive accuracy. The results here are based on the last halves of three chains of 4,000 simulations each (the first half of each chain—considered burn-in—was discarded). Standard diagnostic tests indicated convergence to stationary posterior distributions (all unimodal).

It is also possible to use more informative prior distributions for the MNL models in this application. In particular, since seventy-three models are fit, one after another, it is possible to use normal approximations of the posterior distributions of the explanatory variable parameters for the model fit to predict year t as the prior distributions for the model fit to predict year $t + 1$, and so on. Using such priors produced equivalent, but not better results, than using the noninformative priors just discussed.

The time series nature of the iterative estimation process also permits some modeling flexibility. The process as described uses *all* previous data for predicting any particular year's Oscars. However, it is possible that more accurate models might be estimated if older data were down-weighted in some way relative to more recent data. One approach to doing this might be to *weight* the data and adjust the estimation process to take account of the weights in fitting the model. Experiments with weighting schemes of this nature failed to improve predictive accuracy however. An alternative method for down-weighting older data is to use a *moving window* approach whereby each model is fit using just the previous N years of data. Setting N too low (at, say, 30) for this application produced less stable parameter estimates with correspondingly worse predictions. Setting N too high (say, using all previous data) might have produced parameter estimates that remained overly affected by very early Oscar voting patterns. However, systematic experimentation with the moving window length N ultimately suggested using all previous data.

As indicated in Table 10.1, the explanatory variables enter the models at various points between 1938 and 1996. The main restriction on when a variable enters a model is the earliest date at which the variable is available. For example, since the first Golden Globes were for 1943 movies, the earliest that Golden Globe variables can be used is in the prediction of 1944 Oscars. However, variables were also omitted for years in which they provided little predictive power or counterintuitive parameter estimates. For instance, although a high number of Oscar nominations generally improves the chance of a nominee winning a best picture or directing Oscar, this association only became established for the directing Oscar from 1938 on (so that this variable is only used for predicting directing Oscar winners from 1939 on).

The general modeling strategy follows the maxim that "all models are wrong, but some are useful." We do not claim that our final selected model uniquely represents the actual voting dynamics of AMPAS members during Oscar season. Yet we do hope that our modeling endeavors and results shed some light on interesting questions around the predictability of the four major Oscar categories and whether this can tell us anything useful about the intent of the Oscars to recognize outstanding achievement in film. The approach used to determine which variables are included and excluded for each model for each year is based on standard regression modeling methodology. For instance, variables were initially selected that represent all the phenomena used by Oscar prognosticators in the media (for which data are available). Given the relatively sparse nature of the response data—one choice from a set of five (usually) for each category over a limited time series—and the collinearity between some variables (e.g., Golden Globe for best director and Directors Guild of America awards), many variable effects are poorly estimated (with relatively large standard errors). Such variables were then dropped from the model, although they could re-enter a model later in the time series if their parameter estimates became large enough relative to their standard errors.

Although our approach was rather flexible in this regard (e.g., we did not use a rigid criterion, such as 5 percent significance), we believe our modeling strategy compares reasonably favorably for this application with more formal econometric methodologies. One remaining question is more problematic: Are there any omitted variables that could be biasing the results, as might be revealed through nonrandom, systematic errors? There are undoubtedly factors at play in Oscar voting dynamics that we fail to capture, such as studio advertising, temporal fads, trends, and the like, but there is little evidence to suggest that their absence from the modeling process produces systematic, predictable errors. Residual analysis for logit models is notoriously challenging, but there is little to suggest a serious problem with the residuals for the models considered here.

The two sets of MNL model results (from NLOGIT and WinBUGS) are, in fact, very similar (not too surprising given the relatively uninformative priors used for the Bayesian approach). However, although results for models fit to data up to more recent times are similar under both approaches, results for less recent times (when there were less data) diverged, sometimes considerably. In particular, NLOGIT was sometimes unable to make use of certain variables until a number of years after WinBUGS was able to make use of the same variable. To illustrate, Directors Guild of America awards have been highly predictive of the directing Oscar since their inception (in 1949), and WinBUGS estimates for the corresponding parameter stabilized (with a relatively small standard error) from 1951 on. By contrast, NLOGIT estimates for the same parameter are highly unstable (with huge standard errors) until 1969. Consequently, WinBUGS is able to predict directing Oscar winners over the period 1951–1969 quite accurately, but NLOGIT is far less accurate, relying instead on basing predictions on the Golden Globe best director winner (which is less clearly associated with the directing Oscar winner). WinBUGS is able to obtain stable estimates that NLOGIT cannot because the Bayesian approach can be thought of as "shrinking" the maximum likelihood estimate toward the prior mean (zero in this case), particularly in early years when the data do not (yet) dominate the prior.

Results

The focus of interest for this analysis is the predictability of the single winner for each category in each year, so it seems reasonable to use "percent correctly predicted" as a goodness-of-fit criterion in this context. Thus, to assess the predictive accuracy of the various modeling choices tried, 1-year-ahead, out-of-sample errors were used. For instance, the four major Oscars winners for 1938 were predicted from a model fit to data from 1928–1937. Then, the winners for 1939 were predicted from a model fit to data from 1928–1938, and so on. For example, Table 10.2 provides predictions for the four main categories for the 2010 Academy Awards. The nominees are presented in order of expected probability to win, with the probabilities (in percentages) given in the third column and eventual winners shown in bold in the second column.

Using the MNL model in WinBUGS, 206 of the 292 best picture, directing, lead actor, and lead actress Oscar winners from 1938 to 2010 were correctly identified, corresponding to an overall prediction accuracy of 71 percent. This outperformed both the MNL model in NLOGIT and the ML model in WinBUGS. The main reason for the reduced performance of the MNL model in NLOGIT appears to be related to the inability of the estimation method to use some variables (e.g., Directors Guild of America wins) early in their history. The main reason for the reduced performance of the ML model in WinBUGS appears to be related to the nature of the data in the context of the ML model. In particular, in ML applications with repeated choices, it is possible to condition on an individual's previous choices to improve predictions of that individual's future (out-of-sample) choices. That is not possible here since each Oscar competition is essentially unique, and there are no repeated choices in this sense.

These results favor the MNL model over the ML model and also Bayesian estimation using WinBUGS over maximum likelihood estimation using NLOGIT. This confirms most of the model assessment results comparing the various modeling methods, so we selected the MNL model in WinBUGS as our final modeling method.

With more data available in the later years, prediction accuracy has improved over time. For instance, the overall prediction accuracy for the last 30 years (1981–2010) is 97 correct predictions out of 120, or 81 percent. Figure 10.1 summarizes overall results across the four categories.

In the main, the directing Oscar has been the most predictable, then the Oscars for best picture (until recently), lead actor, and lead actress, respectively. Each of the categories has tended to become more predictable over time, especially lead actress, which was very difficult to predict up until the early 1970s.

Table 10.2 The 2010 Predictions

Category	Nominee	Probability (%)	Notes
Best Picture	*The King's Speech*	84	*The King's Speech* scores high for receiving 12 overall nominations, but *True Grit* (10 nominations), *The Social Network* (8 nominations), and *Inception* (8 nominations) aren't too far behind. However, since *Inception* lacks an accompanying best director nomination, *The Fighter* (7 nominations) and *Black Swan* (5 nominations), which don't, score higher overall. Also, *The Fighter*, *The King's Speech*, and *The Social Network* have nominations in several other "strong" categories, such as acting (lead and supporting), screenplay, cinematography, and editing. Finally, the Producer's Guild win for *The King's Speech* usually carries more weight than the Golden Globe wins for *The Social Network* (drama) and *The Kids Are All Right* (musical or comedy). The remaining three films are real long shots. Overall, this category seems the hardest to call of the four major races this year.
	The Social Network	5	
	The Fighter	4	
	True Grit	4	
	Black Swan	1	
	Inception	1	
	The Kids Are All Right	<1	
	127 Hours	<1	
	Toy Story 3	<1	
	Winter's Bone	<1	
Director	**Tom Hooper** for *The King's Speech*	93	First-time nominee Tom Hooper benefits from his Director's Guild win and 12 overall nominations for *The King's Speech*, giving him a big advantage over the Coen brothers (Joel with two previous best director nominations, for 2007's *No Country for Old Men* and 1996's *Fargo*, and Ethan with one, for 2007's *No Country for Old Men*, while their 2010 film, *True Grit*, has 10 nominations), David O. Russell (first-time nominee for his film, *The Fighter*, with 7 nominations), David Fincher (one previous best director nomination for 2008's *The Curious Case of Benjamin Button*, while his 2010 film, *The Social Network*, has 8 nominations), and Darren Aronofsky (first-time nominee for his film, *Black Swan*, with 5 nominations).
	Joel Coen and Ethan Coen for *True Grit*	3	
	David O. Russell for *The Fighter*	2	
	David Fincher for *The Social Network*	2	
	Darren Aronofsky for *Black Swan*	1	

(continued)

Table 10.2 (Continued)

Category	Nominee	Probability (%)	Notes
Actor in a Leading Role	**Colin Firth** in *The King's Speech*	99	In a reverse from 2009, Colin Firth scores big for his Screen Actors Guild and Golden Globe wins, whereas Jeff Bridges is unlikely to win again this year.
	Jesse Eisenberg in *The Social Network*	<1	First-time nominees, Jesse Eisenberg and James Franco, and Javier Bardem, with a previous lead actor nomination for 2000's *Before Night Falls*, also seem
	James Franco in *127 Hours*	<1	unlikely to win this year. All indications point to an easy win for Colin Firth, but there have been big surprises in this category before, notably Denzel
	Javier Bardem in *Biutiful*	<1	Washington winning over Russell Crowe in 2001.
	Jeff Bridges in *True Grit*	<1	
Actress in a Leading Role	**Natalie Portman** in *Black Swan*	87	Natalie Portman scores big for Golden Globe (drama) and Screen Actors Guild awards and also for being nominated in a movie that has also been nominated
	Annette Bening in *The Kids Are All Right*	9	for best picture. Annette Bening and Jennifer Lawrence also benefit from having been nominated in movies that have been nominated for best picture. Annette
	Jennifer Lawrence in *Winter's Bone*	3	Bening benefits from her Golden Globe (musical or comedy) award, while Nicole Kidman's previous lead actress win for 2002's *The Hours* reduces her
	Michelle Williams in *Blue Valentine*	1	chance of winning again this year.
	Nicole Kidman in *Rabbit Hole*	1	

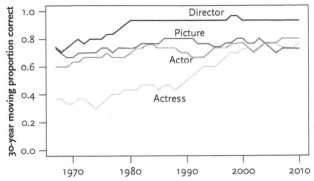

FIGURE 10.1 Thirty-year moving averages of the proportion of correct predictions for the four major Oscar categories (the moving average values are plotted at the end of each 30-year period, e.g., at the far right-hand side of the graph, the proportions of correct predictions for 1981–2010 are 0.93 for directing, 0.80 for lead actor, 0.77 for lead actress, and 0.73 for best picture).

However, the best picture winner has become a little less predictable recently, after the failure of the model to predict the winner from 2004 to 2006.

From the modeling process described earlier, the roles of the explanatory variables in helping to predict Oscar winners can change over time; Figure 10.2 illustrates with LOWESS smooths of posterior medians for the model parameters.

The importance of receiving a directing nomination (for best picture nominees) or a best picture nomination (for directing, lead actor, or lead actress nominees) has tended to increase over time (except perhaps for actors), as shown by the trends in the curves labeled "P." Previous nominations appear to have remained approximately equally important for directing nominees, but were more important for lead actor nominees in the past than they have been more recently (curves labeled "N"). Previous wins seemed to hurt lead actor nominees less in the 1960s and 1970s than in the 1940s and more recently, whereas previous wins have tended to become less important for lead actress nominees over time (curves labeled "W").

The Golden Globes have remained useful predictors of future Oscar success since their inception. The changing fortunes of dramas (curves labeled "D") and musicals and comedies (curves labeled "M") can be traced in Figure 10.2, with musicals and comedies appearing to hold an advantage over dramas in the 1960s with respect to best picture wins, but with acting wins tending to favor dramas, particularly for males. Guild awards have clearly enabled quite accurate prediction of directing winners, and, to a lesser extent, best picture winners (curves labeled "G"). Since they have had a much shorter history, it is not clear whether the Screen Actors Guild awards will be just as helpful in predicting acting wins, although early indications suggest this is so.

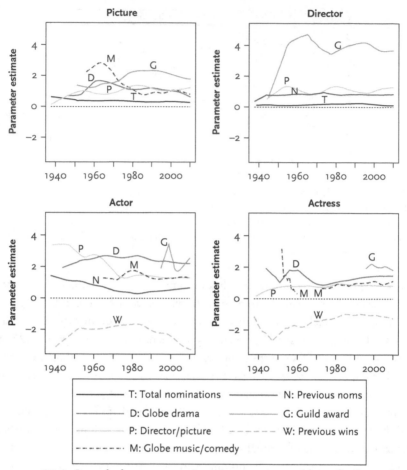

FIGURE 10.2 Smoothed parameter estimates—posterior medians—for the explanatory variables for each of the four major Oscar categories.

The effect of the total number of Oscar nominations (curves labeled "T") on prediction of the best picture and directing Oscars remains reasonably steady. Since the number of nominations that a movie can receive has ranged in the past between one and fourteen, this variable is more influential than it appears to be in the graphs (which show the effects of the number of nominations increasing by 1). The effects of the "front-runner" variables—which cut across all four categories—are not shown in Figure 10.2 (they appeared to be less important than the other variables, having estimates with smaller magnitudes and larger standard errors).

The analysis also reveals which past nominees have really upset the odds (winners with low estimated probability of winning) and which appear to have been truly robbed (losers with high estimated probability of winning). Table 10.3 provides details of the five "most surprising" outcomes in each category (based on

Table 10.3 Five Outcomes in Each of the Major Categories with the Smallest
Estimated win Probabilities for the Actual Winner Relative to the Predicted Winner

Year	Winner	Probability	Predicted	Probability
Best Picture				
1948	*Hamlet*	0.01	*Johnny Belinda*	0.97
2004	*Million Dollar Baby*	0.01	*The Aviator*	0.97
1981	*Chariots of Fire*	0.01	*Reds*	0.88
1967	*In the Heat of the Night*	0.02	*The Graduate*	0.94
1956	*Around the World in 80 Days*	0.02	*The King and I*	0.82
Directing				
2000	Steven Soderbergh	0.01	Ang Lee	0.95
1968	Carol Reed	0.02	Anthony Harvey	0.97
1972	Bob Fosse	0.03	Francis Ford Coppola	0.96
2002	Roman Polanski	0.03	Rob Marshall	0.92
1949	Joseph L. Mankiewicz	0.02	Robert Rossen	0.50
Lead Actor				
2001	Denzel Washington	0.00	Russell Crowe	0.99
1968	Cliff Robertson	0.00	Peter O'Toole	0.88
1974	Art Carney	0.02	Jack Nicholson	0.87
1946	Fredric March	0.02	Gregory Peck	0.85
1944	Bing Crosby	0.03	Alexander Knox	0.79
Lead Actress				
2002	Nicole Kidman	0.07	Renée Zellweger	0.90
1985	Geraldine Page	0.07	Whoopi Goldberg	0.70
1950	Judy Holliday	0.09	Gloria Swanson	0.76
1999	Hilary Swank	0.10	Annette Bening	0.78
1952	Shirley Booth	0.11	Susan Hayward	0.84

the model results). A complete listing of the results is available at the web site
http://www.iainpardoe.com/oscars/ (which is updated with upcoming Oscar
predictions in February of each year).

Discussion

Discrete choice modeling of past data on Oscar nominees in the four major categories—best picture, directing, lead actor, and lead actress—enables prediction

of the winners in these categories with an impressively high degree of success. If recent trends persist, it should be possible to predict future winners with a prediction success rate of approximately 73 percent for picture, 93 percent for directing, 80 percent for lead actor, and 77 percent for lead actress. Curiously, although predictive accuracy has been largely increasing (Figure 10.1), the parameter estimates for predictors often exhibit nonmonotonic trends (Figure 10.2). Thus, the results indicate that the dynamics are more complicated than would be expected if it were a simple matter of the Academy voters gradually converging on the assessments underlying the Golden Globes and Guild awards.

It is also notable that the historical changes in these parameters do not display the same trajectories for the four categories. Most strikingly, the lead actor and lead actress categories not only have different predictors, and different parameter estimates for the predictors that they share, but also the changes in the parameter estimates do not always follow the same trend (e.g., the impact of previous wins). Such contrasts may eventually provide an explanation for gender differences in the degree that acting awards or nominations (whether lead or supporting) are coupled with a best picture award or nomination (Simonton, 2011).

Nevertheless, parameter estimates are generally consistent with commonly held views about the Oscars. Heavily nominated films with complementary best picture and directing nominations tend to do well, and nominees with previous Golden Globe or Guild awards are also favored. To the extent that the corresponding predictors reflect some measure of merit, the Oscar process would seem to be meeting its goal of recognizing outstanding achievement in film. Further, the results support the notion that previous Oscar nominations benefit directors and actors, whereas previous Oscar wins reduce the chance of an actor or actress winning again. However, the actual merit of an acting performance should probably not be contingent on how many times an individual was nominated in the past or on how many times he or she has won the award before. This would seem to indicate that the directing and lead acting Oscars may be as reflective of achievement over a lifetime as of achievement for a particular film. Finally, actors and actresses who are nominated for performances in heavily nominated films (particularly those with a best picture nomination) do indeed fare better than their peers in less highly acclaimed films. Again, this observation might seem to be at odds with a purely objective assessment of the quality of an acting performance.

The recent increase in the number of best picture nominees from five to ten raises the question of whether predictions are strongly affected, either for that category or for the acting/directing categories. There is no clearly discernible change since the model automatically adjusts for the number of nominees in a category, and the prediction method is essentially unchanged. If we were to take out the five "weakest" best picture nominees and rerun the model for the last 2 years, the prediction probabilities for the five remaining nominees would not change all that much. Moving forward, it seems reasonable to expect that the number of best picture nominees with a reasonable chance of winning will probably continue to be just two or three movies each year.

The results also help us to assess those occasions when the Oscars fail to be awarded in a manner consistent with true merit. For instance, there has been much media speculation about legendary individuals who have never won an Oscar, such as Alfred Hitchcock with five directing nominations, Peter O'Toole with eight lead actor nominations, Richard Burton with six lead actor nominations, and Deborah Kerr with six lead actress nominations. According to the predictions, the unluckiest was probably O'Toole, who came closest to winning in 1968 (with an 89 percent modeled probability of winning) and 1964 (with 83 percent probability). Kerr came close in 1956 (with 72 percent probability), as did Burton in 1977 (with 62 percent probability), and Hitchcock's nearest miss was for *Rebecca* in 1940 (with 42 percent probability). In some instances, the Academy decided to make corrections for various inadvertent false negatives. In particular, Hitchcock, Kerr, and O'Toole were eventually awarded honorary Oscars as compensation.

To be sure, sometimes the errors of prediction may be too great, making the Oscars look worse than they really deserve. Although many were surprised when Denzel Washington won over Russell Crowe in the 2001 Oscar race for lead actor, the surprise may not be nearly as extreme as implied by the model predictions of less than 0.01 probability for Denzel Washington versus 0.99 probability for Russell Crowe. Another example is the failure of *Brokeback Mountain* to win best picture for 2005 after winning both Golden Globe and Producer's Guild of America awards. Nevertheless, the surprise of *Crash* winning instead was not as great as that implied by the model predictions of 0.03 probability for *Crash* versus 0.90 probability for *Brokeback Mountain*. Clearly, the model was unable to make use of the late surge that *Crash* made and the apparent backlash against *Brokeback Mountain* (in unquantifiable "Hollywood buzz" terms) as the Oscar ceremony drew near. In so far as such intangibles confound the Oscar outcomes, complete predictive precision is probably unattainable. Nonetheless, it is also conceivable that the addition of new predictors can reduce the number and magnitude of observed errors. Furthermore, it would be instructive to extend the analyses described in this chapter to other Oscar categories, such as the supporting acting and screenwriting awards.

However, future research on this question should not simply focus on empirical prediction. In the long run, theoretical explanation would be no less important. For instance, it would be important to identify any causal process that underlies the various awards. Previous research has suggested two alternative kinds of processes (Simonton, 2011). On the one hand, the various award measures for a given category could be the consequence of a single underlying factor or latent variable that indicates the actual relative merit of the pictures, directors, actors, and actresses. The Oscar awards and nominations would then be a function of this latent factor plus some random shock or error term (sympathy votes, current events, etc.). On the other hand, the diverse awards may reflect a more dynamic process—a reasonable hypothesis given that the award ceremonies are not all on the same day. Because the Oscars are the last awards bestowed in a given year, the Academy voters may benefit in a substantial way from previous awards and nominations or even by rumors of awards and nominations. According to this model, the merit of a picture, director, actor, or actress is not a stable attribute behind all awards, but rather a transient assessment that evolves over time. Although prior empirical investigations have supported the former single-factor model over the latter autoregressive model, these two theoretical accounts have not yet been tested for movie awards.

Improving both prediction and explanation may prove more valuable than just satisfying our intellectual curiosity of a highly visible event. Conceivably, predictive and explanatory models can indicate the specific ways that the Oscars can go wrong. This knowledge might lead to recommendations about how to improve the Academy's selection and voting process. Even if the Academy were unwilling or unable to introduce the necessary improvements—as seems to hold for the notoriously questionable "best foreign language film" category—these prediction methods can provide a useful antidote to the dramatic announcements of Oscar night. In particular, the discrete choice models can help filmmakers and moviegoers alike assess how much faith they can place in the identity of the "best" picture, director, actor, or actress. To what extent does a given award reflect the merits of the actual cinematic performance, rather than represent less relevant processes operating among Academy voters? Given the tremendous consequences of taking an Oscar home, these results would have far more than academic interest.

References

Ginsburgh, V. (2003). Awards, success and aesthetic quality in the arts. *Journal of Economic Perspectives, 17*, 99–111.

McFadden, D. (1974). Conditional logit analysis of qualitative choice behavior. In P. Zarembka (Ed.), *Frontiers in econometrics* (pp. 105–142). New York: Academic Press.

Pardoe, I., & Simonton, D. K. (2008). Applying discrete choice models to predict Academy Award winners. *Journal of the Royal Statistical Society, Series A, 171,* 375–394.

Peary, D. (1993). *Alternate Oscars: One critic's defiant choices for best picture, actor, and actress from 1927 to the present.* New York: Delta.

Simonton, D. K. (2004). Film awards as indicators of cinematic creativity and achievement: A quantitative comparison of the Oscars and six alternatives. *Creativity Research Journal, 16,* 163–172.

Simonton, D. K. (2011). *Great flicks: Scientific studies of cinematic creativity and aesthetics.* New York: Oxford University Press.

11 RESPONSES TO AND JUDGMENTS OF ACTING ON FILM

Thalia R. Goldstein

Although there is theoretical and empirical work on why we like or how we understand a film as a whole, no previous empirical work has specifically investigated how we understand acting on film. Acting, in which a person plays a character as realistically as possible without the intent to deceive, is omnipresent in our popular world; yet it is also understudied. This is particularly odd considering the connections acting has to diverse areas of psychology such as empathy, emotion regulation, theory of mind, imagination, and embodied cognition—connections that acting theorists and actors have long explored (see Roach, 1985).

Despite our attraction to acting, our love of acting, and the amount of time devoted to watching acting, there is very little empirical work on acting. In this chapter, I discuss why we might like acting, how we understand acting, and how we judge acting—whether we notice it at all and how we value it. Next, I present two studies conducted on judgments of acting: the first looked to determine developmentally whether children and adults notice acting differences between similar movies and whether they use acting as a characteristic by which they judge the quality of movie. The second explored whether adults could tell the difference between acting based on different theories and whether lay judgments of an actor's emotionality match the proposals put forward by those different theories of acting. I end by noting some future directions for research on acting and why acting can be a fruitful area of research in the social sciences.

Watching Others Act

Audience members do not passively watch acting as it is occurring, but actively create a world with the actors (Zamir, 2010). This is different from reading fiction, although many theorists combine watching dramatic performances into their theories of processing literature. In acting, we are watching real humans create worlds in front of us; while reading, we create imagined worlds for ourselves, imbuing them with imagined voices and physical embodiment. Yet, by choosing to watch a movie, we choose to watch other people create those worlds for us, and we value when they can do so as closely to the reality of our everyday lives as possible (excepting, of course, broad slapstick and farce).

The question of why we like to watch others act has several possible answers. One is that watching acting allows our *alief system* to work. Alief is an automatic affective reaction to an event that may be at odds with our beliefs (Gendler, 2008a; 2008b). For example, although we full well know that what is happening on screen is false—it is a fictional movie, and the person on screen is a well-known actor whom we have seen in many other movies—our alief system "starts up" our affective and physiological responses before we have a chance to stop them—thus the fear we feel at Freddy from *Friday the 13th*. We have a reaction that is incongruent with our "reasonable" mind. Perhaps this is part of the fun of watching realistic acting. We can have a strong alief emotional reaction without any real-life consequences.

Another possibility for our love of realistic acting is that it is a way to "safely" practice theory of mind (i.e., our understanding of others' minds) (Mar & Oatley, 2008; Zunshine, 2006). Much like dogs and other animals play fight as a way to practice real fighting, individuals' fictionalized worlds are a way to rehearse their real social worlds. The real world is messy and high stakes, and mistakes based on social processing are costly. In comparison, the fictionalized social world is easy and safe. We readily, easily, and constantly process behavior into its underlying intentions and emotions (Baldwin & Baird, 2001); even processing physical characteristics is linked to mental state processing (Teufel, Fletcher, & Davis, 2010). Watching acting allows us to do this while not having to deal with the mess of mixed behaviors, signals, and emotions found in the real world.

A final possible reason we enjoy acting is because we see the craft of it. We appreciate in acting, as in all art, virtuosity, self-expression, and talent (Bloom, 2010). Anyone who believes that acting is easily done is ignoring the large numbers of unnatural and bad performances available in B-movies and quickly cancelled television shows each season (not to mention big-budget flicks with "wooden" performances). The ability of a person to transform him- or herself wholly into another person, physically and emotionally, is something we admire: we call it fearless and have strong opinions over who does it best. But how do we understand it?

Understanding Acting

Although we do it on a daily basis, from a cognitive perspective, acting is hard to perceive. There are no obvious cues to its falseness within the behavior of the actor, and although people in film are acting, an actor may look, sound, and move like the character he is portraying. The perception of acting, particularly the separation of actor and character, has long been discussed in the acting community. There are many anecdotal stories of actors being confused with their characters and approached on the street by angry fans, demanding to know why they broke up with their character's love interest; actors who played doctors on TV have been besieged for medical advice (Gerbner & Gross, 1976).

Several cognitive approaches could explain how we understand acting. One possibility is that we understand it as we do pretend—that we quantify it as false and proceed from there. The problem with this approach is that the behavior on film is often as true to real life as possible. As a culture, we value realistic acting, and most films follow this value by trying to proceed as convincingly as possible. A second possibility for how we understand acting is that we treat it as lying. This solves the problem of the realism of behavior—liars try to show realistic behavior as well. The problem with understanding acting as lying is that everyone involved knows that what is happening on film is not actually happening in real life. When understanding lying, only the liar knows that what he or she is doing is not true. Therefore, acting provides a sort of hybrid for understanding—it is not pretend because the behavior is too realistic. And it is not lying because everyone is in on the falseness of the proceedings (Goldstein & Bloom, 2011).

Other theories taken from the literature on understanding fiction or theatre as a whole could help to explain how we understand the actor. Modern theatre theorists look to cognitive and neuroscience research to build ideas of how we understand acting. A current leading theory, *conceptual blending* (Fauconnier & Turner, 2003), proposes that audience members' blend their understanding. In the mind of the audience member, the concepts of reality, character, fantasy, and narrative are blended (rather than using some other form of cognition such as the "suspension of disbelief") to create the framework in which the audience member then processes and reacts to the work of theatricality happening before him or her (McConachie & Hart, 2006). The blending of the different frames of thought therefore takes on more power than the sum of the parts.

Once an audience member understands acting, the next process that occurs is likely judgment of the actor. Every year, numerous awards are presented for acting in film, with the awardees celebrated in huge publicity campaigns. Yet not much is known about how we judge acting, what qualities we use when specifically considering acting to judge a film, and whether we pick up on subtleties of an actor's technique when comparing actors.

Judging Acting

Most research on judgment of film ratings have focused on the film holistically, taking into account the directors, designers, screenwriters, editors, producers, and actors in one fell swoop. Very little to no work has investigated responses to the most obvious part of a film—the actors in front of you. At an even more basic level, no work has asked two questions: (1) Do we notice acting when making judgments of films? and (2) Do we use acting as a qualification when deciding between two similar films? Although the hand of the director, editor, producer, and other artisans attached to the film is often hoped to fade away so that the audience cannot see their influence, the impact of the actor is meant to be front and center. Publicity campaigns for movies feature actors. It is not often that you see a producer, screenwriter, or director on late-night television hawking his or her movie; few laypersons could name their five favorite film editors. (This is by no means to undermine these persons' influence on the outcome of a film, only to point out that acting should be given weight as a separate area of study).

Although not focusing on lay audiences, some work has shown connections between awards won by acting and overall awards won by films. For example, women's acting performances are less associated with best picture Academy Award winners than are men's acting performances (Simonton, 2004). Acting awards are also associated with adaptations of Broadway shows, initial critics' ratings, and running time but not with adaptations of classics or adaptations by the original author, first weekend gross, or technical awards such as visual effects (Simonton, 2009).

In a study that asked about children's perceptions of acting, Grady (1999) found that 71 percent of children think that childhood roles should not be played by adults and should instead be played by the most realistic actor available. However, no previous work has directly looked at children's use of acting to judge films. The following study looked to whether adults and children attended to acting when making judgments of difference between two movies and judgments of preference, and if so, what aspects of acting they mentioned.

Study: Development of Judgment of Acting of Film

Participants were twenty-eight adults from the human subject pool at Boston College and twelve children (aged 5–12 years; M = 7 years, 6 months) from a suburb of Boston, Massachusetts. Adult participants received participation credit in their introduction to psychology class, and child participants received a certificate of participation. Because this is the first study of its kind, we chose to study a large range of ages to see if any clear developmental trends occurred.

Movies. Participants watched four movie clips from two "sets" of movies, one original and one remake. The first set was *Charlie and the Chocolate Factory* (Siegel et al., 2005) and *Willy Wonka and the Chocolate Factory* (Wolper & Stuart, 1971). The second set were two versions of *The Parent Trap* (Meyers/Shyer Company, Walt Disney Pictures & Meyer, 1998; Walt Disney Pictures & Swift, 1961). These movies were chosen because they were relatively similar in plot and script, were widely released and popular, and were appropriate for children. From the *Willy Wonka* movies, we showed the scene in which one of the children, Violet, eats a piece of meal replacement gum she is not supposed to touch and suffers the consequences by turning into a blueberry during the dessert course. From *The Parent Trap* movies, we showed the scene in which the main character, now switched with her identical twin sister, sees her grandfather and then mother for the first time in many years.

Questionnaire. To investigate as widely as possible what individuals "pick out" from movies as important in their judgments of quality, we simply asked participants to describe every difference they remembered seeing between the two movies. Then participants were asked which version of the movie they liked better, and why.

Procedure. All participants were tested individually in a quiet room. Two children asked to have their parent present as they watched the movies, but parents did not respond or interfere in any way. Participants watched a set of movies, completed the questionnaires about those movies, and then watched the second set of movies and complete a second set of questionnaires. Order of movies and order of movie sets were counterbalanced across participants. Adult participants wrote their own responses whereas child participants told their responses to an experimenter, who completed the response sheet for them.

Results

Because we had no a priori hypothesis about what participants would pick out as differences between the movies or reasons for preferring one movie over another, we developed a coding scheme based on all possible aspects of a movie that could be chosen. Possible codes were then narrowed down based on the actual responses of the participants. All responses were coded by two independent coders, with a third coder (the author) resolving any discrepancies. Each statement a participant made was qualitatively coded into one of eleven categories, which can be found in Appendix 1, along with examples comments from each category. Table 11.1 shows the percentage of participants who made a comment about each of the codes, both when asked about differences between the movies and when asked about preferences between the movies.

The three codes we were particularly interested in were "acting," "actors," and "casting" because they all directly or indirectly referenced the performances of the actors. "Acting" was any comment referencing the quality of the acting, emotional expression, line readings, or physicality of the actors. An "actor" comment referenced the specific person playing a role (e.g., Johnny Depp or Lindsay Lohan). Finally, "casting" comments referenced the person playing a role without mentioning the actor specifically (e.g., "the girl with longer hair" or "there is a mom in this movie, a dad in the last one").

When asked to describe what differences they saw between the two movies, children discussed acting only 12.5 percent of the time, casting 62.5 percent of the time, and actors not at all. When asked to describe why they preferred one movie to the other, children mentioned acting 16.67 percent of the time, casting 12.5 percent of the time, and actors not at all. The comments on acting only came from children over the age of 9: the 5- to 8-year-olds never mentioned acting. Comments about casting were more widespread; children across the age range tested made comments about the casting choices of the movie. Examples

Table 11.1 Percentages of Comments for Each Type of Code

Code	Adult: Differences (%)	Adult: Preferences (%)	Child: Differences (%)	Child: Preferences (%)
Acting	51	57.5	12	16
Actor	1.5	15.5	0	0
Casting	53.5	7.5	62.5	12.5
Scene	46	22	33	4
Prop	14.5	0	33	8
Special Effects	32.5	42	8	8
Music	13	4	8	0
Mood	10.5	9	12	16.5
Plot	57.5	10	45.5	8
Wording	52.5	12	12	4
Viewer	14.5	44	12	37.5

of children's comments about acting included "The new one Willy Wonka was watching everyone carefully, and being a good actor and no one was listening" (12 years old), and "Willy Wonka reacted better in the second version of the movie" (10 years old). Comments about the casting included "The girl looked different" (5 years old), and "The second one had an older girl" (8 years old). When explaining why they chose one movie as better, children were more likely to describe a broad personal preference (e.g., "I just like it more") than any other reason.

When adults were asked to describe what differences they saw between the two movies, they discussed acting 51 percent of the time, casting 53.5 percent of the time, and actors 1.5 percent of the time. When asked to describe why they preferred one movie to the other, adults mentioned acting 57.5 percent of the time (the most of any code), casting 7.5 percent of the time, and actors 15.5 percent of the time. Examples of adults' comments about acting included "[in the] old one—acting appears a bit more forced" and "The expression of the mother was more animated in the new scene." Adult comments about the casting included "Violet was with her mother in the new and her dad in the old" and comments about the actors included "I like Johnny Depp."

Discussion

Although preliminary in nature, from this study, we can see that adults do pick up on and make judgments of preference based on acting and actors in movies. Children over the age of 9 also pay attention to the acting, whereas children between the ages of 5 and 8, at least in our limited sample, do not notice acting or do not comment on it.

When describing preferences between two movies, adults are very likely to mention acting or actors, as well as special effects. Children, meanwhile, are most likely to mention a personal preference, but also may mention the overall mood of a film. This study shows that whereas older children notice and discuss acting, younger children do not. Although studies involving judgment of films often have participants rate holistically, this study shows that it may be important to separate out different components of a film in order to best gage children's judgment of preference.

Study: Judgment of Acting Style: "Technique" Versus "Method" Acting

A second area of judgment of acting, one central to many theorists, is the importance of personal emotional feeling in the performance of a character's emotion.

Although most modern acting is a conglomeration of many theories and techniques as refined by the particular teacher of a particular class, in the Western tradition of acting, there are historically two opposing schools of thought about the proper way to rehearse and create a realistic portrayal of a character. Broadly, these as known as "method" and "technique."

"Method" theory, as known and practiced in the United States is derivative of the "System" of Konstantin Stanislavky (Stanislavsky, 1950). In Stanislavky's system, the way to create emotional realism on-stage and on-screen was for the actor to truly feel the emotions of the character. The most famous of method acting coaches, Lee Strasberg, believed that all of the emotions of a character should come from the emotions of an actor, felt in the moment of a performance and related back to emotional moments in the life of the actor (Hull, 1985). Realism in acting could only be achieved through the connection of the character's life to the actor's life, with the accompanying memories and emotional states.

In contrast, and dating back to the writings of French philosopher Denis Diderot (1957/1770) "technique" theories of acting proposed that to feel real emotions while performing would be disastrous. Instead, the actor should be like a puppeteer, pulling the strings that make the character come alive but keeping a considerable psychological distance. Connecting to the physicality of the character is key, and knowing the outward expression of emotion while keeping one's insides calm is the way to a masterful performance.

Lay conceptions of what good acting is, particularly in the United States, are apt to be closer to "method" theories. We value extreme emotional moments in our actors, and celebrity reporters breathlessly examine how and when actors are affected by their performances. Although there is some truth to the common notion that individuals playing lovers on-screen fall in love, whether this is due to acting as lovers in a movie or merely spending several months together on location is an empirical question still open to study. However, the myths of Marlon Brando's off-screen intensity and Dustin Hoffman's devotion to his roles show a propensity for Americans to think of acting in terms of actors' emotional connections to their characters. This intuition also matches findings in self-perception theory (Bem, 1972) and the facial feedback hypothesis (Soussignan, 2002), both of which would propose that actors blend reality and pretend for themselves as they experience themselves going through the events as a character. We also know this feedback happens to nonactors: the physicalization of certain postures and states can cause feedback to individuals that they are actually in those states (Carney, Cuddy, & Yap, 2010).

Previous work has shown that college students can distinguish between more and less experienced actors, without paying attention to the theory they are using to act. When asked to play a scene with dual meanings (i.e., the character is pretending to have a stomach ache when he is actually fine), as compared to a scene with only a single meaning (i.e., the character has a stomach ache), the less experience an actor has, the less subtle his actions, and therefore the more easily an audience can understand the dual nature of his message (Ando & Koyasu, 2008). The more realistically an actor performed, the more difficult it is for an audience to tell what he was trying to play. However, this study did not ask specifically whether the audience believed that the emotions or physical state of the character were really happening to the actor. Thus, we wanted to investigate whether people can (1) tell the difference between method actors and technique actors based on the actors' connections to the their roles and (2) judged characters played by method actors to have more intense emotions.

Participants. Participants were thirty-four undergraduate psychology students (ten male, twenty-four female) at Boston College, aged between 18 and 21 (M = 19 years, 2 months). Participants received course credit for their involvement.

Movies. Participants watched short clips (less than 2 minutes each) from two different movies. These two movies were chosen because (1) they had the same script, and (2) one version of each movie was created in the United States with American actors and one version was created in the United Kingdom with British actors. Because American acting is traditionally method in origin and British acting is traditionally technique in origin, we wanted to ensure as much as possible that different acting techniques were used by the different casts. To do this, we researched the schools in which each of the actors had received their training.

The first movie, *A Doll's House* (Les Films de la Boétie & Losby, 1973), starred Jane Fonda. Fonda trained at Vassar College and then at the Actor's Studio with Lee Strasberg. Lee Strasberg was a direct disciple of Konstantin Stanislavsky and is considered the strongest proponent of the "method." His "method" involves a deep emotional connection to characters based on real emotional experiences in the actor's own life and a large amount of emotional work on the character before performances begin (Hull, 1985). Paired with this movie was *A Doll's House* (BBC & Garland, 1992), starring Juliet Stevenson. Stevenson trained at the Royal Academy of Dramatic Arts, the top acting school in England, which boasts such luminaries as Peter O'Toole and Vivian Leigh as their alumni. Although no publications have come from this school describing its theory of acting, alumni from the school have often discussed in interviews and their own books how they were trained to focus on the words of the script and the physical natures of the characters and to shy away from emotional investment or feeling the emotions of their characters. From these two movies, participants watched the same scene, in which Nora and Torvald have a conversation just before Nora leaves. The dialogue, setting, costumes, music, and lighting were almost identical between the two movies.

Questionnaire. To test individuals' judgments and reactions to movies with different acting styles, we created a questionnaire that asked about judgments of the *character* and judgments of the *actor*. Participants completed eight questions about each video, four about the character and four about the actor. To judge the character, they were asked "What emotion is the *character* feeling?" (short answer) and "How strongly is the *character* feeling that emotion?" on a 1–7 Likert scale. They then judged "What emotion is the *character* showing?" (short answer) and "How strongly is the *character* showing that emotion?" (1–7 Likert scale). To judge the actor, they were asked "What emotion is the *actor* feeling?" (short answer) and "How strongly is the *actor* feeling that emotion?" (1–7 Likert scale). Finally, they were asked "What emotion is the *actor* showing? (short answer) and "How strongly is the *actor* showing that emotion?" (1–7 Likert scale). Two coders judged the answers to the questions about which emotions the character and actor were feeling/showing as matching (1 point), partially matching (0.5 points) or not matching (0 points).

Procedure. Participants were tested individually in a quiet room. They were given instructions to simply complete the questionnaire on the movie(s) they had just watched and to ask the experimenter if they had any questions. Participants watched the first movie and completed the "acting" questionnaire, then watched the second movie and completed a second "acting" questionnaire. Order of movies was counterbalanced between participants.

Results

To calculate participant's intuitions about the emotions felt by the actor and character, we conducted paired-sample t-tests on each of the questions. Surprisingly, participants judged the character to be feeling stronger emotions in the technique movie ($M = 5.77$) than in the method movie ($M = 5.29$), t (34) = 1.99, $p = .05$. They also judged the actor's internal state as marginally more likely to match the external state of the character in the technique movie ($M = 0.49$) than in the method movie ($M = 0.29$), t (34) = 1.64, $p = .10$, and judged the actor as showing marginally stronger emotions in the technique movie ($M = 5.37$) than in the method movie ($M = 4.91$), t (34) = 1.83, $p = .07$. The participants did not judge the character as showing different strengths of emotion between the two movies (even though they judged them as feeling stronger emotions in the technique movie), nor did they judge the actors as feeling different levels of emotions between the two movies (although they judged the actors to be showing marginally stronger emotions in the technique movie).

Discussion

These results are surprising because they contradict what acting theories would predict. Given the emphasis on personal emotion in method theory and the emphasis on staying away from emotion in technique theory, we hypothesized that audience members would judge the method actor as feeling stronger emotions and matching the emotions of his or her character more often than would the technique actor. However, we found that the technique actor was judged to show stronger emotions than the method actor, and the technique actor's character was judged to be showing stronger emotions than the method actor's character. Finally, and opposite to what technique acting theory would predict, participants judged the actor's internal state to be more likely to match the character's external state for the technique actor than for the method actor.

Of course, it should be noted that we cannot assume the theory that the actors used when creating and performing their characters used in the movies watched by the participants. It is possible that every actor was feeling the emotions of his or her character, or that every actor was having an off day when she filmed the scenes chosen for this study, and therefore was "phoning in" his or her performance. It is also possible that the participants were not responding to the links between feeling and showing emotions in acting, but rather to slight differences in costume, lighting, or other factors explored in the previous study of judgments of acting on film.

However, if what participants are judging are differing levels of emotionality felt by the actors, these results are particularly surprising because they challange what acting theory would predict. Participants thought that the technique actor was more emotionally connected to his or her character and expressing more emotions than the method actor. Perhaps the theory an actor brings to his or her role does not have the effect on performance that would be anticipated. Or, perhaps an emphasis on internal emotional connection to a character does not translate to an external showing of emotion. Likely, there are other factors at work, yet to be investigated.

Looking Forward

The empirical study of acting is a wide open field, waiting to be explored. In work I am currently running, I am investigating children's understanding of the distinction between actor and character: Do they understand that there is a person underneath the character who is a wholly separate entity? And, if so, do children treat the physical characteristics of that person as different from the emotional characteristics of that person (as they relate to the character)? On the one hand, it is easy to understand that the physical characteristics of a character do not migrate to the actor: a character who breaks his leg does not require that the actor also sustains an injury. However, the emotional life of a character is a bit more difficult to comprehend. Due to variations in acting theory, it is possible that the emotional state of a character *is* in fact intertwined with the emotional state of the actor. Also, actors may have gone out and previously trained and gained skills they felt would aid in their portrayal of a character: for instance, learning how to cook when preparing for a role as a professional chef. My current work does not seek to answer the questions of actor–character connection from the actor's point of view, but rather seeks to investigate children's intuitions about the realistically portrayed characters they see every day on their television and film screens.

There is a shared interest among acting theorists, practitioners, and cognitive scientists to understand the workings of the human mind and its connections to the body. Acting, particularly its modern form as a realistic portrayal of our emotions and behaviors, can provide a new lens and a test case for theories of several different areas of cognitive science. Actors could shed light on facial feedback and self-perception because they must inhabit the physicalities of multiple characters in obviously false situations. Acting can provide a test of the development of children's understanding of lying, pretend, and theory of mind and of adults' understanding of layers of knowledge and intention. With clear ties to human behavior already extensively studied in psychology and cognitive science, there is scientific potential in studying why and how we desire the realistic portrayal of fictional situations.

Acknowledgments

Some portions of this material are based on work supported by the National Science Foundation under a grant awarded in 2010, and other portions of this research were conducted while the author was on appointment as a U.S. Department of Homeland Security (DHS) Fellow under the DHS Scholarship and Fellowship Program, a program administered by the Oak Ridge Institute for Science and Education (ORISE) for DHS through an interagency agreement with the US Department of Education (DOE). ORISE is managed by Oak Ridge Associated Universities under DOE Contract Number DE-AC05-00OR22750. All opinions expressed in this article are the author's and do not necessarily reflect the policies and views of NSF, DHS, DOE, or ORISE. Thank you to the many

RAs who helped with data collection and analysis, particularly Nick Ackerman, Kaitilin Mahoney, Emma Racioppo, Lauren Moore, and Lily Lamb-Atkinson for their help with data collection and analysis. I thank Ellen Winner for her guidance with this research and Paul Bloom for helpful discussions on this topic.

References

Ando, H., & Koyasu, M. (2008). Differences between acting as if one is experiencing pain and acting as if one is pretending to have pain among actors at three expertise levels. In S. Ikatura & K. Fujita (Eds.), *Origins of the Social Mind* (pp. 123–140). Japan: Springer.

Baldwin, D. A., & Baird, J. A. (2001). Discerning intentions in dynamic human action. *Trends in Cognitive Sciences, 5*(4), 171–178.

Bem, D. J. (1972). Self-perception theory. *Advances in Experimental Social Psychology, 6*, 1–62.

Bloom, P. (2010). *How pleasure works*. New York: W. W. Norton & Company.

British Broadcasting Service (Producer) & Garland, P. (Director). (1992). *A doll's house* [Motion Picture]. UK: British Broadcasting Service.

Carney, D. R., Cuddy, A. J., & Yap, A. J. (2010). Power posing brief nonverbal displays affect neuroendocrine levels and risk tolerance. *Psychological Science, 21*, 1363–1368.

Diderot, D. (1957) *The paradox of the actor.* (L. Strasberg, Intro, H. Irving, Preface). (Original work published 1770). New York: Hill & Wang.

Fauconnier, G., & Turner, M. (2003). *The way we think: Conceptual blending and the mind's hidden complexities.* New York: Basic Books.

Gendler, T. S. (2008a). Alief and belief. *Journal of Philosophy, 105*(10), 634–663.

Gendler, T. S. (2008b). Alief in action (and reaction). *Mind & Language, 23*(5), 552–585.

Gerbner, G., & Gross, L. (1976). The scary world of TV's heavy viewer. *Psychology Today, 9*(11), 41–45.

Goldstein, T. R., & Bloom, P. (2011). The mind on stage: Why cognitive scientists should study acting. *Trends in Cognitive Sciences, 15*, 141–142.

Grady, S. (1999). Asking the audience: Talking to children about representation in children. *Youth Theatre Journal, 13*, 82–92.

Hull, L. S. (1985). *Strasberg's method: As taught by Lorrie Hull.* Woodbridge, CT: Ox Bow Publishing.

Les Films de la Boétie (Producer) & Losby, J. (Director). (1973). *A doll's house* [Motion Picture]. USA: Tomorrow Entertainment.

Mar, R. A., & Oatley, K. (2008). The function of fiction is the abstraction and simulation of social experience. *Perspectives on Psychological Science, 3*(3), 173.

McConachie, B., & Hart, F. E. (Eds.). (2006). *Performance and Cognition: Theatre Studies and the Cognitive Turn* (Vol. 4). New York: Routledge.

Meyers/Shyer Company (Producer), Walt Disney Pictures (Producer) & Meyer, N. (Director) (1998). *The parent trap* [Motion Picture]. USA: Buena Vista Pictures.

Roach, J. (1985). *The player's passion* Newark, NJ: University of Delaware Press.

Siegel, M. (Executive Producer), Grey, B. (Producer), Zanuck, R. D. (Producer), Dahl, L. (Executive Producer) McCormick, P. (Executive Producer), Berman, B. (Executive Producer), & Burton, T. (Director). (2005). *Charlie and the chocolate factory* [Motion Picture]. USA: Warner Brothers.

Simonton, D. K. (2004). The "best actress" paradox: Outstanding feature films versus exceptional women's performances. *Sex Roles, 50*(11), 781–794.

Simonton, D. K. (2009). Cinematic success, aesthetics, and economics: An exploratory recursive model. *Psychology of Aesthetics, Creativity, and the Arts, 3*(3), 128–138. doi:10.1037/a0014521

Soussignan, R. (2002). Duchenne smile, emotional experience, and autonomic reactivity: A test of the facial feedback hypothesis. *Emotion, 2*, 52–74. doi:10.1037//1528-3542.2.1.52

Stanislavsky, K. (1950). *My life in art.*Moscow: Foreign Languages Publishing House.

Teufel, C., Fletcher, P. C., & Davis, G. (2010). Seeing other minds: Attributed mental states influence perception. *Trends in Cognitive Sciences, 14*(8), 376–382. doi:10.1016/j.tics.2010.05.005

Wolper, D. L. (Producer), & Stuart, M. (Director). (1971). *Willy Wonka and the chocolate factory* [Motion Picture]. USA: Paramount Pictures.

Walt Disney Pictures (Producer), & Swift, D. (Director). (1961). *The parent trap* [Motion Picture]. USA: Buena Vista Distribution Company.

Appendix 1: Coding Guide and Examples

Code	Example
Acting: comment on the acting style, ability, etc	He is sarcastic, rather than just peculiar, in the [newer].
Actor: comment on whether the participant liked the specific actor	I like Johnny Depp a lot.
Casting: comment on the actors being "right" for the role, types of actors used	Violet has a mother in one movie, a father in the other.
Scene: comment on the scenery colors, type, style	The machine/factory was more high tech, bigger and better in the [newer] scene.
Prop: comment on any of the props	[In newer movie] one gum is a strip while [in the older movie] is gold boxy thing.
Special Effects: comment on the special effects	Newer movie had more elaborate special effects.
Music: comment on the background music	More music.
Mood: comment on the general mood of the clip	[Older] movie seemed more serious, darker.
Plot: a comment on an element of plot or change in moments of plot	All the children get gobstoppers in the [older] scene.
Wording: Comment on the script	They switched the words in one scene.
Viewer: a comment about the viewer's general preferences	Probably because it's what I'm used to.

12 AS GOOD AS IT GETS?

BLOCKBUSTERS AND THE INEQUALITY OF BOX OFFICE RESULTS SINCE 1950

Victor Fernandez-Blanco, Victor Ginsburgh,
Juan Prieto-Rodriguez, and Sheila Weyers

This chapter analyses how success, measured by box office revenues, is distributed in the movie industry. The idea that "the winner takes all" is pervasive in describing the high degree of inequality in revenues because we are all subject to the cognitive bias known as "recency effect" and have myopic perceptions that make us think that recent events are more relevant. This makes us believe that inequalities are much more important today than they used to be. Blockbusters such as *Avatar, The Black Knight, Pirates of the Caribbean, Dead Man's Chest,* or even *Titanic* lead us to overestimate revenue inequality. As is the case with many simplifications, this one is also misleading.

The "winner takes all" is an expression coined by Frank and Cook (1996), but the idea was developed by Rosen (1981) in his analysis of the economics of superstars: Only very few artists or cultural products are exceptionally successful. This is especially true in the movie industry, where high levels of risk and uncertainty generate the perception that box office revenues are highly concentrated (see De Vany & Walls, 1996). De Vany (2006, p. 641) suggests that "the top four movies account for 20 percent of revenues and the top eight for nearly 30 percent,...20 percent of the movies earn 80 percent of revenues." The music industry is subject to a similar phenomenon,[1] but the situation is less extreme in publishing where, according to Cowen (1998) the top fifteen books account for less than 1 percent of total sales.

Our perception is fueled by the increased availability and accessibility of information on movies. The web offers weekly and sometimes even daily box office figures; blockbusters make it to the first page of newspapers; and moviegoers pay attention not only to directors, stars, and awards but also to box office results. Presence among the top movies in the US box office is good advertising for a film that is released worldwide.

In nominal terms (current dollars), nine out of the top ten US movies with all-time box office records were released between 1997 (*Titanic*) and 2009 (*Avatar*), and some are far ahead of the pack in each release year. This was the case for *Avatar* in 2009 (with revenues that were 76 percent larger than that of the second 2009 movie), *The Dark Knight* in 2008 (67 percent), *Dead Man's Chest* in 2006 (69 percent), and, of course, *Titanic* in 1997 (140 percent). In nominal terms, these box office numbers look large, but we usually forget inflation, and there are movies produced in the past whose box office is much larger in real terms, as shown in the Appendix, where we list the twenty most successful movies ever. Only three out of twenty were released between 1997 and 2009. We get carried away by our (usually poor) intuition and end up believing that blockbusters released during recent decades made inequality more severe and that the past was more generous to a larger number of producers,[2] even though this inequality was at work a long time ago with *Cinderella* in 1950 (122 percent larger), *Quo Vadis* in 1951 (65 percent larger), *The Ten Commandments* in 1956 (86 percent), *South Pacific* in 1958 (88 percent), *Mary Poppins* in 1964 (96 percent), *Butch Cassidy and the Sundance Kid* in 1969 (98 percent), and *The Godfather* in 1972 (106 percent). These examples are dwarfed by *Ben Hur* in 1959 (200 percent larger) or *Star Wars* in 1977 (217 percent).

Inequality cannot be measured by just looking at two or three most successful movies each year. To clarify this, we analyze how box office inequality has evolved during the past 60 years (1950–2009) using a larger number of movies (twenty to 130 top hits[3]) and find, on the contrary, that inequality decreases after 1975. We relate our findings to the history of the film industry during the same period.

The chapter is organized as follows. The dataset used is described in the next section, and the methodology and results are discussed in the following two sections. Some conclusions are drawn in the final section.

Data

We collected information on the box office performance of top American films in the American market from 1950 to 2009,[4] a period of 60 years. During this period, the industry underwent at least three important changes that will be described in the section Methodology and Results and will be shown to explain, at least partly, our results.

We use two sources with some overlap for the period 1982–1989. For 1950–1989, we collected annual data on rentals for the first twenty movies (Sackett, 1990). There are two problems with this measure: rentals represent only about 50 percent of gross income (grosses)—they are that part of the box office that goes back to the distributor. That is, rentals represent the gross minus the percentage for exhibitors,[5] and the data include total rentals over the life-time of a movie. For instance, rentals of *Cinderella*, a movie released in 1950, but re-released several times (in 1957, 1965, 1973, 1981, and 1987), made $41.1 million in total, but only $12.5 million in 1950. Adding rentals during the whole commercial life of a movie may thus distort the inequality measure corresponding to a specific year. We corrected the data using the information of www.boxofficereport.com and www.imdb.com, which list re-releases, their dates, and their rentals.[6] For the second period, which runs from 1982 to 2009, we use a different set of data acquired from ACNielsen EDI, which gives data on movie grosses, not rentals.

The difference between rentals and grosses matters little here since it does not affect relative measures such as yearly inequality indices as long as these are computed without mixing grosses and rentals within the same year. We exploit the fact that we have both types of data for the period 1982–1989 to show that the "connection" between the two datasets is smooth.

Methodology and Results

Constructing Inequality Indices

To analyze the concentration of box office revenues (rentals or grosses), we use the Gini index, which measures the degree of inequality in the distribution of those revenues. The index is related to the so-called Lorenz curve, which plots the proportion of income (on the vertical axis) that is cumulatively earned by a given percent of movies ranked from lowest to highest rental (on the horizontal axis). If all movies collect the same rental, the curve is a 45-degree sloped straight line. The larger the inequality in rentals, the more the curve will be located below this line, as illustrated in Figure 12.1. The Gini index is equal to the area between the curve and the 45-degree sloped line divided by the area in the triangle below the 45-degree line; that is, A/(A + B). It is easy to see that more equality implies that area A will be small and so will the Gini index. In case of perfect equality of rentals, the index is equal to 0 since the area between the curve and the 45-degree

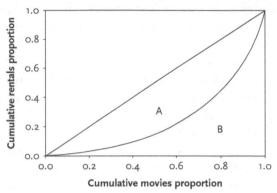

FIGURE 12.1 The Lorenz curve and the Gini index.

line will be zero. If all the rentals go to a unique movie, the Gini will be equal to 1 since area B will be equal to 0.

We compute annual Gini indices using box office data of the top twenty mov-ies for each year from 1950 to 2009.[7] Their values are reproduced in Table 12.1. This table contains two columns of indices, the first based on rentals, the second on grosses, as discussed in the Data section. Note that both rentals and grosses are available for the period 1982–1989. Although the values are not identical, they are fairly close. The largest differences are equal to 0.05 in 1983 and 1989, and the correlation coefficient between both series is 0.84. This leads to the conclu-sion that both sources of data are compatible and allows us to make a consistent analysis of inequality and its evolution during the whole period.

Analyzing the Time Path of Inequality Indices

Plotting the Gini indices as in Figure 12.2 produces a cloud of points[8] that can be analyzed using a technique that produces the smooth curve that summarizes the evolution of inequality over time.[9] The largest and smallest values are 0.498 (in 1965) and 0.137 (in 1998).

Figure 12.2 shows that revenue inequality increased quite substantially between 1950 and 1970, reached a peak in the early 1970s,[10] and then declined until it seemed to stabilize after 1995. Note that, from 1985 onward, average inequality is lower than during the 1950–1970 period. Moreover, there is not a single year in the past fifteen years with a Gini index larger than those observed in the 1960s and 1970s. There is thus no empirical evidence corroborating the insight that box office inequality increased during the last years covered by this study. Even the outlying years—1993, 1994, 1997, and 2004—show Gini indices that would have been considered fairly small during the 1960s and 1970s. [11]

Table 12.1 Inequality in Box Office Distribution, 1950–2009, Top Twenty Movies

Year	Rentals*	Grosses**	Year	Rentals*	Grosses**
1950	0.2325942	–	1982	0.3510830	0.3909091
1951	0.2181276	–	1983	0.2389426	0.2894294
1952	0.2865630	–	1984	0.3440551	0.3449822
1953	0.3272437	–	1985	0.3016339	0.2722659
1954	0.1968220	–	1986	0.2622662	0.2735572
1955	0.1807469	–	1987	0.2329793	0.2258095
1956	0.3943754	–	1988	0.2507338	0.2273294
1957	0.2742566	–	1989	0.2652864	0.2152261
1958	0.2752477	–	1990	–	0.2622763
1959	0.3070923	–	1991	–	0.1994207
1960	0.2690315	–	1992	–	0.1990916
1961	0.3174433	–	1993	–	0.2970535
1962	0.2806175	–	1994	–	0.2710527
1963	0.3303662	–	1995	–	0.1718611
1964	0.4033501	–	1996	–	0.2044936
1965	0.4977183	–	1997	–	0.2893904
1966	0.1760464	–	1998	–	0.1372301
1967	0.3216706	–	1999	–	0.2150607
1968	0.2628515	–	2000	–	0.1459478
1969	0.3177144	–	2001	–	0.1983669
1970	0.3678316	–	2002	–	0.201414
1971	0.3383417	–	2003	–	0.2261665
1972	0.4368801	–	2004	–	0.2510057
1973	0.4120928	–	2005	–	0.2097453
1974	0.2692504	–	2006	–	0.2035921
1975	0.4200232	–	2007	–	0.1884067
1976	0.2276536	–	2008	–	0.2190713
1977	0.4705862	–	2009	–	0.2008289
1978	0.3482638	–			
1979	0.1913785	–			
1980	0.2629073	–			
1981	0.2976786	–			

* Sackett (1990) and boxofficereport.com; ** *ACNielsen EDI.*

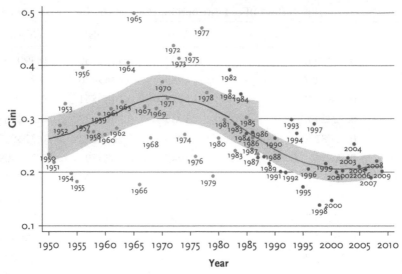

FIGURE 12.2 Evolving inequality of Hollywood movie box office results (1950–2009), twenty top movies.

The annual distribution of revenues became less skewed in recent times, which goes against the "winner takes all" theory, which predicts that the earnings inequality among artists will increase over time. Frank and Cook (1996, p. 121) suggest that "the growing importance of winner-take-all markets thus implies a change in the pattern of incomes observed in the economy...we should see greater income variability now than in the past." This is also what Rosen (1981, p. 855) had in mind in assuming that "an increase in the number of consumers or in the intensity of their demands...increases the market demand for services.... The largest increases (in revenues) accrue to the most talented persons.... Therefore, the distribution of rewards becomes more skewed than before."

Meanwhile, demand dropped since alternatives to cinema were becoming more popular (TV, video, CDs, computers, and video games in more recent years).[12] This is compatible with Rosen's hypothesis, if the decrease in audience affects all movies equally. But it may be that new three-dimensional (3D) technology will lead to an increase in demand (since substitutes will be more distant) and to supply shifts that will generate more inequality in the future. *Avatar* may pave the way for this change.

We now relate the three periods in the curve shown in Figure 12.2 with three turning points in the movie industry that led to important changes in its organization.

1950–1975. From the Paramount Litigation to the Birth of Conglomerates. The 1948 Paramount litigation (*United States v. Paramount Pictures Inc.*) held that movie studios could no longer own movie theaters, thus breaking their vertical integration ties. This had a considerable impact on the industry and changed the way studios produced and distributed films. This was compounded by the fast growth of television, since watching television had replaced going to the movies as the first leisure time activity. Both factors generated a deep crisis in the industry: employment, attendance, box office revenues, and profits during the 1950s dropped very steeply. The industry offered two sequential responses: competing through product differentiation with new formats such as Cinerama, 70mm movies, the first 3D experiments, and collaboration with TV channels.

The crisis, which partly extended to the late 1960s—as illustrated by the failures between 1967 and 1970 of *Doctor Dolittle* (1967), *Star* (1968), *The Battle of Britain* (1969), *Hello Dolly* (1969), and *Tora!, Tora!, Tora!* (1970), among others—forced old-fashioned studios to morph into large conglomerates with economic interests that went beyond the audiovisual industry. The great uncertainty of these years and the responses of the movie industry to changes in social preferences and to the threat of television production companies that were putting efforts in some great movies (in terms of format and budgets) increased inequality.

The end of the 1960s and the early 1970s gave birth to a number of important changes: independent studios appeared and grew, foreign markets emerged, and TV generated increasing income. This period is often called the "golden age" of American movies. Biskind (1998, p. 9) goes so far as to write that, for the young generation, paradise on earth had a name: Hollywood. The movie industry was turned upside down by a series of political and social upheavals that happened during the 1960s. The rapid unfolding of several historical events—John F. Kennedy's assassination in 1963 and the short film documenting it (by chance) by Abraham Zapruder (about which Thoret [2006] writes that it changed the film industry); Martin Luther King's assassination in 1968; widespread social unrest of oppressed minorities; Lyndon B. Johnson's design of the Great Society and his war on poverty between 1963 and 1969; the Vietnam War with its increased deployment of US combat troops in 1965 and subsequent antiwar political activism among students; and Sharon Tate's murder by Charles Manson—shook the American belief in heroes and served to develop the concept of the *anti-hero*. Susan Sontag also strongly underlines the influence of the "vanguard ideas, rooted in the idea of cinema as a craft pioneered by the Italian films of the immediate postwar period. It was at this specific moment of cinema that going to movies, thinking about movies, talking about movies became a passion among university students and other young people. You fell in love not just with actors but with cinema itself."[13]

This is also the time during which the Production Code was abandoned and movies became more permissive. Triggered by aesthetic, political, and historical necessity, producers began to show everyday reality rather than abstract and utopian events.

The audience profile during this period changed in favor of younger, college-educated, and more affluent people, with preferences that were far from those served up by traditional Hollywood. These new audience tastes served to drive the success of new "auteur" films (e.g., *Bonnie and Clyde* [1967], *The Graduate* [1967], and *Easy Rider* [1969]), although it is difficult to establish the direction of causality between new social attitudes and new forms of cinema during this period. The arrival of a new generation of directors (Scorsese, de Palma, Coppola, Spielberg) gave new life to the industry during the next 10–12 years.

The increase in box office inequality (inequality may increase even if the average box office results decrease and vice versa) during these years may be explained as follows. The emergence of conglomerates may have contributed to the growth of inequality, whereas the renewed presence of independent studios did not reduce it. During this period, some blockbusters (analyzed further in the section "Winner Takes All" Movies) reaped much larger revenues than those obtained by other movies present among the top twenty. Blockbusters themselves may be explained by Rosen's superstar phenomenon. When there is competition among talents, very small differences in talent explain large differences in their income, which then leads to large box office differences.

But golden ages never last. In the mid 1970s, movie director George Lucas, after having seen *American Graffiti* (1973), claimed that it was depressing to go to the movies and that it was time to make moviegoers happier. Biskind (1998) is of the opinion that *Star Wars* (1977) marked the recovery of a simple, innocuous, binary (good guys vs. bad guys), and predictable world.

1975–2000. From the Success of Jaws *(1975) and* Star Wars *(1977) to the New Millennium.* This period started with the entry of new directors and producers who were immediately very successful, while at the same time "auteur" projects such as *Heaven's Gate* (1980) or *One from the Heart* (1982) failed miserably. The period is characterized by the importance of famous directors and the need for the majors to develop new strategies to reduce risk: cutting costs, exploiting scope and scale economies, designing new marketing practices, diversifying into merchandising, developing new outlets for audiovisual products, and taking advantage of their transformation into multimedia conglomerates.

Movie audiences changed again. In the 1970s, audiences were extremely young: 60 percent of moviegoers were 12–20 years old and aesthetically more conservative (Belton, 1993). Thus, Hollywood opened its doors to new ideas, genres, tastes, and tendencies—more "arty" movies, in the sense that directors were made more responsible for success, hence the *Jaws* (1975) and *Star Wars* (1977) blockbusters. As can be seen from Table 12.2, audiences become older during the 1990s, and this trend continued during the first decade of the new millennium. As the generation of 12- to 24-year-old from the mid-1970s aged, the industry responded by turning back to the blockbuster policy, looking for standardized productions with sequels (four sequels to *Jaws* after the first 1975 release), prequels (i.e., later productions that describe events that took place before the first production: *Star Wars I, II,* and *III* were released in 1999, 2002, and 2005, respectively, long after *Star Wars IV, V,* and *VI,* produced in 1977, 1980, and 1983, respectively), and franchises (James Bond movies, for instance), or imitating the style, contents, and ideas of previous successful blockbusters. The idea seemed to be that if something runs, try it again, *remake* it,[14] and satisfy those who were young at the time of *Jaws* and *Star Wars.*

Single-screen theaters disappeared and were replaced by multiscreen theaters located in shopping malls at some distance from city centers. After various mergers and acquisitions, the former Big Five (Metro Goldwyn Mayer, Paramount, Twentieth-Century Fox, Warner Bros, and RKO) and Little Three (Universal, Columbia, and United Artists) gave way to the current majors: Paramount, TimeWarner, Sony (which today controls Columbia, Metro-Goldwyn-Mayer, and United Artists), NBC Universal, Fox Searchlight, and Disney.[15] Although they are vertically integrated, majors changed their *modus operandi*: they put their main effort into distribution both in domestic and overseas markets, but also work in other distribution channels.

In trying to decrease risk, the industry made movies, especially blockbusters, more similar, and this is reflected in lower Gini indices, which fall from 0.32 in the middle of the 1970s to 0.22 at the end of the 1990s.

The idea of explaining the turning point of the 1970s by pointing to a new generation of directors is attractive. But Epstein (2010) provides another explanation, one that he calls "the samurai embrace"; that is, the introduction

Table 12.2 Moviegoers (Age Groups in %)

	12–24	25–39	40–59	Over 60
1975	60	26	11	3
1990	43	33	17	7
2005	38	28	25	10

Source: Silver and MacDonnel (2007).

of the VCR by Japanese electronics companies. This was a milestone, making it possible to program and watch movies from your couch. In response, Hollywood began producing teenager-oriented movies especially aimed at the video market. This also contributed to reduce diversity. Again, quoting Epstein (2010, p. 191) "by 2000, Wal-Mart had become Hollywood's single biggest customer, selling about a third of all DVDs, occasioning top studio executives to journey to Bentonville, Arkansas, to find out what ratings, stars, genres, and other attributes would help them win strategic placement in Wal-Mart stores."

2000–Present. Digitization and the motion picture industry. The new millennium defines the beginning of the third stage. Digitization deeply changed the film business. It decreased production, distribution, and transaction costs; improved technical quality; and opened new possibilities, such as downloading music or movies. But this new technology also generated new problems: piracy; the need to invest in new screening equipment (even though previous investments in multiplexes and megaplexes were not yet written off), and a remarkable increase in costs related to marketing, advertising, and copying. In the second half of the decade, uncertainty and high risk shied away banks and investment funds that had put their money on movies. The end of the period was characterized by a recurrence of 3D movies, which seem to be an alternative for the industry even though they represent a new and important increase in production costs.

During this period, the film industry continued to suffer from technical shocks and worked to define its new profile and position. In terms of inequality, this was a period of stability, despite a new small increase of inequality at the very end of the period, which may be due to the effect of 3D movie production. Because 3D production costs are higher, only a few movies could be shot using this technique, thus polarizing the movie market and increasing inequality.[16]

A possible limit to growing inequality is pointed out by Cutting, De Long, and Nothelfer (2010) in their fascinating paper, in which they analyze the pattern of shot lengths in 150 films released between 1930 and 2005 and show that shot lengths, which have an effect on the attention of viewers, and thus movies themselves become "closer" which may also explain why their box office results also become closer.

Robustness Checks

It is useful to verify whether decreasing inequality that began in the 1970s is independent of the number of movies (twenty observations) used to compute the Gini indices. Fortunately, Nielsen's database (1982–2009) is richer than Sackett's in terms of the number of films included so that we can compute alternative Gini indices that are based on more movies. We did this using, respectively, the top 50 and 130 movies produced in each year between 1982 and 2009.[17] Obviously, as we increase the number of movies with smaller box office results (the lower tail of the box office distribution), the values of the Gini indices will be larger with 50 and 130 movies than with 20, since the range of revenues increases. However, the important point is whether the number of movies used in the computations affects the *evolution* of inequality. If this is not the case, we can assume that our results are robust and be confident that they represent correctly the evolution of inequality.

As expected, and as can be observed in Figure 12.3, the larger the number of movies included in the calculation of annual Gini indices, the larger their absolute value. But, and this is the relevant issue for us, the decreasing trend over time is robustly confirmed.

"Winner Takes All" Movies

Outliers

Figures 12.2 and 12.3 include 95 percent confidence intervals (represented by the shaded areas) that inform us about those years that lie far from the smoothed

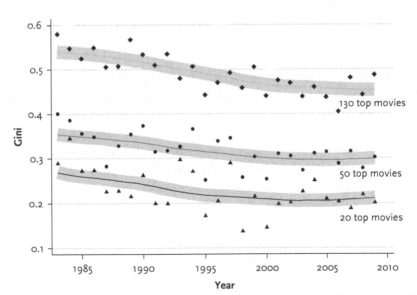

FIGURE 12.3 Evolving inequality of Hollywood movie box office results (1982–2009), 130, 50, and 20 top movies.

curve as outliers. Since we are interested in analyzing "the winner takes all" effect, we are especially concerned with those years that are above the confidence interval. Over the whole period, this happens during 14 years out of 60 (Figure 12.2). However, in the second half of the period (1980–2009), the outlying values of the index are around 0.30—and thus do not contradict the observation that inequality is lower than during the first 30 years—with the exception of 1982 (and 1984, which is almost within the confidence interval).

Some comments on outliers are in order. The largest inequality corresponds to 1965, a year in which two big blockbusters, *The Sound of Music* and *Doctor Zhivago*, largely dominated in terms of box office. *The Sound of Music* rentals were 2.8 times above the third movie (*Thunderball*) and 5.7 times above the fourth (*Those Magnificent Men in Their Flying Machines*).[18]

In seven cases, the top box office movie reaches revenues that were at least twice as large as those of the second movie, showing the strongest "winner takes all" effect: *Cinderella* (1950), *Ben Hur* (1959), *The Godfather* (1972), *Jaws* (1975), *Star Wars* (1977), *Return of the Jedi* (1983), and *Titanic* (1997).[19] Only *Titanic* is reasonably recent,[20] so, once again, this leads us to reject the suggestion that concentration increased during recent years.

New Contracts and Technologies

Many blockbusters are the result of franchising. Disney, Spielberg, and *Star Wars* are the most prominent examples, but this is also so for the franchises of *Superman, Star Trek, Harry Potter,* or *James Bond* films. This is a smart strategy in a highly risky industry: a successful idea has to be milked as much as possible.

The effects of technological tricks—cinemascope, 3D, Cinerama—used to lure people back to the movie theaters did not prove very effective. When used, they merely pushed the first film to use the technology to the top of the box office. *The Ten Commandments* (1956), a cinemascope movie, is one such example.

Cinemascope (and similar technologies to shoot 70mm movies) was probably the only durable and frequently used of these techniques. Cinerama was present in the industry for at least 20 years (from the beginning of the 1950s to the beginning of the 1970s) but only one movie, *This Is Cinerama,* released in 1952, was able to lead the box office ranking; eight other Cinerama movies reached the top twenty. Traditional 3D was less successful: only *House of Wax* (1953) reached a high position (fourth) in the rankings, and there is no other 3D film in the top twenty during the golden era for this kind of movies (the early 1950s). In any case, the high production costs of these technologies and their moderate success certainly contributed to reduce their number.

Disney Studios, Steven Spielberg, and George Lucas

Among the fourteen outlying years in which inequality is especially strong, Disney has two leading movies, although one could also include *The Lion King* (1994), which ranked second but made only $100,000 less than the leader, *Forrest Gump*. If we take into account the whole period, we find nine Disney movies that lead box office results and another 124 movies among the top twenty. Obviously, "Disney" does not guarantee success but seems to improve the probability of being profitable. Disney Studios obviously have a good knowledge of the preferences of US citizens. In addition, the studio followed the policy of re-releasing some of its classical movies, especially animated films. On many occasions, these re-releases were also successful, thus giving the impression that some intergenerational preferences are passed from parents to children and grandchildren.

How did Steven Spielberg perform? Among the 14 years with largest inequality, three of his movies were leaders: *Jaws* (1975), his first blockbuster; *E.T.* (1982); and *Jurassic Park* (1993). He also directed two other top box office movies, *Raiders of Lost Ark* (1981) and *Saving Private Ryan* (1998), and twelve that are included among the top twenty. Starting with *Jaws*, Spielberg directed twenty-three fiction movies, of which seventeen are included among the top twenty.[21] It seems clear that Lady Luck touched this man.

Lucas's *Star Wars* (1977) saga is another interesting case. The movie is responsible for the 1977 outlying Gini index. It was followed by five sequels, of which four made it to the top box office level. *Star Wars Episode II: Attack of the Clones* (2002) "only" made it to third place.[22]

Conclusion

The time series of Gini inequality indices for each year between 1950 and 2009 show that inequality peaked in the 1970s and is lower today than it was during the 1950s. The impression that box office inequality is increasing over time is due to our tendency to give more relevance to more recent events and forget what happened in the past. Therefore, despite the enormous literature on "the winner takes all" and Rosen's "superstar" effects, the idea that box office revenues show increasing inequality over time is an attractive myth rather than a real fact. This evolution can be linked to the history of the movie industry during these years and to changing audiences.

Our findings are consistent with the idea that the 1970s are a turning point in the history of the film industry. In the late 1960s and the early 1970s, the traditional strategy of studios—putting their best efforts into one or a few great movies per year—proved ineffective in improving their financial situation. But because some blockbusters were still successful, this kept box office inequality quite large. Gradually however, Hollywood productions no longer corresponded to the changing demands of the teenagers and young adults who were becoming the main group of moviegoers, nor did Hollywood effectively respond to the social changes in a nation shocked by the Kennedy assassination and the unrest surrounding the Vietnam War. The industry's first response (Biskind, 1998) was to put the reins of the business into the hands of a new group of "auteur" directors such as Coppola and Cimino; this failed and, in the case of United Artists, caused its ruin.

Majors also changed their management procedures. They reduced "in house" productions and increased outsourcing or started dealing with smaller production companies. They found that distribution could be a profitable branch and discovered other sources of income, such as TV markets, merchandising, toys, and, finally, DVDs and video games. In Epstein's (2010, p. 174) words, "Hollywood's future [comes] from creating films with licensable properties that could generate profits in other media over long periods of time."[23]

This business model continues today. Sequels, franchised movies, movies based on comics, or using characters that can be incorporated into video games or other ancillary products dominate the film market. As Finler (2003, p. 6) pointed out, "what the big entertainment companies are selling are not so much blockbuster movies as brands or franchises." The American box office is an increasingly smaller part of the total revenue of a movie, 10 percent in 2007 according to Epstein (2010, p. 23). Therefore, during the past two decades, movie production has been highly standardized and very predictable, so that box office differences become smaller, as the decreasing Gini indices show.

Acknowledgments

Fernandez-Blanco and Prieto-Rodriguez, University of Oviedo, Spain; Ginsburgh, ECARES, Brussels, CORE, Louvain-la-Neuve and ECORE; Weyers, Université catholique de Louvain. Research for this paper was financed by the Spanish Ministry of Science and Technology Project #ECO2008-04659.

Notes

1. See, e.g., Fernandez-Blanco et al. (2007) for Spain.
2. McLean (2009, p. 7), for instance, suggests that "from the 1970s onwards it became apparent to the major studios that the annual box office charts tended to be dominated by one or two films which clearly led over all releases. A studio's income was not coming in equally from all of its releases."

3. Box office results for the full set of movies produced each year is easy to find for recent years, but much less so for the period 1950–1980.

4. See footnote 11.

5. This is the definition of rentals given by the movie website www.imdb.com. Note that the percentage may slightly change if, for instance, the studio, the director, or an actor (Schwarzenegger in *Terminator 3*) have good bargaining power.

6. We found twenty movies that had a major re-release and corrected their rentals to make them compatible with the rest of the data.

7. We also tried other indices such as Theil's index and Generalized Gini indices that corroborate the main results and trends identified by the Gini coefficient described here.

8. Note that for the years 1982 to 1989, both Gini coefficients (computed using grosses and rentals) are plotted.

9. To do this, we use the Nadaraya-Watson nonparametric smoother (Nadaraya, 1964; Watson, 1964) with the Epanechnikov kernel (Epanechnikov, 1969).

10. It is important to note that some Gini indices are quite large (1965 for instance), but, when we construct the trend using the Nadaraya-Watson kernel regression, we obtain a smoothing estimate of the function by locally weighted averages of the Gini values, based on several years. This is the reason the curve reaches its maximum around 1970, although, for instance, the particular indices for 1972, 1973, 1975, and 1977 are larger. The shaded region represents the 95% confidence interval.

11. Since this chapter was completed, we obtained more data for 2009 and new data for 2010 and 2011. This made it possible to update our series of Gini coefficients, which have dropped dramatically in 2010 and 2011 with respect to 2009, so that the light upward trend that we observed for the last years in Figures 12.2 and 12.3 disappears. The artifact was obviously due to *Avatar*'s unusual box office results. The downward trend is thus steady since 1970.

12. "In 1948, when home TV was still a rarity, theatres sold 4.6 billion tickets. By 1958, TV had penetrated most American homes, and theatres sold only 2 billions tickets.... By 1988, tickets sales hovered at 1 billion." (Epstein, 2010).

13. A century of cinema, http://southerncrossreview.org/43/sontag-cinema.htm.

14. Ginsburgh, Pestieau, and Weyers (2005) show that, quality-wise, remakes are not as "good" as originals, generate smaller revenues, but do not seem to lose money.

15. RKO dropped out of the motion picture industry in 1957.

16. According to the International 3D Society, 3D movies have generated 33 percent of the total box office in the United States since the release of *Avatar* (*The Independent*, 9 April 2010, London). See also footnote 11.

17. The number of 130 movies was selected because, in some years, the Nielsen database contains only 130 movies. Selecting a larger number would have shortened the time period for which indices could be calculated.

18. 1998 has the lowest Gini: *Saving Private Ryan* is the top box office movie, but the difference in grosses with the tenth movie (*Patch Adams*) is only $8 million.

19. *Mary Poppins* (1964) and *Butch Cassidy and the Sundance Kid* (1969) could also be added to this list since their rentals were almost 100 percent larger than those of their main challengers.

20. Note that *Avatar,* released in mid December 2009, made most of its grosses in 2010, and our database only include gross revenues before January 20, 2010. Therefore, around one-third of its revenues are excluded from our data. Although this criterion was applied to all movies released at the end of 2009, it is especially important in this case.

21. We do not take into account those collective films in which Spielberg directed only one or two segments.

22. George Lucas is another King Midas in Hollywood. Combining director and producer role, he has seven movies ranked first and three movies ranked second or third.

23. In Epstein's opinion, the origin of franchises, toys, and the like does not come from Spielberg or Lucas but from Disney's *Snow White and the Seven Dwarfs.*

References

Belton, J. (1993). *American cinema/American culture.* New York: McGraw-Hill.

Biskind, P. (1998). *Easy riders, raging bulls: How the sex-drugs-rock 'n' roll generation saved Hollywood.* New York: Simon and Schuster.

Cowen, T. (1998). *In praise of commercial culture.* Cambridge, MA: Harvard University Press.

Cutting, J., DeLong, J., & Nothelfer, C. (2010). Attention and the evolution of Hollywood film. *Psychological Science, 20,* 1–8.

De Vany, A. (2006). The movies. In V. Ginsburgh & D. Throsby (Eds.), *Handbook of the economics of art and culture* (pp. 615–665). Amsterdam: North Holland.

De Vany, A. &Walls, D. (1996). Bose-Einstein dynamics and adaptive contracting in the motion picture industry. *Economic Journal, 439*(106), 1493–1514.

Epanechnikov, V. A. (1969). Nonparametric estimation of a multivariate probability density. *Theory of Probability and Its Applications, 14,* 153–158.

Epstein, E. J. (2010). *The Hollywood economist.* New York: Melville House.

Fernandez-Blanco, V., Gutierrez del Castillo, R., & Prieto-Rodriguez, J. (2007). Analysing author's rights distribution in the recording music industry (mimeo).

Finler, J. F. (2003). *The Hollywood story.* London: Wallflower Press.

Frank, R., & Cook, P. (1996). *The winner-take-all society.* New York: Free Press.

Ginsburgh, V., Pestieau, P., & Weyers, S. (2005). Is it worth producing remakes? (mimeo).

McLean, D. (2009). The evolution of the term "New Hollywood," NEO. Available at http://www.arts.mq.edu.au/documents/NEO_Article_7_2009_Duncan_McLean.pdf

Nadaraya, E. (1964). On estimating regression. *Theory of Probability and Its Applications, 9,* 141–142.

Rosen, S. (1981). The economics of superstars. *American Economic Review*, 71, 167–183.

Sackett, S. (1990). *The Hollywood Reporter book of box office hits*. New York: Billboard Publications.

Silver, J., & MacDonell, J. (2007). Are movie theaters doomed? Do exhibitors see the big picture as theaters lose their competitive advantage? *Business Horizons*, 50(6), 491–501.

Thoret, J. -B. (2006). *Le cinéma américain des années 70*. Paris: Cahiers du cinéma.

Watson, G. S. (1964). Smooth regression analysis. *Sankhya: The Indian Journal of Statistics, Series A*, 26, 359–372.

Appendix: Top US Grosses

Rank	Title	Released in	Studio	Adjusted Gross ($ million)
1	*Gone with the Wind*	1939*	MGM	1,606
2	*Star Wars*	1977*	Fox	1,416
3	*The Sound of Music*	1965	Fox	1,132
4	*E.T.: The Extra-Terrestrial*	1982*	Universal	1,128
5	*The Ten Commandments*	1956	Paramount	1,041
6	*Titanic*	1997	Paramount	1,020
7	*Jaws*	1975	Universal	1,018
8	*Doctor Zhivago*	1965	MGM	987
9	*The Exorcist*	1973*	Warner	879
10	*Snow White and the Seven Dwarfs*	1937*	Disney	867
11	*101 Dalmatians*	1961*	Disney	794
12	*The Empire Strikes Back*	1980*	Fox	781
13	*Ben-Hur*	1959	MGM	779
14	*Avatar*	2009*	Fox	773
15	*Return of the Jedi*	1983*	Fox	748
16	*The Sting*	1973	Universal	709
17	*Raiders of the Lost Ark*	1981*	Paramount	701
18	*Jurassic Park*	1993	Universal	685
19	*The Graduate*	1967*	AVCO	680
20	*Star Wars I: The Phantom Menace*	1999	Fox	674

Source: www.boxofficemojo.com

Grosses are adjusted for ticket price inflation; * are documented multiple releases.

13 SOCIAL SCIENCE OF THE CINEMA

FADE OUT

Joshua Butler and James C. Kaufman

From Creation, to Audience, to Production, to Reception, the sections in this book have endeavored to elevate the conversation of cinema in all its stages. As in a discussion of Picasso's *Guernica* or Shakespeare's *Hamlet,* we have given the great populist medium of the past century the same kind of scholarly analysis. Movies, which since their inception have inspired a visceral response in their viewers quite unlike any artistic medium before them, can engage the brain—think of *Memento* or *12 Angry Men*. They can make your heart swell, like *Somewhere in Time* or *Laura*. Films can inspire absolute joy, like *Singing in the Rain*, or terror, like *Se7en*. And, by capturing the breadth of human emotion, cinema is both populist entertainment and a lucrative commercial enterprise. But it is also an art form, like painting and theater, that inspires its viewers, critics, and scholars alike.

We started off with a section on The Creation. In Chapter 1, Dean Keith Simonton explored how the screenplay contributes to a film's success. Although screenwriters are often a neglected group, the paramount importance of the story cannot be understated. Simonton noted several interesting research findings, such as the box office doom of the drama genre and that the original author's involvement in adapting a work to film actually hurts the final product. Next, in Chapter 2, Stacy L. Smith, Amy Granados, Marc Choueiti, and Katherine M. Pieper analyzed two broad themes: (1) how women are greatly underrepresented as directors, writers, and producers; and (2) how female roles are both marginalized (the authors examine responses to why females comprise less than 30% of all speaking roles) and sexualized. Finally, in Chapter 3, Annabel Cohen analyzed how music contributes to a film. She discussed how our perception, memory, and other cognitive processes enable a core paradox—namely, that film music enhances our interaction with a movie even though the actual presence of music is quite unrealistic.

Smith and co-authors touched on how inequality impacts film viewers; the book's second section explicitly centers on The Audience. First, in Chapter 4, Tomas Chamorro-Premuzic, Andrea Kallias, and Anne Hsu looked at how individual differences in personality impact the reasons why we watch movies. These motivations then influence the types of genres that we prefer. If you love documentaries and your friend prefers comedies, then there may be genuine differences apart from movie preference. Next, in Chapter 5, Jordan E. DeLong, Kaitlin L. Brunick, and James E. Cutting connected the average length of a shot in a movie with how we as an audience can visually perceive the information. They traced how, the over the past 50 years, shot length has been decreasing and the amount of visual activity has been increasing. One wonders if moviegoers 100 years, or even 50 years ago, could begin to process and/or comprehend the latest blockbusters. Finally, in Chapter 6, Gerald C. Cupchik and Michelle C. Hilscher discussed how viewers engage themselves in film. Using the dichotomies of the rational self and the emotional self, they traced the relationships between self and film across time, using both theoretical and empirical approaches. Just like other art forms, cinema is a fluid medium, and films themselves become unique personal experiences for those who engage with them.

The third section, The Production, turns to the business end of movies. The section begins with Joris Ebbers, Nachoem M. Wijnberg, and Pawan V. Bhansing discussing the eternal struggle (the "faultline") between art and commerce in Chapter 7. They looked at the different roles that the director and producer have in making a movie, emphasizing how long-term collaborations help ease such tensions. Next, in Chapter 8, Gino Cattani and Simone Ferriani used Hollywood as a lens to examine how people are recognized within broad social networks. Consistent with past theory and research, they found that those filmmakers high in the social structure of Hollywood (i.e., more connected) are more recognized for their work. Finally, in Chapter 9, Allègre L. Hadida analyzed how American and French film productions differ. Although many components (such as financing or public perceptions) are consistent, the French film director is more likely to be seen as an auteur, whereas the producer has the bulk of the authority in American cinema.

In the final section, The Reception, Iain Pardoe and Dean Keith Simonton led off with the development of an intricate prediction system for gauging the

Academy Awards, in Chapter 10. With impressive success rates for the big four awards (best picture, best director, best actor, and best actress), they confirm the poor luck of Peter O'Toole and Russell Crowe. Next, in Chapter 11, Thalia R. Goldstein looked at perceptions of acting, contrasting technique versus method acting. The counterintuitive results of her study indicate that technique actors are seen as showing more emotion than their method counterparts. Often the artifice of cinema—unlike the immediacy of the stage—can create a greater effect in the viewer than an individual actor's ability to convey raw feeling. Finally, in Chapter 12, Victor Fernandez-Blanco, Victor Ginsburgh, Juan Prieto-Rodriguez, and Sheila Weyers examined how box office success is inequally distributed. Although a common public perception holds that movies today are divided into the studio blockbusters and the small indies, Fernandez-Blanco and colleagues found that such inequality peaked in the 1970s. Indeed, the reception to today's films is more balanced than in the 1950s. Perhaps, in the age of event cinema and huge-budget spectacle, audiences are more likely to be egalitarian in their response to studio product.

Now the traditional conclusion is to fade to black or simply hard cut from the last image of the movie to darkness. Then roll the end credits, or pop them on and off the screen in rhythmic fashion. Or, in some cases, air the filmmakers' dirty laundry and show outtakes and "bloopers" to remind the audience that it's okay to be involved in a movie and then, moments later, to laugh at its pure artifice. Another more current option (as seen in 2012's mega-hit *The Avengers*) is to design an artful collage of graphic elements from the film we've just watched and, in doing so, to relish in the gleeful abstraction of what was so lucid before our eyes just a few seconds before. And perhaps this abstraction is the key to understanding the burgeoning art of filmmaking. By incorporating the visual foundation of painting and photography and design, the probing insight of the written word, the vast complexity of the human image, the aural pleasures of sounds and music, even the grand showmanship of vaudevillian theater—cinema becomes not just its own art form, but a reincorporation of multiple art forms that emerge as much greater than the sum of its parts.

INDEX

absorption, 100
Academy Awards. *See* nominations and
    awards; Oscars
Academy of Motion Picture Arts and
    Sciences (AMPAS), 192, 233
ACNielsen EDI, 271
acoustic spectrographic representation,
    77
actor-character connection, 265
actor performance case study
    modeling strategy, 258
    results of, 258–260
    technique vs method acting,
        260–266
actors/acting. *See also* female actors; male
    actors
    actor-character connection, 265
    adult's perceptions of, 257, 260
    American, 262
    as assets, 210
    British, 262
    children's perceptions of, 257,
        259–260, 264–265
    coding guide and examples, 268
    commercial success for, 168–169
    conceptual blending, 256
    defined, 255
    emotional state of, 265

judging, 257–265. *see also* actor
    performance case study
method acting, 260–266
perception of, 256, 261
realism in, 261
team selection process and, 172–173
technique, 260–266
understanding, 256–257
watching others act, 255–256
actual self is not ideal, 147
adaptations, film, 16–19
Aesthetics and Psychology in the Cinema
    (Mitry), 140
affective covariation principle, 146
affiliation network, 190
ageism, 28
Age of Electronic
    Transmission, 146
Age of Mechanical Reproduction, 146
aggressiveness, 100–101. *See also* sex
    and violence in films;
    violent movies
agreeableness, 91, 93, 99
Aladdin (film), 27
aleif system, 255
Alice in Wonderland (film), 29
All About Eve (film), 130
Allen, M., 41